OXFORD CONSTITUTIONAL T

Series Editors:
Martin Loughlin, John P. McCormick, and

Constitutional Courts and Deliberative Democracy

OXFORD CONSTITUTIONAL THEORY

Series Editors:
Martin Loughlin, John P. McCormick, and Neil Walker

Oxford Constitutional Theory has rapidly established itself as the primary point of reference for theoretical reflections on the growing interest in constitutions and constitutional law in domestic, regional and global contexts. The majority of the works published in the series are monographs that advance new understandings of their subject. But the series aims to provide a forum for further innovation in the field by also including well-conceived edited collections that bring a variety of perspectives and disciplinary approaches to bear on specific themes in constitutional thought and by publishing English translations of leading monographs in constitutional theory that have originally been written in languages other than English.

ALSO AVAILABLE IN THE SERIES

The Cultural Defense of Nations
A Liberal Theory of Majority Rights
Liav Orgad

The Cosmopolitan Constitution
Alexander Somek

The Structure of Pluralism
Victor M. Muniz-Fraticelli

Fault Lines of Globalization
Legal Order and the Politics of A-Legality
Hans Lindahl

The Cosmopolitan State
H Patrick Glenn

After Public Law
Edited by Cormac Mac Amhlaigh, Claudio Michelon, and Neil Walker

The Three Branches
A Comparative Model of Separation of Powers
Christoph Möllers

The Global Model of Constitutional Rights
Kai Möller

The Twilight of Constitutionalism?
Edited by Petra Dobner and Martin Loughlin

Beyond Constitutionalism
The Pluralist Structure of Postnational Law
Nico Krisch

Constituting Economic and Social Rights
Katharine G. Young

Constitutional Referendums
The Theory and Practice of Republican Deliberation
Stephen Tierney

Constitutional Fragments
Societal Constitutionalism and Globalization
Gunther Teubner

Constitutional Courts and Deliberative Democracy

Conrado Hübner Mendes

OXFORD
UNIVERSITY PRESS

Great Clarendon Street, Oxford, OX2 6DP,
United Kingdom

Oxford University Press is a department of the University of Oxford.
It furthers the University's objective of excellence in research, scholarship,
and education by publishing worldwide. Oxford is a registered trade mark of
Oxford University Press in the UK and in certain other countries

© C Hübner Mendes 2013

The moral rights of the author have been asserted

First published 2013
First published in paperback 2015

All rights reserved. No part of this publication may be reproduced, stored in
a retrieval system, or transmitted, in any form or by any means, without the
prior permission in writing of Oxford University Press, or as expressly permitted
by law, by licence or under terms agreed with the appropriate reprographics
rights organization. Enquiries concerning reproduction outside the scope of the
above should be sent to the Rights Department, Oxford University Press, at the
address above

You must not circulate this work in any other form
and you must impose this same condition on any acquirer

Published in the United States of America by Oxford University Press
198 Madison Avenue, New York, NY 10016, United States of America

British Library Cataloguing in Publication Data
Data available

Library of Congress Cataloging in Publication Data
Data available

ISBN 978-0-19-967045-1 (Hbk.)
ISBN 978-0-19-875945-4 (Pbk.)

Links to third party websites are provided by Oxford in good faith and
for information only. Oxford disclaims any responsibility for the materials
contained in any third party website referenced in this work.

For Danuca

Acknowledgements

This book is the corollary of a doctoral dissertation in constitutional theory completed at the University of Edinburgh School of Law. Its asks whether and how valuable collegiate deliberation can permeate the decision-making process of constitutional courts, and argues that "deliberative performance," as defined here, provides a contextual and empirically driven metric to assess the democratic weight of judicial review. I owe many persons and institutions a debt of gratitude for those extraordinary years during which this book has taken shape.

I had the privilege of working with a remarkable trio of supervisors: Neil MacCormick, who passed away before the dissertation had reached a conclusion, was a role model of a variety of academic virtues, among which I would highlight his intellectual openness and curiosity, his argumentative charity and balance and, above all, his collegial character; Neil Walker, with his unrivalled capacity to locate one's inquiry in a broader horizon and to illuminate one's unnoticed assumptions and implications, has made extremely sharp and creative suggestions to this work; finally, Zenon Bankowski has always drawn inspiring connections and analogies between my research and taxing ethical anxieties that probably remain unanswered. I will always be grateful for their unique collective mentorship and friendship.

My special gratitude extends to three other persons that have played a central role in the development of this book's structure and arguments. I have deeply appreciated the constant dialogue with Virgílio Afonso da Silva, whose work on constitutional law and comments on my papers have influenced the very formulation and further development of my inquiry. Cláudio Michelon has also commented on several written pieces and had been the closest interlocutor during the years in Edinburgh. Finally, Mattias Kumm, who had been a supportive sponsor of my research visits to NYU School of Law, Wissenschaftszentrum Berlin (WZB), and Humboldt University Berlin, has encouraged me to refine every argument that I presented to him.

I thank Stephen Tierney and Gianluigi Palombella for a challenging examination panel and for their amiable advices on how to develop the work further. I am grateful for the anonymous reviewers of Oxford University Press, who have made considerate and incisive suggestions for the improvement of this work. I am aware that not all suggestions were satisfactorily met, but I have struggled with them nonetheless.

For very helpful and friendly conversations in different moments and different places, in ways that I cannot fairly measure and duly recognize within this space, I would also like to thank Álvaro de Vita, Barry Friedman, Carlos Ari Sundfeld, Cícero Araújo, Cormac MacAmlaigh, Daniel Augenstein, Daniel Bonilla, David Garland, Diego Lopez, Dieter Grimm, Dimitri Dimoulis, Diogo Coutinho, Esdras Costa, Fernando Atria, Fernando Limongi, Grainne De Burca, Fred Zaumseil, Guilherme Leite Gonçalves, Henk Botha, Jean Paul Veiga da Rocha, Joxerramon Bengoetxea, John Ferejohn, José Garcez Ghirardi, José Rodrigo Rodriguez, Juan Gonzalez Bertomeu, Lewis Kornhauser, Marcos Paulo Veríssimo, Maria Paula Saffon, Matthew Taylor, Niamh Nic Shuibhne, Octávio Motta Ferraz, Oscar Vilhena Vieira, Pasquale Pasquino, Paula Gaido, Rafael Bellem, Richard Stewart, Roberto Gargarella, Roni Mann, Siri Gloppen, Theunis Roux, and Vlad Perju. A special thanks also goes to Wil Waluchow, his students, and other faculty members for a gripping graduate seminar at the Philosophy Department of McMaster University.

As for the institutional support during the doctoral research, I would like to thank the University of Edinburgh for a Ph.D. Research Scholarship and the Brazilian Ministry of Education (Coordenação de Aperfeiçoamento de Pessoal de Nível Superior—CAPES) for a Doctoral Scholarship. At a post-doctoral stage, I would like to thank the New York University School of Law for a Hauser Research Scholarship, the Edinburgh Institute for Advanced Studies in the Humanities, the Research Council of Norway for granting me a Yggdrasil Post-Doctoral Fellowship that made possible a research visit to Christian Michelsen Institute in Bergen, and the Alexander von Humboldt Foundation for granting me a Georg Forster Post-Doctoral Fellowship at Wissenschaftszentrum Berlin (WZB) and Humboldt University Berlin.

I am finally grateful to my Ph.D. colleagues, who helped to keep an active post-graduate research environment at the School of Law. To Francisco Saffie I owe a fond thanks for his zealous engagement with every single idea that I described to him and for a meticulous and intelligent reading. I also thank Maksymilian Del Mar, Oche Onazi, Haris Psarras, Katri Löhmus, and Danielle Rached for our convivial conversations at the Legal Theory Research Group. Their companionship has made the Ph.D. experience much more enjoyable than it would have otherwise been.

Conrado Hübner Mendes

Contents

Introduction	1
The imagery of constitutional courts	1
A methodological vantage point: gains and losses of middle-level abstraction	5
A roadmap of the argument	9
1. Political Deliberation and Collective Decision-making	12
1 Introduction	12
2 The conceptual frame of political deliberation	14
3 Values of political deliberation	19
4 Promises and perils of political deliberation	22
5 Circumstances of political deliberation	36
6 Sites of political deliberation	42
7 Taking stock: the realistic aspirations of deliberative performance	48
2. Political Deliberation and Legal Decision-making	53
1 Introduction	53
2 Deliberation and adjudication: politicizing law?	54
3 Between monocratic and collegiate adjudication	61
4 Conclusion	71
3. Political Deliberation and Constitutional Review	72
1 Introduction	72
2 The singularity of constitutional scrutiny	73
3 The conception of constitutional courts as deliberative institutions	82
4 Conclusion	99
4. Deliberative Performance of Constitutional Courts	101
1 Introduction	101
2 The three-tiered model of deliberative performance	103
3 The core meaning of deliberative performance	105
4 Internal and external deliberation: a reconfiguration	113
5 Prologue to the next chapters	118
5. The Ethics of Political Deliberation	122
1 Introduction	122
2 The character of an ethics of deliberation	123
3 Pre-decisional phase and public contestation	127

    4 Decisional phase and collegial engagement   128
    5 Post-decisional phase and deliberative written decision   136
    6 Conclusion   139

6. Institutional Design: Augmenting Deliberative Potential   142
    1 Introduction   142
    2 Institutional design as a facilitator of deliberative performance   145
    3 Constitutive devices   149
    4 Pre-decisional devices: promoting public contestation, preparing for collegial engagement   159
    5 Decisional devices: promoting collegial engagement   164
    6 Post-decisional devices: drafting a deliberative written decision   169
    7 Conclusion   173

7. The Legal Backdrop of Constitutional Scrutiny   176
    1 Introduction   176
    2 Deliberating about the constitution   177
    3 Responding to law: exoteric deliberation through public reasons   194

8. The Political Circumstances of Constitutional Scrutiny   196
    1 Introduction   196
    2 Devising political strategies   198
    3 Managing the constraints of politics: esoteric political instinct   209
    4 Between prudence and courage: a deliberative court as a tightrope walker   211
    5 Conclusion   219

9. Concluding Remarks   220
    No heroic court, no heroic judges   220
    What is new?   222
    What next?   223

Bibliography   229
Index   247

Introduction

THE IMAGERY OF CONSTITUTIONAL COURTS

The political culture of contemporary democracies has rendered a wealth of images about judges and courts. Such an accumulation of metaphors is unmatched by how we refer to other public officials. The representation of judges is rarely mundane. No wonder why this is so. Unlike legislators, which need to perform the all-too-human task of representing interests and negotiating mutual agreements in the name of collective self-government, we load the judicial shoulders with a more mysterious political ideal, namely, the "rule of law, not of men." When it comes to constitutional courts, the burden gets heavier and the accompanying images and ideals more hyperbolic. As the institution in charge of assuring constitutional supremacy and ultimately checking the constitutionality of ordinary political choices, it is seen as the bastion of rights and the ballast against the dangers of majority oppression. Against a backdrop of mistrust of electoral politics, they became the vedettes inside some circles of liberation movements and of struggles for emancipation.[1] This has happened not always because of what courts have actually done, but often for what they are expected to do.

Images need not only be rhetorical flurries that misguide the big audience about the intangible aspects of adjudication. There usually are concepts and arguments lurking behind them. These concepts prescribe functions, raise expectations, and draw the borders of the judicial job. Legal theorists have been trying to grasp constitutional adjudication in all its guises and, in order to introduce this book, I would like to concentrate on five influential images that have been extensively used in the debate about the character of constitutional courts: the veto-force, the guardian, the public-reasoner, the institutional interlocutor, and the deliberator. They need not be mutually exclusive, but each puts emphasis on a particular aspect of the court's enterprise.[2]

This book attempts to explore the last image—constitutional courts as deliberators—but, to the extent that it encapsulates aspects of the others,

---

[1] See Epp (1998).
[2] In this Introduction, I will henceforth refer to "constitutional courts" or "courts" inter changeably, unless otherwise specified.

I would rather start by sketching each one of them. A veto is a mechanical device to contain the actions of some countervailing force. It is part of the formal logic of the separation of powers and its internal dynamic of "checks and balances," reputedly at the service of liberty.[3] Modern constitutions would bestow upon courts the function of counterweighing the decisions of parliaments and executives. This would be one of the devices through which constitutionalism attempts to moderate different sources of power and institutionalize limited authority. It would prevent tyranny and arbitrariness. Parliaments and governments, under such decision-making machinery, are not all powerful. Courts, in turn, are a negative blockage the accord of which is required for legislative decisions to be constitutionally valid and effective.[4]

A more colorful depiction of courts conceives them as guardians of the constitution. A guardian would be an apolitical adjudicator who carries out the task of checking the constitutional validity of ordinary legislative decisions. There would be no creative or volitional element in such operation, but a disinterested and technocratic application of the law. Unlike the first image, which highlights the physicalist equilibrium between forces and counter-forces, this one is more content-driven. The court is a bound agent on behalf of its principal, a commissarial guarantor of the will of the constitutional founders, however that will is conceived. It allows for the practical meaningfulness of the constitution as the "supreme law of the land."[5] This basic idea somewhat evokes, in the realm of constitutional adjudication, the classical characterization of judges as the "mouthpiece of the law" (*bouche de la loi*).[6]

The remaining images are intimately related, part of a same package of theoretical endeavors to uphold courts on the grounds of their robust argumentative capacity and privileged perspective. Each, however, brings a new nuance to the frontline. A third way to enclose the task of courts envisions them as chief public reasoners of democracy or, in a popular phrase, as

---

[3] The classical reference is found in the Federalist Papers, n 51. See also the distinction between two conceptions of constitution—as machine and as a norm—proposed by Troper (1999).

[4] The "veto" language has also received some conceptual sophistication by other authors, not necessarily to refer to courts. It could certainly be further refined by distinguishing between obstructive and constructive types of veto and so on. A well-known distinction is between "veto-point," a neutral institution that political actors use as instruments to achieve their goals, and "veto-player," an institution that has an identifiable agenda and negotiates with the others to achieve a final outcome. The former would be peripheral whereas the latter would be integrated to the political process. Volcansek: "The court becomes a veto-player if it can say what the constitution means and invalidate both executive and legislative actions" (2001, at 352). See also Tsebellis, 2002, at 328.

[5] This was the formulation of *Marbury v. Madison*, 5 U.S. 137 (1803), which established the putative logical necessity of judicial review for the sake of constitutional supremacy (a necessity later de-constructed and criticized by authors like Nino, 1996, at 186).

[6] "Bouche de la loi" and "pouvoir nul" are classical expressions of Montesquieu to refer to subordinate adjudication. Chapter 2 will come back to this.

"forums of principle."⁷ Due to their insulated institutional milieu and argumentative duties, constitutional courts would be able to decide through a qualitatively unique type of reason. This theoretical stripe claims that judicial review enables democracies to convey a principled political discourse on the basis of which the dignity and force of the constitution are founded. This singular contribution would secure that rights are exercised and protected within a "culture of justification."⁸

The previous images share the assumption of judicial supremacy. Accordingly, as far as the interpretation of the constitution is concerned, courts would have the last word. The fourth image, however, rejects this traditional premise and portrays courts as institutional interlocutors. Judicial review would be a stage in a long-term conversation with the legislator and the broader public sphere. Understanding it as the last word would be empirically inaccurate and normatively unattractive: inaccurate because such an approach would miss the broader picture of an unending interaction over time; unattractive because rather than a monological supremacist, the court should work as a dialogical partner that challenges the other branches to respond to the qualified reasons it presents. In that sense, there would be no ultimate authority on constitutional meaning but a permanent interactive enterprise. The court, here, is still a public reasoner. It does not, though, speak alone and seeks to be responsive to the arguments it hears.⁹

Lastly, the court is also pictured as a deliberator. This image grasps an internal aspect of courts that the others would overlook: they are composed by a small group of individual judges who engage with each other argumentatively in order to produce a final decision. This internal process constitutes a comparative advantage of courts in relation to otherwise designed institutions. Courts allegedly benefit from the virtues of collegial deliberation and, thanks to their peculiar decisional conditions, are more likely to reach good answers upon constitutional interpretation. Thus, apart from a catalyst of inter-institutional and societal deliberation, as the previous image suggested, courts themselves would also promote good intra-institutional deliberation.¹⁰

---

⁷ Dworkin visualizes the court as the "forum of principle," Rawls as the "exemplar of public reason," among several other American scholars with resembling arguments. But this is far from an exclusive American trait. This function is widespread in the constitutional discourses of several other countries. Important examples include Germany, South Africa, Spain, Colombia, among others. Chapter 3 will come back to this.

⁸ This is common currency, for example, in South African constitutional discourse. Albie Sachs summarizes that trend: "we had moved from a culture of submission to the law, to one of justification and rights under the law" (2009, at 33). For an extensive overview, see also Woolman and Bishop (2008).

⁹ For a map of the literature, see Mendes (2009b) and Bateup (2006).

¹⁰ There are numerous articles on judicial collegiality, usually written by judges themseves. A good starting point is Edwards (2003). Specifically about constitutional courts, see Ferejohn and Pasquino (2002).

All images above cast quite optimistic light on what constitutional courts are or should be doing. Detractors of judicial review responded in the same metaphorical voice and furnished, to each of them, a less than praiseworthy flipside. Rather than a mere veto, courts would be political animals with an ideological agenda; rather than guardians, courts would embody an oracle with an inaccessible and armored expertise, would pretend to be mere phonographs and conceal themselves behind a mystifying cover;[11] rather than a public reasoner, courts would be rhetoricians, window-dressers of hidden positions or, at best, paternalistic aristocrats; rather than dialogical partners or deliberators, they would be strategic policy-seekers. These are the cynical counterparts that confront the mainly normative allegories sketched above. Together, they sum up the variegated imagery that constitutional theory has assembled in order to defend or condemn judicial review.

As noted, this book elaborates and tests the idea that courts can and should be special deliberators, that is to say, can and should develop significant deliberative qualities in the absence of which constitutional democracies get impoverished. It seems to me that this apprehension of the function of courts is more insightful than the alternatives. It still lacks, though, a systematic treatment. That is what I will try to do.[12] The other images still pervade the book and help me to explain, by contrast, what I mean. It is helpful, thus, to keep them in mind. The next section sets forth the methodological standpoint of the book and the last summarizes its overall structure.

---

[11] The court would be just a rubber stamp of parliament. Morris Cohen coined and attacked the phonograph theory. I will come back to this in Chapter 2. Here is a good sample of additional pejorative expressions: "bevy of Platonic Guardians" or "philosopher kings" (Learned Hand); "oracles of law" (Dawson); "constitutional oracle" (Stephen Perry); "moral censors of democratic choice" (Scalia); "wise council of tutors in moral truth" (Christopher Zurn); "moral prophet" (Rainer Knopf). Sometimes you can also hear even stronger expressions like "judicial tyranny," "judicial imperialism," among others. This rhetorical misuse of political vocabulary and the spread of an obscurantist anti-judicial lexicon has been misleading the public about the nature of adjudication for decades.

[12] It is opportune to add a quick biographical note. The problem has a personal intellectual history and summarizing my research path may help to make sense of the project in a wider perspective. I condense that research path in three steps. The first was to interpret the debate between Dworkin and Waldron with respect to judicial review. They are paragons of the last word framework and advocate supremacy for either one or the other side of the court-parliament scale. I have applied their arguments to the Brazilian constitutional regime, and although I did not fully embrace Waldron's claims, I showed how his concerns are relevant to problematize extremely rigid constitutions like the Brazilian, which empowers courts to overrule even constitutional amendments (see Mendes, 2008). The second step relativized my previous position and explored what that traditional polarization gets wrong. Such a myopic debate about the ultimate authority misses the interactive and long-term aspect of politics and a binary take on who should have the last word overlooks the variability of political legitimacy. Theories of dialogue, without ignoring the question of last word, would be more proficient to forge a gradualist approach to legitimacy (see Mendes, 2009a and 2009b). Finally, I am now trying to develop a measure of output that can more productively inform a gradualist debate about legitimacy. There are more or less legitimate courts, and hopefully the criteria devised here help to perceive it. That is the horizon of this book.

A METHODOLOGICAL VANTAGE POINT: GAINS AND LOSSES OF MIDDLE-LEVEL ABSTRACTION

This is a book on normative theory. It is concerned with the way constitutional courts should behave in a "well-ordered constitutional democracy," to borrow Rawls' well-known phrase.[13] I departed above from a general canvass about how constitutional courts are visualized in contemporary democracies. I did not give much of an explanation, however, of what I meant by constitutional courts. They are not, indeed, a homogeneous category, but comprise different designs and work under distinct legal cultures, argumentative traditions, constitutional texts, and political environments.

This raises legitimate methodological questions: can normative theory devise prescriptions and guidelines that are equally applicable to any constitutional court? Would such a theory not need to be jurisdiction-bound? Do all extant constitutional courts have a common set of invariants that allow us some generalization? Can something useful be said at this level of abstraction? Is there such a thing as a non-parochial constitutional theory? To what extent can constitutional theory travel across constitutional regimes? Anyone that delves into the literature on the topic may easily come across opening statements like "this is a theory for the American Supreme Court" or "these arguments apply to the German constitution."[14] Whether this is the only productive approach is what I want to thematize here.

For a certain mode of thinking, each court can only be grasped and explained within a very specific context. Contexts, moreover, are never identical across jurisdictions. Judges are different creatures in different settings (for reasons related not only to legal tradition and design, but also to a series of other background factors). Law and politics would be singular phenomena in each place and the boundaries between them diversely set. One can never entirely understand an institution, that thought goes, outside such context, let alone recommend what that institution should do.

This cautious methodological position is not unfounded. Such warning, though, should be taken with a grain of salt. It does not exclude, but rather presupposes, a complementary logical space which, however limited, must be occupied by what I will call "middle-level" normative theory. Or so I shall argue. This book permeates that space (as do so many other theoretical works that, despite not turning this methodological premise explicit,

---

[13] Rawls (1997a). This expression is a variation of "well-ordered society," basis of Rawls' theory of justice (1971).

[14] See, for example, Dworkin (1996) and Alexy (2010). Several authors claim to be doing jurisdiction-bound theory but cannot help slipping into more abstract considerations in order to carve more solid foundations for their normative projects. The fact that they have been usually appropriated by other legal cultures also indicates a certain commonality across jurisdictions.

also advance general arguments on what are the most appealing democratic institutions, on the role of constitutional courts and so on"[15]). Let me briefly explain this idea.

The fundamental task of normative theory is to prescribe, on the basis of values and principles, ideal or desirable states of affairs, or how things ought to be. It founds a judgmental standpoint from where to proclaim what arrangements are attractive and, comparatively, better than others. It equips one with critical lenses from which to assess a concrete object or process. It supplies a militant idiom.

In the sphere of politics, such prescriptions can inhabit distinct layers. At the level of utmost abstraction, it traces the deep values that should regulate the communal life. The proper articulation of values like dignity, autonomy, equality, community, among others, is the goal at this stage. Further down, normative theory also inquires into the secondary principles and institutions that better translate the values defined in the primary step. Democracy and its procedures may be found here. Closing this chain, each political community will make its own tertiary choices in the light of its own context and peculiar dilemmas. These are the constitutive parts of the argumentative tree: the roots strike the balance of abstract values, the trunk proposes its institutional corollaries and the crown comprises the concrete historical instantiations. Each could be further decomposed, but this suffices for the moment.

The modern ideal of constitutional democracy is shaped by an elementary procedural framework that is not strikingly heterogeneous: among others, fair electoral competition, representative parliaments, and the protection of basic freedoms are constants without which, to a greater or lesser degree, the regime is not recognized as such. Constitutional courts are, more often than not, part of that project, or, to use an anthropological jargon, "near universals"[16] of constitutional democracies.[17]

If, on the one hand, concrete instantiations of constitutional courts are products of particular historical narratives, it would be utterly wrong to deny that they are enmeshed in that common wave of political discourse. They are conceptualized under a backdrop of largely equivalent set of principles and signified by similar symbolic references. That project transcended

---

[15] Waldron (2006a) is a good example.

[16] Brown provides a definition of near universal: "one for which there are some few known exceptions or for which there is reason to think there might be some exceptions," as opposed to absolute universals, which is found among all people known to history (2004, at 48).

[17] It is something in between the contrast that Raz, for example, draws between philosophy and sociology of law: "The latter is concerned with the contingent and with the particular, the former with the necessary and the universal" (1979, at 104).

jurisdictional boundaries and, to the extent that it entails a core set of institutional devices, some normative theory had to travel together with them.

The normative arguments this book formulates, once more, intend to be applicable to any constitutional court. I presuppose very little by this term and isolate only three common denominators. For the purposes of this book, constitutional court will be a (i) multi-member and non-elected body[18] that, (ii) when provoked by external actors,[19] (iii) may challenge,[20] on constitutional grounds, legislation enacted by a representative parliament. This body is accountable for the reasons it provides and not for the periodical satisfaction of its constituents. That is my departing assumption. Everything else is up for supplementary institutional imagination.

I take a stand, nonetheless, on the target that such extra imagination should track or, more precisely, on the specific mission that the institution will carry out. Deliberation, or deliberative performance, in the multi-faceted way defined in this book, is my north. It gives my analysis a sense of direction, but remains open-ended. I provide reasons to defend that such a body should be deliberative, and point to the normative implications that ensue. There certainly are many alternative yet valid routes to that north, and only contexts will present the occasional obstacles and shortcuts.

All real constitutional courts, as we know from the repertoire offered by institutional history, despite sharing those three basic features, go much beyond them. Comparative law itself often sets a stricter technical use of that term.[21] Middle-level theory does not supply single detailed solutions for the many further variables that need to be fleshed out, does not determine, in all minutiae, what is the best constitutional court for all times and places. It illuminates, however, what is at stake in each institutional dilemma. It refrains from closing an all-encompassing formula for solving the various trade-offs that spring from each context. At the same time, it is aware of these trade-offs and may even dictate, once the context is known, how they should be balanced and solved. It is a theory for the wholesale, not the retail. That is as far as it can go. Jurisdiction-bound theory will complete the overall normative task by filling in what the other lets open.

---

[18] Some would prefer the umbrella concept of "judicial independence," but I prefer to avoid it not only because it tends to suggest an untenable notion of total "separateness" from political branches, but also because it already commits to other institutional variables that I prefer to leave open.

[19] Inertia is another feature that would promote independence and impartiality. Courts are not allowed to act "ex officio," to have their own initiative, to put forward their own causes.

[20] "Challenge" is a more flexible term that comprises not only the actual power to override or invalidate legislation but also weaker forms of authority like the competence to "declare the incompatibility," as introduced by the UK Human Rights Act (1998) into the British constitutional system.

[21] See Cappelletti (1984).

Middle-level theory, therefore, has an imperfect traction and gains plausibility by candidly recognizing its limits. It should not promise, indeed, what it will not and cannot deliver. In order to have some bite, it must follow at least two requirements upon which the validity of its claims depends. First, it should be malleable and adaptable enough to the specificities of different circumstances. Its versatility protects it from being hostage to jurisdictional particularities and, at the same time, turns it into a context-sensitive normative model. It endorses alternative instantiations of the ideal as long as they make justified choices between the apposite variables. Second, and as a consequence of the first, it needs to identify up until where it can go, that is to say, to employ a measure self-restraint.

Middle-level political theory strays from uncharted normative imagination, which builds the political edifice from scratch. It rather imagines what a constitutional court can be, taking for granted a few consolidated features that can be identified in all courts. Its advantage is to allow for more creative thought-experiments. However constrained by the minimal denominators, it is not tied to real constitutional courts. What it captures in horizontality, though, it inevitably loses in verticality. It does "cover more by saying less," as Sartori would note.[22] That does not mean that I will abstain from climbing or descending, when appropriate, that "ladder of abstraction,"[23] just for the sake of methodological purism. On the contrary, the book's account occasionally addresses ideal theory and offers contextual examples. When it moves upwards and downwards, crossing the boundaries of this middle-level and tilting the argument's centre of gravity, it may lose either in specificity or generality. As long as such gains and losses remain clear, they may enrich the inherently unstable borders of the middle-level.[24] Such instability, though, does not erode its analytical function.

This book advances a pragmatic yet principled case for a deliberative constitutional court or, more generally, a case in favor of a distinctly deliberative institution that is safe from the electoral sort of political pressure and legitimation.[25] A pragmatic yet principled endorsement is probably the only type of normative case one can cogently make for an institution. It is not a defence from an a-historical and deracinated point of view. There is a contingent genealogy of this institution, and it was spread over the reputedly democratic world in the last sixty years. Their differences are significant, but should not be overstated under pains of missing a clear sense of commonality. They are proxies of a similar ideal, not coincidental accidents.

---

[22] Sartori, 1970, 1033.   [23] Sartori, 1970, 1053.

[24] I thank Oxford University Press's reviewer for this clarification.

[25] It is an appeal similar to Pettit's (2005) case for a dualist democracy, one that includes both the exercises of voting and contestation, the "authorial" and "editorial" functions of institutions.

I try to raise conclusions that are applicable to all contexts that share those minimal institutional denominators. For the same reason, however, I stop short of making specific prescriptions. I do not and cannot assume too much by way of common denominators. Neither do I want to derive too essentialistic concepts about the function, structure, and capacity of courts. I leave room for contextual and contingent factors, which cannot be managed at this abstract level.

I believe that this fine line between middle-level and jurisdiction-bound theory, however contested, can and should be drawn.[26] This "virtue of incompletion,"[27] however limited a virtue it might be, allows for a less particularistic approach. Whether this book succeeded on taking up that task is a different story. This section hopefully hinted at a template of criteria by which the reader might assess my attempt to chase that aim.

A ROADMAP OF THE ARGUMENT

The book has nine chapters. In the first chapter, I locate the general discussion about the ideal of political deliberation as a way of collective decision-making within the contemporary literature. Besides an abstract definition of deliberation, the chapter systematizes the intrinsic and instrumental reasons that justify deliberation, supplies criteria to recognize the circumstances in which deliberation might be desirable or not, and shows the specificities that different deliberative sites may have. The second chapter examines how deliberation might relate to law conceptually, by way of legal reasoning, and institutionally, by way of collegiate adjudication. The third chapter dissects the singularity of constitutional adjudication, as opposed to parliaments or ordinary courts, describes how it has come to be perceived and defended as deliberative, and finally diagnoses the gaps in this mainstream approach.

The fourth chapter expounds the key argument of the book and fleshes out the core meaning of deliberative performance. It basically applies the analytical categories of the first chapter to the deliberative phases of a constitutional court and puts forward standards of performance. The fifth chapter will consider the ethical benchmarks that judges should follow in order to

---

[26] There surely is nothing methodologically original in the idea of "middle-level" theory. I could number important authors that engage in exactly such activity. A clear recent example is Waldron (2006a), particularly in his attempt to locate an abstract "core" against judicial review. The idea of a "core" is precisely the definition of hypothetical conditions under which, for him, judicial review would neither be necessary nor desirable. He claims, at a "middle-level," that these conditions obtain in most contemporary democracies, hence the illegitimacy of such institution in all those settings.

[27] These are Walzer's words. He also points to the philosophical tradition that takes up the opposite approach: "Completeness means a closed system, an account of the single best regime, a 'whole' that can be rationally discovered or invented but not rationally contested or revised" (1990, at 225).

animate a court in the deliberative course. These standards correspond to judicial virtues that stand out in each deliberative phase. The sixth chapter focuses on institutional design, the chief facilitator of deliberative performance. More specifically, it will group the devices that are mostly related to the deliberative capacity of courts, and point to the trade-offs that underlie the choice of each device.

Chapter 7 depicts the legal backdrop on the basis of which constitutional courts elicit public justifications for deciding. These boundaries encompass the value-laden character of the constitutional language, the burden of precedent, the argumentative duties towards the inferior courts and towards other branches, and the cosmopolitan reverberations that foreign case-law may have.

Chapter 8, in turn, organizes the political constraints of constitutional adjudication. They comprise the tensions involved in agenda-setting and docket-forming, in defining the degree of cohesion of the written decision (whether single or plural), in calibrating the width, depth, and tone of the decisional phrasing, in anticipating the degree of cooperation or resistance of the other branches and in managing public opinion. The chapter further recommends that the virtues of prudence and courage should help a constitutional court to handle the political pressures it faces. The ninth and last chapter draws some concluding remarks about the repercussions that the overall argument might have for democratic theory.

One may agree or disagree with the book at various stages. First, one can start doubting the general importance of deliberation in politics and collective decision-making. Second, one might raise a relevant suspicion about whether courts are plausible deliberative candidates. Finally, even if one agrees both with the significance of deliberation and with the contribution that a court can make in that matter, one might still reject the model of deliberative performance concocted here, either in its gross structural shape (organized around the ideas of "core meaning," "hedges," and "facilitators") or in its internal components.

If a court is going to be presented in the deliberative mode, I believe these are necessary theoretical steps. I furnish a controlled normative argument that shows what is at stake if a court wants the benefits and burdens of deliberation. I investigate in what sense and to what extent a constitutional court can and should be a deliberative institution, and why a non-deliberative court is inferior to a deliberative one. I lay out, in other words, some patterns of excellence and the potential distinctiveness of constitutional adjudication with regards to its capacity to deliberate and to trigger external deliberation on constitutional meaning. It involves peculiar sorts of failures and achievements.[28]

---

[28] I believe this exercise is analogous to the one made by Lon Fuller in his classical book *The Morality of Law* (1968). There, he devised the principles of excellence in lawmaking and examined how to manage them together in order to build and sustain the rule of law, balancing those standards case-by-case.

The book helps to assess the political legitimacy of judicial review in a gradualist, adaptive, and contextually sensitized way. It has a broad scope and rings several bells in political theory generally conceived. It strives to contribute to different departments of this literature. It may raise a few constructive challenges to the portions of democratic theory that do not assign any role to deliberation; of deliberative democratic theory that accepts the description of courts as mere legalist distractions or deviations from deep moral reasoning; of constitutional theory that do not spell out what a deliberative court entails, that do not pay attention to the politics of adjudication or that, on the other extreme, reductively conceives it as politics by other means. I put forward, in sum, an experimental way of evaluating constitutional courts.

I will not describe the type of deliberative forum that real courts actually are out there. I will rather talk about what sort of forum they can be. I do not furnish an exhaustive list of answers, but a reasonably comprehensive and systematic map of the relevant questions. The answers will legitimately hinge upon alternating circumstances. The model provides me an angle and a heuristic gear through which to compare real constitutional courts.

The book intends not only to forge a pilot "deliberometer," a prototype of the critical equipment that constitutional democracies should develop in order to keep constitutional adjudication under public scrutiny, but also, and first of all, to justify a constitutional court that is specially proficient in deliberating. I probe this stimulating image and envisage some of its promising consequences.

Lastly, a caveat should be stated. The term "deliberation" is used with more than one single meaning along the book. The definition stipulated in Chapter 1, which is my pivotal reference for the concept of deliberative performance, refers to deliberation as an inter personal argumentative engagement. Deliberation, however, has also been used by the literature in slightly different, yet related, senses. Sometimes, deliberation is conceived as mere reason-giving, as the reflexive balancing of reasons, as the exposure to reasons, or as a loose sort of conversation that leads to decision.

Deliberation, therefore, is a term with a large baggage of meanings in the tradition of political philosophy, and also in the contemporary literature of constitutional theory. This instability or variability of conceptual uses may be seen as a problem or rather as a quality of the book. It may be a problem because it risks creating conceptual uncertainty and blurring the very object which I seek to examine. To the extent that these differences are made clear, and that the case for deliberative performance specifies exactly what is entailed by each standard, this risk was hopefully avoided or mitigated. The advantage of this malleable treatment, on the other hand, is to capture aspects of deliberation that, despite relevant for deliberative performance, would fall out of a strict conceptual reach.

1

Political Deliberation and Collective Decision-making

I. INTRODUCTION

Deliberation is believed to evince an appealing ideal for politics. Surprisingly enough, however, the precise benefits it can bring or the harms, if any, it can inflict are not easily discernible. Dialogue and conversation, debate and justification, sympathy and engagement, publicity and rationality, persuasion and openness, transparency and sincerity, respect and charity, mutuality and self-modesty, consensus and common good are but a few hints that allegedly point to what such ideal is about. Self-interest and closure, fixed preferences and aggregation, optimal compromise of pre-political desires, conversely, would negatively indicate what falls short of the deliberative quality threshold. This is an easy black-and-white contrast, for sure. As with every caricature, it does not lead us very far in understanding, evaluating, and illuminating possible avenues for the improvement of contemporary politics.

The fact remains, though, that deliberation, as traditionally depicted, is indeed multicolored and hard to grasp. The persistent resort to such opposition might show that, more than a mere didactic shortcut, it is an unavoidable way to capture this slippery phenomenon. On the grandiose side, politics is praised as a way of life, or at least as the legitimate environment to manage the tensions of pluralism in a wise and respectful manner. On the mundane side, politics is seen as a means to amalgamate and accommodate private ends, to survey the opinions shaped in our individual lives. One is reflective and emancipatory; the other unreflective and solipsistic, fragmenting and disruptive. One operates by channeling voices and weighing reasons of fellow partners in a common enterprise; the other, by counting heads of winners and losers within a minimal agreement of modus vivendi. Collective decision, for one, is a product of strenuous intellectual exercise and cooperation; for the other, just an inventory of individual wills fairly negotiated. And the distinctions could go further. If asked to choose, one would hardly deny the greater attractiveness of the former option. Common sense is on its side. Again, this would be too quick.

The starting point of a book that deals with political deliberation, thus, should unpack this umbrella-concept into its parts. Such systematization is relevant not only for the sake of clarity, but also to set the variables and their connections in an administrable way. Inasmuch as the case for deliberative politics is put forward both through intrinsic and instrumental reasons, so does the case against it. On the side of the advocates of deliberation, there are normative sympathizers, who think deliberation is a political good regardless of its results, and empirical believers, who point to positive effects that are likely to ensue. On the side of the antagonists, conversely, we may have normative critics, who reject the appeal of deliberation, and empirical skeptics, who state that the expected causal connections are simply unfounded or yet to be proven.

This chapter supplies some analytical categories that drive the whole dissertation and describes the cardinal elements of political deliberation. The second section stipulates the conceptual frame of deliberation. The third explains why and how normative sympathizers endorse it and critics oppose it. The fourth advances the instrumental debate and conveys the sorts of positive effects empirical upholders envision, and of negative or innocuous effects skeptics believe to be more accurate. The following fifth and sixth sections help to understand the chasm between advocates and antagonists in a more contextualized way, and two categories illuminate that dispute: the circumstances and the sites of deliberation. In sum, the chapter proceeds in three consecutive steps: definitional, justificatory, and contextualizing.

The contemporary literature, rich as though it may be, has not yet consolidated a comprehensive framework to address political deliberation. In the lack of a set of distinctions, however, it becomes hard to make sense of the controversies surrounding deliberation and of the exact targets at which objections against it are aimed. This chapter tries to do this preparatory conceptual work so that we can talk meaningfully and productively about the several angles of political deliberation. I provide one possible matrix of analysis through which to navigate inside this kaleidoscopic literature.[1] The chapter is an attempt to reconstruct a relevant part of a burgeoning bibliography and to put together the pieces for a comprehensive picture. It goes beyond description and takes a stand on several controversies in order to establish a theoretical foundation for the book.

---

[1] A relevant part of the literature mentioned in this chapter participates in the contemporary family of "deliberative democracy" theories. For the present purposes, I decouple democracy from deliberation and concentrate on the latter. The attempt to conceptualize deliberation regardless of it being democratic has been less common in recent times. More often, both concepts are conflated. For an analysis of the two separate components, see Pettit, 2006, at 156–157. Chambers (2009) also distinguishes between "deliberative democracy" and "democratic deliberation."

2. THE CONCEPTUAL FRAME OF POLITICAL DELIBERATION

Democratic theory has recently revived deliberation as a valuable component of collective decision-making. Deliberation features no less than a respectful and inclusive practice of reasoning together while continuously seeking solutions for decisional demands, of forming your position through the give-and-take of reasons in the search of, but not necessarily reaching, consensus about the common good. Thus, participants of deliberation, before counting votes, are open to transform their preferences in the light of well-articulated and persuasive arguments. Despite a range of variations, both conceptual and terminological, within the literature of deliberative democracy, this can plausibly be regarded as its minimal common denominator.[2]

The previous paragraph wraps up an intricate set of elements. Any political decisional process that fails to tick the boxes of that checklist could be a proxy but still not deserve to be called deliberation. Let me further depict the several components of that stipulative working definition. It bundles together seven major aspects that make up the deliberative encounter: first, it presupposes the need to take a collective decision that will directly affect those who are deliberating or, indirectly, people who are absent; second, it considers the decision not as the end of the line but as a provisional point of arrival to be succeeded by new deliberative rounds; third, it is a practice of reasoning together and of justifying your position to your fellow deliberators; fourth, it is reason-giving through a particular kind of reason, one that is impartial or at least translatable to the common good; fifth, it assumes that deliberators are open to revise and transform their opinions in the light of arguments and implies an "ethics of consensus"; sixth, it also involves an ethical element of respect; seventh, it comprehends a political commitment of inclusiveness, empathy, and responsiveness to all points of view.

Each of these pieces deserves further refinement. I will elaborate one by one a bit more. First, again, the decisional element. We are dealing with political rather than other sorts of deliberation.[3] Politics demands authoritative decisions that command obedience. Decisions compel deliberation with a practical course of action that a group or a political community needs to select. It is a serious choice that faces constraints of time and resources, and hence distinct from other sorts of conversation or inquiry that are not committed to such a drastic burden, like science, philosophy or, less solemnly, everyday cheap talk. Scientists and philosophers do not take decisions of the

---

[2] Several recent publications agree on the existence of a consolidated common denominator within the literature and usually announce it at the outset. See Dryzek, 1994 and 2000; Gutmann and Thompson, 1996; Chambers, 2003; Manin, 2005; Goodin, 2003; Bohman, 1998.

[3] From now on, I will be using "deliberation" and "political deliberation" inter changeably, unless otherwise expressly noted.

same sort. The elements of coercive authority and legitimation are not in question. It does not mean that scientific or philosophical questions cannot be implicated in political decisions. This, in fact, frequently happens. However, when the political dilemmas are framed by scientific or philosophical conundrums, coercive choices will have to be taken regardless of the existence of a right answer in those non-political domains, which conceptually do, and practically should, remain independent. The moment those questions enter the field of politics, they are turned into a different operational logic. Political deliberation has a degree of urgency that faces a peculiar temporal scale. It leads to a closure, provisional as it may be. Moreover, the effects of such a decision directly impact the lives of the deliberators, and possibly, depending of how the deliberative site is shaped, of people that are outside of it.

Second, political deliberation survives a decision and may be reawakened in new rounds of debate. Deliberators do not ignore that decisions are momentous choices that consummate concrete effects in a community's life, but neither do they overlook the element of continuity.[4] There is life after decision and the argumentative process goes on. Fresh practices of contestation, therefore, may well call for new collective decisions, which will always have a taint of provisionality. This tension between the need to decide and the ongoing post-decisional disputes, one could rightly say, is not a singular feature of deliberation, but a fact of politics in general, however way it is practiced and conceived. This observation, acute as it may be, overlooks how continuity has a relevant role to play in explaining the value of deliberation. Continuity, for deliberative theorists, is not just a fact of politics, but an integral part of legitimate politics. It highlights a long run perspective that the justification for other procedures fails to realize. It echoes the popular saying: "A debate is not over until it's over." The following five elements help to configure deliberation more meticulously.

Third, deliberation transcends the act of gathering together to take a decision. It requires the participants to display the reasons why they support a particular stand. It comprehends an exercise of mutual justification that allows a thorough type of dialogue before a collective decision is taken. This means that the participants undertake a process of reason-giving and, afterwards, articulate some adequate combination of those reasons as the justificatory ground for the decision. Silence is acceptable neither during nor after the process.

---

[4] Schmitter rightly points out that "provisionality" cannot do the whole work in exempting deliberation from occasional failures: political decisions are marked by some taint of irreversibility and path dependence, and past mistakes are not entirely corrigible. He wants to counter a sort of "feel-good view" of deliberation, which relies on the continuity of deliberation to correct its own pitfalls (a position that, allegedly, Gutmann and Thompson adopt). "Keep deliberating," therefore, is not necessarily a satisfactory answer for its decisional shortcomings (Schmitter, 2005, at 431).

Fourth, reasons to decide may be of various types and spring from different sources. Not all types and sources are acceptable in political deliberative forums. The collective nature of the decision implies that only reasons that all members could conceivably embrace are compatible with deliberation. This requirement rules out appeals to exclusively private interests, which are not translatable into a language of the common good. Deliberators, as a result, must put themselves inside this chain of argumentative constraints and get out of them consistently.[5]

Fifth, deliberation still demands more. It is not just a matter of giving reasons that are attachable to a plausible notion of the common good. Reason-giving is actually intended to spark an interactive engagement in which deliberators try to persuade each other. A process of persuasion assumes at least three things: one, that its participants are willing or at least open to listen and to revise their initial points of view; two, that there is an ethics of consensus underlying the conversation; three, that coercion is absent.[6] All engage in persuasion because there is a shared belief about the potential existence of a better answer, and that it is worth the effort of trying to unfold it dialogically. The ethics of consensus is the motivational drive that feeds the genuine deliberative encounter. It cannot be confounded, though, with an actual need to craft consensus.[7] Consensus is dispensable not only because of the temporal pressure to decide, but also because deliberators might acknowledge that, as long as their argumentative capacities are exhausted,[8] some points may remain irreconcilable.[9] Again, with or without consensus, which is also inexorably doomed to be provisional, deliberation is always subject to be reignited.

---

[5] This is one of the most controversial domains of deliberative theory. Rawls (1997b) borrows the Kantian notion of public reason for his liberal conception of justice. Because it excludes comprehensive doctrines of the good life, and is formally rigid, it has been criticized on various fronts. For a relevant distinction between inclusive and exclusive public reason, see Rawls, 1997a, at 119, and for his notion of proviso, see Rawls (1997b). This debate has led to expansions and contractions of what is acceptable in this communicative process. Many now defend that non-rational and non-cognitive forms of expression, provided they can be translated into the common good, can be used. See Chambers, 2003, at 322. For Dryzek, rather than a strict conception of public reason, a more tolerant filter would include argument, rhetoric, humor, emotion, testimony, story-telling, and gossip. This would be compatible with deliberation as long as it "induces reflection upon preferences in non-coercive fashion" (2000, at 2). Mansbridge et al. (2010) share this expansive view and think that "mutual justifiability" can be accomplished through less strict reasoning patterns.

[6] See Mansbridge et al., 2010, at 94.

[7] Such ethics requires just "making aim for consensus" (Ferejohn, 2000, at 76). Consensus is seen as an aspirational aim that regulates conduct, not a compulsory end. To what extent the lack of consensus will be considered a failure of deliberation is gradually becoming a less controversial question among authors. Cohen (1997a) recognizes consensus it as an ideal to be chased while Young (1996) rejects it as oppressive. Chambers points out that deliberative theory has dropped a "consensus-centered teleology" and managed to accommodate pluralism and the agonistic side of democracy (2003, at 321).

[8] See Rawls and his idea of "stand off" (1997b, at 797).

[9] Facile criticisms of deliberation sometimes assume two rather implausible views: that deliberation is pointless unless it leads to consensus; that deliberation, regardless of the context, is always unable

The formation and transformation of preferences are, therefore, endogenous and autonomous.[10] They are sterilized in relation to exogenous pressure or heteronomous choices. The deliberative reason recognizes its own fallibility, as opposed to oracular reason, which does not leave room to be contested. The former is modest and dialogical, whereas the latter is dogmatic and usually authoritarian. Deliberative engagement is the opposite of talking past each other, of a conversation between deaf. It is neither, again, idle talk nor a verbal duel.[11] A deliberative institution, to that end, is not simply an ivory-tower reason-giver. The fact that a decision follows a certain argumentative canon, although it may help to justify a certain position, does not turn it deliberative either. This perception fails to capture the kernel of the deliberative clash, which comprises horizontal engagement to find and embrace the arguments that prevail over others on a sincere process of persuasion.[12]

Sixth, deliberation presupposes an ethical attitude based on the presumption that all individuals deserve to be treated with equal consideration. As a matter of inter personal morality, this requires the concrete practice of respect towards every participant and argument that is put forward. This does not mean that such process cannot be heated and conflictive or that it needs to appear amiable and convivial. Neither does it mean that all arguments should have equal weight. It hinges on the recognition, somehow displayed, that there is no hierarchy of status between participants.

Respect towards the individual deliberators, however, does not attain all their moral responsibilities. As a matter of political morality, they are also supposed to adopt an attitude that encompasses three elements: inclusiveness, empathy, and responsiveness.[13] When arguing, deliberators have to include (implicitly or explicitly) the different opinions that were aired, to vicariously imagine the points of view of those who are absent from the

---

to reduce disagreement. Deliberative institutions, however, should be able to make non-consensual decisions, and this feature does not harm its deliberative character. The need of consensus may actually be a disincentive to deliberation and slip into other sorts of interaction (Ferejohn, 2000, at 78–80).

[10] Rostbøll, 2008, at 81, and 2005, at 371.

[11] Walzer proposes a useful distinction between debate and deliberation. Deliberators are persuadable, debaters not; deliberators engage with each other, debaters want to convince the relevant audience that have the authority to grant them the victory. As he claims: "Debaters have to listen to each other, but listening does not produce a deliberative process. Their object is not to reach an agreement among themselves but to win the debate, to persuade the audience...A debate is a contest between verbal athletes, and the aim is victory. The means are the exercise of rhetorical skill, the mustering of favourable evidence and the suppression of unfavourable evidence, the discrediting of the other debaters, the appeal to authority or celebrity and so on...The other are rivals, not fellow participants; they are already committed, not persuadable; the objects of the exercise, again, are the people in the audience" (2004, at 96).

[12] The canonic regulative standard for that claim is the ideal speech situation, which is governed by the "force of the better argument," a maxim of discursive ethics. See Habermas, 1996, at 103, 230, 322–323.

[13] The idea of reciprocity, as defined by Gutmann and Thompson, captures some of these elements (1996, at 53). I believe that my formulation makes some internal components more explicit.

deliberative process but that are equally bound by its result,[14] and to respond (or be prepared to respond) to all counter-arguments. The dynamics between inclusiveness, empathy, and responsiveness, therefore, can be complex and certainly over-demanding. In order to be practicable, a qualitative selectiveness upon whom to expressly include, imagine, and respond to is indispensable. A deliberator, in any event, is aware of these regulative standards and of the abiding possibility that she may be asked to engage with further reasons. The ethical and the political requirements are both embedded in the moral value of equality. The distinction between the sixth and seventh elements is useful, nonetheless, to underscore that the political attitude involves not only respect for the individual, or the shallow recognition that he is a fellow member of the political community, but that it implies a responsibility to take his points of view into account.[15]

Political deliberation, in short, is this large composite. It is a variant of practical reasoning applied to collective decision-making processes. Conceptions of the common good, under this ideal, need to stand the test of argument, not just be numerically assented. It is certainly possible to relax or to tighten the deliberative requirements. One can, for example, conceive of public reason in a more or less expansive way, turn the ethical and political attitudes more or less strenuous and so on. What falls inside and outside the borders will depend on the purposes of each theory and account for its applicability and justifiability.

Different blends of those ingredients might lead to decisional processes that resemble but still fall short of this ideal standard. At another end of the spectrum, however, one could find other types of process that are more clearly opposed to it. Two methods, as briefly mentioned in the introduction, would synthesize, by contrast, what deliberation is not: voting and bargaining.[16] The latter consists in a market-type negotiation where the parties openly put their private interests on the table and trade mutual concessions in order to settle on an agreement that optimizes their respective desires. The former is more chameleonic and not necessarily incompatible with deliberation. Formally, voting is a fair method to aggregate individual positions by

---

[14] I refer to the members of the political community who do not have the power, the chance, the interest, or the competence to present arguments through formal or informal ways, and cannot be included but by empathetic imagination. Later in the chapter, in the section about the sites of deliberation, I will qualify the notion of "deliberator" and distinguish the various actors that may fall under it.

[15] The use of the terms "moral" and "ethical" are by no means uniform or stabilized in the history of philosophy. By "ethical," here, I mean "interpersonal morality" outside the realm of politics. The sixth and seventh elements are based on a distinction between interpersonal and political morality, both grounded on the value of equality.

[16] See Elster, 1998, at 7. Habermas (1996) distinguishes between interest-based bargaining and value-based reasoning.

giving them equal weight.[17] Depending on how this individual position is formed, though, it can shape three different archetypes. If voting is just the end-point of deliberation in order to reach a decision in the light of remaining disagreement, it is not incongruent but rather required by the deliberative ideal.[18] If, on the other hand, it is the aggregation of brute individual preference framed in private, that ideal precludes it. Somewhere in the middle, finally, voting may serve to merge, instead of naked interest, reflective judgments about the common good that did not pass through inter personal scrutiny. However valuable it may be, this third variant surely fails to meet the basic features of deliberation. In this stylized picture, voting may thus aggregate three different entities.

This clear-cut separation between deliberation, bargaining, and voting can be hard to see in real-world decisional processes. These may prove more or less convoluted and the three components oftentimes arise simultaneously in little distinguishable ways. Actual collective decisions are rarely deliberative or non-deliberative in a puristic sense. Impurities are hardly avoidable. Decision-making processes comprise a sum of different practices, each of which having a distinctive ethics and a proper mechanics. It is not always easy to single them out. They may be inescapably enmeshed and it is up to the theorist to dissect how these different components actually operate. It is important, therefore, to keep those uncontaminated categories for the sake of analysis.

3. VALUES OF POLITICAL DELIBERATION

There have been different normative routes to prescribe political deliberation. It has been envisioned through the lenses of political liberalism, republicanism, and communitarianism. The practice does not look entirely different from the perspective of each lens. Each stream of thought highlights distinct values, but end up converging into a fairly similar practice. With slightly distinct colors and emphases, deliberation is resourceful enough to instantiate the pattern of legitimate politics that satisfies such broad range of theoretical outlooks. For all of them, thus, deliberation entails a basis for political legitimacy, irrespective of the outcomes that follow. This reading does not ignore their occasional differences (especially on the boundaries of what constitutes acceptable reason in deliberation), but understands them as marginal variations for the purpose of this section.

---

[17] See Mansbridge et al., 2010, at 85.

[18] Elster addresses this point: "The input to the social choice mechanism would then not be the raw, quite possibly selfish and irrational, preferences that operate in the market, but informed and other-regarding preferences" (1997, at 11). Later he adds: "transformation of preferences can never do more than supplement the aggregation of preferences, never replace it altogether" (1997, at 14). Habermas also distinguishes between aggregation of deliberative or non-deliberative preferences (1996, at 304).

The exact cluster of values this single practice embodies will depend, therefore, on the eyes of the beholder. Deliberation has a magnetic pull to embrace or give expression to different sets of values. Liberals see equality and freedom, tolerance and respect or, more broadly, political justice. Individuals would be free and equals to the extent that collective decisions are grounded on reasons that all members could be reasonably expected to share.[19] Modern republicans see freedom and non-arbitrariness being promoted through contestation, a civic engagement that fosters collective self-government. Under this prism, deliberation would dilute domination.[20] Communitarians see inclusion and a politics of the common good.[21] The full trinity of modern political values—liberty, equality, and community—therefore, would be implicated in political deliberation.[22] At least partially, deliberation reconciles rather than divide diverse approaches to politics.

This mode of inter personal interaction, as defined by the conceptual frame, is valuable in its own right. Such conclusion is shared by a wide spectrum of theoretical persuasions. A normative sympathizer contends that deliberative collective decisions instantiate the best conception of political community. Deliberation, they claim, stands on a dignitarian footing, whatever outcomes may spring from it. It provides intrinsic reasons for authority to coerce, or, conversely, for citizens to comply. This conception of legitimacy is not contingent upon an imaginary contractual consent, but on a concrete practice of considerateness in the midst of disagreement.[23] It is not contingent upon consequences of deliberation, but solely on the value it entails.

Normative critics, however, tell a less glorious story about the attractiveness of deliberation. For them, an across-the-board defense of deliberation is oppressive, anti-political,[24] paternalistic,[25] and legalistic.[26] In trying to suppress

---

[19] This is the basic notion of public reason provided by Rawls (1997a, 1997b and 2005). See also Cohen (1997a) and Freeman (2000).

[20] For definitions of republican freedom, see Pettit's freedom as non-domination (1997, 2004b, 2005), Urbinati's freedom as non-subjection (2004), or Rostbøll's deliberative freedom and its multiple dimensions (2005 and 2008).

[21] See Sandel, 2010, at 242.

[22] Deliberation, as Walzer contends, aspires to be a procedure that turns the participants "free from domination, subordination, servility, fear, deference—from every residue and vestige of historical hierarchy" (1990, at 227).

[23] See Manin (1987).

[24] Deliberation would negate the inescapable role of passion in politics. On agonism, see Mouffe (2000a and 2000b).

[25] Political preferences, thus, are private acts, and in the name of privacy the actors should be exempted to explain it. See Elster, 1997, at 11. Rostbøll denies that deliberation is subject to the paternalistic objection, which he defines as follows: "Some people may want to make their decisions impulsively, without rational deliberation; insisting that they hear rational argument (for their own good) is paternalism" (2005, at 385).

[26] The rationalistic burden of deliberation would force politics to fit into a law-like model of argumentation. See Schroeder (2002).

the agonistic side of politics, it pushes forward an untenable notion of liberty and individuality. Politics would be mostly about conflict rather than consensus. The attempt to drive it in the light of the common good ignores the concreteness and existentiality of political confrontation.[27] The duty to provide reasons and to engage in persuasion removes from individuals the freedom to stay silent and manifest a sheer preference. Sometimes political preferences are what they are. Crude though they might be, there should be no need to attach a rational justification, neither to make it public. Authentic freedom would exempt one from publicly exposing her position and from connecting it to an idea of the common good.

Sympathizers and critics expound two classical visions of legitimate politics. The normative dispute hinges upon which is more defensible and feasible. The advocate of deliberation asserts that a politics of respect is feasible and superior to a politics of unaccountable and detached individuals or of "dictats and fiats"[28] imposed from the top. The freedom to stay silent, for him, when it comes to collective matters, is simply not acceptable. Or, in a more refined vision, as far as constitutional essentials are concerned, stale and untested preferences should not count.[29] Constitutional essentials, at the very least, would need to be grounded on rational judgments, and the obligation to justify is an integral part of judging.

Therefore, it would be the absence rather than the presence of deliberation that fails to fulfill the moral accomplishment intended by that practice. It is not intrusive or unduly rationalistic, but simply a reasonable duty of those who want to construct a kind of community inspired by those values. It is not, thus, anti-political, but distinctly political: it refuses to take politics as the concert of market-driven preferences, which cannot imbue any laudable kind of autonomy.[30] Legitimate collective decisions, in such perspective, hinge upon the exhibition of reasons in the public forum.

If politics is more than the mediation of personal interests, but also a search for the common-good through a practice of reasoning together about collective action, decisions must be publicly justified in this light. On that account, some theory needs to supply a grammar of political argumentation, that is to say, to categorize the different kinds of valid reasons and the rules of priority that regulate them.[31] The provision of such a theory is one central burden

---

[27] See Schmitt (2007).   [28] Pettit (2006, at 153).   [29] Rawls (1997b).

[30] Rostboll asserts: "In deliberation, we must respect the status of each other as free persons, in the sense of persons worth arguing with and as persons who can contribute and respond appropriately to reasons" (2005, at 389).

[31] Political liberalism, for example, sets a priority of rights and liberties over the general welfare. See Rawls (2005). Dworkin's idea of "rights as trumps" is another example. See Dworkin (1978).

of the deliberative literature. Liberals, republicans, and communitarians certainly disagree on the features of such grammar.[32] To enter this dispute is not the purpose of this book. The debate about the reasons that can be used in political deliberation will be addressed in the very precise institutional context of a constitutional court, a task to be discharged by Chapter 7. For the purpose of the current chapter, therefore, it is enough to highlight the common normative core, if contested at the edges, of deliberative theories.

4. PROMISES AND PERILS OF POLITICAL DELIBERATION

There is a difference between what political deliberation is and what it can be expected to produce. There is also a dissimilarity between the values of deliberation itself and its reputed consequences.[33] It is not trivial to reiterate that.[34] In order to avoid circularity, the distinction between what is constitutive of and what is derivative from deliberation cannot be conflated.[35]

If a person wants to participate in deliberation, the conceptual frame indicates what attitudes she should cultivate. The values of deliberation, in turn, furnish their respective intrinsic grounds, the non-consequentialist side of why deliberation is worth pursuing. Both conceptual moves were done by the two previous sections. Political theory, however, has also elaborated on the outputs that this process is likely to deliver. Instrumental reasons are thence part of this theoretical wave, and portray deliberation as a means for attractive external ends. They show what a participant should expect to accomplish collectively. Advocates of deliberation, again, are not speaking alone. Skeptics also claim their place in this canvas and point to the not so positive effects to which deliberation, perhaps counter-intuitively, may yield. Political deliberation, the skeptics submit, is neither riskless nor infallible. Its potential failures are not negligible and, in some contexts, may outweigh the occasional benefits.

Empirical believers point to four kinds of deliberative achievements: epistemic, communitarian, psychological, and educative. From the epistemic point of view, deliberation would promote, at least, clarity about what issues are at stake; at most, it would arrive at the true and best answer. From the communitarian perspective, deliberation would encourage consensus (or at least minimize dissensus), nurture social legitimacy, and deepen a sense

---

[32] Sandel, for example, claims that the rigid requirements of liberal public reason would lead to a "politics of avoidance" instead of a "politics of moral engagement" (2010, 270).

[33] This is not to say that deliberation is purely formal, as Gutmann and Thompson (1996) have argued.

[34] As Mutz maintains: "In practice, good deliberation is often defined as deliberation that produces the desired consequences outlined in the theory. This circularity makes it impossible to use this approach to evaluate the claims of deliberative theory" (2008, at 527).

[35] See the debate between Mutz (2008) and Thompson (2008).

of community. Third, it would instill in deliberators the feeling of being respected. Last, it would educate deliberators both about the respective subject matter and about the deliberative skills themselves. These outcomes may co-exist and reinforce each other. They are not unambitious bets. Their merits are not exclusive of deliberation either. Advocates, however, give credence to deliberation as a more powerful means to foster them.

Deliberative achievements, skeptics warn, might be less praiseworthy than those optimistic promises. The risks would be four-fold too. At the epistemic side, instead of clarifying things, it might be hostage of distorting rhetoric[36] and posturing, end up being obscure, deceiving, and manipulative. At the communitarian, deliberation may deepen disagreement and confrontation. It might empower the rhetorician and the demagogue, while disempowering the already vulnerable. From the psychological prism, deliberators would feel anything but respected equals. Rather, it would serve to reinforce pre-existing hierarchies of status. Contrary to what one might hope, deliberation might educate strategic rather than public-spirited behavior. Finally, deliberation may simply be inefficient, a waste of time, money, and energy among other scarce political resources.

Why should one accept that deliberation fulfills those promises? And under what basis can normative theory predict the results of a certain process of decision-making? These empirical conjectures are made through likelihood estimations, which may be confirmed or falsified by empirical inquiry.[37] Until being disproved, they are granted the benefit of the doubt. At the level of normative theory, on that account, debates about the promises of deliberation are set in terms of plausibility and probability. A reputable tradition of political thought developed such language. The perils, on the other hand, are mostly pointed out by empirical refutations of normative expectations. I will proceed, then, by describing how the promises of deliberation are deemed as plausible.[38]

The act of displaying, from multiple perspectives, the reasons that underlie each conception of the common good, of unfolding premises and subjecting them to critical challenge, would have the manifest virtue of debunking myths, de-constructing prejudices, sanitizing misunderstandings, triggering new ideas and, above all, structuring arguments in a clearer order. It seems sensible to suppose that, except through engaging communication, pre-existing divergent premises would not come to be known, let alone tested or transformed. If we

---

[36] Deliberation is not necessarily at odds with rhetoric, but with a particular kind of rhetoric. See Chambers (2009), Dryzek (2010), and Fontana et al. (2004).

[37] See Thompson (2008).

[38] Partial empirical findings claim that some promises are overstated while others can be confirmed under the right context. For a general review of the empirical literature, see Delli Carpini (2004) and Ryfe (2005).

cannot reach an agreement, at least we are able to know on what and why we disagree. In the same sense, it is through the revelation of the points of view of every participant that this process maximizes the information that might be helpful to decide.[39] Mute amalgamation of preferences formed at home, then, would be a much inferior alternative to pursue the epistemic tasks of (i) premise-unveiling and (ii) information-gathering.[40] Some stop here and consider this to be enough. But others go farther. Deliberation would still fuel the ability of the group to come up with solutions not envisioned by any individual alone. It would be, therefore, a (iii) creativity-sparkling exercise.[41] Finally, it would also perform, better than the alternative methods, a fourth and less modest epistemic mission: if the deliberative process manages to be both a good disinfectant and a competent informer, it cannot but also be a gifted (iv) truth-seeker.

Truth, both in politics and in morals, is predictably not safe from controversy. People disagree about what the true answer is, or whether this very category is at all appropriate in this domain. If truth is really at stake in the search for the common good, what can it mean? Which truth is up for political deliberation? It is not necessary to enter the cognitive or meta-ethical debates to get the point of this epistemic promise. The literature on deliberation itself does not usually pursue that path. More often, they even avoid the metaphysical tone and polemical language of truth, and prefer less contentious expressions as "reasonable"[42] or "better" answer. There is a risk of mischaracterizing or exaggerating their claim, and, indeed, there is not one single version of it.[43]

One of these versions is worth taking seriously for the purposes of this chapter. It states that: since truth about the common good is ultimately undemonstrable,[44] political decisions must all the more have a respectful

---

[39] Silva (2013, at 561).

[40] For Mansbridge et al., when conflicts are irreconcilable, "deliberation ideally ends not in consensus but in clarification of conflict and structuring of disagreement, which sets the stage for a decision by non-deliberative methods" (2010, at 68).

[41] Shapiro argues: "Regardless of possible transformative or cathartic effects on preferences, deliberation may throw up ways of dealing with conflicts that otherwise might not come to the fore" (2002, at 199). See also Grimm (2003).

[42] This is the language of political liberalism. See Rawls (2005).

[43] The classical epistemic arguments are based on the "many minds" idea, not exactly on deliberation: Aristotle (wisdom of the crowds), Rousseau (general will), and Condorcet (jury theorem, a formalization of Rousseau's insight). For Rousseau and Condorcet, in particular, deliberation would disturb rather than help; Mill and Dworkin would fit better. Other contemporary proponents: Estlund (2008), Cohen (1997b), Nino (1996), Martí (2006).

[44] As Dworkin (1986) has pointed out, the fact of undemonstrability or of disagreement does not tell anything about the existence of the right answer. Ontology, therefore, should be severed from epistemology. For Waldron (2001), the ontological question is irrelevant in the realm of politics, which needs to deal with disagreement in a respectable manner. On epistemic proceduralism, see also Estlund (2008).

procedural pedigree; it would be self-defeating, though, to infer from the fact of undemonstrability the conclusion that procedures should be concerned only with its formal respectability and renounce any epistemic pretension; if, on that account, we accept that the legitimacy of political decisions hinges both upon the quality of procedures and outcomes, the procedure needs to somehow fulfill both the moral input-test and the epistemic output-test; the appropriate output-test, due to the fact of undemonstrability and uncertainty, cannot be more than one of likelihood set in advance; deliberation, the ratiocination concludes, is the only procedure that is both morally appealing and, even if fallible, more likely than the alternatives to attain the second test. And why is it more likely? Because it amplifies the scope of points of view, subjects opinions to permanent rational scrutiny, and creates an environment that is logically more hospitable for truth to materialize.[45] We may well find truth by chance, by an astute individual mind or by a number of other means. But reliance on serendipity or individual brilliance cannot be captured by a procedure set *ex ante*, and, in any event, would fail the moral input-test. Thus, the argument goes full circle. Perhaps "truth," for all its universal and ahistorical temper, and for its contested implications, overburdens this fourth epistemic contention. If we switch the terminology from truth to "reasonable," however, lest committing ourselves to a unitary notion of truth, this epistemic claim may regain its purchase power.[46]

This sounds, at any rate, like a "just so story," a reconciliatory narrative that overlooks inevitable trade-offs between conflicting purposes (between respectful input and right output). This would be, however, a premature conclusion in the light of an under-refined summary. In order to make it more persuasive, this epistemic claim would certainly need to clarify, among other things, how it applies to different types of common good[47] and what room it concedes for expertise.[48] To remain attractive, it should also accept that the ideal procedure is still fallible and that it does not exclude an independent substantive criterion to judge the results.[49] Equating the outcome of such

---

[45] On how Marcuse conditionally accepts disruption as a way of political expression, see Estlund (2004).

[46] Gutmann and Thompson (1996) defend the inseparability of procedure and substance in the analysis of legitimacy, and come up with a quite similar formulation.

[47] There are, one could rightly say, collective decisions of different kinds, and it would be misleading to put all of them under a general label of common good. Distinctions between the purely contingent and the essentially value-laden questions that pervade collective dilemmas are necessary to refine this position. Dworkin (1996) draws a similar distinction between "sensible" and "insensible" preferences, or between policies and rights.

[48] I will briefly return to this point on expertise in the later section about sites of deliberation.

[49] A classic presumption made by Rousseau, and more recently reformulated by others like Cohen (1997b). Schauer describes the problems of taking deliberation as constitutive of political truth. For him, there must be a "gap between political truth and constitutional truth, with the latter but not the former defined by the process of deliberation" (1992, at 1201).

a process with truth would suppress the continuous openness to critical challenge that is an inherent property of deliberation. It would go beyond the aim of the section to delve into all this. For the moment, it suffices to say that, for this family of theories, in order to discharge these four cumulative epistemic tasks, people would better talk and deliberate. Alternative means for the same purposes, when they exist, would be inferior. Surely, without specifying who, when, and upon what to deliberate, this remains too crude. These qualifications will come later in the chapter.

So much for the epistemic argument. The second well-known promise of deliberation is the communitarian. It submits that deliberation is a proper means to reach consensus or reduce dissensus. Again, it looks like a steadfast probabilistic prediction: if all participants are committed to pursue the common good and, moreover, to persuade each other through the exchange of public reasons, such an interaction could, over time, more probably than other processes, end up in agreement or, at least, lessen disagreement. Thanks to the force of the better argument, truth would prevail after careful scrutiny and naturally command general assent.

This optimistic idea was supposedly embraced with enthusiasm by a first generation of deliberative democrats.[50] Due to the aberrant implausibility, and even undesirability, of calling for consensus (let alone truth) in a pluralist society, most of them have abandoned that promise, at least in its thick versions.[51] Some critics rejoiced and proclaimed game over. A qualification of the possible meanings of consensus, however, can put the discussion on a more fertile soil. More elaboration is in order here.

With regard to its origins, one can conceive of five types of consensus: spontaneous; product of partnership, pragmatic, or unprincipled compromise; and coercive.[52] Spontaneous consensus may unfold automatically in the exercise of deliberation. Such a muscular version is fairly straightforward: people talk and get convinced by each other, without having to resort to other methods for carving common ground. When deliberation does not achieve this ambitious goal of deep persuasion, then some strategies of less-than-optimal and intermediate consensus-building can be undertaken. Finally, consensus might be reached by the simple use of force.

---

[50] Habermas (1996), Cohen (1997b). To be fair, Habermas actually talked about consensus as a product of a hypothetical "ideal speech situation," not necessarily in a "real" speech situation.

[51] From the perspective of social psychology, unanimity might be a strong evidence of nonautonomous preference formation. As Elster contended: "Collective decision is more trustworthy if it is less than unanimous" (1997, at 17). Thick consensus may be oppressive, inefficient, and unnecessary. Sunstein's notion of "incompletely theorized agreement" (1994) and Dryzek's "working agreements" (2000) were furnished to provide a method to reach second-best accommodations.

[52] Mansbridge et al. propose a somewhat resembling classification. It comprises four types: convergence, incompletely theorized agreements, integrative negotiation, and fully cooperative distributive negotiation (2010, at 70).

Compromise is the motor of intermediate strategies. It can be of three types. You may, as a matter of principle, alleviate your position and concede in two ways. It can be morally laudable to concede to your interlocutor's position if you are not sure about the right answer. It displays cognitive modesty and flexibility. You can also concede because a settlement for a second-best option is sometimes superior to the status quo. It may be prudent to renounce the first-best ideal in order to avoid becoming stuck in the worse scenario. In the former situation, in not having a firm conviction about the common good but agreeing on the soundness of other alternatives on the table, you defer for the sake of partnership and trust; in the latter, despite being sure about your own stance, you perceive that a decision is better than non-decision and paralysis. Both are principled and public-spirited. They have the common good in mind. Third, compromise might be simply unprincipled and be exercised by private-driven bargaining. Unlike the pragmatic type, which still has an ideal conception of the common good on the horizon and defers to what seems politically achievable, bargaining basically trades mutually advantageous concessions.

Finally, consensus may be imposed exogenously. The source of such levying comes from the participants themselves, some of whom may have more or less covert ways to influence or menace the others to converge, which imply actual coercion and domination.

Which of these four non-spontaneous types of consensus, then, are compatible with deliberation? For obvious reasons, when coercion creeps in, the resulting consensus cannot be duly classified as deliberative (indeed, not even as authentic consensus). This practice violates almost all the normative benchmarks put forward by the conceptual frame.

Compromise, in all its variants, is more delicate. If deliberation fails to dissolve disagreements, participants can keep their own position intact and decide by voting. Accordingly, you turn to voting when there is no consensus on the substance of the matter. Politics needs to deal with the fact of intractable disagreement and voting is a practical instrument for reaching decisions. Voting, though, could not take hold if not by an underlying meta-consensus about the acceptability of such a procedure.[53] This constituent meta-level choice, therefore, needs to be resolved first. Still, such a method may simply not be available. Or, besides, the divisions might be as fragmented and obstructionist as to disable voting from settling the issue. There might come a situation where compromise is imperative. The partnership compromise is not only compatible with, but actually presupposes a deliberative process, since, in order to defer to your interlocutor's viewpoint in a principled way,

---

[53] Wollheim (1962) points out that this generates the paradox of democracy: someone may agree (procedurally) and disagree (substantively) with a decision at the same time.

you need to be conversant with it in the first place. The pragmatic type, in turn, although not only achievable through deliberation in the full sense of the frame, is more desirably realized through that process—one could more proficiently tell whether the alternatives on offer are better than the status quo, or compare them with his first-best conception, if he engages with the other decision-makers. Lastly, the unprincipled type, for its very features, cannot be squared with deliberation. It is a wholesale desertion of the common good.

For compromise to be consistent with deliberation, as defined earlier, not only must preference formation be endogenous and autonomous, but also principled.[54] Nevertheless, one could plausibly say that principles are non-negotiable, not subject to concessions. It seems all the more odd, on that account, to conceive of a "principled compromise about principles," a rather enigmatic entity. How can a concession about principles still be principled?[55] A possible way out of that puzzle is to differentiate the two sorts of principles at stake: one might compromise a first-order principle (his particular conception of the common good) in the name of a second-order one (a reason about the benefit of consensus itself).[56]

Consensus-based institutions like some types of juries, for example, pose an interesting question and may help to illuminate the distinction above. In such institutions, decision-makers are forced to converge at any cost, under pain of deadlock or indecision. They cannot decide except by overall agreement. It is one of the situations in which majority voting is not available. This could well be classified as coercive consensus too. However, there is a meaningful difference that calls for a more exact appreciation. Rather than coercion and hierarchy among the deliberators, it is the institution itself that requires that outcome. This feature modifies the nature of the process of will formation. The need of consensus may be a robust incentive for deliberative

---

[54] Principled compromise does not assume that the distinction between principle and expediency or self-interested preference is uncontroversial, neither that people will share views about that. The conceptual distinction is, nonetheless, useful to guide the theorist in evaluating concrete instances of compromise.

[55] One could associate this problem with the practice of "balancing principles," that is common in contemporary rights' jurisprudence, or, more generally, as a constitutive feature of applied ethics. "Balancing principles" should not be mistaken with "principled compromise."

[56] I do not have the intention of providing a full-fledged normative theory of compromise or bargaining (neither do I want to engage with game theory and the economic approaches to it). My insight is that this elementary typology captures basic archetypes. A deep analysis of the phenomenon of compromise would have to delve into the several deriving kinds of concessions and how they fit within a legitimacy standard: there might be mutual concessions with respect to one specific issue, through which participants reach middle-ground; there might be, within a multi-issue case, a concession from A regarding issue X, in exchange of a concession from B regarding issue Y; agents might yet trade concessions across cases. These ramifications are merely rudimentary and exploratory. Other permutations would still be possible. My general claim, again, is that some, but not all, compromises are acceptable, and that deliberation may

engagement and lead to spontaneous consensus.[57] It is paralleled, however, by a competing incentive for other strategies of consensus-building to interfere. Thus, one cannot assume, in every circumstance, neither the spontaneous nor the coercive quality of the consensual decisions rendered by these institutions. Each of the five previous types of consensus is a potential candidate. Spontaneous consensus, indeed, may well emerge. Compromises could also be frequent, and it is up to the procedural designer to create mechanisms that minimize its undesirable types. There are defensible justifications for this kind of institution,[58] but one should be aware of the occasional cost: the need for consensus may occasionally harm the integrity of deliberation.

It might also be the case that consensus, in some institutions, despite not being obligatory and a condition for a decision, is recommended by second-order reasons both of principle and expediency.[59] I will come back to this question later, when dealing with the virtue of collegiality, in Chapter 5, and with the politics of judicial review, in Chapter 8.

There are, yet, other angles through which to classify consensus. It might, in relation to its object, bear upon the procedure or the substance of a decision; with respect to it substance, be based on principles or policies;[60] vis-à-vis its political centrality, be about the constitution or about ordinary politics;[61] as far as its depth is concerned, be superficial or all-encompassing;[62] with regards to its path, be top-down[63] or bottom-up.[64] These categories cut across each other in several ways. They capture, anyhow, further variations that a blunt skepticism against consensus overlooks.

---

be powerful to track them too. Chapter 5 will come back to this by way of fleshing out the meaning of collegiality within the court.

[57] Some institutions, still, might not be internally consensus-based but need to manifest to the public in a unitary manner: when, for example, it is allowed to decide by voting of any sort but only the winning position is publicized as the institutional one. Chapter 6 will briefly address this institutional variation.

[58] The political symbolism or the supra-individual image of unity is one possible example. I will come back to similar considerations in Chapter 2.

[59] The rule of law and its partial demands of clarity and predictability would be an example of the former, whereas the effectiveness and reputation of the institution would be an instance of the latter.

[60] This is the traditional liberal distinction thoroughly elaborated by Dworkin (1978).

[61] There are, in various authors, reasonably similar criteria to distinguish, as a matter of political centrality, the constitution from ordinary politics. This is the crux of constitutional law's enterprise. Rawls' (1997b) notion of constitutional essentials and Ackerman's (1984) distinction between constitutional and normal politics are examples of that. Schmitt (2008), from a different angle, also distinguishes between constitution and constitutional laws.

[62] This is a debate about how far the boundaries of public reason established by political liberalism (Rawls, 2005) should be. Sandel (2010) claims that political deliberations should be all-inclusive, and go as deep as the comprehensive doctrines of the good.

[63] Elster gives an example of top-down when he examines the strategy common to constituent assemblies to agree on the broad political principles rather than detailed practical policies (1998, at 97).

[64] Sunstein's notion of "incompletely theorized agreements" (1994) is an example of bottom-up.

Some detractors of consensus conceptualized it in a rigid and compact manner, assuming it as sweeping and profound. Predictably, in the face of a pluralist society, this version got quickly dismissed, and rightly so.[65] It is over-demanding and misses the indispensable intermediary units of consensus that are constitutive of a communitarian life. The thesis of deep disagreement becomes self-defeating if it intends to go all the way down.[66] A line must be drawn. Some level playing field needs to enable a political community to cooperate.[67] The chief question, then, is whether deliberation helps to draw that line or to furnish some minimal consensus. The advocates can say that, among those various types of consensus, most are compatible with, some are inescapably products from, and, more importantly, others are more likely built through deliberation.

Let me briefly recapitulate. Two types of argument are running side by side here. They should not be obfuscated. In order to refine the well-known instrumental claim that deliberation induces consensus, and to face the skepticism against such claim, I tried to roughly distinguish different sorts of consensus and to examine whether deliberation may help each to come out. In parallel, I also pointed out which are normatively acceptable or not. Knowing the types of legitimate consensus does not imply that deliberation is the necessary means to foster them. Societal consensus, for sure, might also be tacit, a product of routine, self-application, unreflective inertia and so on. My aim is to remind the reader that, even if skeptics are hypothetically right to say that spontaneous consensus is improbable, deliberation may still be consequential for shaping other types of legitimate consensus that may have been overlooked.

All in all, the epistemic and the communitarian promises are key instrumental justifications for deliberation, directly connected to its very conceptual frame: if a qualified group of people is publicly arguing about the best conception of the common good at a given time, one expects that those four epistemic consequences are likely to follow; and if, besides arguing through public reasons, they are also engaged in a process of persuasion, it should not be a surprise if they come up with some sort of consensus. Nevertheless, the co-existence of both tasks, on closer inspection, is not devoid of tension.

Someone may chase the common good without bothering to persuade his interlocutors, or, conversely, track consensus regardless of what the common

---

[65] Manin (1987), for example, rejects the unanimity arguments for political legitimacy, and replaces it with deliberation.

[66] Estlund (2000) criticizes, on this basis, Waldron's over-reliance on disagreement as a ground to defend majority rule.

[67] Similarly, Hart (1961) states that some meaningful level of societal support for the secondary rules is necessary for a legal system. Rawls' (2005) notion of "overlapping consensus" is another example of the social need of at least a thin agreement.

good appears to be. Consensus, for the former, or common good, for the latter, could emerge as a collateral effect. The two behaviors, nevertheless, would not satisfy the standards of the conceptual frame of deliberation, in which both logics—the epistemic search for the common good and the communitarian effort to persuade—work together.

Such an intersected operation, undoubtedly, is not immune from trade-offs. If you engage in public discussion with the sole purpose of finding the best answer, you do not concede unless you are really convinced. If agreement is, hypothetically, your exclusive aim, you do not care about the substantive outcome that finally turns out. Some sort of conversation could be a functional means to either end, but genuine deliberation, in both cases, is absent. If you, however, apart from willing to construct the best answer, also accord some weight to the value of a communitarian shared ground and, hence, engage in persuasion, the epistemic and communitarian pursuits will need to be balanced. Again, as already described, you may have to compromise.[68] This means that there is no pre-eminence of one over the other. If the epistemic and the communitarian enterprises need to be accommodated, deliberation would be, all the more, the proper way to promote this particular joint venture (even if, arguably, not the only way that could promote either venture alone).[69] The right balance between the search for the common good and consensus is a key challenge for deliberators to strike in each particular context.

Political deliberation still promises a psychological effect: people who participate may end up feeling respected and included as equal members of a political community.[70] Deliberation, more likely than non-deliberative practices, would instigate this disposition. It is not about winning and losing after counting the heads of the majority, but rather about being committed with both the process and the outcome. It would create, even on those who disagree, a perception of membership and of equal status.[71] The psychological effect is different from the communitarian one. Instead of bearing upon

---

[68] This tension between the epistemic and communitarian promises may sound similar to the tension between input and output that is inherent to the epistemic promise, as described earlier in this section. There, due to the un-demonstrability of the truth, you resort to the likelihood and respectability of a procedure. Here, despite an occasional conviction that you might have regarding the best answer, you might compromise for the sake of a communitarian value.

[69] One may discern an apparent fallacy in this argument: if deliberation is stipulated as incorporating both an epistemic and communitarian pursuits, it comes with no surprise to state that, more likely than other procedures, deliberation tends to accomplish truth and consensus simultaneously. The premise is smuggled into the conclusion, which brings nothing novel. Therefore, the reasoning would be circular. Circular reasoning is not always logically invalid, and, in any event, is not precisely the case here.

[70] The notion of participation is not straightforward, as it will become clearer when we get down to the "sites" of deliberation. One can participate in deliberation under the status of a decision-maker, or of formal and informal interlocutors who have their arguments listened to by the decision-makers. Be it more or less direct, the psychological effect might well apply, in particular ways, to all of those actors.

[71] See Dworkin's (1995) notion of the partnership conception of democracy.

consensus, it refers to an actual sense of respect despite disagreement. You may not agree with the outcome, but still be inclined to comply. Deliberation, in this case, would also project itself as a means to achieve social legitimacy.[72] Regardless of truth or consensus, this would be a major accomplishment.[73]

There seems to be, one might still note, something tautological here. The conceptual frame defines deliberation as a practice that requires, among other attitudes, respect and inclusiveness towards every other deliberator. The psychological promise, in turn, hopes that every participant will actually feel respected and included. Means and ends become blurred: if deliberation is itself an exercise of respect, there is nothing new in the result of deliberators feeling respected. This inference, however, would confound a normative standard and a potential consequence: it is one thing for a normative ideal to prescribe respect, and another for people feeling respected.[74] The first will be subject to controversy in the realm of abstract theory. The second hinges upon the psychological idiosyncrasies of each participant. Someone may feel respected or included even when the attitudes of the deliberators towards her fall way short of any standard of respect normatively conceived. The converse is also plausible, which indicates that such causal relation does not necessarily obtain. It is neither circular nor farfetched to argue, however, that there can be a mutually reinforcing dynamics between the practice of genuine respect, somehow theoretically defined, and the perception of respect as the result of the process.[75] Even if there is no apodictic causation between the two, some correlation is credible.

Lastly, deliberation expects that people who constantly practice deliberation will increasingly acquire knowledge and skill. There are two dimensions of such learning-by-doing: first, one might get more cultivated in the respective subject matter about which she deliberated; second, and more compelling, one cannot learn to deliberate if not by the very practice of deliberating. The educative promise believes that if a community is to develop an argumentative and respectful politics, its citizens have to assimilate those virtues. And there could not be a better means for that than deliberating.[76]

---

[72] Assuming that we can conceive of different sorts of legitimacy: normative (legitimate because morally right); legal (legitimate because enshrined in the law, however defined); social (legitimate because people actually obey and assent). About this distinction, see Fallon (2005).

[73] For Shapiro, the exchange of justifications generates mutual trust (2002, at 198).

[74] Waldron, for example, criticizes Dworkin for reducing the moral grounds of political participation to the positive consequences that might ensue: the citizens might perceive themselves as equal members of the community, whose views are decently regarded etc. Dworkin would underestimate the intrinsic groundings of participation (see Waldron, 2005b, at 22).

[75] The educative and psychological achievements, in an alternative systematization of the promises of deliberation, could even be seen as appendixes of the communitarian. The two are certainly correlated to the overall realization of a "sense of community" or a "sense of membership."

[76] The educative thesis is advanced, for example, by Mill (1998), Pateman (1970), and Rawls (1997a). Manin shares this view: "Political deliberation and argumentation certainly presuppose a relatively reasonable

Up to this point I have drawn a sketchy portrait of the results that political deliberation is expected to unfold according to the optimistic version of the advocates. There is a less confident way, though, to look through the four angles of the consequences of deliberation. Political deliberation can be less rosy than the above image tries to convey. According to empirical skeptics, deliberation may, and more usually does, fail in each of the four dimensions.[77]

From the epistemic point of view, there is no assurance that deliberation will clarify instead of misleading and obscuring. Attempts to deliberate may often culminate in rhetorical manipulation and demagoguery, which undermine the prospects of an epistemic-type achievement.[78] The constraints of public reason may encourage shallowness[79] and hypocrisy, and the expected gravitational pull of the better reason becomes not more than an innocent myth.[80] Public reason may be cynical rather than public-spirited, and without sincerity there is no prospect to contemplate an auspicious epistemic result.[81] The dynamics of the group-interaction, instead of tracking truth, could lead to various forms of "group-think."[82] The advocate could say, in his defense, that if insincerity slips in, it is not deliberation anymore, but some sort of communication below the threshold of the conceptual frame. In response, though, the empirical skeptic would complain that this is a too safe escape valve for the deliberative case and renders such a theory virtually unfalsifiable.[83] If the threshold is too stringent, deliberation becomes an utterly unrealistic phenomenon, easy to be vindicated as an ideal and hard to be found, and hence tested, in the real world.

---

audience... But they constitute processes of education and or training in themselves." It would be "education without a unique and eminent teacher" (1987, at 354). Sanders goes further on the ideal educative function: "It improves all citizens intellectually, by heightening their ability to consider policy and political problems; personally, by allowing them to realize their untapped capacities for observation and judgment; and morally or civically, by teaching them about the political concerns of other citizens and by encouraging mutual respect" (1997, at 351).

[77] In all fairness, an empirical skeptic is not necessarily an adversary of deliberation. He may even buy the normative stance of the advocates but delve into testing the consequences of such a process, displaying its perils and potential defects. They are trying to map its causality and to determine under what conditions those promises can obtain. Mutual engagement between advocates and critics has produced some convergence. See Mutz (2008), Habermas (2005), Manin (2005), and Chambers (2003).

[78] See Rousseau (1994).   [79] See Sandel, 2010, at 242.

[80] As Schauer contends, it may be that, as a variant of Gresham's Law, "bad arguments drive out good" (1992, at 1200).

[81] Stokes, 1998, at 133. For Przeworski, strategic talk might worsen the results: "Add a dose of self-interest, and the mixture will reek 'manipulation,' 'indoctrination,' 'brainwashing' whatever one wants to call it... Some people are stooges: they know better and are complicit in misleading others" (1998, at 148–150).

[82] Group-think is a psychological phenomenon studied by Irving Janis that is now disseminated in deliberative democratic literature. See Sunstein (2002) and Manin (2005).

[83] See Mutz (2008).

From the communitarian prism, consensus would be unlikely to hold in a pluralist society thanks to the bedrock disagreements that cannot be dissolved by deliberation, as anticipated above. To the very contrary, deliberation may lead, in some circumstances, to polarization and to the strengthening of the conflict.[84] The skeptic still adds to the communitarian downside of deliberation its elitist aspect: it is a process that excludes or disregards the voice of some and privileges an intellectual or social aristocracy.[85] Instead of transforming, it entrenches and perpetuates inequalities and symbolic oppression that already lie in the background. Deliberation would silence and subjugate the weak, rather than empower or channel their voice.

If the two previous objections are sound, the educative and psychological effects of deliberation will not be positive either. Instead of educating for inter personal cooperation, it would rather train political tactics and maneuver. Instead of feeling respected, participants may well feel devalued, misled, or deceived. Deliberation brings in a complex dynamics of personal relationships that may become counter-productive and increasingly degrading, which harms the necessary motivation to keep the process going.

An agnostic approach may still question the evidentiary privilege that advocates try to earn by arguing on the basis of likelihood estimations. A shift in the burden of proof would be fairer and politically wiser: until one clearly uncovers the benefits of deliberation, no convincing case could be made in its favor. Deliberation consumes too much political energy for letting the collective compensations be so ethereal and unpredictable. To indulge in deliberation for its own sake, even if we are not sure whether it is beneficial, would be a damaging way of taking collective decisions and expecting compliance.

The chapter has been rather arid so far. Political deliberation was conceptualized out of any specific context. It is context, however, that ultimately fleshes out both its feasibility and desirability.[86] I have asked, in abstract terms,

---

[84] Sunstein defines polarization: "when like-minded people meet regularly, without sustained exposure to competing views, extreme movements are all the more probable" (2002, at 121).

[85] See Schauer, 1992, at 1200. Sanders points to a similar problem: "Prejudice and privilege do not emerge in deliberative settings as bad reasons, and they are not countered by good arguments. They are too sneaky, invisible, and pernicious for that reasonable process" (1997, at 353). She also reports that empirical studies have demonstrated that, in some settings, quantity prevails over quality (the "talkative promoter" may be perceived as having good reasons simply by talking more), and status prevails over skill (worse deliberators might be more able to persuade by their mere status). Young (2001) also shows that, under unequal background conditions, naturalized hegemonic discourses may thrive in unperceived ways.

[86] Mutz criticizes the celebration of deliberation in the absence of enough empirical knowledge about its exact causalities: "Unfortunately, to date, the 'black box' of deliberation has been exactly that—a morass of necessary and sufficient conditions all thrown together, without specification of why each of these various components is necessary, nor theory that links each of them to a specified desirable outcome" (2008, at 530).

what deliberation is, how to practice it, why it is valuable, and what to expect from it. These questions cannot be satisfactorily answered, though, without further inquiry. The portrait above may have suggested that legitimate politics is all about subjecting people to a process of give-and-take of reasons and letting the force of the better argument hold sway. Disappointingly, this is rarely the case, as empirics have been vehemently at pains to point out. Deliberation, sometimes, is simply not appropriate. Politics, moreover, also involves non-deliberative yet legitimate practices.[87] Contextual elements help to detect how advocates and antagonists may be reconciled and their dispute better understood.

Empirical research, however incipient and complex, already offers important lessons.[88] Deliberation is a double-edged phenomenon. It might, sometimes, produce good consequences, which will be contingent on the circumstances. Other times, it would better be eschewed. An unconditional defense of deliberation, or an unqualified transfer of the desirability of deliberation in the ideal world to the imperfect world of real politics is problematic.[89] To clarify the circumstances when deliberation is desirable, and especially when it is not, is one of the burdens of any theory of deliberation.

A contextual approach to deliberation has to ask when and where to deliberate. Always and everywhere are not tenable answers. A swift and easy solution as such is not available. Further attributes must be added to that abstract picture. To probe "when" turns ourselves sensitive to the circumstances of deliberation, object of the next section. To explore "where" comprises not only who and how many deliberate, but also under what status and with what particular epistemic purpose. These features shape the site of deliberation, theme of the sixth section. If deliberators are able to diagnose and administer the circumstances, and if the sites of deliberation are properly designed, I submit, at least some of the perils indicated above can be set aside. The case for deliberation becomes, however limited, more nuanced and convincing.

---

[87] Walzer asserts: "Politics has other values in addition to, often in tension with, reason: passion, commitment, solidarity, courage, competitiveness" (2004, at 92).

[88] But Chambers warns: "Empirical research can be invaluable in keeping normative theorists on their toes and in zeroing in on some specific institutional design questions. Empirical research cannot be either the last or the leading word in deliberative democratic theory, however" (2003, at 320).

[89] Schauer highlights this aspect: "Do we now make ourselves better by searching for more fora of deliberation? Or do we recognize that deliberation now exists in a nonideal world where talk can oppress as well we liberate, where deliberation can produce majoritarian tyranny as well as individual liberation, and where the social identification of the leading participants in a deliberation is as likely to reinforce as to challenge the existing social structures that in this nonideal world determine who speaks and who is spoken to, who controls and who is controlled, and who has the power and who is subject to it? Until we confront these questions, the jump from deliberation as an ideal to deliberation as policy is far more difficult than Ackerman has yet acknowledged" (1992, at 1202).

5. CIRCUMSTANCES OF POLITICAL DELIBERATION

When, then, should a community invest its scarce political resources in deliberation? Not always, many have alerted.[90] If so, when not? What factors can overrule a default position in favor of deliberation as a chief standard of legitimacy? The value and the promises of deliberation help to envision why its presumptive desirability is sensible, but did not elaborate on the exceptions that cancel out such presumption. There are, I submit, three tests that alleviate that normative call. Each test is the corollary of one of the three variables that shape the deliberative circumstances: the background conditions; the existence and sort of disagreement; and the level of urgency. Together, they detect the contexts that are inimical or favorable to deliberation.

The first test contemplates the very possibility of political deliberation and the disposition of the participants to follow its demands. Deliberation, as already highlighted, does not correspond to every kind of communication about political frictions. The concept adopted here, widely shared by deliberative theorists, is indeed heavily taxing. It does not only insert deliberation in a process of actual decision-making and shed light on the provisional character of every decision. It also adds the requirements of public reason-giving, argumentative engagement, inter-personal respect, inclusiveness, empathy, and responsiveness. Deliberators only make up their minds after rounds of hearing and replying. They must be committed to argumentation, be open to persuade and to be persuaded. In sum, they must take their deliberative burdens seriously and be accountable to each of them. In the absence of all these components, deliberation is not entirely taking place.

Accordingly, the conceptual frame sets the logical condition and the respective boundaries of deliberation. If the practice defined by the frame is to be undertaken, some dilemmas are logically not open to deliberation.[91] The basic underlying agreement cannot be challenged in the course of deliberation without disfiguring it. This second-order question—whether deliberation is valuable—needs to be settled as a pre-commitment, however tacit or not. Only then deliberation takes hold. This conclusion just spells out what the conceptual frame implicitly entails. In a deliberative forum, therefore, not all is up for grabs. Deliberators, to be called so, need to share an allegiance to the ethical and political deliberative principles.

Still, some skeptics warn, the plausibility of this project is contingent on the structural factors that lay in the background. Deliberation is not a

---

[90] The idea of "circumstance" as a variable of deliberative performance is summarized by Sunstein: "The value of deliberation, as a social phenomenon, depends very much on social context—on the nature of the process and the nature of the participants" (2002, at 124).

[91] See Gutmann and Thompson (1996) on what is and what is not open to deliberation.

panacea for pre-existing social diseases, and is more likely to thrive under a certain backdrop. Those attitudinal exigencies and expected achievements could hardly obtain in the absence of a given "social basis of self-respect."[92] These pre-conditions of deliberation are socio-economic and political: as to the former, excessive inequality roots a kind of power hierarchy and self-subordination that cannot be dissolved by deliberation or mere procedural fairness, and opens avenues for surreptitious threats and sanctions that perpetuate injustice;[93] as to the latter, individual interactions regulated by fear, embedded intolerance, and incivility would hamper any attempt to deliberate.[94] In certain scenarios, as a matter of fact, due to degenerated social relations, the attempt to live up to those standards will predictably fail. Deliberation simply cannot occur. The very try, indeed, might lead to unruly consequences.

The test of pre-conditions checks whether that sort of engaging communication is achievable under certain states of affairs. It may realize that the attempt to deliberate has greater chances to be malign (by leading, for example, to enhanced subjection of deprived minorities or to extremist polarization). Or it may, on the other hand, deem deliberation as both possible and, at worst, benign, without a clear risk of deterioration into violence or manipulation. This is a first reconciliatory answer to the critics of deliberation: to the extent that there are precise and convincing evidences about the effects of inequality and intolerance, advocates of deliberation would have to modulate their case and accept that the pre-conditions must be fulfilled in the first place. The defense of deliberation under such scenarios would have to be qualified. That echoes a piece of advice from just war theory: "A war is only a just war if there is reasonable chance of success."

The second test examines how contentious a certain subject matter is and asks whether deliberation will be consequential. If there is a stable agreement over time, it might well be sensible to dispense with deliberation altogether. After all, there is no dispute to argue about. Insisting in it would be worthlessly time-consuming and infertile.

The third is a test of timing and concerns whether deliberation is convenient in the light of the urgency of a decision. A speedy decision carries a value of its

---

[92] See Rawls (1971).

[93] Under such context of power hierarchy, as mentioned earlier, coercive consensus can well be reached, but, again, it cannot be squared with the deliberative ideal.

[94] In presupposing a level playing field on the basis of which deliberation may thrive (which I called, borrowing from Rawls, "social basis of self-respect"), I do not assume that it is possible to equalize all sources of power, to remove all the subtle forms of coercion, or to expel the psychological and physical weaknesses that distort the aspired purity of rational persuasion. To the extent that it is ultimately unfeasible to neutralize these distorting factors, deliberation will always be an imperfect process. This does not mean, however, that the effort to conceptualize and to instantiate that level playing field do not help to illuminate the minimal prerequisites through which, however imperfect, deliberation becomes valuable and productive. See Estlund (2004).

own, which may compete with deliberation. Too much delay and indecision, on the other hand, may unfairly privilege the status quo. Deliberative institutions need to "preserve the capacity of government to act decisively."[95]

The three tests are certainly not that clear-cut. They involve weighing the gains and losses of a deliberative process. The first needs to inquire, in the light of the intrinsic values, how much risk is worth taking in the attempt to deliberate. It consists, moreover, in investigating to what extent the promises simply fall apart, or whether different promises and perils might simultaneously unfold, justifying some trade-off. Conditions are never perfect and results not entirely foreseeable. The second should observe whether, despite an apparent agreement, there is any value in re-awakening deliberation for the sake of keeping arguments alive and protecting them to fall into "dead dogma."[96] Lastly, it would be necessary to verify whether the urgency of a decision outweighs the benefits of deliberation. Sometimes, the costs of deliberation might be justifiable. Even when "Rome is burning," it might be preferable to wait a bit longer before reacting.[97]

To pass the three tests implies that, after balancing, one concludes that deliberation is possible, not incendiary or destructive; consequential, not futile; opportune and rewarding, not ill-timed or distractive. We could yet turn the tests more complex. Oftentimes, the question is not whether but how much to deliberate, and when to stop in order to take a decision (even if the stop is inevitably provisional).[98] The tests boil down to identifying the tipping point where the insistence in argumentation ceases being helpful. The level of urgency and the degree of relevance of the subject matter may indicate diverse solutions as to the amount of desirable deliberation. In certain contexts, the wiser alternative may not be more but rather less deliberation combined with carefully tailored bargaining or some form of silent voting. In others, it may be advisable to let deliberation go on without the immediate prospect of a decision.

In formal settings, part of the tests may be settled in advance by institutional design.[99] Some amount of discretion, however, will always remain in

---

[95] Ferejohn, 2000, at 101.

[96] Like John Stuart Mill famously defined the value of freedom of expression and the importance of one playing the role of a Devil's advocate. Manin (2005) explores Mill's insight and defends the exposure to opposing views as necessary to deliberation.

[97] Shapiro holds: "Sometimes by design, sometimes not, deliberation can amount to collective fiddling while Rome burns" (2002, at 196).

[98] Vermeule and Garrett: "To be sure, deliberation also suffers pathologies, quite apart from opportunity costs: it can reduce candor, encourage posturing, trigger hard behaviour, and silence dissenters. Yet the alternative to deliberation is simply voting without discussion, a procedure that no modern legislature, and few if any collective bodies generally, would ever adopt... The real question is not whether deliberation is beneficial, but how much deliberation is optimal" (2001, at 1292).

[99] Deadlines for decision (which set the level of urgency in advance) and compulsory agenda are but a few examples.

the hands of deliberators. Accordingly, their activity is more intricate than initially imagined, since, before the first-order deliberation, the examination of the circumstances calls for a second-order discussion. That is to say, deliberators should decide, at a meta-level, whether and how much to deliberate. In order to do that, they need, first, to be aware that circumstances matter, and, consequently, be equipped to identify and handle them. These judgments cannot, for sure, be undertaken without hurdles. How can deliberators estimate, in advance, whether deliberation is possible, consequential, and convenient? These are prudential and interpretive tests that highlight when deliberation is demanded or exempted.

The first test, in particular, insinuates a paradox: how can one deliberate about the very possibility of deliberation? The possibility, rather than open to deliberation, would be factually presupposed or instinctively guessed. Counter-intuitive as though it may sound, however, some circumstances may allow second-order without enabling first-order deliberation. The members of a highly divided political community, for example, may be able to come together and, on expediency grounds, decide not to deliberate on the topics that will likely reopen explosive rivalry or animosity. In moments of political reconstruction inside a community with tragic collective memories, it may be wise to postpone such emotionally consuming encounters. Or, to the contrary, some gradual modes of deliberation can be the very instrument to enable the restoring of respectful social bonds.[100] This test may still be conceivable if we disaggregate the agents of first and second-order deliberation.[101] An insulated institution, for example, can deliberate about whether to expand a hot topic to the larger community, or to keep it secret.[102] Considering, moreover, that circumstances are not always stationary, but volatile and mutable, this calculus will once more have a high degree of uncertainty and fallibility. All deliberators can do is draw upon the lessons of their historical records, permanently experimenting and calibrating their deliberative practices, and then comparing, with the benefit of hindsight, their achievements and failures.

The second and third are probably easier to see in the everyday routine of solid political regimes. The second test explores dilemmas that enjoy an apparently broad consensus in the present. It tackles the debates that are

[100] The literature on transitional justice is abundant on what sorts of processes may facilitate the transition and guarantee its moral quality. For a recent example, see Minow and Rosenblum (2003). The literature on institutional design for divided societies also contributes to the examination of how to diagnose and domesticate the circumstances. For an impressively broad set of case-studies in recent transitions, see Miller (2010).

[101] This disjunction between those who deliberate and those who are exposed to deliberation will be more elaborated in the next section, when I will define the sites of deliberation.

[102] There are several reasons that may justify the secrecy of deliberative forums. I will come back to this in Chapter 6, by way of discussing institutional design.

assumed to be over.[103] Sometimes, the deliberative burden thereon has been discharged in the past. The stock of our ancestors' deliberations would ground our current underlying consensus. On the other hand, the option of a new generation to revisit it may be justifiable to avoid that such consensus, instead of a rooted principle,[104] becomes a knee-jerk mantra. Testing how much we really agree on things we assume to agree on may be a healthy political exercise. Or it may be pointless, unnecessary, and even risky. Finally, in the third test, the urgency of the decision determines the amount of justifiable deliberation and helps to identify the moment when the costs of continuing delay are bigger than the potential dividends of further discussion. Since decisions, in a deliberative approach, are understood as open to revision in the long run and not as definitive last words, deliberators can leave some pending quibbles for later. The acuteness to perceive the adequate dose of deliberation for each decision, avoiding both innocuous excess or inappropriate shortage, and, at the same time, being aware that deliberation may also continue after decision, is the heavy charge to be undertaken by deliberative bodies.[105]

There is, in conclusion, a default case for deliberation. It is not, however, an unconditionally recommendable practice, and the burden of proof for bypassing it should be carried out by a second-order deliberation that is in charge of applying those three tests. A competent deliberative forum should aspire to have such versatility and proficiency.

The recognition that circumstances matter is based on an assumption, sometimes alien to normative theory, that contexts short of the ideal require different standards of right conduct. In non-ideal scenarios, it may be deleterious and counter-productive to act as if we were in ideal ones, where prescriptive standards operate as predicted.[106] Deliberation could rather

---

[103] Waldron makes a slightly related point by distinguishing between "debates that are over" (like slavery, torture, and racial segregation) and the pending ones that still deserve attentive consideration: "I think we are now past the stage where we are in need of such a robust debate about matters like race that we ought to bear the costs of what amount to attacks on the dignity and reputation of minority groups...in the interests of public discourse and political legitimacy" (2010, at 1649–1650).

[104] Or instead of a conscious stance from the "internal point of view," in Hart's (1961) terms.

[105] Gutmann and Thompson (1996) are among those who most incisively underlined the continuity of deliberation. Deliberation should precede and follow decisions. Urbinati also highlights this: "Nothing is definitive in a political deliberation scenario whose presumption of legal changeability is its constitutive structure...Openness to revision...is the democratic answer to unsatisfactory democratic decisions" (2010, at 84).

[106] Elster argued forcefully about this dilemma. Some of the early deliberative approaches to politics, for him, failed to absorb the lessons of the "economic theory of the second best" and fell into the "fallacy of the approximation assumption." In his words: "one cannot assume that one will in fact approach the good society by acting as if one had already arrived there...In particular, a little discussion, like a little rationality or a little socialism, may be a dangerous thing" (1997, at 18). Accordingly, if full socialism is not possible, it does not follow that little socialism, or as much socialism as attainable, is desirable.

"entrench nonideality."[107] It is not, thus, invariably the proper remedy, considering that we are never actually in the "ideal speech situation." To put it differently, a little bit of deliberation, paraphrasing another old saying,[108] may be a dangerous thing, perhaps worse than no deliberation at all. Should we still trust deliberation for non-ideal conditions? How do we get from here to there? Is deliberation a wise strategy for getting from non-ideal to ideal?[109]

The three tests rehearse a tentative answer to those questions.[110] They carry a belief, indeed, that deliberation is not just for the ideal world, as long as some risks are set aside and its convenience properly measured.[111] Otherwise, imagining the ideal world as a critical heuristic device would be empty. Such a device, without doubt, may be misused if, as mentioned, it leads to a behavior that is insensitive to the peculiarities of the real political conditions. Or, still, if it produces the opposite side-effect by reckoning that, since we will never get there, an imaginatively fabricated ideal should play no role whatsoever. Correctly understood, this stream of political thinking helps, first of all, to design institutions that clone, as much as possible, the ideal scenario by removing potential sources of hierarchy and hence fulfilling the pre-conditions of deliberation.

This is not to echo the old saying that the perfect is the enemy of the good. The warning of popular wisdom, in this case, is misleading. In politics, the ideal, rightly understood, is not so much the enemy of the feasible, impeding you to move forward. To the contrary, it is a critical standpoint that guides action. Empirical findings are pivotal to fine-tune this institutional-building enterprise and to raise new questions that inspire further normative elaboration. An easy solution to the potential pitfalls of deliberation could be to suppress it in favor of quiet, aggregative, and non-argumentative politics. This would be utterly unwise. The thrilling challenge is to modulate it appropriately.[112]

The concept of circumstance here elaborated has a normative sting. It justifies when deliberators are excused for not deliberating, defends a

---

[107] Schauer, 1992, at 1201.

[108] "A little knowledge is a dangerous thing."

[109] See Fung (2005), Young (2001), Estlund (2004), Sanders (1997).

[110] Estlund (2004) elaborates on the remedial exceptions to the duty of civility. Fung (2005), in turn, proposes an ideal of "deliberative activism" to regulate how the background conditions may temper the duties presupposed in deliberation.

[111] Even in the ideal world, deliberation may not be desirable, as the second and third tests show.

[112] Shapiro gets at something similar by what he calls the "positive sum deliberative thesis": the attempt to maximize the forms of deliberation that enhance our lives and minimize those that do not, thus crafting "optimal deliberation" (2002, at 196). He recognizes that deliberation's benefits are not unequivocal and depend on specific contingencies: "sometimes deliberation creates costs without the attending benefits" (2002, at 201).

second-order deliberation, and sheds light on the tensions that must be handled in each concrete case. This second-order deliberation does not challenge the value of deliberation, but simply accepts exceptions in the light of which first-order deliberation is not commendable (either because its costs are too high, or because the very attempt will collapse).[113]

6. SITES OF POLITICAL DELIBERATION

Finally, let me get down to the variety of places where deliberation may be practiced. Without asking that question, any portrayal of political deliberation remains incomplete. Leaving it to the end of the chapter allowed me to give a general account without tying it with the particularities and limits of each site.[114] It is only by scrutinizing each site, however, that the plausibility of the claims above becomes intelligible and testable. Instead of suggesting a celebratory default case for deliberation, the discussion gains color and texture.

A site is made up of several variables.[115] The level of formality is the elementary component from which I depart. There are informal and formal sites where deliberation takes place. What basically distinguishes both environments is the power of making authoritative decisions in the name of and applicable to the whole political community. Formal sites, unlike the informal, are institutionalized. Law ascribe them a proper competence and jurisdiction.[116]

The informal public sphere comprises, indeed, a variety of practices. In a spectrum, they range from purely spontaneous to controlled deliberations. The latter proceeds through a premeditated construction of amicable conditions to deliberation.[117] The former emerges in ordinary social

---

[113] Sanders (1997), for example, strategically manifests her skepticism about the value of deliberation, that is, on the basis of a second-order assessment of the non-ideal conditions. Instead of rejecting the value of deliberation, she contends that American politics should postpone this goal "for the time being," and first eliminate the inequities of power and status that hamper any attempt to deliberate.

[114] It has also been common to utter, among others, expressions like deliberative "forum," "setting," or "arena." I chose "site," following my idiosyncratic terminological preference, because it refers to the location of deliberation in the loosest way possible, regardless of the level of formality.

[115] The geographic variable (understood as the territorial contours over which deliberation applies—whether local, national, international, or supra-national) would be relevant in a comprehensive approach, which is not the case here. Other variables could still include: between face-to-face and written; synchronic and diachronic; short-term and long-term. I do not consider them here but Chapter 6 will come back to some when listing the relevant devices of a constitutional court.

[116] This echoes Habermas' conception of a two-track political process. It has a center/periphery structure, hinges between formal and informal, between institutions of representative government and public sphere. The latter would contribute to opinion formation, whereas the former would lead to collective will formation. See Habermas (1996) and Chambers (2009).

[117] These could even be called "semi-formal" because, despite the lack of legal authority, their procedures can be highly sophisticated and disciplined. Manin (2005) divides the empirical studies into three general

interactions.[118] One is artificially shaped whereas the other evolves naturally. Spontaneous deliberation is carried out by individuals in their capacity as citizens, irrespective of their personal or professional identities. It simply happens in the social settings they participate in. Controlled deliberation, in turn, fabricates an environment that can be much more mixed in terms of ideological, social, and professional backgrounds. Diversity in all these dimensions is an unlikely quality of the former, but may be successfully assembled in the latter.

The formal milieu of institutions adds a new layer of complexity. Apart from being purposefully designed, it is invested in political power.[119] Hence, legitimacy becomes a chief concern. Its decision-making attribute calls for a theory of authority, a convincing moral story about why to obey or to command. Deliberation can be part of that legitimating story, but not necessarily.

Not all institutions are designed to be deliberative. Of those intended as such, not all are equally so. Not all even ask the same services from deliberation. The way it will be instantiated depends on how the respective site is actually configured.[120] Distinct deliberative institutions deliberate about different things from different angles. The identity, capacity, and quantity of deliberators diverge too. These are truisms worth keeping in mind, as they have oftentimes been overlooked by some of the recent accounts of deliberative democracy that treated deliberation as a one-size package.[121]

The connection between deliberation and democracy is not straightforward. Neither should this conceptual link be reducible to the dimension of "who" deliberates. Under such restricted prism, deliberation would be democratic to the extent that citizens have a voice in it. Populist forums would fulfill such threshold, whereas elitist would not. If the focus turns exclusively to the democratic slice of the equation, assuming that portion is narrowly conceived as "who decides," the putative benefits of deliberation per se can be missed. On top of "who," other variables need to come to the fore.

The primary inquiry of design concerns the definition of the institutional purpose. Every institution, to use the language conventionalized earlier, has an epistemic task, understood as a burden to discharge the best possible

---

categories: "laboratory experiences," "real life experiences" (trial juries, panels of judges, citizen juries), and "quasi-experiments" (like deliberative polling).

[118] Spontaneous public sphere could include: family, private associations, workplace, universities etc.

[119] Schmitter also reminds us that, in formal environments, not only individuals, but also interest-based organizations are part of the deliberative process (2005, at 432).

[120] Infinite configurations are possible: deliberative day, deliberative referendums, deliberative elections, popular assemblies, citizen's assemblies, town meetings, not to mention the conventional institutions of liberal democracies (parliaments, courts, juries, agencies, committees, commissions).

[121] Schmitter (2005), for example, criticizes Gutmann and Thompson for discussing deliberation out of any particular context.

decision in the light of that assigned function. However, at times when the democratic principle has earned chief normative currency, the epistemic task cannot speak alone in determining the other institutional features. Pure and simple epistocracy does not attain that legitimacy benchmark precisely because some core functions of democracy cannot be handled by expertise.[122] Democracy requires that institutions be grounded, directly or not, on some trace of an intrinsic value too, the one of collective self-government.

Accordingly, the stipulation of "who," "how many," and "how" to decide is derived from this mixed gravitational pull, a sensible balance between instrumental and intrinsic reasons. The designer, thus, is concerned both with institutional competence—building capacity to do (or to maximize the chances to do) something proficiently—and with its moral respectability. By this combination, he draws numerous institutional blends. In most contemporary democracies, some version of the principle of the separation of powers, with its interlocking chains of hierarchy and delegation, organizes this overall scheme of authority and the relative role of each forum.

This is a vast subject and getting into more detail would divert from the route taken so far. My intention is to locate deliberation within that institutional-building enterprise. Deliberation is a mode of proceeding on the way to take a decision. Part of its versatile appeal comes from the fact that it contributes both with intrinsic and instrumental reasons to the normative discourse on "how" to decide.

It would be false to claim, though, that deliberation can successfully fulfill a certain epistemic task regardless of who and how many deliberate. What is more, its capacity to craft some kind of consensus, to be perceived as respectful, or to educate deliberators are also contingent on who and how many get to deliberate. Even the claim that it has a value in itself must also be put in perspective. An abstract characterization, as the one provided earlier, fails to notice the infinite possible variations on what deliberation is likely to accomplish, and also its inevitable trade-offs.

Again, every institution has an epistemic purpose. Each purpose will probably demand different achievements from deliberation, diverse types and numbers of deliberators, and a tailored legitimating architecture. No one would believe, for example, that a group of persons, whoever they are, however numerous, by deliberating about whatever subject, in whatever circumstance, will get more informed and creative, unearth deep premises, and reach the best answer.

Earlier in the chapter, I maintained that, for the epistemic claim to be compelling one needs to specify types of common good and the place of expertise within politics. An institution may have to deliberate upon things as

---

[122] See Estlund (2000).

complex as the categorization of facts, the weighing of collective values, the conceptual elucidation of rules, the link between the adequate means to realize certain ends, the accuracy or reliability of scientific predictions, and so on. For some of these tasks, scientific expertise may be indispensable. Others, in turn, are less amenable to it and recommend, instead, laypersons. Whether a body should be technocratic in such sense is, in itself, a crucial political choice.

Depending on how forums are designed, one expectation may be prioritized over the other. No single deliberative forum will entirely excel at the four legs on which the instrumental basis of deliberation was systematized above. For sure, not in the same way.

Once the institutional purpose is clear, and assuming that deliberation is part of its function, defining who participates is a hard assignment. As for their identity, participants might be ordinary citizens with more or less direct interest in the cause, political dilettantes, experts, elected politicians, judges, and so on. They may also vary in terms of their ideological and social backgrounds and of their professional training. Constituting an ideologically diverse body, for example, may invigorate its capacity to amplify the arguments and information on the table. If diversity is a desirable institutional feature for carrying out a particular epistemic task, it can justifiably be pursued. On the other hand, diversity may have downsides too. With respect to certain issues, it can have a lesser capacity to produce agreement. Still, for other epistemic charges, diversity might be irrelevant, or even counter-productive. Chapter 6 will come back to these institutional variables in more detail.

Interestingly enough, deliberative institutions may also interact with the public sphere in special ways. Arguments, intentionally or not, may circulate between formal and informal spaces. This exchange can actually influence how opinions are formed and decisions are taken. A deliberative institution, unlike non-deliberative ones, may be designed to profit from this double-track porosity, to stimulate deliberation outside its boundaries and to benefit from it. This complicates the investigation of who deliberates, of the identity of deliberators.

For this very reason, it is illuminating to explore such porosity and enrich some of the categories employed here. First, deliberators can be conceived as a broadly encompassing class of actors. Actual decision-makers, on this account, are not the only ones. Potential deliberators are all those who can, officially or not, directly or not, engage in the process of persuasion. External interlocutors, despite not having the power to decide, are part of this process, even if vicariously. The political burdens of inclusiveness, empathy, and responsiveness also refer to them.[123] When a deliberator is forming his stance,

---

[123] On that account, the interlocutors may comprise those who are formally allowed to present arguments to the decision-making body, those who simply debate in the public sphere, or even mere spectators or

she includes all the arguments she heard, imagine which hypothetical and unheard arguments could be added, and respond to all of them (either to agree or not).

Consequently, there is more to a deliberative institution than intramural deliberation among decision-makers. Extramural deliberation between the institution and its interlocutors can be an enlightening practice, and any account that disregards such activity would be partial and unfinished. Considering that deliberation involves the interplay between formal and informal actors, and keeping in mind its permanent continuity, an extra refinement could also be made in order to isolate the three phases in which deliberation takes place: the pre-decisional, the decisional, and the post-decisional. Deliberation is an ongoing process marked by circularity, an iterative sequence of unceasing political communication in the long run. Decision is an event along the way. Decision-makers deliberate alone only in the decisional phase (the exclusively intramural moment).[124]

The stylized distinctions between types of deliberators, intra and extramural deliberation, and deliberative phases are helpful to design deliberation, or to give an account of political institutions through the deliberative lenses. By the same token, the symbiosis between formal and informal spheres is fundamental to maximize the plausibility of the four main promises of deliberation.[125] Institutions are more or less permeable to spark and to channel deliberations outside them. They may be deliberative catalysts as much as they are deliberative themselves. A skilled designer takes that into account.

Objections could be raised against this conceptual expansion. If political deliberation has a necessary decisional element, how can mere interlocutors be characterized as deliberators? There are ways to answer this. Deliberation, as defined here, is a process of inter-personal practical reasoning about a course of collective action. This does not entail that all deliberators need to have the power to decide. Reducing deliberators to the ones who have actual authority would be short-sighted. Those who are, so to say, powerless, but willing to engage in argumentation and be subject to its ethical burdens, can meaningfully contribute to the quality of the process. It would be a cognitive loss to miss that. Otherwise, deliberation would be conceivable only in

---

absent stakeholders, whose arguments should be empathetically imagined. Unvoiced, marginalized, and insular minorities, children, mentally disabled, and future generations are examples of the latter. Some institutions, due to their internal culture, may not be open for participation of interlocutors. Others, thanks to institutional devices, are open for participation of formal interlocutors but still deaf to other voices. Any institution, however, may engage in empathetic imagination.

[124] By intramural, I do not mean that the institution is deliberating in secret, free from the scrutiny of the broader public sphere. Secret or public, deliberation will be intramural to the extent that decision-makers engage only among themselves.

[125] As described in the beginning of the chapter: epistemic, communitarian, psychological, and educative.

formal sites between decision-makers. All other communicative processes would fall outside its reach.

This is not to underestimate the greater responsibility of the decision-makers, the pressure they face or the uniqueness of the decisional phase.[126] There is no exact symmetry between both situations. I am not equating these two species of the genus "deliberators." On the one hand, decision-makers have the momentous assignment of settling the issue (at least provisionally). Interlocutors lack that solemn power and its accompanying duties. It would be tempting to say, therefore, that the decision-makers are the only genuine deliberators. On the other hand, interlocutors are deliberators in the weaker yet fundamental sense of presenting the claims that need to be taken into account by decision-makers. Both the interplay between interlocutors and decision-makers, and between decision-makers themselves are distinct and mutually implicated deliberative phenomena. Furthermore, the fact that, among deliberators, some have authority to decide and some have not, is not incompatible with the presupposition, asserted earlier, that all have equal moral status. The institutional contingency that those with authority will prevail does not signify that interlocutors and their arguments are morally inferior.

Lastly, numbers matter too. How numerous should a deliberative forum be? How many decision-makers are necessary for optimal intramural deliberation? The size of any deliberative institution ranges between "the few," "the many," and "the too many."[127] They can even embody "the one," once we take seriously an expansive notion of deliberators.[128] The thresholds are surely inexact, but these types provide evocative size-patterns with an obvious bearing on how uniquely deliberative institutions will be and on what they are able to deliver. Variations in numbers of decision-makers, for better or worse, impact the deliberative achievements.[129] The question hinges, again, on the purpose assigned to the respective body. If representation and diversity are indispensable features for its legitimacy, or if direct participation is valued for the sake

---

[126] The concept, of course, is contingently stipulated and other formulations or terminologies could also perform the same distinctions. The decisional character of deliberation, as an element of the frame, only rules out conversations that are not committed to finding solutions for collective action dilemmas. I separate deliberation from the power to decide, but not from the decision. When academics, for example, are scrutinizing specific public-policy choices, they are also deliberating.

[127] This would be a slight adaptation of Aristotle's classical numeric classification of political institutions (between one, few, and many), from where he derives types of regime. There are different magnitudes of the "many": around a dozen members (like courts, agencies, commissions), some hundreds (like parliaments), some millions (like the electorate).

[128] Monocratic bodies, or "primus inter pares" decisional structures, for example, despite having just one decision-maker, are surrounded by other deliberators.

[129] Studies dedicated to the search of the ideal size of decision-making institutions, though not profuse, have been conducted by the political science and social psychology literature. See Lutz (2006) and Hessick and Jordan (2009).

of its psychological and educative effects, a numerous body would be advisable, despite losing in efficiency, agility, and capacity to promote consensus.[130]

One cannot meaningfully conceive of deliberation, therefore, without knowing, apart from circumstance, the respective site. It provides a clearer picture of the feasibility of the frame, the suitability of the promises, and rehearses an answer to most perils pointed by the critics.[131]

7. TAKING STOCK: THE REALISTIC ASPIRATIONS OF DELIBERATIVE PERFORMANCE

Political deliberation is an intellectual exercise within real politics. It is not a thought experiment to check which principles would derive from a hypothetical original position,[132] or a mere heuristic device to envision what outcomes would emerge from an ideal speech situation.[133] It is an admirable gamble of political imagination. It tries to instill the faculty of reason in a domain of human interaction defined by the exercise of coercive force. It tries to confront brute power with reasons that are publicly acceptable.

One deliberates because, before voting and unilaterally enforcing the majority position, she wants to convince her opponent that she is right, or to be convinced that she is wrong. More modestly, they want to know why they think differently and why they disagree, despite still nurturing respect for each other and sharing enough common ground to be fellow members of the political community. It is a public manifestation of their fellowship,[134] an acknowledgement that they are inside the boundaries of a political community. As old as political philosophy, that enterprise sounds remarkably desirable. At the same time, for the observer of real politics, it seems rather rare and improbable.

Deliberation does not automatically solve the collective anxieties that spring from deep pluralism, from the sense that people should participate in politics, or from the hope that political institutions will make good and appropriate decisions. The deliberative enterprise neither hopes nor intends to extinguish the companion of bargaining, aggregation, and the like. However, it would be incongruous to claim that it should not occupy any space in legitimate politics whatsoever. Whether to deliberate or not is a misleading question to begin with, if not coupled with a particular context. In all fairness, none of the critics has actually gone that far. Their skepticism varies

---

[130] Hessick and Jordan (2009) provides a broad review of the empirical literature.

[131] Estlund grasps it: "The right combination of circumstances, institutional arrangements, and personal character apparently can often minimize the ill effects" (1993, at 72).

[132] From where Rawls (1971) derived his principles of justice.

[133] From where Habermas (1996) elaborates an ethics of discourse.

[134] Which would be captured by Rawls' (2005) notion of "civic friendship."

in exactness, tone and vehemence, but seems to share the idea that when and where, or the scrutiny of circumstances and sites, are the right intellectual and practical tasks to pursue.

The chapter has still left a pending question unproblematized. I prescribed deliberation as a desirable principle of decision-making for some, but not all, circumstances, and contended that each site has a peculiar deliberative profile, contingent on institutional variables. Thus, I provided a set of reasons both for practicing and for suspending deliberation, when and where appropriate. Deliberation, under this instrumental framework, might be cast aside in virtue of a cost-benefit analysis.

If I concede that some circumstances outweigh the value of deliberation and liberate the members of a political community from that duty, I am assuming a more intricate and casuistic justificatory relation between intrinsic and instrumental reasons than the initial sections might have suggested. It is comforting to argue that deliberation has an intrinsic ground that exempts it from displaying any instrumental leverage. However tempting, this would be a hasty answer. Consequentialist considerations are inescapable and shake the intrinsic foundations by revealing their relativity. It is incorrect to say that deliberation is a good in itself and hence its consequences, whatever they are, do not matter. Other values countervail the putatively intrinsic value.[135]

Jon Elster has once criticized a specific non-instrumental view of politics. For him, a purely intrinsic view is self-defeating and narcissistic. His argument sheds light on the question above:

> Politics is concerned with substantive decision-making, and is to that extent instrumental. True, the idea of instrumental politics might also be taken in a more narrow sense... but more broadly understood it implies only that political action is primarily a means to a non-political end, only secondarily, if at all, an end in itself... The nonbusiness part of politics may be the more valuable, but the value is contingent on the importance of the business part... Although discussion and deliberation in other contexts may be independent sources of enjoyment, the satisfaction one derives from political discussion is parasitic on decision-making. Political debate is about what to do—not about what ought to be the case. It is defined by this practical purpose, not by its subject matter.[136]

That being so, decision-making uncovers what politics is for. It may not be an instrument for accommodating our given private desires, but is still a means for a proper collective action. It is about doing something. If people

---

[135] At least in circumstances 2 and 3, when deliberation is arguably possible. As for circumstance 1, it could be argued that the value of deliberation is not even at stake because the very attempt to deliberate will fail. Any communication will fall short of the conceptual frame.

[136] Elster, 1997, at 19, 24, and 25, respectively. And, later, Elster adds: "Politics on this view is not about anything. It is the agonistic display of excellence, or the collective display of solidarity, divorced from decision-making and the exercise of influence on events" (at 26).

enter it regardless of this something, they would betray that bottom line. Politics for its own sake, like political deliberation as an end in itself, would ultimately be nonsensical ideas.[137] Intrinsic reasons cannot go all the way down. Neither do, however, the instrumental ones. Either reason, alone, is not enough to capture why deliberation is meaningful. If isolated, they provide a somewhat precarious ground. There is a level of interdependence between them.

If the justification relied only on intrinsic reasons, it would fail to diagnose that some circumstances cancel those reasons themselves. Deliberation, moreover, would still lack a functional point. If, on the other hand, the justification comprised only instrumental reasons, it would fail to see that there is something worthwhile happening, along the way for a decision, irrespective of the results that ensue. Deliberation, if grounded exclusively on instrumental grounds, would still be vulnerable to empirical objections and remain too fragile in the economy of trade-offs involved in decision-making and institutional design. Neither of both alternatives exhausts the justificatory job.

What, then, is the relation between both kinds of reasons? What is the proper equilibrium? The balance, as it happens, involves a controversial interpretive exercise. As long as deliberation does not excessively hurt, it should be practiced even if clear benefits are not brought about. Deliberation may occasionally not help to get to a certain result and still be valuable. Valuable, however, only inasmuch as it does not cause harm to an unacceptable degree. The notions of "harm" or "hurt" require a delicate judgment, according to the particularities of the case. Abstract formulas will not do. Intrinsic reasons, on that account, are subordinate to an instrumental threshold, but not a mere appendix. From that threshold onwards, the logical priority is inverted, the burden of proof shifts. The challenge for institutions is to detect that precise frontier.

Deliberation is valuable in its own right, therefore, up to a point.[138] Once we are assured that nothing extremely disruptive will emerge, deliberation can be undertaken regardless of whether the positive consequences finally ensue. Deliberation gains a freestanding status at this precise moment, not before. The switch from the instrumental condition to the independent intrinsic grounding, like the old saying about just wars, "Only winnable wars are just," depends on a difficult and serious political judgment.

There is a limit, therefore, to the acclamation of deliberation for its own sake. It is, as politics in general, a servant of collective decision-making. If one proves that, in some circumstances, deliberation is damaging, any putative

---

[137] Shapiro has a somewhat similar hostility against this fetishistic view of politics: "Doing things democratically is important, but is should rarely, if ever, be the point of the exercise" (2002, at 207).

[138] Shapiro, 2002, at 203.

duty to pursue it should be revoked. Once there is need to decide, we should choose the method that is morally superior among those that meet the minimum requirement. Deliberation is a praiseworthy way of getting to the decision, but is conditioned by that test. In order to avoid the risk of a narcissistic view of deliberation, one should undoubtedly be attentive to its consequences, but only to a certain degree. Carving this middle ground, again, is a task both for the designer and for the deliberators themselves.

Advocates of deliberation gradually learnt to refine the understanding of the circumstances and the non-trivial variables behind each site. In a masterfully designed forum, several empirical objections fall apart. Institutions are imperfect devices and do not eliminate, *ex ante*, all traces of latent perils, which will need to be tackled, *ex post*, by deliberators themselves in a second-order deliberation. However well the site was designed, circumstances cannot be entirely anticipated or domesticated.

The book does not insinuate a steadfast faith in deliberation, neither does it submit a wholesale and unmitigated case. This should have become clear. Deliberation, as I tried to convey, must be put in perspective. Instead of a fetish, it can inspire a self-aware belief. Deliberation is not only imperfect because it cannot neutralize all sources of illegitimate influence that distort frank persuasion and furtively harm autonomy, but it is also fluid: one single discussion may oscillate between deliberative and non-deliberative stages. It is a permanent achievement and serves as an important index for the quality of a political community.

Deliberation, on that account, is a slippery and multi-dimensional phenomenon. A serviceable model of deliberative performance must capture that complexity. Performance, in politics, entails the accomplishment of cherished political goals. Deliberative performance, in turn, regards the fulfillment of certain standards of excellence in deliberation. Before one can measure the deliberative quality of the different sites from where political will emanates, there is a significant theoretical work to be done. Parliaments, courts, executive cabinets, technocratic bodies, citizen juries, or popular assemblies will require a specific theoretical grasp. All things being equal, an institution that maximizes its deliberative performance intensifies its political legitimacy. This output indicator, I submit, should be part of any legitimacy assessment.

The literature on deliberation roughly adopts three general approaches towards current democratic institutions: to supplant them; to supplement them with new institutions; to invigorate their deliberative capabilities and performance. This book fits into this third path and looks to one particular site. Through the categories put forward by the current chapter, one can have a clearer bird's eye view of the remaining parts of the book. Chapters 2 and 3 describe the basic features of the peculiar site that a collegiate court and, more specifically, a constitutional court instantiate. Chapter 4 makes a general case for the deliberative performance of constitutional courts. Chapter 5 spells out the ethics that the conceptual frame presupposes, while Chapter 6 maps the institutional variables that facilitate deliberation in that particular site. Chapter 7 rehearses the sort of public reason that is up for constitutional courts. The content of judicial deliberation must be fleshed out with a theory about legal reasoning, and that chapter tries to draw the basic tenets of such a theory. Chapter 8 deals with some of the circumstances that permanently shape constitutional decision-making. Any promising position on political deliberation needs to come to grips with all these questions, and show how the answers can hang together. This is the challenge of the book.

2

Political Deliberation and Legal Decision-making

I. INTRODUCTION

Prominent advocates of judicial review have claimed that constitutional courts are deliberative forums of a distinctive kind and have grappled to show the plausibility and implications of this commonplace.[1] Surprisingly enough, however, they have not entirely come to grips with the sorts of requirements that should be met if courts want to live up to that promise. Important questions remain unanswered while others endure unasked. Constitutional talk is thus deprived of a set of qualitative standards that guides us in assessing how different courts, for better or worse, may do and are actually doing in terms of that presupposed and esteemed decisional virtue.

This under-elaborated assumption needs to be fleshed out. The current chapter examines how a court of any kind can be imagined as deliberative. This is surely not an indisputable feature of law and adjudication. Before one can talk intelligibly about a deliberative court, some theoretical objections must be put out of the way.

To connect adjudication with deliberation is a delicate task. There are two main angles through which this question can be conceptualized. First, there might be a conceptual link within legal reasoning itself: law is deliberative to the extent that it allows for the weighing of various reasons for action, rule-based or otherwise. It would not be possible to live under law without discursively engaging with it. Second, there might be an institutional link as well: judges deliberate with each other within collegiate adjudication.[2] Deliberation, in the latter sense, corresponds to the inter-personal argumentative engagement as defined by the preceding chapter; in the former, to the mere character of reflexivity.

---

[1] This commonplace will be diagnosed and thoroughly described later in the chapter.

[2] I will use the words "collegiate" and "collegial" with different meanings throughout the book. Collegiate is a formal and technical definition: the mere fact of a multi-member decisional body, with all of them sharing responsibility for the decision. Collegial is an ethical and cultural definition: an attitude towards deliberators, pursuing a supra-individual and de-personified decision. "Collegiality," in turn, may refer to both.

This chapter will put forward both theoretical assertions: the second section argues that law is inherently deliberative and the third maintains that collegiate adjudication should be so. Not everybody believes in both contentions and I will seek to show what they assume and in what sense these objections are unsound. Chapter 3, in turn, will delve into the unique character of constitutional courts and describe how they have been envisioned as deliberative institutions.

The point of the expository strategy of the current and the next chapters is to lay the foundations for the positive steps that follow, refining and delimiting the theoretical battlefield before advancing the main arguments of the book. The trajectory of questions and the positions I take along the way are instrumental for making judicial deliberation meaningful, acceptable, and desirable before proposing an evaluative model of deliberative performance.

2. DELIBERATION AND ADJUDICATION: POLITICIZING LAW?

Does deliberation fit well with law and adjudication? Some have discomfort with that mixture. The previous chapter considered the claim that deliberation, with all its protocols, would legalize politics. I argued that a defensible conception of politics turns such a statement down. This section deals with the reverse hypothesis: deliberation would politicize law and adjudication, transfigure it into an unbound exercise of practical reasoning, and, essentially, open it to non-legal cogitations. Let me explore what this remark might actually convey.

An account that tries to combine deliberation with law, or to advance the idea that legal reasoners deliberate, needs to be anchored in a conception of law (or at least reject those which are at odds with deliberation). This conception will not be entirely uncontroversial. Deliberation, for some, would be more in tune with politics and morals, not with law; with legislation, not adjudication; with lawmaking, not law-application; with hard, not easy cases. Accordingly, for certain modes of thinking, law would be anti-deliberative. But what can that radical stance actually signify? In order to highlight how the articulation between law and deliberation may be plausible, and how judicial deliberation may be tenable, I need to set that position aside.

The first version of this class of objection is premised upon a rudimentary dichotomy. It depicts an unbridgeable gap between lawmaking and application, a strict division of labor between the legislator and the adjudicator. The two functions would be entirely matched by the two institutions. Whatever deliberation might have happened, it would have preceded law. The moment a collective decision is enacted into law, the legal machine would operate in an automatic and self-sufficient way, without much further consideration. Law would be complete and certain, leaving no room for a hard case, no chance for argumentative confrontation in the shadow of dubious and unsettling rules. Rule-application, as opposed to rule-formation, would involve a rigid kind of mental process mastered by trained experts and insulated from dense reflective exercises. Only then would the rule of law fulfill its promise of certainty and predictability.

Morris Cohen gave an eloquent label to such stand and, almost a hundred years ago, denounced its perversity. He called it a phonograph conception of adjudication,[3] the view according to which judges merely vocalize the rule they are supposed to apply.[4] For him, this is a damaging myth that leads to confusion, a demagogic mask that "shuts off a great deal of needed light."[5] Law cannot operate, for him, except by a "continuous process of supplementary legislation and gradual amendment" that judges daily administer.[6] They have no choice but to continuously make law, and by not being candid about it, they protect themselves from public criticism.[7] Such "theory of judicial passivity," with its stark split between an "active creator" and a "passive declarer," spares judges from a burdensome responsibility.[8]

There are innumerable other accounts of this simple idea. It is not just a caricaturesque construct fabricated for pedagogical purposes. Implausible though it may sound today, this "gap between saying and doing"[9] survives as a fraudulent maneuver that facilitates judicial legitimation at the cost of collective self-deception, as a resilient immaturity symptom of a democratic public culture.[10] Thanks to its seductive and sticky quality, it bravely remains in the lay public minds.[11] The beauty and tidiness of its arrangement seem intimidating. Modern state created a legal division of labor that looks too neat to be false. It promotes a curious type of political obscurantism by hiding in public what many, at worst, seem to know in private.

---

[3] For this view, a judge would be "a sort of impersonal phonograph who merely repeats what the law has spoken into him" (Cohen, 1915 at 475).

[4] For Neumann, the "phonograph theory" of adjudication describes the act of judging as a mere "act of recognition" of what is "already contained in the general norm in an abstract way." The judge is in charge of a "logical subsumption" that connects the major premiss—the law—with the minor premiss—the facts—in order to reach a decision. This theory would supposedly avoid "the establishment of a rule of judges," but end up hiding their creative power (1986, at 225–228).

[5] Cohen, 1914, at 175. And he still adds: "The accepted theory thus prevents judges from changing the law when they should and disguises the process when they do."

[6] Cohen, 1915, at 479.

[7] Cohen: "so long as they are bound to make law, it is better that they should do so with open eyes rather than wilfully blind themselves to what they are doing by the use of plausible fiction" (1915, at 475).

[8] Cohen, 1914, at 195.

[9] See MacCormick and Summers, 1997, at 500.

[10] Even the French codifiers, to whom some attribute that vulgar naivette, were actually sensible to the creative aspect of adjudication (Atria, 2009, at 128–129).

[11] Perhaps the most intriguing example of the resilience of that view is American constitutional law and its crude versions of originalism as a method of interpretation. The two last Senate hearings of

Thus, the first objection—that there can be deliberation in lawmaking, but not in law application—is, at the very least, empirically flawed. Its gross mistake is not exactly the very distinction between lawmaking and law application, but rather the notion that, in the latter case, there is no room for debate, no latitude for reasonable controversy. There is, though, a more sophisticated objection. It openly dismisses the mechanical view above, but may still seem to refuse the blend law and deliberation. It reads like this: legal reasons are pre-emptive of other sorts of substantive considerations behind rules. On that account, there could hardly be deliberation when arguing about law.

Joseph Raz elaborates his version of positivism on these terms. For him, law may be at odds with deliberation in a very specific sense: it excludes the reasons that were counted to justify the enactment of a rule in the political debate. Once this "decisive moment" has passed, those premises are not available for further legal reasoning anymore. Law facilitates social coordination and complexity exactly by settling dilemmas in advance and by economizing open-ended deliberation. The rule-based reasons for action supplant rather than supplement the background reasons that may have been pivotal for enacting the rule. Thus, when dealing with law, one needs to avoid "double counting."[12]

Legal reasons, as legitimate authoritative reasons, would preclude independent deliberation about whether they should apply. The existence of a legal rule is not a merely ancillary reason for action. Instead, it is an autonomous ground that substitutes for the other occasional motives that originally justified the rule. Legitimate authority is founded on that protected scaffolding and it denies access, to the province of law, of the reasons that were raised in the province of politics and that do not directly emanate from the text of the rule itself. One should not reignite the pre-legal debate.

Non-positivists discard that depiction. For them, there is a conceptual connection between law and morality that inexorably breaks down such attempt of separation. Dworkin translates this through his encapsulating ideal of integrity.[13] Alexy, in turn, expresses it through the inherent "claim to correctness" that would lurk behind any argument that one can make about

---

US Supreme Court nominees, Justices Sottomayor and Kagan, provided several fresh instances of the obsession with an idea of "fidelity to law" elaborated in those terms (see Dworkin, 2009 and 2010a). The distractive and un-theorized slogans that poison these sessions ("to apply, not to make the law," "impartial justice, not a personal policy agenda," "law, not politics") have been subverting the public debate at least since the rejection of Robert Bork's nomination in 1987.

[12] As Raz sums up: "When considering the weight or strength of the reasons for an action, the reasons for the rule cannot be added to the rule itself as additional reasons. We must count one or the other but not both...To do otherwise is to be guilty of double counting...This fact is a reflection of the role of rules in practical reasoning. They mediate between deeper-level considerations and concrete decisions. They provide an intermediate level of reasons to which one appeals in normal cases where a need for a decision arises" (1986 at 58).

[13] See Dworkin (1986).

law.[14] The concept of law, for the latter, is overarching: it combines a factual and an ideal dimension in realizing an "optimal coupling of legal certainty and justice."[15] You cannot know law just by reading its public and printed black-letters, neither argue about law without steering an ideal theory and engaging your own values, as Dworkin could say.[16] This does not lead to a mere exposition of individual preferences, but rather to a structured and constrained type of reasoning.

Hard cases are the conventional reference to grasp what is at stake between these contenders, the "sensors by which the nature of law can be established."[17] Each school yields an approach to hard cases. Positivists, unlike the phonograph myth-makers, are prepared to defend that nothing but discretion subsists in the situation when rules and legal reasons run out. They do not indulge in the legal-mouthpiece story, neither do they offer alternative "dignified exits from the agony of self-conscious wielding of power," as expressively put by Bhagwati.[18] They accept that fidelity to law is a more onerous ideal than a regurgitating of rules.

Discretion notwithstanding, positivists do not derive an untrammeled power to decide. Neither Hart nor Raz, for example, accept that the judge is authorized to decide arbitrarily, out of his own naked will. For them, the life of law is not machine-like, but still does not dilute legal reasons into whatever consideration seems adequate to solve a hard case.[19] Even when rules run out, there is rational discipline and, be it inside or outside the confines of law, it constrains judges.

---

[14] Alexy basically transfers the formal requirements of discourse theory to law, which amounts to instilling the demands of correctness, justification, and generalizability to legal claims: "in the process of enacting and applying the law, a claim to correctness is necessarily made by the participants, a claim which embraces a claim to moral correctness" (1989, at 173). See also Alexy, 2002, at 35.

[15] Alexy, 2007, at 336.

[16] As stated by Waldron in a review of Dworkin's *Justice in Robes*: "We need to know what legal reasoning would be like at its best, in order sometimes to be able to make it better" (2006b).

[17] Alexy, 1989, at 181.

[18] P. N. Bhagwati, former Chief Justice of India, 1992, at 1262.

[19] Hart's notion of discretion is subtler than the one Dworkin apparently took him to have defended. "Judicial decisions, specially on matters of high constitutional import, often involves a choice between moral values, and not merely the application of some single outstanding moral principle; for it is folly to believe that where the meaning of law is in doubt, morality always has a clear answer to offer. At this point judges may again make a choice which is neither arbitrary nor mechanical; and here often display characteristic judicial virtues, the special appropriateness of which to legal decision explaining why some feel reluctant to call such judicial activity 'legislative.' These virtues are: impartiality and neutrality in surveying the alternatives; consideration for the interest of all who will be affected; and a concern to deploy some acceptable general principle as a reasoned basis for decision. No doubt because a plurality of such principles is always possible it cannot be demonstrated that a decision is uniquely correct: but it may be made acceptable as the reasoned product of informed impartial choice. In all this we have the 'weighing' and 'balancing' characteristic of the effort to do justice between competing interests" (Hart, 1961, at 204–205).

Hart, for example, has provocatively classified American theories of adjudication between two poles. At one, "the nightmare," judicial decision would be pure creation from scratch, like "crypto-legislation." At the other, the "noble dream," it would be entirely contained by the linguistic boundaries of the law. The real decisional context of judges lies, for Hart, somewhere between both extremes. He characterizes adjudication as continuous with legislation and, embracing Holmes' phrasing formula, as having a "genuine though interstitial lawmaking power." The open texture of legal language creates penumbra and this leads judges to make creative choices at the edges of the rules' "core meaning." Judges fill this vacuum by reflecting on what ought to be. It is a purposive and intelligent decision rather than an arbitrary one.[20]

Raz follows exactly the same direction. Although law, according to him, is not a "system of absolute discretion," it does not mean that judges are "computing machines." Neither does it mean, though, that they ought not to "exercise their judgment in order to reach the best solution."[21] "Unregulated cases" arise from the incompleteness and vagueness of law but they are not "pure law-creating" either.[22] Applying and creating co-exist.

Non-positivists, in turn, call for an investigation about the underpinning principles of law, and refuse to call this disciplined exercise discretionary. Even in hard cases, constraints of legal reasoning do not fade away. Law as a justificatory enterprise is complete in a precise sense: you need to unearth its background principles without which it becomes senseless and unarticulable. One cannot understand what the law is in a hard case without uttering the ultimate values that account for the rationality of such system. These are not visible at the surface of legal materials, but are rather tacit and can only be unleashed through interpretation. According to non-positivists, to say there is discretion gives an inaccurate apprehension of the phenomenon and underestimates the burden of justification that goes all the way down. The judge cannot discharge it by making a silent choice, and the reasons he evokes should be none but legal ones.

With or without discretion, with or without legal reasons properly conceived, what invariably remains is a more or less vigorous exchange of arguments that tries to come up with the best solution to both easy and hard cases. This

---

[20] For Hart, the occasional errors of a formalistic and mechanical view of law do not impact on the soundness of the separability thesis: "It does not follow that, because the opposite of a decision reached blindly in the formalist or literalist manner is a decision intelligently reached by reference to some conception of what ought to be, we have a junction of law and morals" (1958, at 610). The inevitable creative aspect of adjudication is not incompatible with the assumption that adjudication consists in rendering a judgment (an inter-subjective claim for correctness) rather than expressing a preference or desire (Kornhauser and Sager, 1986, 83).

[21] Raz, 1979, at 197.   [22] Raz, 1979, at 195.

should be enough for reconciling, at least in the weak sense defined in this section, law with deliberation in both views presented above. In hard cases, there is deliberation, call it extra-legal or not, when constructing a solution argumentatively. In easy cases, where that polemical opposition loses much of its practical grip, there can also be deliberation, however permeated by limiting rule-based reasons. Deliberation is sensible where the decision is neither obvious nor purely arbitrary. Legal decision-making does not have either quality. Thus, judges cannot be painted as phonographers or slot-machines, the antipodal images that were devised to convey, for the former, the hope of total certainty and, for the latter, the misery of absolute arbitrariness in the law. Positivists and non-positivists come together against both distorting caricatures.

Institutions, I submitted in the last chapter, constitute the deliberative theatre and, by doing so, constrain deliberation not only from the procedural point of view, but also in terms of the reasons that are valid in such a setting. The functioning of any legal system denotes a proper degree of formality, a capacity to select the reasons that are acceptable in legal discourse regardless of their substantive caliber. When arguing in the domain of law, something is excluded from our portmanteau of "all-things-considered reasons."[23] Some filter reduces the number and quality of reasons available.[24] Such closure of legal language, presupposed by the rule of law, corresponds to a "canon." As this canon of legal argument varies, so do the boundaries of deliberation within law. The formal character of law should not be overstated though. Any deliberative forum, be it adjudicative or not, needs to select what the acceptable reasons are, or, as earlier contended, to parse public from non-public reasons. Democratic politics, too, presupposes a formality in political argumentation. Parliament is no different.

It would be wrong to read either positivism or non-positivism, therefore, as excluding either the formality or the deliberative character of law. The point of controversy is not whether, but how deliberative law is, a matter of degree rather than of kind. They will differ on what would be appropriate to classify as legal or non-legal reason, what would be controllable by legal directives. Some adopt a more expansive approach to law's formality and relax the filter to allow a deeper digging into the subterranean assumptions of rules. Others restrict that scope.

---

[23] Atria defines: "a kind of normative discourse where participants are justified in not considering substantive questions that are, or might be, relevant for an all-things-considered decision" (2002, at 218).

[24] For Atria, to know what arguments will be classified as legal or not, you need to look not to the rules themselves but to the "image of law," a social construct embedded in a legal culture that sets the legal apparatus in motion (2002, at 218).

Easy associations of the positivist tradition with the phonograph conception of adjudication are grossly erroneous. They are worlds apart. One is a noxious fiction whereas the other remains as a prestigious theoretical stance. The mistake of the objection from which I departed was to infer from the quality of pre-emptiveness a totalizing conception of law, one that exhausts, beforehand, what can be argued in actual cases. Once we lose that cornerstone (which was never actually there but to mystify), we put in place a conception of law that is candid to its inherent arguable character.

Neil MacCormick has also and more bluntly pursued that path. He strived to reconcile the ideal of the rule of law with the contestable character of legal cases. He concurs that this ideal consists in setting a normative framework in advance, thereby enabling individuals to plan their conduct according to public normative expectations. It is not intriguing for him, however, that such capacity of planning is inevitably tainted by a grain of uncertainty. Rather than a regrettable imperfection, this feature is an integral part of what is valuable about that ideal. Thus, he harmonizes two dignitarian bases of the rule of law: on the one hand, certainty; on the other, the right to defense, "letting everything that is arguable be argued."[25] In other words, MacCormick refutes a monolithic account of the rule of law which sacralizes one dominant value and the expense of the other,[26] and sheds light on its "chain of putative certainties that are at every point challengeable." As he summarizes the dynamism of the ideal: "Law's certainty is then defeasible certainty."[27]

The recognition of an "element of principled evaluation" in legal reasoning is, for MacCormick, a "corrective to a merely narrow legalism." Moreover, it approximates legal reasoning of moral reasoning, without eliding the distinction between both. The former, as opposed to the latter, has a measure of heteronomy. Law's authoritative institutionality is the key for realizing its aims. Unlike moral deliberation, legal deliberation does not entirely bind us to our own will. Law provides a set of texts that constitutes a "fixed starting point for interpretive deliberation."[28]

One could say that the non-positivist approach to law enhances law's deliberative character, and this perception may be right if we define and measure deliberation by the kinds of reasons that are accessible. It does not follow, nevertheless, that the positivist approach is non-deliberative. Whichever conception of law a theorist endorses, therefore, deliberation will be part of what the life of law is about. There is nothing in law's formality that makes

---

[25] MacCormick, 2005, at 31.

[26] This imbalance is thus captured: "the original representation of the rule of law as antithesis to the arguable character of law was a misstatement in the emphasis it gave to the certainty of law" (MacCormick, 2005, at 28).

[27] MacCormick, 2005, at 28.   [28] MacCormick, 1995, at 83.

it anti-deliberative, although different degrees of formality entail diverse grades in law's deliberativeness. Deliberation does not disappear under either of these comprehensions.

The claim of this section is largely negative. I want to do away, at the outset, with a suspicion that deliberation might not be of law's business. This is the product of a conflation of distinct questions: the relation between law and morality; the argumentative character of law; the reasons that should count in hard (or even easy) cases. Does deliberation politicize law? Not necessarily, or not in any objectionable sense. To insist on that doubtful division between positivists and non-positivists, the latter would assert that law is inevitably politicized inasmuch as we understand it as the articulation of deep political principles; the former would maintain that it may get more or less politicized in hard cases, when non-legal reasons are inescapably taken onboard to fill the space of discretion in a non-arbitrary way. What is more, easy cases may also involve deliberation among strictly rule-based legal reasons, and there is nothing disagreeably political about that.

This claim is not entirely trivial. Still, the more fertile controversies relate to the kind and amount of reasons that are available to the legal reasoner. Chapter 7 advances a more constructive moralistic account of constitutional law that may better inform deliberation, but this is enough for the moment.

3. BETWEEN MONOCRATIC AND COLLEGIATE ADJUDICATION

There is another way to ventilate skeptical doubts about the deliberative character of law or, more precisely, of adjudication. This springs from its institutional side: collegiate courts promote the encounter of judges that need to take a joint decision. There are several procedural equipments that enable a collegiate body to come up with a collective decision. The question is whether deliberation, as I defined it in the first chapter, should integrate such equipment, hence regulate judicial behavior and inform our expectations upon collegiate adjudication.

In such institutional context, one might say, even if judges adopt the crudest notion of the phonograph theory and see adjudication as a simple discovery of what the law already is, some sort of deliberation, however weak, would still be possible. Thanks to the fact that, despite the supposed completeness of law, phonographers may still disagree, they may well opt to deliberate among themselves. Contrariwise, assuming that judges embrace an openly principle-based conception of law, it does not automatically follow that they do or should deliberate. Accordingly, judges may or may not deliberate regardless of the conception of law that stirs the judicial decision. Once judges adhere to this mode of inter-personal interaction, however, one could still claim that deliberation would be enhanced if they all share that latter vision about law. The conceptual and the institutional sides are, thus, relatively but not entirely independent.[29]

A collegiate court is not, in and of itself, a deliberative body. I submit, nonetheless, that there are good reasons for courts to espouse that aspirational practice. This section outlines a case for the deliberative character of collegiate adjudication. It focuses on adjudication in general and avoids, for now, some complications of the constitutional adjudicative genre. Before specifying the intrinsic values that undergird and the beneficial consequences that may, more likely than not, emerge from judicial deliberation, there is a preliminary question from where I should start: why should adjudication be collegiate in the first place? Raising this question helps to set aside the tempting inference that would derive, from the mere collegiate character of courts, a duty to deliberate. The case for deliberation, I shall note, is not that simple.

This question invites an interpretive exercise, an attempt to put that practice under the best conceivable light.[30] Collegiate courts were not created by historical fortuity, and their documented traces are, to some extent, particular to each political community. Contingent institutional choices, though, should not be normalized as if tradition, by itself, could fulfill this justificatory requirement. Path-dependence may explain how an institution evolved, but is not enough reason to warrant its subsistence. Irrespective of the actual causal factors and original intentions, one needs to further investigate whether this sort of collegiate body can still be maintained on the basis of fresh principles. Such exercise dissects and updates the values that ground a traditional organizational form.

There are different ways to institutionalize the activity of applying the law to concrete disputes. The elementary dichotomy between monocratic and collegiate adjudication is a basic step. Contemporary state judiciary systems usually adopt some mixture of both formats. As far as decisions of last resort are concerned, however, it is a fact that, in most instances, collegiate bodies are accorded the ultimate legal authority. The collegiate structure raises peculiar and non-negligible theoretical consequences that are absent in the monocratic setting.

One set of problems is operational: as any multi-member institution, a collegiate court needs to frame a procedure that allows for the conversion of the "many" into "one," to define what shape "the opinion of the court" will have. Questions related to the rules of aggregation, to the style of judging

---

[29] This variable connection between the shared conception of law and its impact on the deliberativeness of collegiate adjudication will be addressed in Chapter 7.

[30] Dworkin provides the definition of an interpretive exercise through the example of the institution of courtesy: you seek the contemporary reasons that may justify, or indicate the need of adjustment, of that practice (1986, at 47).

and to the drafting of the decision, among others, will need to be confronted and consciously solved. There is, moreover, a question of institutional ethics, of the moral standards that should inform the interaction among judges. Finally, there is a justificatory demand, the articulation of the reasons why a collegiate court, in each scenario, is the right pick over a monocratic option.

Deliberation is not the most obvious candidate for framing the justificatory discourse that grounds collegiate courts. We have strong deliberation-independent reasons to institutionalize adjudication in a multi-member body. By recognizing such reasons, it becomes possible to avoid a one-sided defense of the collegiate form. These deliberation-independent reasons are not just ancillary, but essential components of the overall edifice. They provide self-standing normative footing for the adoption of collegiate courts, irrespective of whether they deliberate or not. There is more to be told in favor of collegiate adjudication than just its greater amenability to deliberation. These deliberation-independent reasons shape part of the answer as to why a single clever judge is no adequate substitute for a deliberative court.

Hence the question that launches this exercise: why a multi-member court instead of a wise, self-reflective and monological judge? There are four interrelated deliberation-independent reasons for placing, at least at the highest positions of the judiciary, multi-member courts.

First of all, a collegiate body profits from the phenomenon of de-personification. Instead of putting all the weight of declaring what the law means on a single man's shoulders, such arrangement permits the decisional responsibility to be detached from the individuals and coupled with the institution, which gains an identity of its own, dissociated from its members. The "rule of law" would sidestep the "rule of men" by domesticating individual idiosyncrasies through the institutional impersonality.

Impersonality is Janus-faced though. It has an ambivalent relation with the monocratic or collegiate structure of adjudication. If, on the one hand, the monocratic type personifies because it gets, at least symbolically, associated with one official, it de-personifies by producing a cohesive single decision; if, on the other, a collegiate body de-personifies because it involves several persons and dilutes the association with particular individuals, it personifies to the extent that it delivers an unsystematic patchwork of individual opinions instead of a unitary one. Inasmuch as they do not reach an "opinion of the court" but a potpourri of opinions, it could rather be the personal face that catches the eyes. One may personify by the number and de-personify by the content, and vice versa (in case the collegiate opts for a *seriatim*).

Second, a court may be collegiate on the grounds of political prudence, in two complementary senses. For one, its supra-individual character avoids the concentration of too much power in the hands of one single person and prevents abuses; for another, at the same time that it inhibits undue overstepping and holds the authority of each "one" in check, it also empowers the institution to take the momentous and sometimes politically controversial decisions that law requires. A judge, alone, could hardly have political strength to affirm, for example, that hundreds of legislators were wrong, or to confront influential socioeconomic power. A group of judges, conversely, if not powerful enough to knock down or resist a highly disciplined anti-judicial offensive, is still better safeguarded than the solitary judge.

Third, there is a symbolic recognition about the nature of law, an acknowledgement that interpreting the law, let alone the constitution, is a complex task that should be open to diverse voices and leave room for disagreement. This justification would probably be at odds with a phonograph-type grasp of law, which repudiates the putative multivocity of law's directives. Still, if we set that archaic vision aside, a collegiate forum can publicly express, better than a monocratic judge, the open-ended and argumentative character of law. This symbolic attribute, indeed, might raise a tension with the first one: to the extent that de-personification succeeds, that desired multivocity would be watered down. Still, the mere fact that a group of judges reach a joint decision may already express this desirable permeability of law to diverse individual perceptions. Some balance between pure *seriatim* and *per curiam* opinion might carve a reasonable space for both virtues.

Fourth, it may be a shrewd option to have a collegiate court for reasons of epistemic likelihood. The logic is well-known: two heads, more often than not, would think more acutely than one, and there would be lesser fallibility if a group of judges, rather than a loner, is granted the power to decide intricate legal questions. This is a purely numerical and Condorcetian epistemic claim that does not depend on deliberation.[31] The larger the number of members of a decisional body, provided some personal qualifications obtain, the better they perceive nuances of the case and bring more points of view to the fore. It is an upgrade to its informational porosity. Besides, more heads are more likely to cover a broader range of legal expertises as law becomes increasingly complex.

It is arguably possible, yet less likely, for a single judge to attain such standard. For the institutional designer, to rely on a single and expectedly astute judge would be risky. Thus, even by a purely aggregative mode of decision-making, as the number of judges increases, the less fallible the decisional organ turns out to be. This is a "many minds" epistemic argument. As long as courts are composed by just a "few," they may have less traction than

---

[31] Condorcet's jury theorem requires independence between the heads that will be counted. See Condorcet (1976). See also Estlund et al. (1989).

a body formed by the "many." Still, a "few" would be more competent than "one" and minimize the danger of the lack of individual insight.[32]

These four arguments lay the theoretical structure for a sufficiently grounded collegiate body. They reduce the dangers of setting the size of an institution on the magnitude of "one" and collect the benefits of the "few." Nevertheless, some mode of plural decision-making must yet be put into effect. Again, it is not accurate to claim that a collegiate court does not have a choice but to deliberate. Non-deliberative alternatives are available. For a joint decision to be feasible, indeed, judges have to interact and communicate in some way. Granted, there is no aggregation without some communication. Still, it does not need to be of that onerous kind.

The chief alternatives to deliberation were already stated in the opening chapter. First, a multi-member body may opt to bargain, but the same general objection against bargaining is all the more applicable in the domain of adjudication: private-driven interests do not meet the impartial reasoning standards of law. Therefore, negotiating personal agendas, trading votes across cases or mitigating arguments within the case, if motivated by self-interest, are plainly incompatible with adjudication. Two other sorts of compromise—partnership and pragmatic—can still be squared with collegiate adjudication, but they are a product of rather than a substitute for deliberation.

Bargaining is a too easy target. If impartiality is required at least to some specific departments of political reasoning, legal reasoning as a whole is certainly one of those. The second option—aggregation—is not so simple, however, to discount. The same earlier qualifications are in order. There are three kinds of aggregation. It can be the sum of either of three entities: raw private interests; self-reflective preferences;[33] fully deliberated, yet divergent, preferences. The first, for the same reasons that cast bargaining aside, is out of the question. The crux of the matter, therefore, revolves around the two remaining types. Or, to put it more straightforwardly: should a group of judges prefer to aggregate their legal opinions right away, or should they, first, engage in deliberation and subject their initial positions to the deliberative filter?[34] Why aggregation after deliberation rather than aggregation without any tint of deliberation?

---

[32] I am using the classical categories of "one," "few," and "many" to convey imprecise but yet useful conceptual measures to classify the size of decisional bodies. I assume that collegiate courts, in general, have a size that is way below the usual number of members of elected parliaments (on the scale of hundreds) and that normally amounts to a number below 10, or hardly exceeds a number around 20. Whatever the exact number, it is indubitable that these bodies are organized in different orders of magnitude, and this has implications for the sort of epistemic promise it can plausibly make.

[33] Kornhauser and Sager would call that a "hermetic generation of judgments" (1986, 100).

[34] An aggregation of the former type would materially result in a "non-deliberative *seriatim*" decision, a patchwork of individual pre-given opinions. An aggregation of the latter type would, in turn, culminate in either a "deliberative *seriatim*" or in a single opinion of the court with occasional concurrent and

If collegiate judicial deliberation is to be sustained, this is the focal question to be answered.[35] Deliberation-independent reasons are untroubled with aggregation. In order to answer that question, the intrinsic and instrumental rationales for deliberation must be retrieved and tailored to this particular site.

There are courts of diverse sizes, jurisdictions, and competences, handling disparate kinds of legal dispute, immersed in heterogeneous legal traditions. Moreover, they may be located in different spots of the judicial hierarchy. Despite this large range of variations, it is useful to start by considering courts in this generic sense. In the next chapter, and for the rest of the book, we will delve into the more precise confines of constitutional courts, some of which have noteworthy implications to the limits and possibilities of the deliberative political ideal. At this stage, it suffices to uphold very basic assumptions: courts are bodies with the function of settling disputes of law when provoked by external actors or litigants; the decisional collegiate (be it a panel or the plenum itself) is composed by a small group[36] of judges that, be they formally recognized as experts or not, are supposed to reason on the basis of the applicable rules of law.

Let me examine whether those rationales are still applicable to a site largely defined by these preliminary features. I shall start by the instrumental ones. The four dimensions of the epistemic promise seem to be as plausible to collegiate adjudication as they are, all other things being equal, to any deliberative body. The sort of inter-personal engagement defined by the conceptual frame is able, more likely than silent aggregation, (i) to clarify and structure the premises that are in play, (ii) to maximize the information that might be useful to decide, (iii) to allow for creative solutions not anticipated by any of the deliberators alone, and, finally, (iv) to reach a substantively superior decision. Even if one remains reluctant to believe in the ambitious epistemic promise of crafting the right answer, the empirical appeal of the three others is hard to dispute.[37] If all other things remain constant, a group

---

dissenting opinions which communicate with the majority opinion. These variations will be further explored in the coming chapters.

[35] Orth defends the deliberative mode: "Judging appeals, on the other hand, is viewed as a deliberative process, benefiting of the contributions of many minds" (2006, at 15).

[36] The number of deliberators impacts the quality of deliberation and thus the plausibility of the deliberative promises. There is a tension between what the logics of the deliberative and the aggregative epistemic arguments require in numerical terms. Whereas optimal deliberation needs to be made by "not too few, but not too many," optimal aggregation, provided the Condorcetian provisos are met, needs to be made by as many as possible. To consider the implications of the various sizes of courts would add another layer of complexity that I do not want to pursue here. I ground my assertions, again, on approximate generalizations that might be more or less applicable to outlier cases. For an extensive discussion between court size and accuracy, see Kornhauser and Sager, 1986, at 97. Chapter 6 will further address this institutional variable by referring to some empirical researches.

[37] Indeed, epistemic arguments like the ones advanced by Rousseau and Condorcet were mainly aggregative and, for some, anti-deliberative (see Estlund et al., 1989). This point was already raised in Chapter 1.

of judges that deliberate tends to outperform, most of the time, an uncommunicative group or, even more so, an individual judge. In line with this belief, "heads deliberating" have a better chance of reaching a good decision than "heads aggregating" (even when they aggregate careful and thoughtful individual positions).[38]

The second promise of deliberation stresses its capacity to, through rational persuasion, construct consensus or minimize dissensus between deliberators.[39] In a judicial body, which, by definition, needs to find some level of agreement in order to decide, deliberation may be an indispensable resource not only to reduce disagreement, when that is achievable, but also to let legitimate compromises, if necessary, arise. Both pragmatic and partnership types of compromise are hardly obtained without deliberation. In the context of adjudication, moreover, some pivotal values of the rule of law, like intelligibility and uniformity, may work as relevant second-order reasons that push partnership compromises. If a judge does not have a firm opinion about a subject matter, he may well defer to a majority position in the name of a more cohesive legal decision. Courts are operative agents of the rule of law and their judgments mold the societal comprehension of the law. The provision of rationality to rules and principles is one of their chief responsibilities, and compromises might be acceptable for that purpose.

The psychological and educative promises of deliberation may also have a bearing on collegiate adjudication, though a less clear one. Unlike the two first promises, which are supposed to have an impact on the quality of the decision itself, these other two are expected to cause a beneficial effect on the persons involved. This personal involvement may refer both to those who directly participate in the strenuous practice of deliberation and to those outside the forum but whose interests are at stake in the decision.

Thus, judges who take part of deliberation would tend to, as stated by the psychological promise, feel respected by his peers. This sense of respect is a volatile condition of inter-personal relations, and its maintenance can foster a collegial environment that facilitates the daily internal workings of the institution. What is more, it enables the institution to remain able to deliberate (which would be advantageous, of course, if deliberation is regarded as

---

[38] Kornhauser and Sager highlight the epistemic point of collegiate adjudication: "Thus, if we favor deliberation as a means of improving group judgment, it must be because we assume that its judgment-enhancing aspects outweigh its judgment-impairing features." Despite the lack of empirical proof, they concede, "the general assumption favoring deliberation as an aid to correct judgment seems reasonable *in light of common experience*" (1986, 102, emphasis added).

[39] Kornhauser and Sager, again, note this communitarian virtue of persuasion: "Unless one presupposes that judges enter this process either fully aware of all points and counterpoints, or obdurately fixed on both result and rationale without reference to the full range of possible argumentation, it must be the case that some judges emerge from the deliberative process with judgments about the appropriate result or rationale *different from their initial ones*" (1986, 101, emphasis added).

desirable in the first place). Besides, some sense of respect may also be felt by the litigants themselves. The perception that your point of view, as a litigant, was given due weight, contributes to the acceptance of the decision as much as the content of the decision itself.[40] As empirical researches have shown, the perception that procedures were fair are, in the main, at least as important as a favorable decision for the satisfaction of the parties with the judicial outcome.[41]

Finally, advocates of deliberation also expect it to produce two sorts of educative effects on those who are involved in the process. It would train both the deliberative skills and inculcate the subject matter on them. To what extent are these effects plausible in the context of collegiate adjudication generally conceived? Judges are supposed to be knowledgeable on the subject matters of law and, that being the case, deliberation would not necessarily strengthen such trait. However, deliberative skills can only be developed through their very practice (and this result would be attractive, again, if deliberation is deemed positive in the first place). As deliberation is routinized, this educative attribute may turn gradually less significant for judges, but it cannot be neglected with respect to newcomers and neophytes. Finally, the educative effects that deliberation, rather than aggregation, would produce on litigants may probably be uncertain and remote, apart from contingent on very specific institutional features that each court may have. At this level of generality, not much can be said, but I will return to it by way of assessing the deliberative potentials of constitutional courts in the forthcoming chapters.

These promises of deliberation, if sound, further revitalize most of deliberation-independent reasons. A deliberative collegiate body de-personifies because its product is different from the sum of pre-deliberative opinions (even if the decision is still *seriatim*); turns law's openness to a plurality of voices even more unambiguous (since deliberation make present voices that are not in the room); and switches the epistemic key from a purely quantitative to an argumentative mode.

This set of beneficial consequences, in sum, is more likely to ensue through deliberative engagement than through aggregation. But that is not all. There might be more to say in favor of deliberation. Apart from these consequentialist reasons, inherent values are also at stake. The remaining question is whether, in this generally conceived collegiate site, any credible intrinsic reason still subsists. Is it valuable that judges deliberate regardless of any putative beneficial consequence?

---

[40] For Kornhauser and Sager, on top of accuracy, the psychological dimension is also a central measure of performance of judgment aggregation. They call it "appearance," the ability of the decision to inspire belief that it is proper (1986, 91). Leflar follows the same line: "Reasonable assurance of sound decision and public confidence in that soundness support the multi-judge system" (1983, at 723).

[41] The literature on the psychology of procedural justice offers evidence on that direction. See Thibaut and Walker (1978).

The first chapter contended that there is a non-consequentialist normative case for deliberation, provided that some tests of circumstances are satisfied. On that account, as long as excessively disruptive results are not likely to occur, and provided that there is a relevant level of disagreement to be faced and that the decisional urgency is manageable, deliberation should be practiced even if the cherished potential effects are not likely to eventuate either. I argued that beyond some threshold, after these second-order tests are satisfactorily worked out, intrinsic reasons outweigh those consequentialist warnings. The priority basis of the normative case switches from one category of reason to the other. In other words, once the procedure is shielded from an unruly repercussion, it becomes valuable for its own sake. Both sorts of reasons, thus, are interconnected. The actual circumstance is what sets the priority for one or another side of the scale.

That said, when we get down to a court, assuming it has already crossed that conditional threshold and passed those second-order tests, the henceforth presumptive dominance of intrinsic reasons, as that ratiocination commended, does not automatically follow. That line of argument is not easily transplanted to the institutional milieu without further qualifications. Institutions operate a disjunction between decision-makers and the political community, between deliberators and spectators. The abstract normative case of the previous chapter did not take such disjunction into account.

If a political regime praises the equal status of its members, formal or informal political engagement should respect the standards prescribed by the conceptual frame of deliberation. That was the normative concept of political legitimacy that the prior chapter took up. An inter-personal interaction regulated by those parameters recognizes the equal rank of each individual. More precisely, it displays considerateness and sympathy for each one's point of view. That is probably why the key assertions of many deliberative democrats are addressed either to the informal public sphere or to the participatory formal institutions. In both settings, genuine deliberation embodies a civic achievement that, whatever consequence supervenes, is politically significant. It matters for the identity of a political community as a whole and incarnates a general ethics of citizenship.

The moment a sub-group of citizens becomes decision-makers, is granted authority, and gets segregated inside an aristocratic body, as courts, administrative agencies, or elected parliaments,[42] the occasional intrinsic value behind the way they interact becomes pale. That potent intrinsic element cannot

---

[42] To equate parliaments and courts as aristocratic bodies is inaccurate indeed. As a distinction is created between governing bodies and governed citizens, between formal bodies and informal public sphere, an indelible aristocratic element is inserted into a political regime (on this Janus-faced character of parliaments, see Manin, 1997, at 149–150; on the "distance between the people and law-determining decisions," see Waluchow, 2007, at 16–18).

simply be transferred en bloc. Not, at least, with the same self-standing force. The breach between citizens and decision-makers cannot be ignored. Courts, like most institutions, discharge a political function that has a predominantly epistemic commitment. The fact that judges deliberate with each other does not carry anything autonomously laudable in that taxing sense. If not by the rewarding results that may succeed it, judicial deliberation would be, from a political point of view, beside the point. The recognition of the equal status of citizens does not, by itself, transpire from inter-judges deliberation.

Accordingly, before anything else, there must be a point in intra-institutional deliberation. Judges, or any other decision-making official, do not and should not deliberate for its own sake. They rather do and should do so for coming up with the best outcome they can on the respective decisional task that was bestowed on them. The thrust of judicial deliberation is primarily epistemic. If that is right, the plausibility of the epistemic promise is a necessary condition for demanding that judges deliberate. If, in turn, this probabilistic expectation is really sound, it may be possible to rescue, in a conditional way, that intrinsic grounding: since deliberation increases the chances of a better decision, practicing it denotes considerateness. This will be valuable, therefore, even if, eventually, judges fail to fulfill that epistemic promise. Once it is accepted that, probabilistically, deliberation is the most plausible means to reach the best answer, the mere attempt has a value in itself.

All in all, the case for a deliberative court is grounded on the marriage between the deliberation-independent reasons for a collegiate body and the promises of deliberation themselves. Together, they offer noteworthy advantages over the alternatives. One could still say, for the sake of the argument, that if the deliberation-independent reasons were not plausible, a "primus inter pares" arrangement could equally respond to the call for deliberation. That setup could retain the positive aspects of deliberation without having to dilute authority. A highly deliberative cabinet with ministers led by a president or by a prime minister, for example, could also benefit from deliberation in order to take appropriate decisions. A single judge, too, could have similar "primus inter pares" conditions: clerks and expert witnesses, in their own ways, may deliberate with him. That is true: a deliberative forum does not have to be rigorously collegiate. In a collegiate body, all share equal responsibility to decide, and deliberation does not presuppose that.[43] It should still be tested, though, whether the asymmetry that shapes the dialogue in such a formally hierarchical setting may temper some of the promises, especially the epistemic and the communitarian ones.

---

[43] The distinction between interlocutors and decision-makers, as two types of deliberators, accepts that. Chapter 4 will explore that further.

4. CONCLUSION

Law, adjudication, and legal reasoning, some may believe, are not open to deliberation. They are associated with expertise, closure, and elitism. I have tried to clean up the terrain for this seemingly explosive combination. Deliberative adjudication would be a contradiction in terms. Phonograph theories have kept that damaging myth alive and inspired a tacit agreement: judges purport, perhaps sincerely, not to be lawmakers; the audience seems, perhaps sincerely, to believe. This line of thought, despite being dated and obsolete, is sporadically resuscitated. I argued that, once that implausible mechanical view is removed, the question of whether law is hospitable to deliberation turns into one of degree. The spectrum of available reasons for legal argumentation fluctuates according to the proper canon of legal argument. However variable this canon might be, there is no impediment to square it with deliberation.

Collegiate adjudication, in turn, is not necessarily deliberative. I argued, yet, that there is a respectful prima facie normative case for such decisional approach. This case comprises the instrumental benefits of deliberation, which, with several qualifications, remain plausible in the context of collegiate adjudication, and is further enhanced by an inherent value.

3

Political Deliberation and Constitutional Review

I. INTRODUCTION

One cannot presume the judge as a loner. In fact, she rarely happens to be. This matters for a theory of adjudication.[1] Constitutional adjudication, in particular, is not a solitary act either.[2] Nonetheless, the current mainstream seems to have largely neglected this institutional trait.[3] Quite a few theories carry on being indifferent as to whether, or to what extent, it is acceptable that such collegiate body decides in a non-deliberative fashion. The question appears not to have prompted a relevant inquiry.

This is not to say that monocratic adjudication does not have anything to do with the ideal of deliberation. From a different perspective, an individual decision might follow some general deliberative standards, regardless of any inter-personal dialogue. Reflexivity is not exclusively a potential feature of group interaction, but rather a general approach to practical reasoning.[4] This latter intra-personal sense, however, was not the one defined by the conceptual frame and is not the focus of this book. Collegiality is a fact of constitutional courts, and constitutional theory needs to take that into account.

---

[1] Theories of adjudication, for Kornhauser and Sager, are "curiously incomplete." And they add: "Appellate adjudication, the common, almost exclusive focus of theories of adjudication, is thus essentially a group process, yet extant theories neither explain the group nature of the process nor take it into account." The "fact of group decision-making" needs to be incorporated into the analysis (1986, 82–83).

[2] A caveat might be worth reminding. Some systems of constitutional review accept that first instance monocratic decisions challenge the constitutionality of legislation in a concrete case, which is usually called "diffuse" as opposed to "concentrated" control. This book, however, is concerned with constitutional review of last resort that is operated by a collegiate body.

[3] Kornhauser and Sager (1993). Barak also reminds us that: "Scholars do not sufficiently consider the fact that the judge often acts as part of a panel" (2006 at 209).

[4] That is why some prefer to avoid the term "deliberative" and rather use "discourse" or "conversation" to refer to this enhanced ideal of democracy (see Dryzek, 1994). "Deliberative," on its own, would not specify the interpersonal character of the phenomenon. Goodin emphasizes this "internal reflective" side: "Deliberation consists in the weighing of reasons for and against a course of action. In that sense, it can and ultimately must take place within the head of each individual" (2003, at 169).

The considerations of the previous chapter have to be re-addressed, thus, in the light of constitutional law and adjudication. This task will be divided in three parts. The following section approaches the singular nature and political specificity of the function played by constitutional courts as opposed to ordinary courts and elected parliaments. The third section then grasps how the ideal of political deliberation has been tied, though yet incompletely, to constitutional courts, and diagnoses what is missing in these tentative connections. The next chapter will then discuss whether and how that distinctiveness reinforces the call for deliberation and will conceive of the core elements of the ideal of deliberative performance.

2. THE SINGULARITY OF CONSTITUTIONAL SCRUTINY

"Adjudication" is a misleading label to examine what constitutional courts do. This conventional term refers to a form of decision-making that is usually associated with a bilateral confrontation of pleadings that informs and delimits the judgment by a disinterested third-party to the dispute. Or, as Fuller has put it, adjudication is a process that accords the affected parties an "institutionally protected opportunity to present proofs and arguments for a decision in his favour," or to give them their "day in court."[5]

Adjudication finally proves to be an inappropriate word for reasons that will become clearer. The job of constitutional courts is, at best, a sui generis stripe of that decision-making pattern. In a constitutional court, the chief coordinates of adjudication wane. Disputes at such institutional context go beyond the adversarial forensic battle. Even when the process is formally structured around a plaintiff and a defendant, and even if the court is asked to manifest itself through the binary code of constitutionality and unconstitutionality, these adjudicative-type dichotomies are peripheral. Some environmental formalities and rituals, indeed, make them look like adjudication. Since that function has been mostly operated by "courts," which are staffed by "judges," usually located within a "judiciary" and, in some cases, accumulate ordinary judicial responsibilities, that confusion is natural. Such perception, however, passes over the gist of what is actually happening. There is something distinct behind that camouflage.

Henceforth, I will adopt a fresher expression that, if not faultless, at least liberates the function of constitutional courts from the technical meanings that accompany adjudication. Constitutional courts are in charge of operating the constitutional scrutiny of the acts of parliaments.[6] To probe whether they have a justified function to play is a more illuminating inquiry than

---

[5] Fuller, 1960, at 3.
[6] Zurn also tries to detach the function from the label and calls it "constitutional review" (2007).

straining to fit it within any definitional straitjacket. For the purposes of this book, that would be a diversionary route to follow. I will attempt to grasp that function.

Let me specify, first, what I assume as the institutional structure of a constitutional court. I am not using this term in the technical and minute sense conventionalized by a major part of the literature.[7] My definition is rather minimal. A constitutional court has three institutional properties. First, it is a small collegiate organ formed by non-elected members who are thus deprived of the periodical and competitive certification of authority. Instead, they are appointed through distinct political methods. Second, it does not have its own motor and is typified by inertia: cases are brought by external provocation, not by internal initiative. These devices are supposed to nurture the institutional conditions for non-biased judgment. Judicial election and the power to act *ex officio* would tear impartiality apart. Third, it has the power to challenge, oversee, and usually override the acts of elected parliaments in the name of constitutional supremacy. These are the institutional contours that all constitutional courts, as far as I can tell, share. This definition has a level of generality that evades any parochial attachment to a specific system. It remains at the level of institutional design writ large.

Constitutional scrutiny is different both from parliamentary legislation and ordinary adjudication in a variety of perspectives. I will inquire about some traditional ways of comparing and drawing both functional distinctions and demarcate what I consider to be the fundamental criterion to discriminate the nature of constitutional scrutiny.

The dichotomy between lawmaking and law-application cuts across both comparative exercises: constitutional scrutiny would be, according to a certain common sense, more creative and discretionary than ordinary adjudication, but less than legislation. In a spectrum polarized by the two ideal categories, it would stand somewhere in the middle. This, however, is a somewhat inaccurate depiction of the essential difference I am searching for.

If juxtaposed to ordinary adjudication, what is new in constitutional scrutiny? One common way to answer that question appeals to the abstract character of the constitutional language. Due to the open texture of the normative text that drives such examination, and to the morally and politically overloaded concepts that it contains, constitutional interpretation would be a whole different territory, where an abnormal amount or a stressful sense of

---

[7] I equate, for the purposes of this book, a relevant distinction between "supreme courts" and "constitutional courts" *stricto sensu*. The differences regarding the type of constitutionality control (diffuse and concrete as opposed to concentrated and abstract), how they are situated in relation to the overall judiciary system, among others, are not trivial. However, I assume that the kernel of their role is coincidental and use "constitutional courts" in a *lato sensu* way. Their differences, indeed, might require adaptations in my argument but do not invalidate its general normative claim.

discretion comes forth. To instantiate those "essentially contested concepts,"[8] a court would inescapably engage in a constructive and therefore contentious activity, supposedly absent from ordinary adjudication. Syllogistic reasoning, if plausible at all, could hardly be applied in the same way. The court would be less bound by the law and less controllable by the dictates of the legal system.

This contrast between untrammeled discretion and non-volitional application does not work well to isolate constitutional scrutiny. Open texture is not a peculiar quality of the constitutional language and similar open-ended concepts abound all over the legal system. The adjudicative activity, rooted on the constitution or not, is not about the discovery of hidden meanings imprinted in the normative text. It comprises, to different extents, will and justified preference.[9]

One could still say, further dissecting this contrast, that it is a matter of emphasis: while constitutional scrutiny would envision this wholly discretionary legal landscape, ordinary adjudication would resemble it less frequently. However didactic and perhaps accurate part of the time, the criterion is repeatedly falsified by concrete counter-examples. Hard cases are not the monopoly of constitutional scrutiny, neither does ordinary adjudication have exclusivity over easy cases.[10] Not only can the ordinary judge deal with disputes that grant her substantial interpretive leeway and lawmaking power, but also can the constitutional judge be faced with a legally uncontroversial conflict. This criterion provides a fragile grip and relies on unstable borders. By wearing these lenses, one will see, in both settings, shades of not so dissimilar activities. If there really is something different going on, the normative language is a too easy suspect to single out the specificity of either one.

It is also commonly contended that constitutional courts are not concerned with resolving a dispute by the application of the law to facts, like ordinary adjudication, but rather with analyzing the textual compatibility between two hierarchically different norms, a purely abstract exercise. Moreover, their outlook is mainly prospective, not retrospective. These are genuine differences in several jurisdictions. They fail to apprehend, though, those systems where ordinary courts and monocratic judges engage with a constitutional-type reasoning and even have power to disavow the application of a statute on the grounds of its reputed unconstitutionality.

---

[8] See Gallie (1964).

[9] For a radical de construction of neutral adjudication, see Kennedy (1998).

[10] For Dworkin, it is not the open texture per se that typifies constitutional hard cases, but rather the special political divisiveness of the constitutional language, as opposed to the relative technical or less polemical character of the ordinary statutory language. Again, statistically accurate though it may be, this criterion still needs to face many counter-examples (2004, at 80).

The remaining variance between ordinary adjudication and constitutional courts, in a system of such diffuse mode of constitutionality control, is the scope and effect of the decision: the ordinary court's decision impacts only the parties of the case (intra partes), whereas the decision of the constitutional court is valid erga omnes and practically removes the statute from the legal system.[11] This opens a more productive avenue to finally differentiate both enterprises. To declare the unconstitutionality of legislation, or to specify the interpretations that might be constitutionally valid, denotes a species of power and prompts a repercussion that is incomparably heavier. The political voltage of such cases potentially soars and requires political sensitivity to anticipate reactions and modulate the decision accordingly. The aseptic habitat in which law is supposed to operate becomes clearly subverted.

The linguistic standard suggested earlier as a discriminating yardstick is weak and unconvincing, but the distinction between the varying scales of the decision's impact is, indeed, a crucial one. Yet, it does not exhaust this analysis. Before proceeding with this quest, the comparison between the activity of constitutional courts and that of parliaments may add some light. What constitutional courts do has sometimes been associated with legislation. Kelsen famously argued that the court, when cancelling the validity of a statute for its incompatibility with the constitution, would be legislating in a negative sense. He later conceded, though, that there was an inevitable element of positive legislation too.[12] The potential lawmaking character of such activity has gradually become clearer as courts started to impose stricter interpretive limits on parliaments. Even the compromising idea of "interstitial legislation,"[13] once

---

[11] As it inevitably happens with middle-level theory, exceptions to the general rule, or to the minimal denominators that I assume to universally obtain, may exist and betray those assumptions. These exceptions might be more or less important for the argument I develop. This association between, on the one hand, concentrated control and *erga omnes* effect, and, on the other, diffuse control and *intra partes* effect, may prove false or relative in some cases. Three recent examples in the United States show the potentially larger impact of district judges' decisions: *Perry v. Schwarzenegger*, decision in which the district federal judge Vaughn Walker invalidated Proposition 8, which banned gay marriage in California State (04/08/2010); *Log Cabin Republicans v. United States of America*, case in which the district federal judge Virginia Philips issued an injunction banning the enforcement of the infamous "Don't ask don't tell" policy against openly gay persons in the US Army (12/10/2010); *Cuccinelli v. Sebelius*, case in which the district judge Henry Hudson ruled part of the healthcare plan (namely, the requirement for individuals to have insurance) as unconstitutional (13/12/2010). In Brazil, the federal judge Julier Sebastião da Silva prompted the creation of the "Brazil Visit" policy by ordering the immigration officials in all Brazilian international airports to dispense to arriving Americans, in the name of reciprocity, the same rigorous identification procedures through which Brazilian citizens had to pass in American airports due to post-9/11 anti-terror policies (01/01/2004).

In addition, other technicalities may be invoked to differentiate the formal ways to "remove the statute from the legal system." The US Supreme Court does that through *stare decisis*, without formally withdrawing the statute from the official rulebooks, whereas most continental systems do that by actually overruling a statute. This technical difference does not have a practical import in this book.

[12] Kelsen (1931, and especially 1942).

[13] Justice Holmes, dissenting opinion in *S. Pac. Co. v. Jensen*, 244 U.S. 205, 221 (1917).

wittily suggested by Holmes, became unrealistic. A judicial declaration of unconstitutionality shapes, to an extent contingent on the decision's holdings, the meaning of the constitution. It delineates the perimeters of future legislation, if parliament is to comply with the court's directives.

Legislation, in the abstract sense of unbound lawmaking, is not a sharp enough category to distinguish the functions of both institutions.[14] For sure, substantial differences cannot be ignored. Parliaments legislate in a very precise sense. Whereas it enacts wholesale and overarching regulations, courts act in the retail, through piecemeal and surgical infusions into the legal system. The court has an incremental and usually less perceptible lawmaking power: it does so in slight doses rather than in sweeping offensives, in quite definite controversies rather in comprehensive legislative packages.[15] Furthermore, parliaments can be proactive and have power to work ex officio, whereas courts are chiefly reactive and cannot govern their own agenda (even when they can delimit it through some filter[16]).

Despite significant structural differences, both share, in a dynamic way, a lawmaking role.[17] Both can be seen, so to say, as co-legislators. This conclusion, if sound, points to a seemingly eccentric institutional intelligence and reveals a turbulent division of labor within the separation of powers. The curious fact of their functional redundancy, though, does not make them institutional equivalents. Their structural and procedural peculiarities forge markedly different decisional settings: they diverge in their epistemic capacities, their symbolic import, their political capital and their decisional tempo. Their co-existence despite functional overlap can be justified on the basis of their diverse designs: two institutions should partake an analogous function provided that something valuable lurks behind their interaction. There are historical and theoretical rationales for that, which are articulated by the logic of the checks and balances and constitutional supremacy. The next section will outline this logic by way of summarizing the pertinent literature to my subsequent inquiry.

So far, I have maintained that constitutional scrutiny deviates from ordinary adjudication mainly because of the impact it promotes and the consequent

---

[14] It is already commonplace that constitutional courts legislate in a specific sense. Many authors share that perception. See Ferejohn, 2008, at 204. Stone-Sweet also points out how constitutional courts, far from exercising a simple veto to legislation—"immediate, direct and negative"—also do legislate in a positive sense—"prospective, indirect and creative" (2000, at 73).

[15] Waluchow heavily relied on this criterion of this case-by-case character of judicial review.

[16] Like the writ of certiorari in the US Supreme Court.

[17] Historically, the "materialization" of the law through welfare policies is considered to be one crucial cause of the breakdown of the liberal distinction between legislation and adjudication (see Habermas, 1996, chapter 5). However, in the realm of constitutional scrutiny, this gray zone has become clear much earlier.

political susceptibility that a constitutional court needs to manage. Due both to the delicate political context and to the grandness of its cases, constitutional courts face constraints that are different in kind from ordinary adjudication. This is not to say that, as invoked at the outset, the phraseology of the normative standards that calibrate the discretion of constitutional courts are unimportant for distinguishing it from ordinary adjudication. Equivocal and polemical terms, indeed, abound in the text of modern constitutions. The more objective the normative language, one may plausibly say, the less the court gets embroiled in the political thicket. Statistically, perhaps, the linguistic angle may explain why constitutional courts are, more often than ordinary courts, invested with far-reaching discretion. However, this is still a too error-prone angle from where to draw the contrast. On the other hand, to reduce constitutional scrutiny to politics, as a clash of forces, misses the point too, and falls short of answering the question about its proper nature. Such apprehension correctly grasps the trees, but still disregards the forest.

I have asserted that, leaving epiphenomenal, yet no less important, design variances aside, constitutional courts and parliaments share, at least part of the time,[18] a very similar role. A widespread common sense could probably add that the court, as opposed to the parliament, has the unparalleled responsibility of guaranteeing the supremacy of the constitution. This statement would depict that function in a strictly formalistic frame, concerned with normative hierarchy rather than content. A substantive comprehension is largely absent from this common sense. A less dry perception, however, would discern that constitutional courts do not simply engage in lawmaking *tout court*. They operate a unique sort of lawmaking that creatively builds on the borders of the political. This idea requires careful formulation.

Morris Cohen, honing his attack on the phonograph theory, argued that "our constitutional courts are continuous constitutional conventions, except that their decision do not need the ratification by the people."[19] "Continuous constitutional conventions" is a vivid phrase to encapsulate the weight of that function and the deeper meaning of its political facet, but perhaps it sensationalizes too much and lets rhetoric curb conceptual clarity.

Put in a different way, constitutional scrutiny is one institutional technique to set in permanent motion constitutionalism's "meta-political function" of "constituting the body politic," to use Walker's phrase.[20] It may be that, according to the variations of each system of constitutional scrutiny, a court will not play this wide-ranging constitutive function all of the time. After all, the texts of modern constitutions contain several provisions that do not

---

[18] Whereas constitutional courts may accumulate ordinary functions, parliaments often spend most of the time dealing with legislative issues of a non-constitutional nature.

[19] Cohen, 1915, at 484.   [20] Walker, 2009, at 8.

pertain to any plausible notion of "material constitution," but can still serve as the basis for a judicial inspection of legislation.

Therefore, a notion of material constitution is indispensable to detect when constitutional courts and parliaments are undertaking this thick constitutive function or when they are enmeshed in the everyday business of politics. A material constitution not only empowers and disempowers the governmental institutions and their officials, not only enables and disables individuals for pursuing their public and private lives, but, in doing all that, founds the collective identity of a political community. It molds the polity and hence influences without exhausting what policies are acceptable.

How can constitutional courts, by way of constitutional lawmaking, affect the material constitution? Some further conceptual refinement is necessary to classify the quality of lawmaking at stake. In constitutional courts, lawmaking can be groundbreaking, but not limitless. They do not effectuate lawmaking of any sort or extent. I understand constitutional lawmaking as comprising five gradually wider and politically tougher phenomena: lawmaking as interpretation, when filling the semantic void of the constitutional text; as transformation, when changing the consolidated meanings of past settlements; as invention, by creating a provision that is out of the semantic borderlines of the text but without disturbing the core constitutional structures;[21] as amendment, by reforming the text itself; and as a re-foundation, by inaugurating a novel form of political organization.

It would strain too far to claim that a court upsets the founding political decision that lurks behind the constitutional text. A court cannot transfigure the very "type and form of political existence," as Schmitt defined the constitution.[22] Constitutional scrutiny is a constituted power, not an act of brute political will, independent of and prior to any normative backdrop. If it is true that a constitutional court engages in a sort of constitutional lawmaking, it is also accurate to recognize that it does not have such grand notability. Neither does it amend the constitutional text itself. Nevertheless, comparative constitutional jurisprudence is replete of examples of the other three phenomena. By switching, inflating or deflating the practical meaning of fundamental concepts, it promotes subtle non-textual reconfigurations of constitutional law and inevitably shakes the edges of the adopted "type and

---

[21] In conventional constitutional law doctrine, "interpretation" is the only concept acceptable, and can sometimes comprise the idea of "transformation," but hardly the one of "invention."

[22] See Schmitt, 2008, at 125, 130. In the same way that Schmitt distinguishes the constitution from constitutional laws, it is possible to conceptualize acts of "constitution-making" and of "constitutional lawmaking." It is mainly with the latter that a constitutional court is concerned. However, to the extent that there are interconnections between constitutional law and the constitution so defined, constitutional scrutiny will also impact the latter.

form of political existence." Whether this is properly called interpretation,[23] transformation,[24] or invention,[25] and to what extent this is "constitutive" or not, will be a matter of controversy, but the categories help graduating undeniable nuances.

The court is surely not framing the margins of the political alone, and is not free to reinvent the political identity from the very bottom. It faces not only legal limits, but also political ones, in the Schmittian physicalist sense. It is in charge, however, of the routine demarcation of the meaning of the constitutional project. The constitutional court speaks on behalf of and towards the whole political community, not just towards a limited number of litigants. And it speaks not only about the community's quotidian policy affairs, but rather about its very character. Still, its function is far from the all-inclusive and total power that manifests itself in the critical moment envisioned by Schmitt.

Constitutional hard cases are qualitatively different from ordinary hard cases because of politics, not because of law. And politics, in this instance, must be qualified. It resounds not just the power struggle dimension, the tint of *realpolitik* by which the court is surrounded and with which it needs to get away, but rather the communitarian momentousness of re-signifying the constitution. The court, therefore, is not only a political force gauging its strength and severing its allies and adversaries. It is first and foremost a co-framer of the political.

This line of thought also echoes Ackerman's influential concept of "constitutional moment," which helped him to narrate American constitutional development, to debunk the myth of its constitutional continuity, and, normatively, to defend the idea of a dualist democracy.[26] Constitutional moments are events of intense civic mobilization that lead to constitutional change

---

[23] South African Constitutional Court, *Grootboom* case: *Government of the Republic of South Africa & Ors v. Grootboom & Ors* 2000 (11) BCLR 1169. This is a landmark social rights case in which the South African Constitutional Court, on the basis of section 26 of the constitution, recognized the right of a person to demand the state to act reasonably in framing a housing policy.

[24] US Supreme Court, *Brown v. Board of Education of Topeka*, 347 U.S. 483 (1954). This is a good example of when interpretation leads also to transformation: the reversal of *Plessy v. Ferguson*, 163 U.S. 537 (1896), which accepted the constitutionality of the "separate but equal" doctrine.

[25] Canada Supreme Court, *Reference re Secession of Quebec* [1998] 2 S.C.R. 217. The Canadian Supreme Court recognized the right of secession despite the lack of any remotely clear constitutional provision. See Choudhry (2008).

[26] A dualist democracy is characterized by the alternation between two qualitatively different moments of political significance: in times of "normal politics," the "people" is concentrated in its private affairs and collective decisions made by elected politicians basically to coordinate self-interest; in times of "constitutional politics," the people awakes to the common good and lead changes of exceptional civic engagement and deliberative quality. The role of the Supreme Court, in this frame, is to protect the voice of the people manifested in such "constitutional moments." In US history, for Ackerman, they were three: the Founding, the Reconstruction, and the New Deal periods (see Ackerman, 1984 and 1995).

without formal constitutional amendment. The constitution mutates and its regular amendment procedure is bypassed. The Supreme Court can be, for Ackerman, a legitimate protagonist of such process by recognizing the deliberative quality of the civic engagement that triggered such modification. The normative purchase of that idea was controversial though. For Choudhry, these moments account for "unconstitutional acts of constitution making." The *Quebec Secession* case, decided by Canada Supreme Court, offered an unrivalled example of an act that, for him, was tantamount "to amend[ing] the Canadian Constitution extralegally under the guise of constitutional interpretation."[27]

Still, the concept supplies a good approximation of the proper nature and potential scope of constitutional scrutiny. In Ackerman's version, actual constitutional moments are rare and extraordinary. But the basic properties of such a "thick constitutional event" do not need to be so strictly selective.[28] It is possible that the "process of extratextual amendment is continuous," "more fluid than sporadic."[29] Parliaments and constitutional courts are permanently oscillating between "polity-generative questions" and "policy-programme questions,"[30] which are not easily distinguishable. Widening the notion of constitutional moment to embrace these apparently ordinary lawmaking events, and detaching it from the too demanding deliberative involvement of the public sphere that Ackerman requires, may equip us to better perceive subtle shifts in the inconstant borders of the political and to observe how the court participates in it.

Whatever alternative expression might sound more palatable and truthful to refer to constitutional courts—a "third legislative chamber," a "derivative constituent power," or a "subordinate constitutional demiurge"—the striking aspect to be noted is that they interact with elected parliaments in a dynamic and higher lawmaking process that transcends the walls of legislatures. Their activity does not suit rigid notions of legislation and adjudication, *simpliciter*. Desirable or not, constitutional scrutiny is, in relation to parliament, an exogenous test with constitutional lawmaking attributes.[31] However, the purview of this exogenous test should not be overstated. It operates under significant constraints. Attempts to rigidly demarcate the province of constitutional scrutiny from legislation on the basis of the arid lawmaking *versus* law application dichotomy slip through the hands of the

---

[27] Choudhry, 2008, respectively at 229 and 198. [28] Walker, 2003, at 8.
[29] Schauer, 1992, at 1194–1195. [30] Walker, 2003, at 3.
[31] One may be reminded that the French Constitutional Council is rather an endogenous test of the legislative process. However accurate this might be, and despite the qualifications that one needs to do with respect to the French model, the fact remains that it operates a review of the decision of the elected parliament.

observer. Constitutional scrutiny plays a revisory function that might be distinguished from the activity of parliaments only in temporal and structural terms rather than functional.

If we assimilate constitutional law as the "combination of canonical texts, interpretive cases and political understandings," the constitutional court is obviously participating in the making of it.[32] Depending on political circumstances, a constitutional court is able carry out constitutional moments of lower and higher calibers. Whether it is justified in doing so is part of a different story. This book will address that question by devising the idea of deliberative performance as a measure of comparative legitimacy. So far, I simply recognized the lawmaking power of courts as a fact that is already spread, in different degrees, over contemporary constitutional democracies. The move from the analytical to the normative was not yet done.

3. THE CONCEPTION OF CONSTITUTIONAL COURTS AS DELIBERATIVE INSTITUTIONS

Political frictions between parliaments and courts were not born in North-American soil with the advent of judicial review of legislation in the beginning of the nineteenth century. The chronicles of the modern rule of law show that their origins can be traced further back.[33] Neither have these quarrels been always formulated in the perspective of the democratic legitimacy of an unelected body with the legal competence to overrule the acts of an elected one.

Nevertheless, the emergence of judicial review, and specially its gradual enhancement over time, has significantly dramatized that historical tension. It resonated in constitutional theory and triggered new sorts of questions then inspired, indeed, by the democratic ideal. What was originally a US feature became, later in the twentieth century, through the burgeoning of constitutional courts and the accompanying judicialization of politics in Western democracies, a multinational one.

The canonical genealogy of judicial review has three important masterminds: Hamilton, who announced the rationale years before judicial review was implemented;[34] Chief Justice Marshall, who derived that power from

---

[32] See Schauer, 1992, at 1189.

[33] Some historical marks thereof are usually mentioned. A classical one is attributed to judge Edward Coke who, before the English Glorious Revolution of 1688, established the doctrine of the supremacy of common law over statutory law (Bonham case). This doctrine reverberated in the pre-independence English colonies in North America to face the colonial parliaments and also, after independence, to counter the activist states' legislative assemblies under a fear of majoritarian despotism (see Gargarella, 1996, at 17, and Thayer, 1893, at 139).

[34] As stated by Hamilton: "No legislative act therefore contrary to the constitution can be valid. To deny this would be to affirm that... the representatives of the people are superior to the people themselves... It

what he understood as an implicit logic of the constitution;[35] and Kelsen, who deeply theorized about its role and inspired the creation of a new model of constitutionality control in Austria.[36] They were concerned with institutionalizing the supremacy of the constitution, and the kernel of their suggestion was basically the same: the validity of a statute is contingent upon its compatibility with the constitution; the judiciary is in charge of applying the law and therefore authorized to disregard statutes that are unconstitutional. Without this outer extra-parliamentary agency, constitutional supremacy would not obtain, and parliament would be free to amend the constitution under the formal guise of ordinary legislation.

The alleged logical necessity of judicial review was sold without ample theoretical contestation. The fallacy of that ratiocination was pointed out much later.[37] Besides logical soundness, however, other reasons might be invoked for the existence of an institution. The convenience of judicial review was historically consolidated, if not as a product of logical inference, at the very least as an "edifice of liberal political prudence."[38] In this modest version, judicial review is a necessary evil to be tolerated for the community's self-protection against abuses of power.

This prudential stance, nevertheless, is surely not a conversation-stopper. The dispute upon the democratic legitimacy of the existence of judicial review, and upon the valid scope of its practice, has been fervent in the US ever since. It was first Thayer and then, decades later, Bickel, who ventilated this concern in the most notorious way. The fear of "democratic debilitation,"[39] to the former, and the nuisance brought by the "counter-majoritarian difficulty,"[40] to the latter, just furnished catchier slogans to the ingrained Jacksonian conception of democracy that perseveres in part of the American political mind.

This populist take on democracy was not entirely embraced by later cycles of constitutional fertility in Western democracies. The constitutional courts created by the post-war, post-fascist, or post-communist constitutional regimes were not seen as "deviant institutions."[41] Neither has the "counter-majoritarian

---

is far more rational to suppose that the courts were designed to be an intermediate body between the people and the legislature" (Hamilton, Madison, and Jay, *The Federalist* 78, at 379). See also Brutus, Letter XII, at 507.

[35] See *Marbury v. Madison*, 5 U.S. 137 (1803)   [36] See Kelsen (1931) and Nino, 1996, at 187.

[37] For a thorough analysis of the fallacy behind the arguments of both Marshall and Kelsen, due to the conflation between two different conceptions of legal validity, see Nino, 1996, at 193. For a historical overview of the legacy of *Marbury v. Madison*, see Nelson (2000).

[38] These are Michelman's words (1999, at 135). Grimm shares this opinion. For him, the point of judicial review "is not one of principle, but one of pragmatics" (2000 at 105).

[39] Thayer (1893).   [40] Bickel, 1961, at 16–18.

[41] Another expression of Bickel, 1961, at 18. About the cycles of constitutionalism, see Grimm, 2000.

difficulty" automatically traveled together with them. One cannot assume, however, that the general theoretical justification of constitutional courts is settled, or that these courts do not face resembling challenges in their everyday operation. The argument, indeed, is far from over.

Advocates for judicial review of legislation often conceive it as a reconciliatory device of (liberal) constitutionalism and (representative) democracy.[42] It would be an institutional compromise that recognizes the priority of the right over the good,[43] or the co-originality of individual rights and popular sovereignty.[44] It institutionalizes the irreducible tension between procedures and outcomes in the concept of political legitimacy, and recognizes that the electoral pedigree is not enough reason, all of the time, for decisional supremacy in a democracy.

Variations of this simple idea abound. But there is nothing, so far, that connects constitutional courts with deliberation. As a matter of fact, deliberativists are, more often than not, suspicious, if not forthrightly unsympathetic, of the deliberative prospects of courts. For Gutmann and Thompson, for example, the question about whether the protection of rights should be ascribed to courts is an empirical rather than principled one, and requires more concrete evidence than some have been able to offer. Their theory of deliberative democracy does not seek to find, in any event, the "primary province of deliberation," but to spread out forums of deliberation as much as appropriate. Courts may be one of them, but hardly the main one.[45] Promoters of deliberation should indubitably look "beyond the courtroom" if the quality of democracy is to be augmented in that direction.[46]

Deliberative democrats resist putting too much weight on courts not only due to their elitist character. They do so because of the supposedly restrictive code that shapes the argumentative abilities of this forum. Courts would be handcuffed to the apparently stringent vectors of legal language. Nothing could be more at odds with the openness of the deliberative ideal than this. Waldron, Glendon, Zurn, and others have expressed misgivings about the possibilities of legal argumentation to encompass deeper moral considerations.[47] Judicial discourse would be legalistic and myopic, a distraction from the nub of the matter. Their patterns of reasoning would impede judges to see what is genuinely at stake. Their professional duty to take legal materials into account would harm straightforward deliberation. The operation of law

---

[42] Or, in Grimm's words, as a "necessary completion of constitutionalism" (2009, at 23).

[43] See Rawls, 1971, at 31.   [44] See Habermas (1996).

[45] As they state: "To relegate principled politics to the judiciary would be to leave most of politics unprincipled" (1996, at 46).

[46] Gutmann and Thompson, 1996, at 47.

[47] See Waldron (2006a, 2006b, 2009a, 2009b,), Glendon (1993), Zurn (2007).

would simply not comport with the transformative claims to which deliberative politics should be permeable.[48] This concern is a serious one, but cannot be too quickly generalized as an inevitable or universal feature of constitutional courts.[49] Moreover, it is little comparatively informed and typically based on the reasoning habits of the US Supreme Court.[50]

i. Constitutional courts as "custodians" of public deliberation

That caveat does not entail that no deliberativist accommodates constitutional review within a deliberative democracy. Many actually do. However hesitant and refusing to accept any deliberative eminence of the process of constitutional review, it may have a room to occupy in the background. Habermas, for example, calls on the court to assure the "deliberative self-determination" of lawmaking and to assess whether the legislative process was undertaken under decent deliberative circumstances.[51] The court, in his account, needs to mediate between the republican ideal and the degenerate practices of real politics. It is a tutor that guarantees the adequate procedural channels for rational collective decisions rather than a paternalistic regent that defines the content of those choices. It does not substitute for the moral judgments made by the legislator, but investigates the procedural milieu under which these judgments were formed.[52] Zurn largely reproduces this justification. He carves a space for constitutional review within his "proceduralist version of deliberative democratic constitutionalism." He accepts an external agency to enforce procedures but, like Habermas, refuses to accord it substantive moral choices. The court would not second-guess parliament, but just make sure it is in good working order. Their notion of "procedure," though, is a robust one and the extent to which it is successfully severed from substance remains an open question.[53]

Nino and Sunstein, in their own ways, play in unison with the logic of this account. Nino does not doubt that a constitutional court is an aristocratic

---

[48] Chapter 7 presents a minimal conception of constitutional law that tentatively mitigates this feature of constitutional reasoning.

[49] Kumm, for example, rejects this generalization by showing how the "rational human rights paradigm," employed by several European courts, avoids this legalistic trap (see Kumm, 2007).

[50] Glendon explicitly recognizes that the US Supreme Court adopts a peculiar "dialect" of the language of rights, which is not necessarily reproduced elsewhere. Waldron's and Zurn's claims, on the other hand, seem to have a more general scope, despite invoking almost only US examples.

[51] See Habermas, 1996, chapter 6.

[52] Habermas is supplementing and polishing the classic argument put forward by Ely two decades earlier. For Ely, the court should be restricted to a "representation-reinforcing" role, which he defined as not more than the protection of freedom of expression, the right to non-discrimination and to vote freely (see Ely, 1977). See also Silva and Mendes, 2008.

[53] Dworkin once objected Ely's pioneering attempts of finding a "route from substance" (1985, at 58).

body and that the assumption of any judicial superiority to deal with rights evokes "epistemic elitism."[54] However, he accepts that the belief on the value of democracy presupposes certain conditions. The exceptions to the default preference for majoritarian processes constitute the mandate of courts, and they are of three kinds: first, the court needs to draw the line between a priori and a posteriori rights and to protect the former if genuine democratic deliberation is to ensue; second, in the name of personal autonomy, the court needs to quash perfectionist legislation that oversteps the domain of inter-subjective morality and establishes an ideal of human excellence; finally, the court needs to preserve the constitution as a stabilized social practice against abrupt breaks.[55]

Sunstein also defends that the Supreme Court has a role to play in the maintenance of the "republic of reasons" to which, for him, the American constitution committed itself. His advice for "leaving things undecided" through a minimalist strategy to kindle broader deliberation by the citizenry is the best-known part of his account. The less-known portion is its complement: when "pre-conditions for democratic self-government" are at stake, a maximalist take is, according to him, the pertinent one.[56] In some enumerated circumstances, rather than crafting "incompletely theorized agreements," the court should look for complete ones.[57] Nonetheless, he supposes, the cost of maximalism is the consequent impoverishment of deliberation in the public sphere with respect to these judicially bared issues.

Despite defending constitutional review, the deliberative concern of these authors lies actually elsewhere. Such function, for them, is justified only to the extent that it unlocks, safeguards, and nurtures deliberation in other arenas. The court is just the warden of democratic deliberative processes, not the forum of deliberation itself. This is not the angle I want to illuminate at the moment.

ii. Constitutional courts as "public reasoners" and "interlocutors"

There are three more robust ways to couple constitutional courts with deliberation. They are related to the imagery portrayed in the introduction of the book. Rather than a mere custodian of democratic deliberative processes, the court may be a more intrusive participant of societal deliberation either as a "public reasoner," as an "interlocutor," or yet as a "deliberator" itself. The public reasoner and the interlocutor supply public reasons to

---

[54] Nino, 1996, at 188.   [55] Nino, 1996, at 199–205.

[56] This is not the only hypothesis for allowing maximalism to supplant minimalism (see Sunstein, 2001, at 57).

[57] Sunstein (1994).

the external audience. Both images ignore, however, how judges internally behave and disregard whether they have simply bargained or aggregated individual positions to reach common ground. The qualifying difference is that an interlocutor, unlike a public reasoner, is attentive to the arguments voiced by the other branches and dialogically responds to them. Finally, the court can be imagined as a deliberator. Apart from being an inter-institutional interlocutor, it is also characterized by the internal deliberation among judges. When courts are referred to as "deliberative institutions," it is not always clear which of these three specific senses is under reference. I will sketch these three images a bit more so that their occasional weaknesses become clearer.

"Public reasoner" is an evocative umbrella-term that encompasses a prolific dissemination of derivative images. They all share a very similar insight. Rawls and Dworkin are probably the leading figures on that account. Their proposal of a court as an "exemplar of public reason" or as a "forum of principle" is not only a description of the American Supreme Court, but also a prescription of how this function should be incorporated into a democracy. Two other creative accounts fit in this category too. Alexy thinks of a constitutional court as a "venue for argumentative representation" and Kumm, in turn, conceives it as an "arena of Socratic contestation." I proceed to condense each one.

Rawls is largely enthusiastic about constitutional review. He asserts that, "in a constitutional regime, public reason is the reason of its supreme court."[58] He even assumes that "in a well-ordered society the two more or less overlap."[59] Or, yet, in his most confident passage, he suggests a litmus test for knowing whether we are following public reason: "how would our argument strike us presented in the form of a supreme court opinion?"[60] For him, the constraint of public reason applies to all institutions, but in an exceptionally burdensome way to constitutional review: "the court's special role makes it the exemplar of public reason."[61] In other moments, he moderates his terms and remarks that the court "may serve as its exemplar," as well as the other branches.[62] The comparative advantage of courts, however, is to use public reason as its sole idiom. The court would be "the only branch of government that is visibly on its face the creature of that reason and of that reason alone."[63]

In such account, the court is a key device for the regime to comply with the liberal demand of legitimacy: a politics of reasonableness and justifiability deserved by each and every citizen as equal and free members of the political community. Coercion is admissible to individuals only if based on reasons that all "may reasonably be expected to endorse."[64] Public reason is

---

[58] Rawls, 1997a, at 108.
[59] Rawls, 1997a, footnote 10.
[60] Rawls, 1997a, at 124.
[61] Rawls 1997a, at 95. See also Rawls 2005, at 231 and 1997b, at 768.
[62] Rawls, 1997a, at 114.
[63] Rawls, 1997a, at 111.
[64] Rawls, 1997a, at 95.

thus the linchpin of such machinery.[65] The readiness and willingness to listen and to explain collective actions in terms that could be accepted by others is the pivotal democratic virtue, labeled by him as "duty of civility" or as a manifestation of "civic friendship." Not all reasons, therefore, are public reasons, but only those which refuse to engage in a comprehensive doctrine of the good, and remain within the bounds of a strictly political conception of justice. Such discipline, moreover, does not apply to any issue, but only to constitutional essentials and matters of basic justice.[66] The role of the court is to ascribe public reasons "vividness and vitality in the public forum," to force public debate to be imbued by principle. There would reside its educative quality too.[67]

Dworkin adopts a similar approach. The distinction between principles and policies is at the core of his theory. Principles ground decisions based on the moral rights of each individual, whereas policies inform decisions concerning the general welfare and collective good. Both co-exist in a democracy. They embody two different types of legitimation, one based on reasons, the other based on numbers. The catch is that, when in conflict, the former trumps the latter. Neither law as integrity, nor democracy as partnership (which, in Dworkin's "hedgehog approach" to values, are interdependent[68]), can be exhausted by arguments of policy. They cannot be squared with this purely quantitative perspective.

For Dworkin, judicial review is democracy's reserve of principled discourse, its "forum of principle." Only a community governed by principles manages to promote the moral affiliation of each individual. Political authority becomes worthy of respect thanks to its ability of voicing arguments and displaying "equal concern and respect," not to its techniques of counting heads. The institutions of such a regime need to foster communal representation, apart from a statistic one. Judges, on that account, do not represent constituents in particular, but a supra-individual entity—the political community as a whole. An elected branch cannot be sufficiently trusted as the "forum of principle" because of the counter incentives it faces.

To remove questions of principle from the ordinary political struggle, then, is the court's mission. Other types of argument may obfuscate the centrality of principle. There is no legitimacy deficit on that arrangement because democracy, correctly understood, is a procedurally incomplete form of government—there is no right procedure to attest whether its pre-conditions are fulfilled. The promotion of preconditions can emerge anywhere. When it

---

[65] Rawls, 1997b, at 765.
[66] Rawls, 1997a, at 93. Constitutional essentials refer to the central rights and liberties and the structures of power. Matters of basic justice are related to socio-economic matters.
[67] Rawls, 1997a, 112–114.   [68] Dworkin (2010).

comes to principles, the legitimacy test is a consequentialist one. We measure it *ex post*, by assessing whether a decision is correct, or at least attempting to provide the best possible justification. Procedural inputs do not matter for that purpose. The court is not infallible, but the attempt to institutionalize an exclusive place for the promotion of principle cannot be illegitimate because of its inevitable fallibility.[69] Lesser fallibility, if plausible, is enough. The legitimacy of the court depends, then, on its independence from ordinary politics and, most of all, on its "responsiveness to changes in public opinion and public principle."[70]

Alexy keeps the same tune. Judicial review is reconcilable with democracy if understood as a mechanism for the representation of the people. It is representation, though, of a peculiar kind: rather than votes and election, it works by arguments.[71] A regime that does not represent except through electoral organs would instantiate a "purely decisional model of democracy." Alexy, however, believes that democracy should contain arguments in addition to decisions, which would "make democracy deliberative." Elected parliaments, to the extent that they also argue, may embody both kinds of representation—"volitional or decisional as well as argumentative or discursive"—whereas the representation expressed by a constitutional court is an exclusively argumentative one. The two conditions for argumentative representation to obtain are the existence of, on the one hand, "sound and correct arguments," and, on the other, rational persons, "who are able and willing to accept sound or correct arguments for the reason that they are sound or correct." The ideal of discursive constitutionalism, for him, intends to institutionalize reason and correctness. Constitutional review is a welcome device if it is able to do that.[72]

For Kumm, at last, judicial review is valuable because it institutionalizes a practice of Socratic contestation. This practice engages authorities "in order to assess whether the claims they make are based on good reasons."[73] Liberal democratic constitutionalism, he contends, has two complementary commitments: for one, elections promote the equal right to vote; for the other, Socratic contestation guarantees that individuals have the right to call public acts into question and receive a reasoned justification for them. Parliaments and constitutional courts are the respective "archetypal expressions" of both commitments. If legitimacy, on that liberal frame, depends on the quality of reasons that ground collective decisions, judicial review is a checkpoint that

---

[69] The pieces of this argument are dispersed over many Dworkin's publications. See mainly Dworkin 1985, at 34, 1986 (chapter 6), 1990, 1995, 1996 (introductory chapter) and 1998.

[70] Radio interview at <http://www.podcastdirectory.com/podshows/868705>, accessed in October 2010 (no longer available).

[71] Alexy, 2005, at 578–579.   [72] Alexy, 2005, at 581.   [73] Kumm, 2007, at 3.

impedes this demand to dwindle over time. The Socratic habit of subjecting every cognitive statement to rigorous doubt helps democracy to highlight and test the quality of substantive outcomes, instead of passively resting merely on fair procedures. Constitutional courts, through this "editorial function," hold parliaments accountable for the reasons upon which they decide. They probe collective decisions and, by doing that, have the epistemic premium of casting aside, at least, legislative decisions that are unreasonable.[74]

The cursory description above does not do justice to the complexity of each author. It shows, still, the similar logic of their arguments. All equally tackle a monotonic picture of democracy that relentlessly pervades objections against counter-parliamentary institutions like constitutional review. Their chorus intones: "democracy is not only that." Democracy is rather shaped by a duality. Whatever this less intuitive component is called (public reasons, principles, rational arguments, contestation), there would be no genuine democracy without it. The court does not have a monopoly of such code, but has the virtue of operating exclusively on that basis. It is a monoglot. There lies its institutional asset. It avoids the danger of political polyglotism, the cacophony of reasons that may lead to harmful trade-offs and prostrate this cherished yet permanently endangered dimension of the complex ideal of collective self-government.

I do not plan to discuss whether their arguments on the legitimacy of judicial review are sound.[75] Neither am I interested in thematizing whether elected parliaments or other institutions could play that function as much as courts. The description of the expectations they place on courts, however, enables us to grasp some implications later.

Courts as "public reasoners," therefore, entail much more than what was prescribed by Habermas and other deliberativists. Courts as "interlocutors" too. This image springs from "theories of dialogue," which echo an old insight of Bickel, for whom the court should prudently engage in a continuing "Socratic colloquy" with other branches and society.[76] These theories have developed through many sophisticated stripes since the 1980s.[77] Some of their statements underline what other aforementioned authors also claimed: the court can catalyze deliberation outside it. For these theories, though, the court is not an empty ignition of external deliberation and neither a pontifical source of right answers to be submissively obeyed. It is rather an argumentative participant. And unlike ivory-tower reason-givers,[78] as the previous image

---

[74] Kumm, 2007, at 31. Kumm is interestingly articulating the liberal requirement of public reasons advanced by Rawls, with Alexy's rights' discourse structured around proportionality and Pettit's republican definition of democracy as "contestation" (see Pettit, 1997).

[75] I did it elsewhere. See Mendes (2009a and 2009b).   [76] See Bickel, 1962, at 70–71.

[77] See Mendes (2009b).

[78] This image is more akin to the handful of pejorative images that spread in the literature (philosopher-kings, bevy of platonic guardians, etc.).

suggested, "interlocutors" join the interaction in a more modest and horizontal fashion. They do not claim supremacy in defining the constitutional meaning. Dialogical courts know that, in the long run, last words are provisional and get blurred in the sequence of legislative decisions that keep challenging the judicial decisions irrespective of the court's formal supremacy.

iii. Constitutional courts as "deliberators"

Constitutional courts have so far been seen as deliberation-enhancing, but still not, necessarily, as deliberative themselves. Those accounts, I submit, are unsatisfactory and incomplete. They fail to open the black-box of collegiate courts and to grasp whether those taxing expectations are plausible, or under what conditions they are achievable, and to what degree. They rely on an optimistic presumption: since judges are not elected, their superior aptitude to deal with public reasons eventuates. This inference conceals several mediating steps. There is a lot to be said and done between the premise and this putative effect. It is intriguing how that presumption could overlook the internal dynamics of this conflictive multi-member institution.

This question was not prolifically discussed in constitutional theory. Apart from some thoughtful testimonies from famous constitutional judges,[79] the specific value of collegial deliberation for constitutional courts has not been fully explored yet. Do the roles of "public reasoner" or "interlocutor" require some sort of internal deliberation? Are they compatible with non-deliberative aggregation? If the practice of Socratic contestation between branches is likely to improve the outcomes of the political process, is it not plausible to argue that deliberative engagement among judges is likely to improve, in turn, the substantive quality of Socratic contestation? Would it be acceptable to replace a collegiate court by a wise monocratic judge that produces well-reasoned decisions? Michelman hints as to why this may not be the case:

> Hercules, Dworkin's mythic judge, is a loner. He is much too heroic. His narrative constructions are monologues. He converses with no one, except through books. He has no encounters. He has no otherness. Nothing shakes him up. No interlocutor violates his inevitable insularity of his experience and outlook...Dworkin has produced an apotheosis of appellate judging without attention to what seems the most universal and striking institutional

---

[79] Sachs, 2009, at 270: "We discover that a collegial court is more than the sum of its parts. It has its own vitality, its own dynamic, its own culture. We subsume ourselves into it." Barak, 2006, at 209: "When the judge sits on a panel of multiple judges, the judge must consult with his colleagues. The judge must convince them. A good court is a pluralistic court, containing different and diverse views. That is certainly the case in a multicultural society. There are always mutual persuasion and exchange of ideas." Grimm, 2009, at 31: "Legal arguments mattered and it happened quite often that members of the court changed their minds because of the arguments exchanged in the deliberation." Grimm, 2003: "the United State Supreme Court wastes this source of illumination by not deliberating enough."

characteristic of the appellate bench, its plurality. We ought to consider what that plurality is for. My suggestion is that it is for dialogue, in support of judicial practical reason, as an aspect of judicial self-government, in the interest of our freedom.[80]

"Plurality" and "dialogue," in the light of "judicial practical reason" and for the sake of "judicial self-government," resound some of the deliberative virtues listed earlier. We ignore how courts deliberate at our own theoretical peril. We may be missing something potentially valuable and immunizing judges from critical challenge when they decide to turn a deaf ear to the arguments of their peers and opt to act as soloists or strategic dealmakers. We remain deprived from any critical template. It might be appropriate to demand from judges more than what we have seen so far.

The superficial yet widely accepted assumption that courts are special deliberative forums calls for refinement. Not much is said about what a deliberative forum entails. That contention simply stems from the institutional fact that courts are not tied to electoral behavioral dynamics, hence their impartiality, hence their better conditions to deliberate. We should certainly not underestimate that courts occupy an apposite institutional position for deliberation. It is still not clear, though, whether courts are being as deliberative as that presumption believed, or why they should be motivated to deliberate in the first place. In contemporary regimes, we will find all sorts of constitutional courts, some better than others in the deliberative exercise, some absolutely null. The normative underpinning, let alone the causal forces, of such goal were not yet specified.

Rawls and Dworkin conceived the deliberative ability of courts merely as reason-giving. They do neither elaborate on how courts may oscillate when pursuing that function nor, indeed, on how we may discern that oscillation. They would certainly agree that some courts are better reason-givers than others, or that the same court might attain or frustrate those expectations in different cases. To assess that volatile quality, nevertheless, they do not offer much analytical resource apart from a liberal theory of justice. For them, we would have to confront the substantive controversy on its face: whether the outcomes are right or wrong, better or worse, closer to or farther from their conception of justice. Alexy and Kumm, in turn, offer the structure of proportionality reasoning. Though less substantive, it still does not tell much about what else surrounds the decision-making process.

The court as an interlocutor gains a subtle attribute in relation to the reason-giver: it is more cautious in modulating the decisional tone and in demonstrating that all arguments are given due regard. It displays that, apart from being a good arguer, the court is also a good listener and digests the

---

[80] Michelman, 1986, at 76. Habermas incorporates Michelman's criticism of Hercules (1996, at 223).

reasons from the outside. Both images catch, in any event, a still defective picture of a constitutional court's potential as a deliberative institution. Courts can be and, to various extents, often are, deliberative in a more fecund sense. Its institutional context and procedural equipment create peculiar conditions to do so. To grasp only the reason-giving aspect is to miss a broader phenomenon. Constitutional watchers need to measure these variances and to see whether they have any implication for the legitimacy of constitutional review.

Ferejohn and Pasquino pushed that debate to a richer stage.[81] They agree that courts face a tighter regulation with respect to the delivery of reasons. For them, the separation of powers encompasses various kinds of accountability, each of which occupying distinct spots of a "chain of justification." The longer the thread of delegation, or the more distant an authority is from election, the greater will be its duty of reason-giving "in return." On one extreme, a weightier deliberative burden compensates for the electoral deficit. On the other, the deliberative deficit is counterbalanced by the closeness to the people.[82] These varying charges are "inversely correlated with democratic pedigree."[83, 84]

Thus, they share with Rawls the claim that courts are "exemplary deliberative institutions."[85] They note, though, that there is not just one way to be deliberative. Deliberation, for them, can be internal or external and has a distinct target in each case: "to get the group to decide on some common course of action," in the former, and "to affect actions taken outside the group," in the latter. One "involves giving and listening to reasons from others within the group," whereas the other "involves the group, or its members, giving and listening to reasons coming from outside the group."[86]

This distinction is a useful one and sheds light on separate functions and settings. The recognition of the court as an actual "deliberator" becomes more evident. Judges deliberate internally while striving to reach a single

---

[81] See Silva (2009).

[82] This conception of accountability is derived from what Ferejohn calls a "folk theory of democracy," one that demands thin Schumpeterian procedures, as opposed to stronger substantive requirements. "A well functioning political/legal system can be expected to exhibit a range of accountability relations that runs roughly from the political to the legal or, if you prefer, from the arbitrary or wilful to the reasonable or deliberative" (Ferejohn, 2007, at 9–10).

[83] Ferejohn, 2008, at 206. There is a scale of decreasing deliberative demands according to four degrees of separation from the people: courts, public agencies, legislatures, voters. The ballot box is a "reason free zone"—at this stage, only numbers matter (Ferejohn and Pasquino, 2002, at 26).

[84] "Courts are expected to deliberate and are given elaborate deliberation-forcing procedures to ensure that they do... Put another way, because courts have no direct access to political power, they are forced to rely on reasons" (Ferejohn, 2008, at 205).

[85] On top of being a principled directive of accountability, reason-giving is also a pragmatic necessity: it allows the court to be predictable and to play a coordinating role (Ferejohn and Pasquino, 2002, at 24).

[86] Ferejohn and Pasquino, 2004, at 1692.

settlement, and externally while exposing their decision to the public. The authors then compare the features of a set of courts through these lenses. From what they managed to see, two main patterns are inferred: the US Supreme Court, which represents a model that centers on external deliberation, with little face-to-face engagement among judges and a liberality to express themselves in multiple individual voices; and the Kelsenian courts, which would value clarity and hence tend to communicate, after struggling in secret deliberation, through a single voice in most cases.[87] One archetype is outward-looking whereas the other prioritizes the inside. Despite all the dissimilarities between the courts under inspection,[88] the authors observe that all, in their own ways, "retained the exemplary deliberative character" proclaimed by Rawls.[89]

This description is then followed by some intriguing explanatory hypotheses. The Kelsenian model, where the authority of review is concentrated exclusively in a special court, would require more unity "if ordinary courts are to be able to apply" the constitutional court's decisions.[90] The US model, characterized by a diffused authority to declare unconstitutionality across the judiciary, would require greater coordination between the Supreme Court and inferior judges. Hence the multiple individual voices, which allow the other actors of the legal system to anticipate the court's actions, to identify who is who within the court and how each member is likely to decide.[91]

Each deliberative pattern would be contingent on the political situatedness of the court. This independent variable would determine how deliberation looks in each context. Both the internal and external aspects are always present, but "partly in conflict": "If the individual Justices see themselves as involved in a large discussion in the public sphere, they may be less inclined to seek to compromise their own views with others on the Court."[92] In that light, the US Supreme Court would be much more "externalist" than its European counterparts.

---

[87] Ferejohn and Pasquino, 2002, at 35.

[88] They are considering the US Supreme Court, and the German, Italian, and Spanish constitutional courts. They also examine the French Constitutional Council, but it does not fit these patterns because a system of parliamentary sovereignty brings variables that impede such stable categorization.

[89] Ferejohn and Pasquino, 2002, at 22. This is not a precise reading of Rawls, who has actually said "exemplar of public reason" (Rawls, 1997a, 1997b). The fungibility between "public reason" and "deliberative," apparently assumed by both authors, hints at their limiting take on deliberation.

[90] Ferejohn and Pasquino, 2002, at 33.

[91] "In part this is made necessary by the fact that the Court has no monopoly on constitutional interpretation and mostly acts to regulate the process by which the Constitution is applied by other courts. This coordinating or regulatory role forces the Court to do its work in a public and transparent manner" (Ferejohn and Pasquino, 2002, at 35).

[92] Ferejohn and Pasquino, 2004, at 1697–1698.

Once the two patterns are elucidated, Ferejohn and Pasquino culminate in a critical assessment of the US court and in a normative appeal for denser internal deliberation, à la European courts. American justices "ought to commit themselves to try hard to find an opinion that everyone on their court can endorse."[93] Reforms would be necessary to galvanize justices to "spend less time and effort as individuals trying to influence external publics" and to focus on finding common ground, like genuinely deliberative bodies would do.[94] Despite the positive aspects that multiple opinions might have in some circumstances, they believe the US Supreme Court to have gone too far. The advisable step back, for them, comprises the two fronts that influence political behavior: first, the authors recommend an institutional reform to make the court less partisan, namely, a new mode of appointment and tenure; second, they urge the legal community to demand from judges the compliance with deliberative norms oriented towards the pursuit of consensus and towards an ethics of compromise and self-restraint with regards to the public exhibition of personal idiosyncrasies.

Their series of articles, without doubt, made significant progress. They furnished a broader understanding of how courts might or should be deliberative. The conceptualization of two sorts of deliberation and the call for reforms that confront both design and ethical issues are noteworthy achievements. Their concern is fair: the liberality for multiple voices, and the absence of any constraint, ethical or otherwise, against such practice, harms the capacity of the US Supreme Court to play a deeper deliberative role in American politics. However, they have not gone far enough in fleshing out what that role is. In addition, the way they suggest a partial conflict between internal and external is often misleading.

To start with, their definition of "external deliberation" is unstable. One can capture, in their writings, at least three senses of that concept: as reason-giving in public *tout court*, which is a common trait of any court; as multiple reason-giving in public, through individual opinions; or as an individualist attitude towards the public through the disclosure of atomized and non-deliberated disagreement.[95] Sometimes, therefore, the authors seem to imply that external corresponds to the soloist US style, which permits individual justices to publicize

---

[93] Ferejohn and Pasquino, 2004, 1673, footnote 9.   [94] Ferejohn and Pasquino, 2004, at 1700.

[95] Some extracts give an idea of the variety of definitions of external deliberation: "The Court rarely tries to speak with one voice, apparently preferring to let conflict and disagreement ferment" (Ferejohn and Pasquino, 2002, at 36); "part of the wider public process of deciding what the Constitution requires of us as citizens and potential political actors." Or later: "It may lead citizens and politicians to take or to refrain from actions of various sorts, or perhaps to respect the Court and its decisions. There is, however, no singular focus on a particular course of action that politicians or citizens must take." Finally: "to engage in open external dialogue about constitutional norms with outside actors" (Ferejohn and Pasquino, 2004, at 1697–1698). "Its aim is to convince those who are not in the room" (Ferejohn, 2008, at 209).

their own statements regardless of internal dialogue. In other passages, they adopt a more flexible notion and accept that there are different manners to be externally deliberative, even through single opinions.[96]

The relation between external deliberation and the formal style of decision publicly delivered is, thus, ambiguous: if it means simply the use of reason with the purpose of prompting and affecting the public debate, either single or multiple-voice decision could potentially do; if it means exposing the court's internal disagreement, then, indeed, multiple-voice would be the only way to go.

The connection between internal and external is also problematic. They suggest two unconvincing or, at best, under-demonstrated causalities. First, a bond between, on the one hand, a *per curiam* decision and the prevalence of internal deliberation at the expense of external; second, between a *seriatim* decision and external deliberation, which would overpower the internal.[97] Even if the descriptive portrait of that handful of courts were relatively accurate, the inference of an inevitable causal link between the way judges interact among themselves and the way the decision is formally presented to the public remains strained and little illuminating.

Such formal criterion does not convey much about the substantive quality of the decision and its ability to spawn and shape citizenry discussion. Whether the court manifests itself through *seriatim*, *per curiam*, or something in between rarely matters that much for the sake of public debate. As long as it is not oracular or hermetic, any decision may and has actually provoked external deliberation as they defined it.[98] A court could arguably struggle internally, but still manifest itself *seriatim*,[99] or be internally non-deliberative and speak *per curiam*. The degree of external deliberativeness, therefore, does not derive exclusively from the form, but more likely from the content of the decision and from the other circumstances that surround it. Comparative constitutionalism has several examples of *per curiam* decisions that electrified societal argumentative engagement, or, conversely, of *seriatim* decisions of which no special notice was taken.

Again, from the supposed descriptive accuracy of both patterns, it does not follow that there are inevitable trade-offs between the two, or that the maximization of one precipitates the respective minimization of the other.

---

[96] "There are various ways in which a court may play a role in external deliberation" (Ferejohn and Pasquino, 2004, at 1698).

[97] But they apparently contradict themselves here too: internal deliberation "may or may not be regulated by a shared expectation that the court will publish a single opinion or that multiple opinions will be published as well" (Ferejohn and Pasquino, 2002, at 23).

[98] Even narrowly reasoned decisions may stir deliberation up. This is, for example, Sunstein's defense of minimalism (Sunstein, 1994, 1996, 2000).

[99] One classic example is the House of Lords (see Paterson, 1982).

It is yet to be verified that a court could not excel on both. One might certainly claim that the more the court deliberates internally, the greater chance it would have to reach a consensus and manifest itself through a single opinion. This would not, however, discourage external deliberation as I understand it. Otherwise, the mostly consensual European courts could not be said to motivate external deliberation.

Unless the court simply refuses to offer reasons that ground its decisions, the possibility of prompting external deliberation is not a choice. The outside audience will be able to argue with those reasons regardless of the particular form through which they are communicated—*per curiam* or *seriatim*. But two fertile dilemmas still remain. First, the court needs to ponder whether to have internal deliberation, which, unlike the external, is indeed a choice. Second, the judges should still contemplate, in the light of many other considerations, whether, after deliberation, they should express themselves individually or collectively. European courts certainly diverge from the US Supreme Court in that matter. This is not due, nevertheless, to their lack of capacity or willingness to spark external deliberation, but to a cultural factor: a thicker "aim at unanimity" animates their internal processes, and a minimally divided decision is expected from them.[100] The American practice, consolidated in the last decades, notoriously strays from the European predominant allegiance, whenever possible, to a single voice.

Overall, Ferejohn and Pasquino have raised important empirical and normative questions, but have not entirely answered them. Their endeavor to relate constitutional review to deliberation remains, if not too hasty, surely unfinished. There are at least six aspects to be further explored. First, the notion of external deliberation, if excessively tied to one of the forms of public display (the *seriatim*, in their case), fails to capture how the substance of the decision, be it *seriatim* or *per curiam*, may be important from both the empirical and normative prisms. There are ways of reasoning that, even if communicated in the *per curiam* mode, sensibly incorporate disagreements and respectfully engagewith them. A cryptic *seriatim* would obviously obtain a lower score in that respect and would simply prevent the faintest external discussion. The next chapter proposes the notion of a deliberative written decision to address such normative concern. Rather than a causal trade-off between internal and external, I work with the hypothesis of mutually reinforcing phenomena.

Second, their notion of external deliberation still overlooks two different stages and practices in this public setting: the pre-decisional phase, where the court may competently inflame public debate and administer various

---

[100] Ferejohn and Pasquino, 2004, at 1692.

techniques for receiving argumentative inputs, and the post-decisional, where the court delivers its product until a next round of deliberation on the same issue ensues. The task and value of each moment, and the respective virtues that are necessary to carry them out, are not coincidental. The distinction between pre-decisional and post-decisional, thus, is not trivial. To equate both as "external," or to simply ignore the former and highlight only the latter, misses key deliberative aspects.

Third, Ferejohn and Pasquino, despite defending internal deliberation, do not give a sufficiently comprehensive account of why it may be desirable, except for the values of uniformity, predictability, and coordination. In other words, internal deliberation would be valuable only for the sake of these conventional formal principles of the rule of law. This is a partial perspective though. There might be more benefits to deliberation than intelligible reason-giving.[101] It is not only about the supply of certainty, not only a service to rule of law. The willingness to persuade and to be persuaded in an ambient of reciprocity, as deliberation was earlier defined, may not lead to consensus, but is no less important when dissensus withstands.

Fourth, when considering institutional design, they call for a qualified legislative quorum in the appointment process and for a fixed term of tenure. For them, this reform would approximate the US Supreme Court to the European ones, because its composition would be less driven by partisan behavior. Despite being crucial, this device still does not exhaust the set of incentives that may push the court to be more deliberative. It remains too reductive and narrow.

Fifth, they rightly add to their suggestion of institutional design a call for deliberative norms, that is, for an ethics that acknowledges the importance of deliberation. However, they do not flesh that out. Behind the abstract exhortation to engage in the process of persuasion, there are minute virtues that can make such a task more discernible.

Finally, assuming that the legitimacy of constitutional courts is somehow connected to their deliberative quality, as many submit, and since deliberation is a fluctuating phenomenon, a theory must be able to measure different degrees of attainment of the ideal. Put differently, it needs to conceive of measures of deliberative performance. Therefore, if a constitutional court is to become a plausible deliberator, and not only a reason-giver or an interlocutor, these additional questions have to be tackled. The current book aims

---

[101] Shapiro points to the distinction: "Some commentators try to capture this aspect of deliberation by reference to reason-giving, as when courts are said to be more deliberative institutions than legislatures on the grounds that they supply published reasons for their decisions. But significant though reason-giving is to legitimacy (particularly in the unelected institutions in a democracy), it does not capture the essence of deliberation" (2002, at 197).

to fill, if only partially, these six gaps. This diagnosis is the point of departure of the forthcoming chapters.

4. CONCLUSION

In a constitutional democracy, there are a variety of more-or-less deliberative institutions. They stand on some point between lawmaking and law-application, between broader or narrower discretionary compasses. Trivial though this may be, judicial tribunals, by a conventional definition, stand closer to the latter end of the spectrum. Closer, at least, than legislatures, most of the time. Constitutional courts, however, make this convention more complicated. They are situated at a unique position of the political architecture. The distinctions between legislation and adjudication, on the one hand, and between politics and law, on the other, become much less stark than in ordinary instances. There is hardly a sharp criterion to draw that line. This is not due, as it is generally contended, to the open-ended phraseology of the constitutional text, but rather to the underlying quality of constitutional scrutiny: it frames, in a conflictive partnership with the legislator, the boundaries of the political domain.

Efforts to enclose constitutional scrutiny within the rigid dichotomy between lawmaking and law-application are thus anachronistic. Contemporary constitutional case-law makes such inadequacy strikingly visible. The inaptitude to talk about it in a descriptively meaningful way reflects the deficit, to some extent, of our modern lexic of political concepts and evidences the need for further elaboration on the function of constitutional courts.

Constitutional scrutiny consists in delineating the moral limits of collective decisions by unearthing the principles that originally gave rise to and keep making sense of a political association. It is a step back to the basics of communal life, not prosaic political talk. Behind prosaic talk, one could say, conscious yet tacit decisions upon those basic principles may also be made. The virtue of open constitutional scrutiny, however, would be to articulate them explicitly, to candidly test collective choices against the background commitments that embodied the political alliance. The immediateness of ordinary politics usually blurs that broader horizon. Constitutional scrutiny, in turn, retains this dimension of political existence awaken.

Constitutional courts have no exclusivity over constitutional scrutiny. It is a fact, though, that they participate in such an enterprise. This peculiarity has naturally charged courts with a heavy justificatory burden. The apprehension of a constitutional court through the lenses of its allegedly special deliberative circumstances and capacities may be a significant component of such a justification. That basis, though, remains fragile so far.

If deliberation enhances the existential condition of constitutional courts, such courts need to be more than "exemplars of public reason" or "forums of principle," more than reason-givers or interlocutors. These expressions, and the respective expectations that they convey, are still superficial. They lack more teeth. The next chapter introduces a model of deliberative performance and, by doing so, better explicates the magnitude of such incompleteness.

4

Deliberative Performance of Constitutional Courts

So if I'm asked, "Do you miss the Court?"
I say, "Yes, I miss the deliberations."[1]

I. INTRODUCTION

As a judge of the German Constitutional Court, Dieter Grimm had a privileged vista of the strengths and weaknesses of that body in German politics. Unlike outside observers who, despite being unable to attest it, trust that court to be a highly deliberative body,[2] he had been an insider. His testimony of what that court does in secret, encapsulated by the epigraph above, apparently confirms that common-sense belief. But what exactly does he miss? And what is the value of what he misses for the legitimacy of constitutional courts? He did not specify it much, apart from exalting this "source of illumination"[3] and pointing to the fact that, "quite often," he and his colleagues did change their departing positions in light of mutual arguments. This chapter tries to imagine what he might or, ideally, should be suggesting.

Advocacy for judicial review strolls around a theoretical comfort zone. Its premises are relatively stabilized, as the previous chapter has shown. Constitutional courts have been praised as unique deliberative forums without much refinement of what that involves. That portion of literature did not develop a meticulous inquiry into this exact institutional property. It quickly assumes that, thanks to the insulation from electoral politics, and because of the expectation that judicial decisions are grounded on public reasons (a demand supposedly less stark in parliaments), the court would have better conditions to protect rights and, more generally, to enforce the constitution.

---

[1] Grimm (2003).   [2] Among others, see Ferejohn and Pasquino (2004).
[3] Grimm (2003).

Both attributes are not, in fact, merely peripheral features of a court's institutional context. Absence of elections and tougher argumentative burdens is likely to induce a whole new setting. Nevertheless, these factors still do not, by themselves, unfold what is, can, or should be the judicial contribution to the constitutional process.

This strand of normative theory, admittedly, does not buy judicial review at any price. It grants legitimacy under the condition of a singular deliberative performance. Or so I understand it. A constitutional court, in this light, becomes a paramount candidate for the "exemplar deliberative institution." This burdensome title cannot be presumed. It needs to be earned. The difficulty, again, is to have a precise idea of what that implies. Constitutional theory has to come to grips with this lacuna. We still do not know what to ask for, neither what to expect from, a deliberative court. Not much beyond, at least, the cursory call for a public justification grounded on constitutional principle. Little is said about the practices that should precede it, the values that should guide it, or the implications that might follow it.

I have already diagnosed the incompleteness of that position. The present chapter goes a step further and unpacks what a deliberative court minimally entails. It points to the additional prescriptive work that is yet to be done. If political deliberation, as I claimed, is a good thing and if, on that account, it does also follow that a constitutional court ought to be deliberative, one still needs to investigate what the components of such an endeavor are, instead of taking that for granted. Deliberation is a case-by-case achievement, not an automatic reflex of those meager institutional features from where those theories set off. I try to bridge this gap by forging an evaluative model of deliberative performance.

Its purpose is not to insinuate the superiority of judicial deliberation in relation to any other institution, but to justify its place in an overall system of collective decision-making. The book makes that mainstream stance more complex, and highlights its potential vulnerability and vigor. It tells a more colorful story about the meaning of a deliberative court, with a more intricate plot and diverse characters. It does not promise a happy ending, but believes that courts can contribute to the task of value-based reasoning that underpins the constitutional dilemmas of a democratic community. How and when courts can proficiently do that are questions not to be answered in the abstract. Answers will undoubtedly vary according to context, and context is shaped by a series of legal, political, and cultural variables. Middle-level theory, however, can devise normative standards about what is appealing and acceptable for this kind of institution to pursue.

Unlike the three first chapters, which tried to demarcate the different threads of theoretical questions and respective literary references, this chapter kicks off a more constructive and essayistic venture. This transition puts together the pieces so far outlined and rehearses a project of theoretical investigation the backbones of which are developed here. It is structured in four additional sections: the second advances the anatomy of a three-tiered model of deliberative performance; the third spells out the first tier of that model—the "core meaning"; the fourth explores the implications what the structure of the core meaning may have to the distinction between internal and external deliberation outlined in the last chapter; the fifth sums up the steps so far taken and prepares the terrain for the two following chapters.

2. THE THREE-TIERED MODEL OF DELIBERATIVE PERFORMANCE

Of the three images of constitutional courts explored in the last chapter—namely, the reason-giver (an actor that speaks and justifies its decisions through public reasons), the interlocutor (which not only speaks, but listens to and incorporates the reasons of other actors), and the deliberator—the last one remains the most mysterious. This is so not only because very few authors have yet gone that far, but is also due to the more composite questions that such images incite. There may be alternative ways to fill that void. I propose one particular model to measure deliberative performance. It is structured around three interrelated tiers: the "core meaning," the "facilitators," and the "hedges" of deliberative performance. This section articulates the definitions and the structure of this general canvas.

The "core meaning" corresponds to the immediately observable behavior of a deliberative court in operation, the kernel of deliberation itself. This first tier provides conceptual tools to detect the basic set of deliberative commitments taking place in the particular setting of a constitutional court. It locates who can be regarded as a deliberator, specifies who, among them, has power to make decisions, identifies the distinct stages of that process, their respective targets and values.

The second tier contemplates the institutional devices that may trigger and galvanize or, alternatively, hinder and discourage deliberation. The idea of "facilitators" relies on the empirical assumption that political behavior is a function of an intricate and inconstant friction of institutional incentives and mentality. A certain array of traits and dispositions that sets those devices in motion must be part of that explanation. In this regard, a political community needs to decide which procedures will channel its collective deliberations, and additionally, must be able to select and train those who will occupy such positions of authority. If courts are indeed expected to be deliberative, procedures and virtues should also be appreciated under this prism.

The third tier conceptualizes the "hedges" of deliberative performance. It delineates what a court should deliberate about. They comprise the legal backdrop and the political circumstances of deliberation. The former dictates the sort of public reasons that are acceptable for an institution to deliver, which are derived from a minimal concept of constitutional argumentation. The latter maps the political dilemmas that the institution needs to handle so that its decisions are accepted and effectively enforced. In a constitutional democracy, every political institution is somehow empowered and constrained by the normative directives of law and the unwieldy forces of politics. Courts too, in their own way.

The three tiers are thus interconnected. Deliberation is not a rule-bound conversation of whatever sort. It presupposes a substantive perimeter, outside which this conversation falls short of the deliberative threshold, and a political sensitivity, without which deliberation may be risky, inopportune, or innocuous. The core meaning, therefore, is not enough to affirm that deliberation is prospering. Without noting how the hedges mold the particular deliberative event, the core meaning would only give rise to a façade for deliberation. To check whether a constitutional court is deliberating, therefore, presupposes a scrutiny of its specific content and context.

Facilitators, in turn, are not deliberation per se, but indicate its prospects and elucidate its causalities. They flesh out what lurks behind the core meaning. One does not explain the performance of a certain institution without having this additional component in mind. The ways the quality of deliberation and the institutional devices interrelate in practice are possibly hard to formalize or to predict. The mere existence of favorable procedural routes does not guarantee a constant deliberative performance, but constitute the basic conditions for such aim.

Whereas the core meaning, joined by the hedges, corresponds to the *actuality* of deliberative performance, the facilitators gesture to its *potentiality*. The two former categories help to appraise whether the outcome produced by an institution was, as a matter of fact, deliberative, whereas the latter reveals the likely set of correlative causal agents.

It would be wrong to conclude, though, that the hedges do not play an explanatory role or does not help to gauge the deliberative potential too. In prescribing what the substance of deliberation should be, hedges, at the same time, helps to indicate the likelihood of deliberation itself. A high deliberative performance will be more likely, for example, when a court handles a concrete case that touches on highly controversial matters of law and faces little political obstacles for effective decision. If, on the other hand, the case relates to reasonably settled questions of law and raises foreseeable political obstruction, an ensuing low deliberative performance would not be unexpected. This dual nature of the hedges—both prescriptive and explanatory, both delimiting the actual and illuminating the potential performance—will become clearer when Chapters 7 and 8 flesh them out. Deliberative performance, therefore, is the consequence of a complex interaction between the institutional devices, the ethical traits of deliberators, the legal materials, and the political landscape.

This formal three-fold skeleton may be serviceable for the assessment of deliberative performance of any institution. Its founding categories, indeed, could plausibly be replicated to other decision-making settings. The next section, and also the coming chapters, will further dissect how these formal notions may have a bearing on constitutional courts. Let me start by the core meaning.

3. THE CORE MEANING OF DELIBERATIVE PERFORMANCE

The core meaning tracks down two preliminary categories advanced by the first chapter. First, the distinction between three deliberative phases—pre-decisional, decisional, and post-decisional. It corresponds to three moments in which performance might be discerned and appraised, three slices of an overall enterprise. The model isolates three activities in order to diagnose and assess diverse sorts of problems and accomplishments, distinct instances of deliberation.

A deliberative court, in this respect, manifests itself in three consecutive instants. It might be deliberative in one, but not in the other. An ideal-type deliberative court, as we shall see, is masterful in all three phases. Through these diachronic categories, the model incorporates and slightly refines the notions of internal and external deliberation. The internal deliberation would correspond, under the typology suggested here, to the decisional phase, whereas the external deliberation would refer mainly to the post-decisional phase. The pre-decisional, under that frame, is overshadowed. The heuristic disadvantage of that dualist division is its monotonic character, which overlooks the precise deliberative aspects that can and should be observed in the pre and post-decisional phases. That duality is indifferent to this temporal dimension.

In a loosely informal sense, the post-decisional phase could be seen as the pre-decisional of the next case (and both be coalesced into the generic category of "external" deliberation). For the sake of analytical clarity, however, this book stipulates that the pre-decisional is tied to an existing formal case

Deliberative phases	Deliberative tasks
1. Pre-decisional	"Public contestation"
2. Decisional	"Collegial engagement"
3. Post-decisional	"Deliberative written decision"

and is hence prompted by the concrete litigation. The post-decisional, in turn, comprises, first, the drafting of the written decision, and then the whole set of debates that follow in the informal public sphere, regardless of a particular new lawsuit. The sorts of deliberative tasks of the pre- and post-decisional phases may have similarities that should not, however, obscure their own peculiarities. Amalgamating both as "external" deliberation, in an undifferentiated way, could miss important facets.

This neat distinction, moreover, might prove more or less artificial if we look to the operation of real-world courts, in which the three phases are usually intermingled to varying degrees (sometimes, for example, phases 1 and 2 can alternate, 2 and 3 can overlap, and so on).[4] In the same vein, it may be misleading if we understand it as a linear time-line, with clear boundaries between when one stage stops and the following starts. Still, for the sake of the analysis, it is useful to keep these categories at hand. They turn us sensitive to distinguishable factors and times in which actual performance might be gauged. Despite mutually permeable, there is something unique happening in each phase, and this should be appropriately grasped by a competent model of deliberative performance.

Second, one should discern between who deliberates. The decision-makers (judges) and the interlocutors are the two relevant types of deliberators. The community of interlocutors comprises all social actors that, formally or informally, address public arguments to the court and express public positions as to the cases being decided. They provide external argumentative inputs for the judicial decision. They can influence and persuade, but not decide. Formal interlocutors involve all those parties who are qualified and entitled to participate of the specific constitutional case (litigants, *amici curiae* etc.). Informal interlocutors are those who, in the attempt to exert an indirect influence on the court, engage in the debates through the various communicative media of the public sphere. Deliberative performance in the pre-decisional moment is, to a large extent, contingent on how interlocutors discharge their responsibility. Deliberative failures at this stage may thus be attributable to interlocutors too, and even implicate the quality of deliberation in the subsequent phases.

Political deliberation is a demanding decision-making process through which reasons of a specific kind are exchanged in the attempt to persuade and reach consensus. If it is pertinent to qualify those three phases as deliberative, the very concept of deliberation must be malleable enough to permit such parsed instantiations. The give-and-take of reasons in each phase is not done among the same characters and in the same spirit. The cluster of

---

[4] The distinction between the three well-defined phases fits well, for example, the continuous process between hearing sessions, conference meetings, and drafting in the US Supreme Court.

values and promises that is encompassed by a general definition of deliberation, like the one sketched in the first chapter, may also need to be adjusted to each of the three.

With these distinctions refreshed, an ideal-type deliberative court, put straightforwardly, is one that maximizes the range of arguments from interlocutors by promoting public contestation at the pre-decisional phase; that energizes its decision-makers in a sincere process of collegial engagement at the decisional phase; and that drafts a deliberative written decision at the post-decisional phase. In other words, if someone wants to check whether a constitutional court is fulfilling its deliberative duties, she should inspect the written and face-to-face interaction among interlocutors and judges, then the interplay between judges themselves, and finally the written decision delivered by the court. Each of them deserves a proper examination, according to tailored indicators. Each would have a specific score.

A constitutional court, therefore, conforms three slightly distinct sites of deliberation. Each one should face taxing deliberative patterns. In the pre- and post-decisional phases, the institution itself interacts with the public sphere. Interlocutors are expected to be active participants by presenting their cases and, afterwards, scrutinizing the court's decision. In the decisional phase, there is an intramural deliberation among judges, and interlocutors remain as spectators. The exact layout of each site will ultimately depend upon details of the design of each court, but any decision-making process fits into these elementary iterative categories.

The model breaks deliberation into three practices that, for the sake of phrasal simplification, will henceforth be dubbed as "public contestation," "collegial engagement," and "deliberative written decision." They are qualitative indices of this three-phasic process.

i. Public contestation

Public contestation is prompted by one or by a group of political actors that have the formal power to, through appeal or direct intervention, submit a case to a constitutional court. From that moment until the judges sit together to reach a final settlement, the dialogical process among interlocutors and decision-makers contains beneficial deliberative potentialities.

In practice, the quality of public contestation will predictably vary according to the salience of the case and to how a political community mobilizes itself to contribute to the collective issues being addressed. Interlocutors, therefore, share responsibility for the overall performance in this phase.

As a prescriptive aspiration, public contestation corresponds to, on the one hand, the actual involvement of all interested actors in presenting arguments to the court and, on the other, to the earnest attention of the court in receiving these arguments and probing them publicly. Interlocutors speak while decision-makers actively listen and question.

A constitutional court may have strong institutional devices for channeling those voices. In the lack of formal mechanisms, though, nothing prevents it from being alert to the plurality of positions that are aired in the informal public sphere.[5] Interlocutors, therefore, may be included through both the institutional and extra-institutional argumentative channels that are offered by a political community.

On this account, the court should steer the pre-decisional phase with a series of purposes in mind: to collect, as much as possible, arguments from interlocutors; to publicly challenge these arguments so that interlocutors have the opportunity to further refine them; and, above all, to display an institutional openness to the actors that may have something to add to the stock of arguments that bears upon the case. The performance of the court, at this stage, should be judged by these three general patterns.

ii. Collegial engagement

Collegial engagement is the guiding aspiration of a constitutional court as far as its decisional phase is concerned. It is the proper standard to discipline and evaluate the intramural process that occurs among decision-makers themselves. Rather than looking outwards to collect and test arguments that interlocutors might forge, judges interact with each other to make a decision.

The proper institutional asepsis is assumed to be in place when decision-makers gather to deliberate. Otherwise, collegial engagement would not be a plausible guideline. This setting should thus mitigate, as much as one can anticipate, some of the objections against the dangers of deliberation: by involving professional colleagues, the risks of entrenching and reproducing social inequalities through deliberation is obviously not at stake; by expecting that all decision-makers have the proper argumentative insubordination and mental endurance, the risk of oppression and other types of non-autonomous will-formation are controlled; by requiring decision-makers to be adequately versed in constitutional matters and jargons, the peril of epistemic hierarchy is unlikely to thrive.

---

[5] The formal mechanisms, as we will see in Chapter 6, may be written, comprising different sorts of petitions, or face-to-face, which may include public audiences or typical hearing sessions. According to Paterson, the hearing sessions of the House of Lords were, at least during the period he studied, the primary moment in which the actual persuasion happens. It was an oblique type of deliberation, in which judges did not address each other directly. Through the questions to the litigants, however, they usually intended to convince their colleagues (Paterson, 1982, at 72). Depending on how flexible and versatile such mechanisms are to capture various sorts of arguments and enable various actors to vindicate their positions, public contestation could be seen as a mechanism of participatory democracy.

Deliberation is not a verbal duel. It is not, thus, conducted in the same spirit of a competition.[6] The standard of collegial engagement mandates judges to listen and to incorporate their peer's reasons into theirs, either to adhere or to dissent. They are not obliged to hide or suppress disagreement, but committed to frank argumentation in search of the best answer. It is relevant that the court "try harder to arrive at common opinions," like Ferejohn and Pasquino would like the US Supreme Court to do.[7] The formal properties of the rule of law may well be second-order reasons that push for compromises where substantive agreement is arduous to come about. Deliberation, still, is not only an instrument for fabricating consensus, but also for trying to arrive at a good decision irrespective of unanimity.

A deliberative court does so by being permeable to a wide range of reasonable arguments that may have been propelled by various sources. It should assimilate not only the reasonable arguments that were officially presented by interlocutors, but also those that were informally ventilated on the respective topic by other interlocutors and those that can be empathetically imagined. The court, therefore, has the burden of representing and inspecting both actual and vicarious positions in the heat of decisional deliberation. The occasional procedural deficits that impede interested interlocutors of formally submitting their reasons, and hence hinder the court's capacity of enlarging its argumentative repository at the previous phase, may be compensated by the court's ability to listen to the outer public sphere and to imagine other possible points of view. This is the only way to counterbalance or even neutralize an occasional poor performance of interlocutors in the preceding phase.

The driving-force of collegial engagement is, accordingly, three-fold: the effort to take into account all positions the court was able to collect and to empathetically conceive; the search for the best principled answer; and the pursuit of consensus or, if it does not come forth, minimal dissensus. It is up for each court to balance these demands when they pull in different directions.[8] Especially with regards to the epistemic and communitarian promises, as Chapter 1 described, serious dilemmas are likely to arise.

iii. Deliberative written decision

A deliberative written decision is one that translates the ethical commitments of deliberation into a written piece. Apart from well-reasoned, it has the burden of being responsive and readable by the public. Assessing whether a

---

[6] As Shapiro believes American judges to do: "Rather they try to show that they have the most cogently reasoned view, the best argument. This is a competitive justificatory enterprise, not a cooperative one. Argument is about winning, which is what lawyers are trained to do. Deliberation is about getting the right answer" (Shapiro, 2002, at 197).

[7] Ferejohn and Pasquino, 2004, at 1702.

[8] As Sachs summarized: "The goal is to reach a principled consensus wherever possible" (2009, at 243).

written decision is deliberative, in the sense defined here, requires more than the pedestrian exercise of examining whether the court has addressed the arguments of the litigants, more than simply counting the bullet points of a checklist. This sort of decision is characterized, above all, by its literary style.

As opposed to the two previous phases, in which the court was concentrated in collecting, digesting, and imagining diverse points of view in order to take a decision, the focus here is to communicate, in a considerate way, the decision already taken. A deliberative written decision, thus, is not a cryptic and arcane announcement of an allegedly right answer.[9] Neither is it an apodictic assertion of what the constitution means by virtue of the court's putative interpretive superpowers. It is rather the product of an effort to deal with all points of view in a thorough manner.

A deliberative court is aware of its fallibility and of the inevitable continuity of deliberation in the public sphere and in possible future cases. The written decision needs to convey this attitude through a careful and laborious rhetoric. Despite consummating concrete effects, the decision also invites new deliberative rounds. Sachs has tellingly expressed how he managed to face such challenge. The decision, for him, instead of dividing the nation between the "enlightened" and the "benighted," should demonstrate a special respect to the ones who are having their deep beliefs affected by it. In other words, it has to chase a literary style that avoids treating the parties as winners and losers of an interpretive contest. Interlocutors need to be regarded as fellow members of a community that will keep talking about that specific controversy as long as disagreement persists.[10]

The text of a deliberative decision will usually be an embellished rearticulation of collegial engagement. It needs to render a convoluted process of interpersonal argumentation, face-to-face or otherwise, into an accessible discourse. As Sachs, again, has recommended, the drafting process has a "preening" quality that is fundamental to the prominent function that is played by constitutional courts.[11]

---

[9] This contrast resembles Llewellyn's well-known distinction between two styles of judicial reasoning: the *Formal Style*, which would "run in a deductive form with an air or expression of single-line inevitability," and the *Grand Style*, which is concerned with the principle behind the rule, resort to "situation-sense" and provides guidance to the future (see Llewellyn, 1960). Each would have distinct "aesthetic urges": while the formal style seeks cold clarity, the grand style strives for "functional beauty—fitness for purpose" (Twining, 1973, at 210).

[10] Sachs exemplified this challenge with the decision of the South African constitutional court that upheld same-sex marriage: "While unequivocally upholding the right of same sex couples to be treated with the same respect given to heterosexual couples, it would at the same time acknowledge and give constitutional recognition to the depths of conscience belief held by members of faiths that took a different view" (2009, at 7). "Courts should seek wherever possible to engage with the whole nation. It's not for court judgments to divide the nation between progressives and reactionaries" (2009, at 254).

[11] "We work with words, and become amongst the most influential story-tellers of our age. How we tell a story is often as important as what we say. The voice we use cannot be that of a depersonalized and

This drafting stage should strive to turn collegial engagement into a supra-individual decision, to produce the special kind of de-personification that only deliberation conveys. A deliberative court, in this phase, has to balance between the need to construct an institutional identity and to respect the place and value of resistant dissenting opinions. It grants special weight to institutional authorship but does not shy away, as far as circumstances commend, from exhibiting internal discord. A deliberative court does not publicly display any sort of discord, but those that withstand collegial engagement. Divisions, when they persist, are serious and respectable ones.

From the formal point of view, a deliberative decision may be manifested both as a single voice or multiple voice. It may be a pure *seriatim*, a *per curiam*, or stand somewhere in the middle, composed by a joint majority opinion, plus the occasional concurring and dissenting opinions. There is no immediate or foolproof causality between collegial engagement and a single voice, neither between the lack of internal deliberation and multiple voice decision. The presence or the absence of deliberation at the decisional phase are not automatically determinative of the *per curiam* or *seriatim* formats. Good quality collegial engagement cannot be easily presumed from that formal surface.[12] The permutations of these two variables produce a typology of written decisions. The four types can be graphically represented like this:

Format Deliberativeness	*Seriatim*	*Per curiam*
Non-deliberative	1	2
Deliberative	3	4

A non-deliberative *seriatim* may symbolize not only the failure but, most likely, the sheer lack of the effort to converge that should animate collegial

divine oracle that declares solutions to the problems of human life through the enunciation of pure and detached wisdom" (Sachs, 2009, at 270).

[12] There is a genuine difference between the traditional common law *seriatim* and the US Supreme Court style. In the former, opinions both for the majority and minority are almost always separate. In the latter, unless the majority opinion is diluted into a series of concurrences, there is usually a single "opinion of the court," joined by occasional dissents and concurrences. As Kornhauser and Sager contend, the move from the English to the American style "entails more than the mechanical fact of an economy in the number of opinions... It involves a commitment to, and a demand for, collegial deliberation, and supports an ideal of a multi-judge court acting as an entity, not merely an aggregation of individual judges" (1993, at 13). With respect to the format, therefore, there seems to be a difference of degree along a continuum between the *seriatim* and *per curiam* (because the American court may well reach, even if exceptionally, an extreme *seriatim*). Behind the format, however, lies an essential qualitative difference related to the internal ethos of the court, as pointed out by Kornhauser and Sager. If we too quickly attach a *seriatim* with the lack of deliberation, these nuances may get overlooked.

interaction. Even if preceded by some thin informational communication that is requisite to any aggregation, it falls short, as a written piece, of the normative standard outlined above. It down-rates the institution under the shade of its individual members, who tend to become public personas: they end up being perceived for what they personally think, not for what they are able to come up with when acting as a collegial forum. Such institutional indolence is regrettable for downright abdicating the promises of deliberation (even if each fragmented opinion strives to reason in the best way) and therefore trivializing the dignity of constitutional dilemmas. A non-deliberative *seriatim*, on this account, is the archetype of personification and is composed by a patchwork of individual opinions that do not mutually converse. The lack of communication between opinions makes it all the more damaging, in addition, to the rule of law by not providing a clear *ratio decidendi*.

A non-deliberative *per curiam*, in turn, is a single opinion that does not meet the ethically loaded literary style earlier described. Even if it is able to de-personify and meet some demands of the rule of law, like clarity and coordination, it does not meet the test of responsiveness and empathy. It stands closer to a hermetic and obscurantist exposition of legal directives. Empirically, it may even be preceded by collegial engagement, but may still be adopted by virtue of some other consideration. In the canonical comparative types, the French dry and synoptic style of judicial reasoning approximates it more patently.[13]

As for the two other strands, both the deliberative *per curiam* and the deliberative *seriatim* follow that full-throated reasoning style.[14] The former, however, is de-personified in a thicker sense, whereas the latter contains multiple voices that, unlike the non-deliberative version, communicate among themselves.[15] Instead of a frail patchwork, its opinions are sewn in a more explicit fashion. Mutual arguments are faced, objections are answered, and stands are taken.

All written decisions delivered by a collegiate court will fall into one of these four categories. A deliberative court should, in principle, favor either the third or the fourth type, both of which share that cherished style. It does not mean, nevertheless, that this is a peripheral dilemma, or that a deliberative court should be indifferent with respect to the choice between them.

---

[13] Lasser (2004).

[14] MacCormick considers the *seriatim* tradition of the British system a better way to communicate the whole range of arguments and counter-arguments: "One strong reason for clearly articulating these counter-arguments is that a dissenting judge may have articulated in a strong form the very reasons which need to be countered for the justification of the majority view to stand up ... Certainly, it is a consequence of the dialectical setting of the British appellate judgment that, characteristically, a much more thorough exploration of arguments one way and the other is set forth than in those systems which in effect express only a set of sufficient justifying reasons for what may be only a majority decision, and which need neither rehearse nor counter any possible opposed arguments" (1978, at 10).

[15] The extent to which a deliberative *seriatim* can be de-personified depends on other variables of design, like the alternative of anonymity. I shall consider it in Chapter 6.

Different contexts may call for other sorts of considerations that could push for one or the other. To the extent that the exact political context of the decision is unknown, both formats are compatible with the deliberative ideal. For middle-level normative theory, there is not enough information for an unassailable choice.

Probably with the exception of a non-deliberative *seriatim*, the choice between the other three formal options might get more complex due to the politics in which constitutional adjudication is enmeshed. Even a non-deliberative *per curiam*, despite lamentable for reasons already articulated, might be commendable when political circumstances so indicate. The political element of the hedges of deliberative performance will orient that choice. The third section below will return to this question.

In short, promoting public contestation, fostering collegial engagement and crafting a deliberative written decision are the three basic tasks of a deliberative court. Chapter 5 further fleshes them out by decomposing the specific virtues that these three tasks require from judges. For the purposes of this chapter, it is still worth exploring how the promises and values of deliberation, generically described in Chapter 1 and indistinctly applied to collegiate courts in Chapter 2, can still have something to say about a constitutional court in each of these three moments of deliberation.

4. INTERNAL AND EXTERNAL DELIBERATION: A RECONFIGURATION

The preceding chapter has uncovered the reasons why we should prefer a multi-member court to a single judge at least for legal decisions of last resort. The answers invoked concerns of political prudence, de-personification, symbolic recognition, and epistemic likelihood. Whatever actual historical causes led to the adoption and evolvement of collegiate courts, there is a number of compelling normative reasons for choosing this arrangement instead of alternative ones. But why should a multi-member court deliberate? I argued that most promises of deliberation are applicable to collegiate courts and that, as long as the epistemic likelihood is reliable, there is an intrinsic value in the attempt to fulfill it. In sum, a set of deliberation-independent reasons justifies collegiate adjudication, and additional reasons inform the case for a deliberative court.

That defense of a deliberative collegiate court is entirely applicable to a constitutional court. In such a setting, however, there is more at stake. The momentous function of constitutional scrutiny makes the pre-decisional and post-decisional phases relevant from perspectives not earlier appreciated. Ordinary adjudication is deprived of such political weight.

Constitutional courts, therefore, should be deliberative institutions in a richer sense. There is more to be gained from them. This claim is not self-evident. It needs to disclose why deliberation, in constitutional matters, is exceptionally valuable. The following table enumerates the potential deliberative qualities of the three phases.

Public contestation	Collegial engagement	Deliberative written decision
- weak epistemic	- strong epistemic	- strong epistemic
—	- communitarian (internal)	- communitarian (external)
- strong psychological	- weak psychological	- strong psychological
- strong educative	- weak educative	- strong educative
- strong intrinsic	- weak intrinsic	- strong intrinsic

This compartmentalization should not be taken to suggest a discontinuous process with tight and segmented characteristics. They underscore, however, the different ways and degrees in which the values and promises of deliberation are in play.

As far as there is an epistemic point in what deliberative courts do, a share of it can be identified along the three phases. Public contestation contributes to the multiplication of points of view on a certain controversy. It can, at the very least, be a strong practice of information-gathering. This is consequential and also indispensable for the epistemic potential of the collegial engagement that should follow. At the decisional moment, an argumentative interaction in the search of an institutional opinion, rather than mere non-deliberative aggregation, is more likely to reach a fine-tuned decision and to let a transparent construction of the disagreements that genuinely remain. Premise-unveiling, creativity-sparkling, and truth-seeking, as defined in Chapter 1, are more likely to result from collegial engagement than from alternative aggregating techniques. Finally, the delivery of a deliberative written decision has the still non-negligible epistemic function of supplementing the next cases with densely drafted precedents. Without such precedents, a future case would have to re-inaugurate the deliberative chain from scratch, wasting the argumentative accomplishments and progresses of previous cases. It would waste, in other words, the deliberative dividends that current cases can receive from the accumulation of precedents.

The communitarian goal of consensus is less of a concern for the pre-decisional phase, which basically provides inputs to a forthcoming decision. Public contestation, undoubtedly, is inspired by the purpose of persuasion.

However, at this early stage, it cannot properly have a special commitment to reduce disagreement. This is an adversarial moment of litigation, mostly concerned with collecting arguments and exposing positions. Collegial engagement, on the other hand, has the responsibility of constructing an institutional and de-personified decision. Deliberation, here, is a fitting (even if not the only conceivable) way to reach consensus among decision-makers. Finally, to the extent that a written decision is able to document the institutional identity out of the interpersonal deliberation, it is more likely than a non-deliberative decision to reduce disagreements among the court's interlocutors.

As for the psychological promise—the sense of respect instilled among the participants of deliberation—a deliberative constitutional court is more likely to do a good job both through a genuinely porous public contestation and a carefully drafted decision. Intra-institutional respect, as already argued in the previous chapter, enables the court to remain collegial and to keep up its capacity of deliberation.

Deliberation may also be a means to educate the deliberators themselves.[16] The active participation in the process of public contestation and, later, of scrutinizing the final judicial decision can educate interlocutors in the argumentative skills and moral attitudes required by deliberation, and, in addition, illustrate them in the subject matter itself. As for the judges of a constitutional court, who deliberate on a routine basis, the enhancement of skills would be a frivolous expectation. Deliberation, still, may be a peculiar way of refining their knowledge on the respective topic.

Instrumental reasons for deliberation, thus, are largely applicable to the three activities in focus. Each has something to tell about the potential roles and desirability of each deliberative task. They furnish one palpable justificatory route for the deliberative enterprise of constitutional courts as conceptualized by the core meaning. This sort of reason is set in terms of a likelihood calculation about the chances of the court realizing those ends. Even if deliberation occasionally fails, its practice, I submit, makes it more likely that the court: reaches a better decision from the epistemic point of view; carves a supra-individual opinion; includes and responds to all arguments in play; nurtures a sense of respect and enlightens the participants of this process.

These instrumental groundings, if plausible, are possibly enough. One can still look, however, for a more vigorous footing on which judicial deliberation, in its various manifestations, can rest. Instrumental reasons enable the normative theorist to assume the probability of certain dear results. She is not usually at home with the fluctuating currency of mere plausibility,

---

[16] See, for a more recent statement, Stone-Sweet, 2000, at 194–204. The pedagogical function of constitutional courts is an old point already made, among others, by Bickel, Dworkin, and Rawls.

with speculating non-demonstrated or, sometimes, non-demonstrable causal links. Intrinsic reasons, if persuasive, alleviate the burden of proving causalities in a peremptory manner. They change the code of the debate and survive, to some extent, an occasional empirical evidence that affords to demonstrate that deliberation is less likely to fulfill those optimistic promises. They are resistant to that kind of confrontation.

What intrinsic reasons, if any, can endorse and push for public contestation, collegial engagement, and deliberative written decisions? It has been popular to argue, in line with last chapter's description, that the point of judicial review is, as a matter of respect for citizens, to offer public reasons for decisions that bear upon the constitutional essentials of the community's political identity. Irrespective of whether citizens assent to the particular content of decisions, they deserve, as equal members, this collective feedback. The idea of a deliberative written decision deepens this commitment and is thus more ambitious. We request such a densely responsive decision for the sake of how interlocutors, according to this demanding standard of legitimacy, should be treated by political institutions. This claim justifies judicial review on the basis of the estimable service it can do to interlocutors.

A very similar argument applies to public contestation. A court that opens institutional channels for interlocutors to argue displays not only an epistemic commitment to deliver a good decision, but respect. Interlocutors have the chance to make themselves heard and realize their argumentative autonomy before the court. One could state that the value of deliberation in the pre-decisional phase is contingent, to some extent, on the actual performance of the court in the post-decisional. They would be somehow inter-dependent because the court would only manage to craft a genuinely deliberative response if it has engaged with interlocutors in the first place. In other words, public contestation would hardly be valuable if, ultimately, the court hands down an oracular and fiat-like decision. The pre-decisional phase would not be valuable if not for the sake of a deliberative outcome. Separated or combined, nevertheless, the performance in both phases has a more visible intrinsic value.

It seems less difficult to illustrate the moral gravity of deliberation in the pre- and post-decisional phases. A court that operates constitutional scrutiny interacts not only with the litigants, but also with the public sphere broadly conceived and vicariously imagined. It has the chance to act as a catalyst of external deliberation and to work as an open and accessible "forum of contestation."[17] It is valuable to have a forum where the moral imperative of equal respect is not derived from the right to vote, but from the right to be heard and to receive a rigorous answer.[18]

---

[17] Kumm (2007).   [18] On a dualist conception of democracy, see Pettit (2005).

A constitutional court would be welcome, then, if it ignites a process of deliberation among citizens. Judges, though, do not need to deliberate among themselves to achieve it. Arguably, a single judge or a collegiate yet internally non-deliberative court could also fulfill that expectation. As long as they do so, one could maintain, the way judges interact among themselves does not matter. Let them behave in whatever style they want, this story goes, provided that they deliver what we duly ask from them in the pre- and post-decisional phases—the appropriate opportunities to argue and a pertinent written outcome. One could not automatically infer, therefore, that a collegiate court, in order to spur external debates, should be internally deliberative in that ambitious sense. The internal dynamics, for the purpose of prompting societal conversation, would be superfluous.

Why should interlocutors deserve the institutional commitment of the court to craft, deliberatively, the best response the judges are able to give together? The capacity to stimulate external deliberation should not, indeed, be neglected as an unimportant achievement of under-deliberative yet good reason-giver courts. Any suggestion of causal interdependence between collegial engagement and deliberative written decisions seems, however credible, slightly overstated at this theoretical level. The former practice, indeed, is not indispensable for the latter. Nonetheless, in the light of the set of reasons earlier compiled, deliberation is still more reliable than the alternatives to pursue the best decision. A court that renounces deliberation loses this epistemic "source of illumination."[19] A court that embraces it, in turn, signals that it does its best to reach the most reasonable decision. Judges surely do not and should not deliberate for the sake of deliberation. There is a point to this practice in the first place. Inasmuch as this point is likely to include an epistemic quality, the mere attempt to fulfill it is valuable. Although less strongly, an intrinsic grounding resonates here too.

According to the core meaning, again, a constitutional court will be fully deliberative if it excels at those three tasks. The model sheds light on the three goals without establishing any normative hierarchy between them. It would sneak beyond the proper domain of middle-level theory to do so. Various circumstances can demand and justify those goals in different scales or intensities. Causal hypotheses that attempt to empirically relate these phases could also be rehearsed and tested in various courts. Occasional synergies and trade-offs between public contestation, collegial engagement, and a deliberative written decision could be unveiled and help construct a more jurisdiction-sensitive case for a deliberative court. Such inquiries would extrapolate my purposes.

The core meaning improves some of the underdeveloped conclusions of Ferejohn and Pasquino, which I diagnosed in Chapter 3. Their distinction

[19] Grimm (2003).

between internal and external, despite being sensible, still fails to capture the specific properties of the pre-decisional phase. Their characterization of external deliberation as multiple-voice decisions and of internal deliberation as consensual decision-making had the misleading effect of suggesting an inevitable trade-off between both tasks. Their distinction between single and multiple-voice decisions, moreover, was purely formal, without any consideration of how, sometimes, the content and style of the decisional text may be even more important to trigger external deliberation than the mere exposition of a set of separate opinions, however drafted. Finally, they ignore that internal deliberation, besides increasing the chance of reducing disagreement, which would be important for the sake of the formal requests of the rule of law, cumulates a whole set of other plausible promises that, sometimes, may even outweigh its putative consensus-building virtue. Collegial engagement is desirable for many other reasons beyond the sole attractiveness, in some circumstances, of a clear and unitary opinion of the court.

5. PROLOGUE TO THE NEXT CHAPTERS

A constitutional court could aspire to be a pragmatic problem-solver and to settle disputes regardless of reasons. It could step beyond that and play the role of a reason and consistency-provider of the rule of law. Or it could, more ambitiously, be both a deliberator itself and an igniter of larger societal argumentative processes about a community's political identity. Only a deliberative court, through the facets identified above, attains these three cumulative accomplishments. We are better off, as a political community, if judicial reason is deliberative rather than oracular, if it contains good arguments rather than fiat-like statements. And the scheme of government by which we abide would be more legitimate if constitutional scrutiny were undertaken in that way.

Judicial deliberation, for sure, is highly structured. As is every deliberative institution, a court is constrained both by procedural rituals and by reasoning canons, which will become clearer in the next chapters. This should not lead to quick conclusions about its merits or defects.[20] Forums of collective decision-making are all framed by formal and tacit rules, by canons of reasoning, and conventions of interpersonal interaction. These rules shape the opportunities for arguing and deciding. Informality and spontaneity are not typical qualities of political institutions. Each may be deliberative in its own constrained way.

---

[20] Waldron, for example, derives some pessimistic generalizations about the judicial capacity for good moral reasoning, taking the US Supreme Court as its main source of reference (2009a and 2009b).

Traditional jurisprudence has not taught us to assess judicial decisions in terms of performance. It is more preoccupied with finding the correct answer. Tools for achieving it—methods of interpretation and theories of justice— abound. Such enterprise gets stuck in a straightjacket between the right *versus* the wrong interpretation. Besides, jurisprudence does not usually pay attention to the fact that constitutional courts are collegiate institutions. Normative theories of adjudication remain largely unmoved about this vital institutional feature and have not duly perceived its non-superfluous implications.

This chapter presented the three-tiered model of deliberative performance and concentrated on the first tier. The first tier sketches what a regime is likely to gain with, or lose without, a deliberative constitutional court. This model cherishes, but cannot guarantee, a substantively good decision. It relies on a plausible probability of deliberation generating a better outcome, but there is more to a deliberative constitutional court than that.

Substantively flawed decisions, as rated by some critical observer, may well come out from a highly deliberative court. Deliberative performance, after all, is an output test of a procedural kind. Yet, it is not apathetic about the decisional substance, because the epistemic promise is one of its central groundings. Both are goals to be jointly pursued. By being deliberative, constitutional courts aim at the right answer. However, the full-blown substantive theory that determines such answer will be, itself, subject to contested deliberation.

A deliberative constitutional court is committed to substantively good decisions expressed, when possible and desirable, in a single voice, or, when justifiable, in multiple voices, as long as they are thoroughly responsive and preceded by serious public contestation and collegial engagement. Deliberation should not be underestimated as a means for those attractive external ends. It strives to gain respect and prestige, nevertheless, not only by these substantive and formal qualities of its outcomes, but by the way it treats its interlocutors.

Doubtlessly, such hopes may be frustrated. The circumstances in which those epistemic and communitarian expectations are likely to fail or to succeed may even be possible to predict. Again, a good and unitary decision is not necessary to attest deliberative performance. The three deliberative tasks, in principle, should be tracked even when we are arguably able to foretell it is not likely to meet those promises. Up to a point, the three tasks are self-standing and radiate important intrinsic values: the institutional effort to take interlocutors' claims considerately and to produce an ethically acceptable response, despite remaining disagreement. The attempt itself, regardless of the outcome, is a laudable achievement of a pluralist political regime.

The reader may agree or disagree with the model in different levels. First, one needs a generic account of deliberation in order to make sense of its promises and of the benchmarks that can be used to assess this particular aspect of institutional performance. The three previous chapters helped on that. Chapter 1 clarified how deliberation is associated with several virtues in politics and its conditions. Chapter 2 delimited how deliberation could be squared with adjudication in general, and Chapter 3 contemplated constitutional adjudication in particular.

Second, it is fruitful to distinguish between three tiers of institutional performance. The current chapter advanced the core meaning of an ideal-type deliberative court, but assessing genuine deliberative performance, as I envision it, puts forward two additional tiers. This three-tiered structure forges the backbones of the model.

Third, it is possible to further disaggregate each of these tiers and criticize their internal components. Initiatives of improving constitutional adjudication must, nevertheless, address all these dimensions. The three tiers indicate one path for increasing the deliberative capacity of courts.

This model is flexible and comprehensive enough to capture, from a certain angle, most variations in comparative constitutional adjudication. By shedding light on the judicial ethics and on aspects of institutional design (writ large and writ small), on the legal backdrop and on the political circumstances of constitutional deliberation, it intends to enable comparisons between the deliberative potential and actual performance of constitutional courts. It offers a holistic portrait of what is at stake in a deliberative institution, and of how a deliberative constitutional court, more specifically, may look like.

A curious observer could conjecture, after inspecting the surface of most contemporary democracies, that constitutional courts are the place from where, on average, the most thoroughly considered collective decisions about political principles have been emerging. These decisions reputedly forge the chief compendium of applied political philosophy produced by these regimes.[21] Nothing comparable to that, he may note, emanates from parliaments. This perception is in line with the flood of comparative studies on constitutional courts and with the vacuum of publications on parliaments, especially with regards to rights promotion and public reasoning.[22] This conclusion might be precipitate though. Jurists have traditionally been less prone to scrutinize the various channels of legislative reasoning. Parliamentary debates, moreover, are not documented and publicized in the same way. Judicial decisions are usually accompanied by a relatively structured set of arguments that justify the outcome. The reasons that back statutes, on the other hand, can only be loosely identified in the messy debates that precede

---

[21] See Robertson (2010).

[22] Recent comparative studies on courts include Goldsworthy (2006) and Robertson (2010). On parliaments, see Bauman and Kahana (2006).

legislative voting. These diverse styles do not prove, by themselves, that parliaments are inferior to courts with regards to principled decision-making.

I do not assume, at any rate, the conjectures of the curious observer. The book is not courting deliberation at the expense of other potential deliberative forums, but is highlighting what judicial deliberation might be at its best. It consists in a normative exhortation for constitutional courts to promote public contestation, collegial engagement, and deliberative written decision: different doses and mixtures of institutional design and of deliberative ethics may end up excelling on those three goals. Chapter 5 spells out the virtues behind the three components of deliberative performance and Chapter 6 sheds light on the institutional contours that might motivate them. The normative postulate from where the next chapters depart is that constitutional courts are to be deliberative. Henceforth, the very desirability of a deliberative court steps out of the spotlight.

5

The Ethics of Political Deliberation

I. INTRODUCTION

Public contestation, collegial engagement, and deliberative written decision are institutional achievements. They embody the three indices of deliberative performance, the three targets to be aimed for by this collegiate body. It is still necessary, however, to investigate the individual attitudes that lurk behind such collective pursuit, to translate those three targets into a set of micro-virtues that judges should develop and practice if committed to those goals. The inquiry shifts from the group-level to the individual-level. What sort of behavior should one expect from the judges that happen to participate in the process of a deliberative constitutional court?

Political deliberation, as it was defined in Chapter 1, and deliberative performance of constitutional courts, as further decomposed in Chapter 4, imply an ethics, that is, a set of criteria that draws a line between the rightness and wrongness of action. Of the several elements that shape deliberation, according to the definition in Chapter 1, some more immediately invoke ethical attitudes. Deliberation denotes absence of coercion, interpersonal argumentation detached from egotistic interests, tolerance towards enduring disagreement after the exhaustion of the argumentative horizon, presumption of equal status among participants, and clear display of respect. Deliberators are prone both to listen and to speak, and are disposed to change their previous preferences in the light of the new arguments that are raised during discussion.

These statements, part of the mantra of the deliberative literature, are yet too blunt. They still do not solve the difficulties deliberators face and the polemical choices they need to make in the course of that activity. The way deliberators behave and engage with each other must be more deeply theorized. Further behavioral guidelines are needed to face the several dilemmas that routinely emerge out of such complex interaction. Deliberation takes place in diverse sites, each of them with distinct priorities and expectations. Circumstances are mutable, and those of a constitutional court may, indeed, request different ethical responses.

This chapter intends to illuminate this more intricate ethical phenomenon that underlies deliberation in constitutional courts. It has four additional sections. The second approaches a preliminary discussion about the character of an ethics of deliberation. The three following sections, then, deal with the specific ethical burdens that may get more or less pronounced in each of the three phases of deliberation. In sum, the chapter expands on what is requested, by the three indices of deliberative performance, from judges of a constitutional court devoted to deliberation.

2. THE CHARACTER OF AN ETHICS OF DELIBERATION

Normative ethical inquiries often start by positioning themselves somewhere within a classificatory triad. "Virtue ethics," "deontology," and "consequentialism," with their respective internal variants, are the generic alternatives offered by the philosophical tradition.[1] The ethics of deliberation could arguably be elaborated in different ways and hence approximate itself from each of these three branches of ethical thought.

If devised in consequentialist terms, for example, deliberation would be better or worse, and deliberators would be more or less praiseworthy, inasmuch as the four expected results—epistemic, communitarian, psychological, and educative—unfold. Important though the consequences of deliberation might be, that focus would be, if not mistaken, surely impoverishing. The ineptness of an exclusively consequentialist formulation is not due to the fact that deliberation, also having a value in itself, should supposedly be practiced anytime, anyplace, irrespective of its outcomes.

That simplistic moral case was already cast aside. When it comes to a decision-making institution, that stand-alone justificatory path gets even weaker. Institutions should not deliberate for the sake of deliberation. There must be some instrumental purchase, even if just in probabilistic terms, as already contended. Deliberation is not consequence-indifferent. The difficulty, still, is that a focus solely on the consequences does neither portray nor explain the proper actions that are likely to produce those cherished effects. It does not do justice to the phenomenological experience of a deliberator. Even if deliberation authorizes the participants to expect more or less beneficial outputs, or even require them to seek those outputs, its very definition is indifferent to what consequences, in practice, ultimately ensue.

A robust ethics of deliberation, if that trichotomy holds, would thus have to be further fleshed out either in deontological terms or as an instance of virtue ethics. This division is more intricate. To rigidly matriculate the

---

[1] Aristotle, Kant, and Bentham are regarded as, if not originators, the spiritual fathers of these traditions. See Oakley (1996).

propositions of the current chapter under any of these headings would require a more technical analysis of moral philosophy than the one I am prepared or need to engage with.[2] I do, still, resort to the notion of virtue in order to elaborate my claims.

It is hard to talk about deliberation without uttering the vocabulary of virtue. Virtues inspire a sincere act, rather than a strategic obedience to a rule. Doing the right thing, in deliberation, is not simply to abide by the duties or patterns of right conduct. The "spirit" of deliberation calls for more than conformity "to the letter of a rule."[3] It conveys something beyond a sheer duty to exchange arguments. Individuals cannot deliberate but with the right motivations (apart from the consequentialist expectations embedded in the promises of deliberation). Otherwise, a relevant part of the normative appeal of deliberation would melt away. The ambitious epistemic and communitarian promises, at the very least, would become fake. The search for the best answer and the attempt of persuasion need to be genuine, not "just for the show."

Whether a virtue is just a sincere "disposition to act" for the sake of a certain reason, or an unhesitating predisposition derivative from deep and entrenched character traits is a discussion in normative ethics on which I do not plan to embark. The ethics of deliberation cannot entirely be grasped in crude deontological terms, but this claim, alone, does not suffice to solve that classificatory dispute.

The distinction between motivations, deeds, and consequences of deeds is indispensable to better understand deliberation. If not accompanied by the right motivations, an argumentative interaction cannot be regarded as veritably deliberative.[4] Deliberation, in this sense, collapses deeds and the motivations behind them. If we were to elaborate the ethics of deliberation in the form of a set of duties or to codify it through a list of rules, the rules themselves would have to include character traits. This, in turn, would

---

[2] To call it a virtue ethics, I would need to enter the debate about emotions and moral remainder, the possibility of emerging out of resolvable, irresolvable, and tragic dilemmas with clean or dirty hands etc. (see Hursthouse, 2002, chapters 2 and 3).

[3] "The Devil, after all, can quote scripture to serve his own purposes; one can conform to the letter of a rule while violating its spirit" (Hursthouse, 2002, at 32). Or in another passage: "Clearly, one can give the *appearance of being* a generous, honest, and just person without being one, by making sure one acts in certain ways. And that is enough to show that *there is more to the possession of a virtue than being disposed to act in certain ways*; at the very least, one has to act in those ways for certain sorts of reasons. But, in fact, we think of such character traits as involving much more than tendencies or dispositions to act, even for certain reasons" (Hursthouse, 2002, at 11, emphasis added).

[4] Deliberators must first believe there is a point in deliberating. A useful analogy can be borrowed from Wolfe's provocation against conservatives: "Conservatives cannot govern well for the same reason that vegetarians cannot prepare a world-class boeuf bourguignon: If you believe that what you are called upon to do is wrong, you are not likely to do it very well" (Wolfe, 2006).

apparently break down the distinction between deontology and virtue ethics itself. As Hursthouse shows, however, that is not necessarily the case.[5]

Virtues are not an overly explored issue in contemporary jurisprudence. Solum, though, has been emphasizing the role of virtues in the practice of judging. He advances a normative theory of judging that is "virtue-centered" rather than "decision-centered," "thick" rather than "thin."[6] Instead of conceiving of judicial virtues—like temperance, courage, temperament, intelligence, and wisdom—as serviceable means to reach good legal decisions, which he believes to be shared by every plausible theory of judging, he accords virtues a weightier role.

Such a role is specified by two controversial propositions: (i) "A lawful decision is a decision that would characteristically be made by a virtuous judge in the circumstances that are relevant to the decision." (ii) "A just decision is identical to a virtuous decision."[7] He wants to counter a position that envisions the just decision as logically prior to the virtue of justice. To be truly "virtue-centered," then, a theory of judging could not rely on an independent standard of the right legal decision.

Duff praises Solum's effort to identify the "substantive qualities of character that will equip or enable the person to make right decisions."[8] Nevertheless, he claims, virtues are still derivative and dependent of a previous account of the good decision.[9] Judicial virtues, in his account, retain an important epistemological function, but not metaphysical. A judge, for him, could not justify her own decision by appealing to her alleged virtues, but only through some prior explanation of what an accurate or reasonable interpretation of law is.

Duff's critique may have been too quick. Solum contends: "Although we might say that a just decision is independent of the virtue of the particular judge who made the decision, it is not the case that the justice of the decision is independent of judicial virtue."[10] Solum seems to propose a distinction that Duff may have missed: the right decision is determined not by a "particular judge" who claims to be virtuous, but rather through a reflection about what an ideally virtuous judge would do in a specific situation. Therefore, *contra* Duff, Solum may say that a judge, indeed, could not justify her decision by

---

[5] For a clear explanation about these nuances, and also about how the mere reference to virtue does not makes an ethical theory part of "virtue ethics," not more than the mere reference to "duties" makes it deontological, see Hursthouse, 2002. Virtues, as much as rules, generate prescriptions and prohibitions. It is not correct to claim that virtue ethicists, in being "agent-centered," do not provide action guidance or a notion of right action, or that deontologists, in being "rule-centered," cannot have a notion of character or judgment, or that neither care about consequences (because sometimes, to know what is virtuous or right depend on estimating its consequences) (Hursthouse, 2002, 28–29).

[6] Solum (2003).   [7] Solum, 2003, at 198.   [8] Duff, 2003, at 218.

[9] "We might need virtue to discern what justice requires, but what constitutes an outcome as what justice requires is not that this outcome is discerned by the eye of virtue" (Duff, 2003, at 221).

[10] Solum, 2003, at 199.

saying that she is virtuous, but by showing that the decision accords to what a hypothetical virtuous judge, in those circumstances, would do.

However charitably we read it, though, Solum's stance seems to beg the question. His conceptual trick is to incorporate into the set of judicial virtues the virtue of lawfulness—the ability to understand and adequately apply the law. If the virtuous judge is one that, thanks to his lawfulness, is able to come up with acceptable legal decisions, one will first need to discuss what a lawful decision is in order to know how a virtuous judge would decide. Solum, therefore, does not really manage to circumvent the need for a virtue-independent criterion of just outcome: in order to fill in the meaning of "lawfulness" in each case, one would proceed through the route he was trying to avoid.

A normative theory of judging, as far as it seeks to specify the right outcomes of law application, cannot be "virtue-centered" in the way Solum defines it. Nonetheless, a normative theory of deliberation can. Virtues are not just a means for good deliberation. Rather, the practice of a specific set of virtues instantiates deliberation itself. Virtues, indeed, are a means for the cherished results that are supposed to ensue from deliberation, and the correctness of these results should be rated, unlike Solum would suggest, by an independent criterion. But they are not merely that. The plausibility of the epistemic promise of deliberation, in other words, depends on frankly virtuous acts. Virtues, though, are not the appropriate standard to assess what is epistemically right.

I will elucidate the virtues that are conducive to deliberation and the occasional dilemmas that may arise in the course of promoting public contestation, furthering collegial engagement and drafting a deliberative written decision. All enumerated virtues, to some extent, are in play along the three phases, and disentangling them too much would be artificial. It is useful, however, to underscore which virtues outstand in each phase.

This set of virtues furnishes the court with a sense of direction. Together, they construct a decision-making culture that is indispensable to the credibility of a deliberative court. Without this shared belief on the potential benefits of deliberation, deliberative performance would be hindered. The following diagram illustrates the virtues to be described by the next sections:

Phases	Virtues
1. Pre-decisional	Towards interlocutors:
	i. Respectful curiosity
2. Decisional	Towards fellow colleagues:
	ii. Collegiality
	iii. Cognitive modesty
	iv. Cognitive ambition
	v. Empathy

Phases	Virtues
3. Post-decisional	Towards interlocutors: vi. Responsiveness vii. Clarity viii. Sense of fallibility and provisionality

3. PRE-DECISIONAL PHASE AND PUBLIC CONTESTATION

How is public contestation translated into the attitudes of judges? Judges of a deliberative court do not only address the court's interlocutors when delivering a written decision. Their interaction with interlocutors during the pre-decisional phase is essential for what deliberation can mean at this point.

Contemporary constitutional courts, as a matter of fact, for the sake of independence and impartiality, tend to restrict the opportunities for such interaction and prioritize judicial passivity. Formal design, to be sure, can nourish or prevent the potential of public contestation. This question, in any event, will be dealt with in the next chapter. For present purposes, I imagine what public contestation entails under the assumption that design variables do not levy any unbridgeable obstacle against it. Public contestation is characterized, as far as the role of judges is concerned, by the virtue of "respectful curiosity."

i. Respectful curiosity

A deliberative constitutional court should have the capacity to hear a plural group of interlocutors and be porous to various sorts of outside arguments. It should maximize the points of view that can profitably inform its subsequent deliberations, but not in an unqualified "the more, the better" sense. It gives a broad range of interlocutors an opportunity to speak, and develops a qualitative filter for the reasonable arguments that will have to be better digested later.

At this stage, judges are concerned with actively listening and understanding what interlocutors have to say, instead of properly arguing with them. They may incidentally argue with the purpose of probing the consistency and clarifying the interlocutor's contentions, which is, in itself, part of "active listening." Their purpose, yet, is not so much a persuasive one as it is inquisitorial and informative.

Respectful curiosity, therefore, consists in putting "active listening" into practice, taking care of the risks it can bring. In spite of their natural pre-deliberative inclinations, judges must resist forming their positions before they experience the sequence of argumentative interaction they are supposed to attend subsequently. Apart from being open to listening before sticking with their occasional pre-deliberative inclinations, they must be sensitive enough to *show* that their decision is not already taken and that they are disarmed. It does not mean, again, that they cannot raise sharp questions and challenge the quality of the arguments being aired.

The technique for raising these questions in a non-tendentious way, considering the respective social positions and political vulnerabilities of interlocutors, and also the originality of their arguments, will demand skill and acute judgment. Respectful curiosity does not necessarily mean, therefore, that each interlocutor will need to be granted exactly equal opportunity and time to manifest his case. This flexible and selective treatment may be justified in the light of all promises of deliberation. Even fairness can sometimes recommend that flexibility, if one assumes a less formalistic take on deliberation. A rigidly ritualized procedure, which prevents the court from calibrating the adequate participation of each interlocutor, can hamper public contestation. This dilemma, however, concerns a calculus of institutional design to be addressed by the next chapter.

Public contestation, for sure, cannot be guaranteed by the judicial respectful curiosity alone. It is contingent on the contribution that interlocutors are able or willing to make. That virtue can, nevertheless, steer judges on mustering arguments in a way that is serviceable to the constitutional court's role as a deliberative forum.

4. DECISIONAL PHASE AND COLLEGIAL ENGAGEMENT

Collegial engagement is a complex mode of deliberation. It is oriented to consensus but does not depend on it. It deals with the tension between the epistemic and communitarian promises, and also with second-order reasons for reaching unanimity. Decision-makers have the burden of reaching an authoritative solution to the case, of converting individual positions into an institutional one, without suppressing disagreement. In order to discharge their responsibility in the deliberative way, judges should take four virtues into account: collegiality, empathy, cognitive modesty, and cognitive ambition, as follows.

ii. Collegiality

Collegiality is the primary and usually the sole virtue addressed by the legal literature that connects courts with deliberation.[11] There is a commonplace assumption according to which collegiality leads to a *per curiam* decision

---

[11] There are a number of articles about collegiality in American literature. The major bulk of them written by judges themselves, reminiscing on their own experience in a collegiate court. The discussion

whereas individuality prompts a *seriatim* decision. Unanimity, thus, would signal its presence whereas multiple opinions would echo its absence. These inferences, however credible, should be handled with care. In courts where multiple opinions are proscribed, the presence or absence of collegiality is not a matter of concern. In those where multiple opinions are allowed, the effects of collegiality may be various. In any event, a deliberative court is collegial in an ethical rather than in a numerical sense. But what does this virtue entail?

There are manifold definitions of collegiality. In its primitive forms, collegiality evokes camaraderie, clubbiness, and exclusivity, or yet narrow-mindedness and self-interested corporatism.[12] It would consist in the nurturing of close personal relationships for the pursuit of private-oriented goals.[13] Slightly refined, it may also mean the "constructive use of relationships with other professionals in the making of professional decisions."[14]

Collegiality as a virtue of deliberation has a more precise sense. It remains, indeed, attached to a collaborative project, but one that is concerned with the internal institutional culture that favors deliberation and the search of unity.[15] It generates the conditions for "comfortable controversy"[16] and develops an "intimacy beyond affection,"[17] in the eloquent expressions of American judges.

Edwards offers a more useful understanding. For him, rather than consensus, collegiality implies "that we discuss each other's views seriously and respectfully, and that we listen with open minds."[18] In a more elaborated version, he claims that collegial judges are prepared to "listen, persuade, and be persuaded, all in an atmosphere of civility and respect," and that such process "helps to create the conditions for principled agreement."[19]

Collegiality, therefore, is an umbrella that could be decomposed into several other virtues. It comprises a certain level of respect, a commitment to argue and to cooperate, and a disposition to strive for a supra-individual decision. It is more encompassing and nuanced than the "ethics of consensus,"

---

usually concentrates on whether, how, and when to dissent. It does not thoroughly touch on the other qualities of deliberation.

[12] See Edwards, 2003, at 1666, and Collier, 1992, at 7.   [13] Silva (2013).

[14] Collier, 1992, at 4.

[15] "Collaboration and deliberation are the trademarks of collegial enterprise" (Kornhauser and Sager, 1993, at 2).

[16] "Collegiality is lively, tolerant, thoughtful debate; it is the open and frank exchange of opinions; it is comfortable controversy; it is mutual respect earned through vigorous exchange" (Tacha, 1995, at 587).

[17] "Collegiality has several faces. One is intimacy. But it is intimacy beyond affection... It is fed from the spring of our common enterprise" (Coffin, 1980).

[18] Edwards, 1998, at 1361.   [19] Edwards, 2003, at 1645.

mentioned in the first chapter, but certainly includes this shared "aim at unanimity."[20]

A collegial enterprise involves a "shift in the agency of performance from the individual to the group."[21] In the case of collegial adjudication, the agency of performance is the court, not the judge. Collegiality is a magnetic needle that pulls towards convergence. Without this gravitational force, the interaction turns to mere mutual justification and occasional passive acquiescence rather than deliberation. Collegiality, therefore, is clearly at odds with a judge that, despite carefully studying the case and elaborating well-reflected reasons to decide, does not feel any responsibility to interact and communicate with his colleagues. This is an easy example of the lack of collegiality. This virtue may have to arbitrate, however, more intricate ethical dilemmas. Such dilemmas materialize when, despite the mutual effort to argue and persuade, disagreement persists. In such situations, deliberators can compromise and find common ground, concur or, as a measure of last resort, dissent. These alternative getaways from consensus turn courts "imperfectly or at least complexly collegial" if compared to totally collaborative enterprises.[22]

When spontaneous consensus, or even a minimal majority, does not come forth, compromise may be an acceptable solution. Second-order reasons can push a judge who believes he is right to alleviate his first-best choice and join the group. Sometimes, judges may concede in the name of the symbolic and political power of a unanimous decision, as opposed to the susceptibility of divided ones. Managing this political variable is part of the everyday diet of constitutional courts that allow dissenting opinions, but I will postpone this discussion to Chapter 8. For now, I return to a more general point about the acceptability of compromise.

Compromise, especially in the domain of adjudication, may call to mind a suspicious moral aura. More often, this notion gets embroiled with less legitimate kinds of bargaining that, although stimulated in other fora, could not be tolerated by the standards of impartiality that the application of law is supposed to involve. Brennan, for example, is deemed to once have said: "my business is to form majorities." Many have understood it to confirm a model of judicial behavior which identifies nothing but strategic bargaining in a collegiate court. This apparently cynical statement, though, should not be taken at face value. It can also be read through a deliberative prism. In

---

[20] While they "do permit dissenting opinions, there seem to be strong internal norms against such public display of disagreement. Indeed, in most of the European courts most of the time, the justices seek to deliberate to a consensus or common decision. They *aim at unanimity* wherever that is possible" (Ferejohn and Pasquino, 2004, at 1692, emphasis added).

[21] Kornhauser and Sager, 1993, at 5.

[22] Kornhauser and Sager have in mind, for example, scientists that develop a research project together, writers that co-author a novel, and so on (1993, at 56).

order to reach a majority or a consensus, judges may deliberate and reach principled compromises. Chapters 1 and 2 have already maintained that there are non-objectionable types of compromise.[23] Such compromises, however, presuppose a level of interpersonal trust that only collegiality can plausibly engender.

Collegiality pushes deliberators to find principled compromise where spontaneous agreement proves unviable. Disagreement survives only when principled compromise is not possible.[24] A collegial body induces a spirit of accommodation, a default preference for compromising instead of concurring or dissenting, a willingness to locate points of conflict and dissolve them.[25] It implies a pressure to deflect "in deference to one's colleagues."[26]

Digging deeper to find common ground may be easier in a court that shares some methodological backbones of interpretation, like, for example, the German Constitutional Court and its usual recourse to balancing and proportionality.[27] In a more polarized setting like the US Supreme Court, where the dispute between originalists, textualists, and the like are cashed in such an adversarial (and even partisan) fashion, common ground is harder to find. There are levels of analysis in which communicability is simply broken, which is regretful for the prospects of deliberation.

Collegiality, in sum, is a virtue that cannot be imposed by design, although some procedural constraints may stimulate it; a question for the next chapter. It leads a judge to act "in concert with colleagues,"[28] or expects judges to "behave as colleagues."[29] But is not incompatible with an occasional individual manifestation, where such is institutionally allowed. A judge may concur or dissent and still be collegial.[30] This will depend, among other variables, on the

---

[23] To recapitulate, a deliberator may strike a partnership compromise (she defers because, not having deep feelings about her own position, she values institutional unity) or a pragmatic compromise (she defers to change the status quo in a favorable direction, although the solution still falls short from her ideal position). The frontier between principled compromise and bargaining may become less clear when concessions are made not within a controversial issue of a case, but inter-issues (in a multi-issues case) or even inter-cases.

[24] Brandeis hints to an idea of compromise: "I can't always dissent. I sometimes endorse an opinion with which I do not agree. I acquiesce" (Bickel, 1957, at 18). Holmes is also cautious to dissent: "if I should write in every case where I do not agree with some of the views expressed in the opinions, you and all my other friends would stop reading my separate opinions" (Ginsburg, 1990b, at 142).

[25] "In most cases, we debated the issues until there was enough common ground for a unanimous judgment to be produced" (Sachs, 2009, at 209).

[26] For Kornhauser and Sager, collegiality is not at odds with compromise, but it obviously rejects strategic behavior: "For a collegial judge, strategic behavior is behavior that transgresses both her own convictions per se, and her convictions as appropriately modified to respond to the pressures of collegial unity and sound collegial outcome ... A judge is entitled, indeed obliged, to deflect her conduct in deference to her colleagues. But she is not entitled to misrepresent her views or redirect her voting conduct in order to better advance her own candidates for rationale and outcome" (1993, at 56).

[27] Grimm (2000).   [28] Edwards, 2003, at 1661.   [29] Kornhauser and Sager, 1993, at 2.

[30] There are ways and ways to dissent. Some are compatible with collegiality and others are not. See O'Connor (1998) and Stack (1996). Minority opinions do not detract from an authentic collegial enterprise

effort he initially exerts to converge, on the perceived reasonableness of the separate public statement he wants to make, and on the frequency in which that happens.[31] Genuine collegiality avoids the risk of "overindulgence in separate opinion writing"[32] and nurtures an institutionally minded style of judging, even in case of dissent.[33] It refuses turning the decision into a "showcase of the autonomous minds of the justices."[34]

If the right to dissent is guaranteed, collegiality turns its exercise burdensome and conditional. A collegial dissent is perceived to be a measure of last resort.[35] Its licentious use would undermine collegiality and, as a consequence, the very conditions for deliberation. How to distinguish a justified dissenting opinion from a self-regarding, vain and gratuitous one?[36]

Collegiality is what inspires the dissenter's dilemma. This is a charged moral choice that an individualist judge ignores. It involves an intricate balance between competing claims.[37] Zobell believes that the judge has a duty to dissent when he thinks that his opinion "may contribute to the eventual correction of a decision which he believes to be wrong," provided this is less costly than the "appearance of a disintegrated Court."[38] For Pound, dissents are welcome to the extent they provide a "useful critique of the opinion of the court."[39] Even the American Bar Association had once recommended

---

as long as the minority judges do consider the majority opinion as the "opinion of the court." The dissenter implicitly declares: if I were to decide for the court, I would decide like this. That is why dissents would "read in the subjunctive" (Kornhauser and Sager, 1993, at 38). Kornhauser and Sager insightfully underscore the internal and external aspects of a collegial dissent: "Internally—within the Court itself—dissent promotes and improves deliberation and judgment. Arguments on either side of a disagreement test the strength of their rivals and demand attention and response... Externally—for lower courts, the parties, and interested bystanders—concurring and dissenting opinions are important guides to the dynamic 'meaning' of a decision by the Court" (1993, at 8).

[31] The discussion about the dilemmas of dissenting is by no means an exclusively American one. This is a relevant question, for example, for most Latin American and European constitutional courts. The French Constitutional Council and the Italian Constitutional Court remain as the few exceptional cases where dissent is absolutely forbidden.

[32] Ginsburg, 1992a, at 1191.   [33] Ginsburg, 1992b, at 199.   [34] Kelman, 1985, at 227

[35] Sometimes the right to dissent is seen as a corollary of "judicial independence." This is a risky and atomistic view of collegiate judging, that mixes up insulation of the institution against external pressure and a freedom to be soloist within a multi-member body. The effective dissent, for Ginsburg, "spells out differences without jeopardizing collegiality or public respect for and confidence in the judiciary" (1992a, at 1196).

[36] Many consider the practice of dissent by the US Supreme Court as pathologically personalized (Quick, 1991, at 62; Ginsburg, 1992b). "Dissent became an instrument by which Justices asserted a personal, or individual, responsibility which they viewed as of a higher order than the institutional responsibility owed by each to the Court, or by the Court to the public" (Zobell, 1958, at 203).

[37] Ginsburg, 1990b, at 150. "The judge should balance the advantage of insisting on his opinion with the disadvantage created by the very expression of dissent;... balance the advantage of expressing a dissent that may in the future become the majority opinion with the disadvantage of the uncertainty that dissent may create within the legal system" (Barak, 2006, at 209–210).

[38] Zobell, 1958, at 213.   [39] Pound, 1953, at 795.

an effort of self-restraint: "Except in case of conscientious difference of opinion on fundamental principle, dissenting opinions should be discouraged in courts of last resort."[40] For Bickel, only instinct will tell how to strike the balance between these abstract standards.[41]

The dissenter's dilemma may actually be more taxing due to a relevant temporal dimension. After dissenting once, should a judge keep dissenting in cases that raise similar issues in the future, or simply defer to precedent? Does it make any ethical difference to persist with dissents that were already clearly stated in the past? The pull of collegiality, in such circumstance, becomes even starker.[42]

Collegiality nourishes the presupposed group psychology of a deliberative body.[43] It does not welcome soloists, who do not hesitate to use petty and capricious dissents. A deliberative forum must be immunized against the cult of celebrity. The collegial atmosphere may, for sure, oscillate over time. Its maintenance cannot be taken for granted. The abuse of dissents and other kinds of individualist attitudes deteriorates the court's deliberative capacity. Judges of a deliberative court get to know each other's intellectual personas quite well.[44] Their quotidian interaction may entrench theoretical divisions and lead to a deadlock. Deliberation shrinks when differences become fossilized and collegiality evaporates, a challenge that can be tackled by some institutional devices.

Being collegial in a court, to sum up, is different from being collegial in a golf club. Collegiality in a court does not imply interacting with colleagues for the sake of mutual enjoyment. It also implies more than deferring to

---

[40] "Canons of Judicial Ethics," ABA, 1924.

[41] Bickel, for example, recognizes the tension: "Thus the dilemma. To remain silent, not drawing attention to a possibly nascent doctrine which one deems pernicious, not assisting, despite oneself, in its birth; or to speak out. Silence under such circumstances is a gamble taken in the hope of a stillbirth. The risk is that if the birth is successful, silence will handicap one's future opposition. For one is then chargeable with parenthood. Yet dissent may serve only to delineate clearly what the majority was diffident itself to say... Instinct, a craftsman's inarticulable feel, which must largely govern the action in such a matter, dictated now one choice, now the other" (Bickel, 1957, at 30).

[42] Kelman for example, distinguishes between a dissent that is "superseded" by *stare decisis*, a "sustained" dissent and a "suspended" dissent, which is characterized by temporary acquiescence (1985, at 238). Bennett also sees the sustained dissent as problematic: "There is an important institutional purpose served by dissent the first time some issue arises... The matter is very different when an issue already decided arises again" (1990–1991, at 259). For Kornhauser and Sager, there would be an "unencumbered license to dissent in a case of first impression," whereas dissents in subsequent cases would be "encumbered by the contrary obligations of precedent" (1993, 8–9).

[43] Grimm, again, narrates how collegiality is ingrained in the German Constitutional Court's decisional culture. The reluctance to file a dissenting opinion or even to ask for a postponement of the judgment, according to him, would be perceived as "very unfriendly to one's colleagues" (Grimm, 2003).

[44] Coffin has suggested a dichotomy that captures this: anticipatory collegiality entails "sensitivity to one's colleagues' sensibilities," whereas responsive collegiality corresponds to the "written acknowledgement by a justice of the feelings of another colleague" (Coffin, 1980, at 181–192).

colleagues in order to find common ground, regardless of what that common ground is. It indicates the belief on a supra-individual good that they can only reach together, and on which the external respectability of their decision will depend. This good should normally outweigh their preferred individual position. Renouncing that good deprives the institution of an important source of legitimation.

iii. Cognitive modesty

Collegiality is a central virtue if the decisional phase is to fulfill its deliberative job. However, collegial engagement is not reducible to it. Three complementary virtues help typify this practice more sharply. The first one is cognitive modesty, a logical and moral condition of preference transformation. This virtue could be seen as underlying collegiality, but it is worth taking note of its particular role in shaping deliberation.

Deliberation assumes its participants do not stick to their pre-deliberative dispositions and are not too self-assured about conclusions individually reached. Deliberators, therefore, make themselves vulnerable to the scrutiny of their fellow colleagues. Modesty is often what persuasion and mutual concessions logically and morally entail.

Cognitive modesty exhorts judges to investigate deeply what they share and to clean up their misunderstandings, to take each other's opinions seriously and exercise, to the limit, the method of self-doubt.[45] Judicial deliberation requires, apart from the virtue of "judicial intelligence,"[46] that is, the appropriate intellectual equipment to understand and to cope with legal complexity, an unassuming attitude towards knowledge itself. The character and role of modesty resembles the notion of "interpretive charity": its point is not to "pay homage, deference or respect to our interlocutors," but rather to inspirit a constructive attitude for the acquisition of insight.[47]

iv. Cognitive ambition

Cognitive ambition is the flipside of cognitive modesty. Deliberation asks for their co-existence. It consists in the institutional willingness or the collective disposition to strive and persist in the search of the best possible decision. It

---

[45] "There is a modesty inherent in the judicial function that prevents me from being convinced that I necessarily am right, or, rather, that there is only one right answer to a legal problem...My modesty is institutional, not personal" (Sachs, 2009, at 143).

[46] As proclaimed by Solum (2003).

[47] "The aim of interpretive charity is not generosity towards others, or anything like that. It is not to pay homage, deference or respect to our interlocutors, or to avoid giving offense...The aim is to learn. It is aggressively to learn what there is to be learnt from puzzles the interlocutors pose to us, by assuming there is method in their madness and doing our best to ferret that out" (Michelman, 2008, at 4).

fuels collegiality with an investigative energy without which the epistemic promise of deliberation gets anemic and fatigued. Cognitive ambition furnishes deliberation, therefore, with a more powerful epistemic drive than sheer collegiality.[48]

Deliberators inspired by that virtue are not content, thus, with reaching agreement, but try to subject an occasional convergence to further tests of argument. If uncomfortable with a too hasty agreement, they return to the counter-arguments that a "Devil's advocate" could make. Deliberators, in this sense, are not "advocates of a position" but "students of an issue,"[49] and are relentless in the search of the best decision.

Collegial engagement is the setting where the ideal of non-hierarchy but of the best argument gets most closely instantiated along the three-phasic decisional structure of a constitutional court. The articulation between cognitive modesty and ambition, that is, between the deliberator's attitude of self-doubt and the commitment to persist in searching the right answer and challenging superficial agreements, is what maximizes the epistemic plausibility of judicial deliberation as far as judicial attitudes are concerned. Institutional design, as we will see, can provide adequate conditions for this articulation to flourish.

v. Empathy

Finally, empathy qualifies cognitive ambition. This virtue relates to the ability of vicariously imagining the points of view that were not formally voiced in the course of the judicial process, or of "submerging in other people's narratives."[50] It is the principal corrective a constitutional court can have against a poorly deliberative pre-decisional phase. When institutional hindrances impede interlocutors to fully argue their positions, or when the interlocutors themselves do not manage to do justice to the complexity of the case, empathetic judges can, to some extent, fill that gap.[51] Empathy enables the

---

[48] Edwards, for example, considers the epistemic benefit that derives from collegiality alone: "since collegiality fosters better deliberations, collegial judges are more likely to find the right answer in any given case" (Edwards, 2003, at 1684). Tacha also goes in the same direction: "Often these deliberations do not change a judge's vote or a case's outcome, but the rationale behind the vote is more fully informed and intellectually sound because of the collegial interaction" (Tacha, 1995, at 587).

[49] Tacha, 1995, at 587.   [50] Wills (2010).

[51] Empathy is implicit in Kornhauser's and Sager's concern with the need for "just treatment of unrepresented parties," which would indicate the complementarity between adversarial exchanges in the pre-decisional phase and deliberation in the decisional: "While each party will advocate positions most favorable to it, this advocacy ensures that any biases of the judges are exposed to conflicting arguments and views...Our understanding that judicial decisions affect parties not before the court and our conception of just treatment of these unrepresented parties argues that judges should *consider the interests of those parties not before the court* because the adversarial process will not necessarily produce arguments and options favorable to these persons" (Kornhauser and Sager, 1986, at 101, emphasis added).

court to amplify "whom the judges listen to before they decide, and whom they encourage to speak after they decide."[52]

A constitutional court, in this sense, can go beyond the arguments it was able to collect in the pre-decisional phase through empathetic imagination of the potential community of interlocutors. This may be particularly relevant for an institution that is usually seen as "elitist" and with comparably weaker capacity to be heterogeneous and representative (although design can slightly mitigate it, as we shall see in the next chapter).

Sachs elaborated on the empathy of a constitutional judge with remarkable acumen. As a judge, according to his memoirs, he tried to be sensitive not to the actual but to the "potential readership" his opinions could have. That implied, for him, taking the widest imaginable audience into account[53] and developing an "enlarged mentality."[54]

5. POST-DECISIONAL PHASE AND DELIBERATIVE WRITTEN DECISION

A deliberative written decision concludes the process by communicating to the public what decision collegial engagement was able to produce and the broad set of arguments that were duly weighed. It expresses a de-personified institutional identity, whatever format it might take. Again, the choice between *per curiam* and *seriatim* is a serious one, and should be made according to contextual criteria. However counter-intuitive it may sound to claim that a *seriatim* can be de-personified, there arguably are institutional devices to accomplish that.

More important than format, a deliberative written decision embodies an argumentative style. And an argumentative style, as Walzer reminds, is also a moral style.[55] The court has the responsibility to tell its story about the case in a particular way.[56] Such story-telling will depend on the exercise of three main virtues: responsiveness, clarity, and a sense of fallibility and

---

[52] Thompson, 2004, at 84.

[53] Sachs defines his audience in a broad, non-formalistic sense: "It is a *notional community*, made up by all those who feel they are wearing legal hats when dealing with a problem" (2009, at 143, emphasis added). And regarded "potential readership" as his chief criterion: "however reduced the actual readership of any judgment of mine might be, its *potential readership* is vast." "The objective is not to please or displease anyone, but to converse with as much rigour, integrity, and awareness of our constitutional responsibilities as possible, with *as wide an audience as can be imagined*" (Sachs, 2009, at 149, emphasis added).

[54] ". . . active vision that enables him or her to rise above individual idiosyncrasy to cover the standpoint of others belonging to the community to be persuaded" (Sachs, 2009, at 143).

[55] Walzer summarizes the deliberative moral style: "a form of political argument that is nuanced, probing, and concrete, principled but open to disagreement: no slogans, no jargon, no unexamined assumptions, no party line. This argumentative style, which is also a *moral style*" (Walzer, 2008, at ix, emphasis added).

[56] "We work with words, and become amongst the most *influential story-tellers* of our age. How we tell a story is often as important as what we say. The voice we use cannot be that of a depersonalized and

provisionality.⁵⁷ The deliberative promises at stake in this phase will hinge, again, upon the court's capacity to embrace these virtues.

vi. Responsiveness

Responsiveness entails a capacity to select which of the arguments raised by formal and informal, actual and vicarious interlocutors, deserve a proper reply. Rather than a duty to respond to everything that was publicly voiced, the court has to exercise, as a matter of practicality and fairness, sensible judgment. This is the corollary of the qualitative filter applied at the stage of public contestation. Responsiveness, therefore, unlike its common sociological sense— a mere reaction to some prior action—is content-driven. Apart from interlocutors, a responsive court has to consider the chain of precedents in which the case is inserted, so that the decision contributes to the coherence and systematicity of law, a question to be addressed in Chapter 7.

Moreover, responsiveness also concerns the tone of the answer. Constitutional courts make decisions in the name of and addressed to the whole political community. Controversial moral choices have to be made, which are doomed to spark disagreement.⁵⁸ The decision has the arduous and sometimes unachievable challenge of making the interlocutors on the losing side of the conflict realize that their positions were taken seriously and that their equal moral status was not disregarded. It has, in other words, to "speak with equal voice to both groups."⁵⁹ This is a dignitarian side of the decisional tone. The decisional tone also has a political side, which will be dealt with in Chapter 8.

vii. Clarity

"Simple, clear, persuasive to the legal community, that is my dream."⁶⁰ Clarity is probably a much too obvious virtue to ask from judicial decisions. Adding

---

divine oracle that declares solutions to the problems of human life through the enunciation of pure and detached wisdom" (Sachs, 2009, at 270, emphasis added).

⁵⁷ These three virtues resemble the three demands Thompson requires from an ethically responsible court: recognition of agency, justification, and interlocution. As he contends: "Citizens are better able to respond to a judicial decision if the judge acknowledges it as his or her own; gives reasons for it that citizens can understand; and supports practices that permit challenges to it" (Thompson, 2004, at 74).

⁵⁸ " . . . adjudicating such disagreements involves choosing for the whole society one set of values and rejecting others" (Thompson, 2004, at 72).

⁵⁹ "The judgment should attempt to *speak with equal voice* to both groups... To discover the humanity, the integrity, the honesty, in everybody, and to present your response in a way that everybody can say 'I understand what is being said; I have grave doubts about the result; but the judgments acknowledges what I'm thinking, knows where I am, and takes account of my convictions and respects my conscience and dignity; I'm not being defined out of the answer by what purports to be a completely neutral way of framing issues and arriving at conclusions; my convictions, values and perspectives are being taken seriously and treated thoughtfully and with respect'" (Sachs, 2009, at 239, emphasis added).

⁶⁰ Sachs, 2009, at 58.

that platitude would not tell much about its deliberative specificity.[61] Sachs' dream, however, reveals that achieving this pre-requisite of communication in the realm of legal reasoning is an arduous job. Clarity demands more than shallow intelligibility. It qualifies responsiveness: a deliberative written decision is the opposite of an oracular statement, and cannot indulge in rarefied legalese, however hard this may prove to realize in practice.

Clarity is a virtue that presupposes good writing, but goes beyond that. It stems, first and foremost, from the assumption that legal decisions, and especially constitutional ones, need to speak to a broader audience than the professional legal community. Closure and opacity are not inevitable features of the decisional text. A measure of rhetorical self-restraint and candor contributes to the potential readership of a decision.[62]

A deliberative judge, when in charge of drafting a decision, takes public readership as his primary responsibility. If a constitutional court is going to attract and enable the broader community to join in the political deliberation about fundamental principles, it needs to convey an accessible message that includes non-experts in law. It is this stern devotion to open communication, rather than through its supposed legal expertise, that a deliberative court pursues to obtain public trust.

viii. Sense of fallibility and provisionality

Lastly, and further qualifying its tone, a deliberative written decision expresses a sense of fallibility and provisionality. It recognizes that the decision is historically situated, that the court might have made a mistake, and that deliberation should continue as long as disagreement perseveres or whenever it re-emerges. This virtue requires a careful calibration of how the court envisions or announces judicial supremacy.[63] In other words, the decision reflects the court's awareness of the "continual moral challenge"[64] upon which the legitimacy of collective decisions, taken through whatever procedure, depends.[65]

---

[61] Clarity is a inherent quality of the rule of law itself (Fuller, 1968, at 63).

[62] "It would, of course, be reprehensible to go in for the headline-seeking. The temptations of judicial populism, which offer shallow judicial sound bites without any real jurisprudential content, are great... But I do not feel there is anything wrong in employing a resounding phrase or sharp image that is potentially memorable" (Sachs, 2009, at 57).

[63] Thompson, 2004, at 91.

[64] "If neither citizens nor judges can finally justify making the authoritative choice of fundamental values for society, we must preserve the possibility of *continual moral challenge* to the choices of values that public officials inevitably make for us" (Thompson, 2004, at 73, emphasis added).

[65] For Thompson, responsible judicial decisions need to offer "genuine opportunities for citizens to respond" (2004, at 84). "Responsible officials *encourage response* to their decisions" (Thompson, 2004, at 73, emphasis added).

There is something morally and politically relevant in a decision that expresses, in whatever subtle form it may find, the awareness of its potential reversibility in the future (even if actual reversal turns out not to be the case). Political deliberation is an incorrigibly iterative process. The prospect of incessant iteration constrains the judge to account for her decision and to explain herself in public.

One conventional technique to convey such message of continuity is a dissenting opinion.[66] Dissents may sow the seeds of a potential jurisprudential shift in the future, or so it has been largely believed, for example, by a slightly over-idealized history of judicial dissents in the US Supreme Court.[67] In spite of this romantic view, and even if actual jurisprudential changes cannot be attributable to the existence of courageous dissents in the past, one should not ignore their role in signaling fallibility and provisionality. Dissents may serve as a critical benchmark from which the quality of the decision can be assessed.[68] In any event, with or without dissents, a deliberative decision should find its proper way of inviting responses.

6. CONCLUSION

Deliberation requires a moral, intellectual, and psychological disposition that are hard to develop, let alone to regularly maintain over time. Persuasion is a long-term process, not the conclusion of an afternoon conversation. The chapter described the moral experience of deliberators in the language of virtues and set indicators for the assessment of deliberative performance. Deliberation is a way of doing things. It is, as it were, a virtue-based procedure. It must be distinguished from the outcome that follows it, and there will be independent criteria to judge the substantial rightness of such outcome. The notion of virtue is certainly not the criterion to appraise the rightness of the outcome (as Solum tried to do with respect to judging in general). It

---

[66] Minority votes would have a "concurrent jurisdiction over the future": "For a dissent is a formal *appeal for a rehearing* by the Court sometime in the future, if not on the next occasion" (Kelman, 1985, at 238, emphasis added). The opposite of this potential quality of divided decisions would be the French tradition of corporate opinions: "foster the myth of law's impersonality and inexorability" (Kelman, 1985, at 227).

[67] The three most epic dissents in US Supreme Court history (published by Justices Curtis in *Dred Scott* [1857], Harlan in *Plessy* [1896], and Holmes in *Lochner* [1905]) form the pantheon of the "Great Dissenters." Cardozo, among others, helps to nurture this heroic view of the dissenter, whom he sees as a "gladiator making a last stand against the lions" (1934, at 34). Holmes, by his dissents, is deemed to have contributed to debunk the myth of judicial certainty, at the cost of invigorating the myth that "dissenting justices are anticipating future trends" (Zobell, 1958, at 202).

[68] "Dissent for its own sake has no value, and can threaten the collegiality of the bench. However, where significant and deeply held disagreement exists, members of the Court have a responsibility to articulate it...A dissent *challenges the reasoning* of the majority, *tests its authority* and *establishes a benchmark* against which the majority's reasoning can continue to be evaluated, and perhaps, in time, superseded" (Brennan, 1985, at 435, emphasis added).

is, however, the appropriate standard to assess the quality of the interactive process that precedes decision. A deliberator does not simply follow duties. One cannot search for the best possible answer, imagine vicarious interlocutors, be open to persuasion, and so on, simply as a matter of duty.

Deliberation cannot be reduced to one single virtue either. Collegiality is not the only one at stake. If one were to summarize those virtues through the lenses of their respective vices, an anti-deliberative judge would be passive and ritualistic rather than respectfully curious; individualist and pedantic, rather than collegial; cognitively over self-confident rather than modest and susceptible to persuasion; cognitively indolent, rather than ambitious; egocentric rather than empathetic. An anti-deliberative decision would mirror an ivory-tower reason-giver, rather than grappling to respond to the relevant arguments; would be obscure and cryptic rather than clear and transparent; would offer an apodictic and supremacist statement of the right answer instead of recognizing the continuity of deliberation. The anti-deliberative attitude, in sum, is stubborn and confrontational. However well designed it might be, a constitutional court will only deliberate if judges are dedicated to tackle these vices.

In a non-deliberative court, there cannot be agreement or disagreement properly so called. Decision-makers celebrate individual authorship and do not exactly care about what others happen to think. They do not acknowledge that a supra-individual decision embeds any special value. Agreement or disagreement are mere accidents of a fragmented and personalized decisional process.

Does Hercules have the virtues required by deliberation? Or is he the stereotype of the anti-deliberative judge? Michelman, as we have seen earlier, understood Hercules as a loner, a criticism that Habermas embraced.[69] Hercules would be too self-assured and self-centered to participate in a deliberative encounter. Even when he reaches the Olympus (that is, when he gets promoted to the Supreme Court[70]), he seems not to be very concerned with his colleagues. This might or might not be a fair and charitable reading of Dworkin. Whatever the appropriate understanding of the role that Hercules plays in Dworkin's theory of adjudication, it would be refreshing to think, with the same idealistic vitality, about how a mythical judge with such intellectual vigor should behave in a collegiate body.

A deliberative judge does not seek a single goal, but balances a whole set of considerations. When to compromise, to concur, or to dissent, which interlocutors deserve a more thorough response, for how long to deliberate, among others, are but a few of the ethical dilemmas she faces. The decisional

---

[69] Michelman, 1986, at 76; Habermas, 1996, at 223.   [70] Dworkin, 1986, at 379.

body in which she participates can be reduced "neither to one nor to the many,"[71] and crafting this middle-ground requires dense moral reflection.

Public contestation, collegial engagement, and deliberative written decision are not hard and fast targets, but complex and interconnected ones. They all play a part in making the promises of deliberation more plausible. The virtues described above better capture those goals themselves, and are also instrumental to achieve the promises of deliberation. Cognitive modesty and collegiality, for example, are indispensable for any sort of communitarian persuasion to take place. Cognitive ambition, in turn, is an essential part of what collegial engagement entails, and is also a necessary means for the epistemic promise of deliberation to obtain.

The existence of the right answer in constitutional interpretation is irrelevant for a further question: considering that we disagree about what moral or legal truth is, and that we cannot demonstrate to have reached the truth, what ethical attitude is owed to any fellow citizen who has a different understanding of the constitution? The chapter argues that he deserves to be treated as an interlocutor. This implies an earnest recognition of the moral complexity of constitutional conflicts. In the right circumstances, deliberation is, compared to alternative decision-making methods, and all other things remaining constant, a powerful way to reach good legal decisions. On top of this key epistemic task, however, deliberation has a non-negligible remainder: it involves agents gravely committed to go through this strenuous process for the respect it symbolizes. Deliberative institutions, deciding in the name of the whole political community, take this moral complexity seriously. In trying to produce the right answer, they deliver supplementary political goods.

The ethics of deliberation was outlined here in a comprehensive way. I have described a list of traits that characterize how deliberators are morally inclined to act, not just a list of skills to be technically mastered by them. These traits embody a relevant part of the phenomenological experience of a constitutional judge that is concerned with the ideal of deliberation. Chapter 8 will add to this phenomenology some dilemmas created by the political circumstances of constitutional deliberation, which should be faced by two further virtues: prudence and courage.

---

[71] To slightly rephrase Kornhauser and Sager's title "The one and the many" (1993).

6

Institutional Design: Augmenting Deliberative Potential

I. INTRODUCTION

A constitutional court was earlier defined in a rather minimal way.[1] That concept is often used, admittedly, in a more precise sense. For the purposes of this book, such institution corresponds to a relatively small non-elected body that has the power to challenge, oversee, or even override legislation on the basis of the constitution. Inertia typifies its propulsion system: instead of acting *ex officio*, it needs to be provoked before it takes up a case and is allowed to decide. Beyond these three common denominators of institutional design, which could be reasonably generalized to most systems of judicial constitutional scrutiny, existing courts are naturally more colorful. Innumerable other devices shape their peculiar format. In contemporary democracies, they are not reducible to a single institutional package.

The variances that were overlooked or omitted by that minimal definition are not unimportant. On the contrary, they determine the very chances of a court being more or less deliberative. Comparative constitutional law has consolidated some canonical taxonomic categories to organize the systems of judicial constitutional scrutiny. While serviceable, these mainstream grand classifications are still not sufficient to grasp the set of incentives or disincentives to deliberation. Those classifications look at macro-variables that actually have a limited, if any, bearing on deliberation.[2]

---

[1] See Chapter 3. As already stated at the outset of the book, for the lack of a better term with sufficient degree of generality, "constitutional court" is used in a non-technical sense. It is the genus of which the European constitutional courts and the US and other "supreme courts" are species. I could arguably use "constitutional adjudication" or "judicial review" to circumvent that conventional dichotomy. That choice, however, would still be misleading, because these alternatives highlight the function (which can be spread across different bodies), not the specific body that I want to single out.

[2] Virgílio Afonso da Silva (2009) has cogently argued in favor of such refinement in this mainstream taxonomic template: "In the legal domain, the debate about constitutional review usually concentrates upon procedural actions or upon the effects of judicial decisions, and the only possible conclusions end up

Three conventional distinctions are worth mentioning. First, systems of judicial constitutional scrutiny may be classified by how they allocate such revisory authority across the judiciary. Under such a prism, systems can range between concentrated and diffuse types, that is, between the exclusive jurisdiction of one single apex court or spread over the judiciary.[3] In the former, only a constitutional court has the power to declare the unconstitutionality of legislation. In the latter, any judge would be able to do that in a concrete case, and the constitutional court would have the last word at a final appeal stage.[4]

Some have argued, indeed, that in a diffuse system the top court would benefit from the accumulation of arguments in lower instances. At that ultimate appeal stage, the case would be as dense and mature as possible, hence ripe for deliberation. This contention, however plausible, overlooks that a "progressive distillation of argument"[5] can also be obtained by other means. The dichotomy, thus, remains too distant to have a self-evident bearing on deliberation.

Second, with respect to the type of case it handles, a constitutional court may be in charge of abstract or concrete review. Traditional descriptions usually conflate this dichotomy with the previous one. As a matter of fact, in the most prestigious and well-known constitutional systems, they do tend to come together. However, they refer to different jurisdictional aspects. Here, the basic criterion is the existence of a concrete conflict or not. Abstract control appraises the compatibility of the statute with the constitution without the need for a real and individualized conflict to have emerged. Concrete control, in turn, occurs as an incident of actual litigation involving interested parties and specific facts that, unlike the abstract control, supposedly add palpable flesh to the controversy. Roughly speaking, the combination of the two variables gives shape to the two prominent models: the American, which is both diffuse and concrete, and the Kelsenian, which is both concentrated and abstract.[6]

Some have also argued, similarly to the defense of a diffuse model, that concrete review would enable the court to take advantage of the richer texture

---

being restricted to the choice of this or that model, to the resort to this or that legal action... The moment has come to go beyond that focus" (author's translation).

[3] Ferejohn and Pasquino (2003).

[4] A further distinction about the effects of the decisions taken through concentrated or diffuse control (between *erga omnes* and *intra partes* reach) could still be invoked, but are less relevant for the purposes here (see Cappelletti, 1984).

[5] Le Sueur and Cornes, 2000, at 13.

[6] Ferejohn and Pasquino give some attention to this variation, and claim that the Kelsenian model emphasizes the legislative rather than the judicial side of judicial review (2003, at 256). One needs to be careful, however, not to overstate this contrast and derive from it too strong differences, since the legislative aspect can outstand in the context of the American model.

of facts that a real case supposedly conveys. This inference, though, seems overstated and does not give much attention to the counter-empirical claim that the factual richness of a constitutional controversy may not necessarily depend on the individual case. Concrete review may be, at least sometimes, as dry as abstract review, whereas abstract review may be, at least sometimes, as factually multicolored as concrete cases. Even if, statistically, this contrast holds some grain of truth, the quick causal inference is unconvincing.

Last, recent institutional creations, undertaken by a movement that came to be known as "commonwealth constitutionalism," gave rise to a third and fresh distinction that tries to apprehend the weight of judicial review: extant systems would range between weak and strong models. Weak models respond to and seek to alleviate the populist anxiety with judicial supremacy vis-à-vis elected parliaments. That is, instead of granting the court what is believed to be the "last word" on constitutional meaning (as "strong" models would do), it creates an institutional escape valve for parliaments to react against the judicial decision. This dichotomy runs parallel to the two previous ones: the classical versions of both the American and the Kelsenian models are instantiations of "strong" review, as opposed to the "weak" ones.[7]

The angle I want to focus on in this chapter does not stem from these large classificatory categories. I do not assume they are inconsequential for deliberation.[8] However, there is much more to be told about the differences and similarities of the extant systems.[9] The emphasis on those categories tends to obscure rather than illuminate.[10] Behind them, many less visible micro-devices are more significant in assisting a court to deliberate. They offer a richer template for institutional improvement than these dichotomies might suggest. These devices do not necessarily follow those orthodox

---

[7] See Gardbaum (2001 and 2010). "Weak" models of judicial review are the ones created by the "Canadian Charter of Rights and Freedoms" (1982), the "New Zealand Bill of Rights Act" (1990), and the "UK Human Rights Act" (1998). One could still mention a fourth relevant distinction, between the a priori or preventive and the a posteriori or repressive mode of constitutionality control. Basically, the former takes place before the enactment of a legislative bill into law, and the latter may happen afterwards. Despite being important, all well-known systems of judicial scrutiny are repressive, whereas preventive mechanisms are usually located elsewhere, especially within an elected parliament. The French Constitutional Council is the usual example of a quasi-judicial body located inside the legislature and operating a priori review (Stone-Sweet, 2000).

[8] When Ferejohn and Pasquino praise the European model for being internally more "deliberative," they are actually pointing to other causal factors (mainly to the mode of appointment and the pressure for consensus), not to those grand variables (2003).

[9] Silva (2009) has already advanced such point: "as important as these dichotomies is the analysis about how deliberation takes place within courts in charge of probing the constitutionality of legislation" (author's translation).

[10] Comparative politics provide a useful analogy to the obscuring causal diagnosis that canonical categories may generate: the distinction between presidentialism and parliamentarism, for example, has usually been thought to be the definitive factor to establish the relationship between parliaments and executives. Later research, though, demonstrated a less linear picture (see Przeworski et al., 1996)

dichotomies and are not prototypical of any of them. They can enrich the classificatory repertoire of comparative law.

What, then, are the central incentives to deliberation? At the macro level, some of the common denominators assumed at the outset—the absence of elections, the small multi-member format and inertia—outline a decision-making setting that, according to the proponents of such arrangement, is more favorable to deliberation. But what else may trigger a distinct deliberative performance? What set of institutional devices may enable the court to spark public contestation, promote collegial engagement, and craft a deliberative written decision?

This chapter furnishes a tentative answer. It offers a comprehensive, if concise, picture of the most relevant choices a designer needs to make. Apart from those three minimal features, everything else is open to question. If deliberation is a goal to be pursued and strengthened, none of the following choices should be taken for granted.

The chapter is structured in five additional sections. The next section explores the notion of facilitators of deliberative performance. The four subsequent sections then enumerate four types of institutional devices: those that have a constitutive function, and those that mold the pre-decisional, decisional, and post-decisional phases.

2. INSTITUTIONAL DESIGN AS A FACILITATOR OF DELIBERATIVE PERFORMANCE

Isolating the chief institutional predictors of political behavior would be the central ambition of hardcore institutionalist studies. They try to map the causalities of political processes by controlling the variations between procedural devices, treated as independent variables, and the respective outcomes. Culturalist studies, at the other end of the spectrum, adopt the opposite approach to political behavior. It is culture, or a set of shared beliefs and values, rather than institutions that can ultimately diagnose what causes what in politics. Such dichotomy may be overstretched, but it does illuminate one important theoretical axis through which social sciences read and elucidate political phenomena. To avoid the risk of cultural or institutional determinism, hybrid approaches tend to reach a mix of both types of explanation. They make concessions on both sides.

Any prescription of institutional design presupposes some sort of explanatory theory of political behavior.[11] The notion of facilitators of deliberative

---

[11] This stance is valid even to those institutional devices that are justified by an intrinsic value. One cannot be ignorant of the likely results that institutions, however morally laudable, may produce. As Ferejohn and Pasquino have contended: "If we want to encourage restraint and judicial patience and forbearance

performance, presented by the current chapter, espouses that mixed methodological premise. It recognizes that there are limits to how far deliberation can be improved by way of inventing or reforming institutions. Deep improvements would also demand proper ethics—shared commitments that regulate conduct—of the type described in the previous chapter.[12]

Institutional design is, as modern law, a "purposeful enterprise."[13] It engineers processes in the shadow of some plausible assumption of political behavior. I do not assume judges are paragons of virtue, in perfect line with the ethics described earlier. That would, to some extent, turn design futile.[14] One of the tasks of deliberation-oriented design, therefore, should be to minimize the incentives for judges to behave otherwise.

Procedural devices are forces among others to exert pressure on political behavior. The resultant vector will depend on how the devices and the attitudes of the individuals who operate them interact. In any event, it is of fundamental importance to perceive whether and how institutional devices favor or hinder deliberation, or, borrowing the words of Duverger, whether they function as an "accelerator" or a "brake."[15] Irrespective of the attitudes of judges, as Ferejohn warns, it is sensible to search for an institutional setting that is not obstructive of the deliberative project.[16] The link is bi-directional: proper devices tend to encourage deliberative attitudes; the right attitudes may lead to a constant refinement of the procedures themselves. A well-designed court might surely

---

to deliberate internally, we need to understand the circumstances in which courts will tend voluntarily to adopt internal deliberative practice. That is, we need an explanatory theory of deliberative practice. Drawing upon the European experiences, the elements of such a theory seem close at hand" (2004, 1702). As noted earlier, however, they reduce their analysis to the mode of appointment and tenure as the chief mechanisms from where deliberation would tend to follow or not.

[12] "Going further will require more attention to what we might call democratic ethics—norms that aim to regulate how people behave in deliberating, deciding, interpreting, criticizing, and carrying out public courses of action" (Ferejohn, 2000, at 87).

[13] Fuller (1968). The very idea of design, of rationally intervening in the political world to accomplish desirable ends, is part of the modernist ambition that constitutionalism evokes in the realm of politics (Hirschl, 2008). Lutz sums that up: "Constitutionalism says that we must do the best we can in an imperfect world that we hope we can improve" (2006, at 244).

[14] Not entirely futile, for sure. Although a proper ethics is an important part of deliberative performance, there must be some "procedural assurance" for deliberation to be constituted in the first place. As Ferejohn warns, "what shape that ethical system would need to take will depend on what it is that institutions cannot reliably do" (2000, 75). And Murphy points out to the limit of design itself: "Indeed, all constitutional designers must take culture into account. It may be malleable, but not infinitely so" (2008, at 1320).

[15] As Duverger argued with respect to electoral systems: "The influence of electoral systems could be compared to a brake or an accelerator. The multiplication of parties which arises from other factors is facilitated by one type of electoral system and hindered by another" (1964, at 205). I thank Silva (2006, at 37) for such reference.

[16] "I have nothing negative to say about an approach aimed at finding better deliberative norms or practices and instilling them in leaders as well as the broader public; indeed, I think this inquiry is equally necessary. But I think it is unwise to place too much weight on the likelihood of achieving improvements in democratic practice solely through the ethical transformations of citizens" (2000, at 100).

perform poorly, and vice versa. But this should not hide the fact that a good design is a helpful starting point.

When engaged in such an *ex ante* calculus, the institutional designer attempts to maximize the likelihood that a certain performance will be achieved (however this performance is defined). If deliberative performance is at stake, institutional design should, therefore, increase deliberative potential and block anti-deliberative tendencies. The two preceding chapters advanced three indices of deliberative performance: public contestation, collegial engagement, and deliberative written decision. I will consider each device in the light of the particular contribution it can give to these abstract goals.

The basic criterion that steers the further sections replicates the division between the three phases of deliberation: there are devices that have a specific bearing on the pre-decisional, the decisional, and the post-decisional stages. And there is, in addition, an institutional concern that comes before the pre-decisional phase. It relates to the devices that are constitutive of the core features of the institution itself.

The list, for sure, does not exhaust all that must be handled in designing a court, but selectively comprise those that more directly impact, among other tasks, deliberative performance. It combines, to some extent, institutional design "writ large" and "writ small."[17] The former refers to large-scale choices—like the ones that inspire the mainstream classifications briefly described above—whereas the latter is related to small-scale rules that need to be enacted once the grand variables are set. They allow us to envision incremental reforms that can be done outside the polemical foundational variables.[18] The distinction, for sure, is not one of kind but of degree. And as we move along the spectrum from the constitutive to the post-decisional devices, their nature also tends to move from writ large to writ small. Most variables will show that significant deliberative improvements may require "institutional tinkering"[19] rather than monumental redesigns.

Finally, devices should also be perceived according to whom their designer is or should be. When considering the amalgam of elements that shape a constitutional court, we can note that some are defined exogenously (by an exterior actor, which can be both the constitutional maker and the legislator) and others endogenously, through self-regulation. And among the endogenous elements, one should still distinguish between those devices that are set in advance as general internal rules, and those that are set in a case-by-case basis.

---

[17] See Vermeule (2007) and Vermeule and Garrett (2001).

[18] Vermeule and Garrett, for example, bypass the controversy upon foundational design. As small scale and incremental reformists, they try to improve the interpretive capacity of Congress through institutional mechanisms that all interpretive theories would share, mechanisms that may stimulate "the right quantity and quality of congressional deliberation on constitutional questions" (2001, at 1277).

[19] Murphy, 2008, at 1336.

There might be an institutional wisdom in letting some devices be subject to flexible self-regulation, which enhances the notion of design as a permanent endeavor rather than a fixed master plan. It enables the court to adjust different strategies to different circumstances, to test and manage its own procedures without the need for outer mobilization for reform.[20] How much of the institutional design should be decided by external sources (constitutional or legislative) and by the court itself is an important normative question that is answered locally.

The exact causal relationship between the listed variables of institutional design hinges on empirical test. Due to the lack of stock of empirical evidence about the connection between judicial behavior and each device, let alone the interaction between variables, the chapter plays with conjectures that draw upon largely accepted knowledge about plausible correlations.[21] The state of the art of our discipline forbids categorical conclusions on each one. If, on the one hand, we are still not able to discern strong causalities, some correlations are visible from comparative experience.[22] We can, at least, single out the main causative agents that matter for deliberation, even if we are not sure about the aggregate weight or the exact net effect they will have in each circumstance.

Institutional design invariably comprises trade-offs. That is why the language of balance pervades such discussion, a recognition that the multiple conflicting purposes cannot be simultaneously obtained. The tensions may happen within a single device or across different devices. I will try to illuminate the non-optimal choices the designer needs to make, the comparative costs and benefits she would need to handle. There is no golden bullet for shaping a deliberative constitutional court. Variables must be contextually tailored according to the priorities and emphases of each political community. The following sections, in sum, chart the institutional devices that increase or decrease the likelihood of deliberation. They provide a deliberative toolkit from which diverse courts could be customized. The main building blocks, I believe, are certainly there.

The following analysis, in sum, raises a set of empirical questions but does not seek to answer them. It does so not only because specific recommendations would depend on empirical tests and, as an argument for middle-level

---

[20] The leeway of self-regulation enables the court, as the horticultural metaphor provided by Eskridge and Ferejohn suggests, to be its own "gardener": "the horticultural perspective requires that the designer or her associates be stakeholders with an ongoing relationship to the design" (2008, at 1273).

[21] What Vermeule claims about the incorporation of "lay justices" into the US Supreme Court could certainly be more broadly generalized: "On the present state of empirical knowledge we can do little better than guess at these things. What I have emphasized, however, is that our current practices already and inevitably embody a guess about the same questions" (Vermeule, 2006, at 33).

[22] See Ferejohn and Pasquino, 2004, at 1702.

normative theory, it should overstep that boundary. It does so also because a constitutional court can be more than one type of deliberator. Choices on the different emphases and priorities are hardly, in the abstract, better than others. I do not, therefore, make concrete suggestions for reform.[23] Neither do I take a definitive stand on any of the alternatives. If anything, the chapter demands a conscious choice with regard to each of the variables.

3. CONSTITUTIVE DEVICES

Devices	Dilemma
i. Institutional location	Between specialized and non-specialized jurisdiction
ii. Number of decision-makers	Between the few and the "too few"
iii. Character of decision-makers	Between plurality and homogeneity
iv. Mode of appointment	Between partisan and consensual
v. Tenure	Between life tenure and fixed term

i. Institutional location

The introduction of the chapter outlined the traditional comparative categories of constitutional courts, but it omitted an important one: whether the apex court is a specialist in constitutional matters or a generalist. The two "ideal types" of existing constitutional courts, according to this conventional typology, actually conflate a triad of features: the Kelsenian model places concentrated and abstract review in a specialist court, whereas the American model corresponds to diffuse and concrete control, with a non-specialist apex court in charge of processing the ultimate appeal.[24] From this biased classificatory starting point, outlier systems are classified as "mixed."[25] Again, these are different features that need to be disaggregated.

Specialist constitutional courts have usually been associated with civil law countries, whereas generalist supreme courts have been connected to the common law tradition, which has resisted specialization. The reason for this

---

[23] Reforms like the ones proposed, for example, by Vermeule (2006), Zurn (2007), or Ghosh (2010).

[24] Walker provides a more refined typology of comparative constitutional design. He points to two axis of variation: on the horizontal, related to functional organization, we find generalist and specialist courts; on the vertical, related to the different levels of government, appellate jurisdiction may be centralized of decentralized. Crossing these two axes, he finds four archetypes (2010, at 34–35).

[25] Specialist constitutional courts may do more than just abstract control, in which the litigants have direct access to the court's original jurisdiction. Some also do concrete review, when ordinary cases that raise a constitutional incident are referred to the court, which is the case of Germany, Spain, and Italy (Walker, 2010, at 42).

coupling is less derived from the logical necessity of either legal family, and more attributable to the historical tendencies at the moment these courts were created.[26]

The pertinent normative inquiry, here, asks whether there is any deliberative benefit in a specialized jurisdiction. Conventional wisdom on this matter holds that non-specialist courts, which cumulate constitutional and ordinary jurisdictions, let the former type of case submerge under the latter type. Constitutional review becomes just one more competence diluted among many others. This would have two downsides.

First, from the epistemic point of view, the non-specialist court would be likely to have a lower capacity to grasp the "distinctive type of constitutional case" and its corresponding "distinctive type of constitutional reasoning."[27] Some anecdotal evidence supports the hypothesis, for example, that the existing non-specialist supreme courts tend to get more entangled in the technicalities of legalist reasoning than specialist ones, and to miss the constitutional complexity of the case. Nevertheless, such undesirable consequence cannot be attributable to the mere lack of specialization so quickly. Other underneath variables had not been investigated.[28] The advantage of non-specialized courts, one could retort, would be the possibility of dealing with the legal system as a comprehensive unit, rather than just a fraction of it. That, in turn, could be a more effective institutional strategy to pursue the ideal of integrity.[29]

Second, the objection to a generalist court maintains that, regardless of the greater or lower epistemic capacity of judges, the public would tend to ignore the constitutional distinctiveness and salience of cases that get intermingled with others. The lack of focus on the cases of constitutional magnitude, therefore, would hamper the court's ability to play a more relevant function from the educative point of view.

ii. Number of decision-makers

Historically, the size of a constitutional court, let alone other institutional factors, has rarely been determined by a theoretically informed reflection

---

[26] As Walker recognizes: "Read differently, therefore, the overall trend may be a common historical one rather than a family-specific one. The specialist constitutional courts, including the new South African court, are typically a phenomenon of the 20th and 21st centuries as much as they are products of the civilian tradition, while the generalist Supreme Courts are typically creatures of the 18th and 19th centuries as much as they are products of the common law tradition" (2010, at 43).

[27] Walker, 2010, at 46–47.

[28] To investigate who the judges are, for example, may also raise plausible correlations. Irrespective of the court's specialization, differences in legal reasoning can also be found between courts that are composed by career judges and courts composed by judges that have a more plural professional background. While the former would be more inclined to arcane legal details, the latter would be more open to a flexible argumentative approach.

[29] As Dworkin (1986) defines it.

about institutional function.[30] Instead, political struggles,[31] path-dependence or managerial concerns can better explain why numerical choices were made.[32] The question of the optimal size of a deliberative forum, however, defines one of its crucial features and circumscribes what such a forum can plausibly be expected to do.[33]

There is an abundant literature in political science, inspired by Condorcet,[34] that discusses how the number of heads may impact upon the epistemic capacity of decision-making bodies. Some defend the benefits of "the many" while others point to the qualities of "the few." There is no body of research, however, with precise recommendations with respect to constitutional courts and the specific role they are supposed to discharge.

Specifying the exact number of a decision-making body presupposes a clear notion of what expectations are in play. The outcomes that deliberation is deemed to produce, as we have seen, are multiple. What is more, we may perceive that the variation in number may favor one objective at the expense of the other. There is no way out of a cost and benefit analysis of the many and of the few. Such a purely quantitative question does not have to reach a clear-cut number, but distinct patterns tend, indeed, to produce different implications. Collegiate bodies of 3, of 15, of 50, or of 500 members are, each of them, better at performing some tasks rather than others. Courts have historically ranged between the two first magnitudes, but one does not need to take it as a given.

Conventional wisdom, again, states that the main trade-off exists between the purpose of uniformity and consensus, on the one hand, and, on the other, the promotion of the openness and multivocity of the law, which would also raise the probability of a more accurate decision.

As the group grows, the greater would be the chances of someone expressing disagreement and, even if falling short of consensus in the end, of refining the conflicting positions.[35] Larger groups, moreover, tend to increase, other things considered, the amount and quality of available information. These epistemic gains with size are not illimitable though. At some point, the group "may become so large as to inhibit the productive exchange of information

---

[30] See Hessick and Jordan (2009).

[31] Court-packing plans are not just an anecdotal episode of Roosevelt's tense relationships with the US Supreme Court during the 1930's, but can be found as a recurrent measure of other authoritarian regimes to curb the authority of courts (see, for example, the cases of Brazil and Argentina).

[32] For an introductory account about the question about this quantitative question, see Orth, 2006.

[33] "Whether chosen deliberately or by happenstance, the size of the court has institutional consequences" (Hessick and Jordan, 2009, at 708).

[34] On the "jury theorem," see, for example, Estlund, Waldron, Grofman, and Feld (1989), or Kornhauser and Sager (1993).

[35] "The presence of a devil's advocate forces a group to test assumptions and can generally reduce the incidence of deliberative failures like groupthink and informational cascades" (Hessick and Jordan, 2009, at 681).

through deliberation, thus undercutting the informational benefits of a larger size."[36]

The likelihood of agreement, if not entirely dependent on the number of deliberators, certainly has a plausible bearing on it. A small size reduces the danger of the "too many cooks in the kitchen syndrome," as Shapiro has put it.[37] The lesser the number, however, the more a body can be perceived as non-representative of the plurality of positions that a heterogeneous society may have, and the lower the chances to come up with solutions that adequately respond to that heterogeneity.

Some pathologies of will-formation,[38] which lead to less than autonomous individual decisions, are more likely to emerge in large bodies, others in small bodies.[39] This fine-tuning may be made by a flexible regulation of the circumstances when the court should decide in a more numerous plenum, or in smaller colleges or panels.[40]

The numerical question involves, therefore, not only a delicate balance between the communitarian and the epistemic promises of deliberation, but also between what aspects of the epistemic promise itself (which comprise informing, clarifying, creating original solutions and reaching the best answer) should be prioritized.[41] Deciding on "which bundle of

---

[36] Hessick and Jordan, 2009, at 649. This article surveys an extensive social science and social psychology literature on decision-making and its relationship with size. Furthermore, increasing the size of the group may generate a free-rider problem: the more diluted the individual weight, the lesser incentive to be informed and the lower the individual competence (Mukhopadhaya, 2003).

[37] Shapiro, 2002, at 199.

[38] Like group-think, herding, cascades, polarization, and adaptive preferences (see Vermeule, 2006).

[39] The size will be important for reaching accuracy, thus, inasmuch as the group dynamics does not lead to deliberative failures. Alarie, Green, and Iacobucci note that: "Certain kinds of deliberation call for fewer judges, all things equal. For example, suppose that one judge tends to be consistently persuaded by another. Having both on the same panel does not add to accuracy relative to one, since in effect there is only one decision that affects both votes. On the other hand, other kinds of deliberations call for more judges. Suppose that each judge has some probability of thinking of some insight that when shared with other judges is not decisive, but increases other judges' probability of reaching the correct outcome" (2011, at 11).

[40] One advantage of a court that sits *en banc* is to prevent criticisms about how the composition of the panel was determinant for the outcome. This has been a cutting discussion in the context of the UK Supreme Court. For a description of the debate about the number of judges that should sit in panels of the UK Supreme Court see Le Sueur (2008). Alarie et al. (2011), for example, carry out a case-study on the Canadian Supreme Court and defend the discretionary definition of panel size. Such leeway would empower the institution to tailor the appropriate kind of deliberative environment for each circumstance, and intelligently allocate its scarce institutional energy.

[41] A larger size, for Hessick and Jordan, tends to promote diversity and accuracy at the cost of decreasing the prospects of consensus and efficiency, of inhibiting participation and impairing collegiality. Hence, the inevitable cost-benefit balancing: "The Court is of optimal size when the marginal benefit of the addition of a Justice equals its marginal cost. But ascertaining that size is easier said than done. To start, it is difficult to determine what size would maximize any particular benefit in isolation. That difficulty is greatly exacerbated by the interaction of competing benefits... How to set the size therefore depends on how we prioritize the goals of the Court" (2009, at 696).

institutional goals is most valuable"[42] does not admit a universally valid answer.

iii. Character of decision-makers

One of the most striking flags of judicial reform debates in recent times accents the value of diversity.[43] The previous section dealt with numerical diversity. However, this is not just about numbers.[44] Who should sit in a constitutional court matters in a more serious way. What other sorts of plurality should the designer of a deliberative court promote? Diversity has an obvious connection to the deliberative potential of an institution. It is widely contended and, other things considered, empirically demonstrated,[45] that plural forums tend to be more deliberative and more proficient in bringing a greater variety of experiences and perceptions to the fore.[46]

Diverse groups, it is believed, create a tension that is somewhat analogous to the one that exists between the purely numerical variations seen above: a more plural body would be more porous to the variety of arguments that a controversy may have; nonetheless, the prospects of communicative breakdown, intractable disagreement, and resistance to persuasion, again, are higher.[47]

The character of deliberators is an institutional variable that encompasses the tension between the epistemic and communitarian promises of deliberation, but goes beyond them. A plural court, even more than a simply numerous one, can symbolize the recognition that interpreting and applying the law is an enterprise that includes different kinds of voices. The psychological and educative promises, therefore, are also at stake. To have an African descendant, a "wise Latina woman,"[48] an ex-refugee, or anti-apartheid fighter[49] within the court would be an expressive achievement of courts in heterogeneous societies.

[42] Hessick and Jordan, 2009, at 649.

[43] In the UK, for example, the case for a more diverse judiciary does not just seek equality of opportunity or to reflect the diversity of the society. It also has an epistemic reason: "Judges drawn from a wide range of backgrounds and life experiences will bring varying perspectives to bear on critical legal issues" (see "The Report of the Advisory Panel on Judicial Diversity 2010"). Walker has also asserted the importance of a non-homogenous court. For him, it should be "broadly representative of the population it serves" and incorporate "diverse range of backgrounds, experiences and perspectives" (Walker, 2010, at 51).

[44] "A court may be both large and homogeneous" (Hessick and Jordan, 2009, at 682).

[45] Williams and O'Reilly (1998) provide an extensive literature review on the effects of diversity on decision-making. There is consolidated evidence showing that diversity can increase group performance, depending on the nature of the task.

[46] On how that standard would apply to measure the deliberative quality of the UK House of Lords, see Parkinson, 2007, 380.

[47] Hessick and Jordan, 2009, at 689.

[48] As Justice Sottomayor professed in a lecture in 2001: "I would hope that a wise Latina woman with the richness of her experiences would more often than not reach a better conclusion than a white male who hasn't lived that life" (Sottomayor, 2009).

[49] Like Justices Sachs and Yacoob, from the South African Constitutional Court.

Diversity, then, is expected to play a heavy role. It is defended as an end in itself, since it reputedly nurtures symbolic inclusion of various groups,[50] and as a means both to social acceptance and to accuracy of decisions. A diverse court would not, thus, simply represent multiple demographic groups and, hence, be more likely to attain their compliance. It would also make their voices actually partake in the final decision, the content and quality of which, as a consequence, would likely be superior.[51]

The difficulty, however, is that demographic diversity and symbolic representation do not necessarily lead to informational diversity or productive communication upon which the epistemic promise depends. Such happy overlap is not at all obvious. On the contrary, in certain contexts, diversity may, among other things, raise "communication barriers" and trigger "stereotyping."[52] A court could only evade such traps and fully capitalize on diversity if some measure of collegiality impregnates its decisional culture.[53]

There are, thus, multiple signals of diversity that can be taken onboard to boost deliberation: gender, race, ethnicity, geographical, and socio-economic origin are the most obvious. Its disruptive tendencies may be domesticated or reduced by a collegial culture. There is, though, a less intuitive signal that deserves serious consideration. It is usually assumed that constitutional courts should be populated with professional lawyers or career judges. Constitutional scrutiny, under this assumption, would be a matter for trained experts in law. This is a central reason why courts are seen as elitist bodies that operate under a narrow frame of mind. What benefits, if any, are there in a court that, alongside lawyers, is also composed by non-elected historians, ethicists, natural scientists, economists, and so on? Does professional

---

[50] "If the value of diversity is symbolic inclusion, then the only forms of diversity we value are those whose symbolism matters" (Hessick and Jordan, 2009, at 659).

[51] Willi argues that diversity does not only promote "physical representation" but "representation of voice" (2006, at 1274). Iffil shares such view and reminds that looking at minority judges just as role models would serve to legitimate the status quo and fail to perceive the transformative contribution they can make (2000, at 479). For Edwards, diversity would produce "a powerful impact on how non-minority judges, lawyers, and litigants view minority persons" and broaden "the variety of voices and perspectives in the deliberative process" (2002, at 329). Sherry, for example, claims that women can make a peculiar contribution by their (i) presence—helping to break the gender stereotypes, by their (ii) participation—reducing the gender-biased outcomes due to their greater empathy to women's problems, and by their (iii) perspective—adding a unique way of seeing the world, one that is more contextual and virtuous-based, as opposed to the abstract rights-based views. Their presence and participation are important as a corrective for non-ideal conditions, i.e., situations where discrimination is entrenched. Their perspective, however, is desirable even in ideal contexts (Sherry, 1986).

[52] Hessick and Jordan, 2009, at 682.

[53] Edwards, 2003, at 1669. In another article, Edwards also indicate the epistemic benefit and collegiality: "A deliberative process enhanced by collegiality and a broad range or perspectives necessarily results in better and more nuanced opinions" (2002, at 329). Hessick and Jordan echo the same idea: "Collegial groups are better at promoting participation by all members, at avoiding stereotyping and communication breakdowns that can accompany demographic diversification" (2009, at 684).

plurality aggregate competence to constitutional scrutiny? Do we lose something by relaxing the assumption that all constitutional judges should be professional lawyers?

For Vermeule, professional diversity would alleviate the "likemindedness that arises from common professional training"[54]—an elementary cause of deliberative collapse—and further increase the epistemic capacity of the court.[55] It would, in other words, on top of "diluting groupthink" and avoiding deliberative pathologies like herding, cascades and polarization, internalize sources of non-legal knowledge that are functional for good constitutional decisions.[56] The harms of professional homogeneity and pressure for conformity cannot be compensated by the conventional case-by-case mechanisms for the incorporation of expertise (like amicus briefs, expert witnesses, and so on). Interlocutors and decision-makers play distinct roles in deliberation, and having one or more non-legal experts among the decision-makers would be, according to Vermeule, a substantial technocratic improvement.[57]

To sum up, the size of the body and the plurality of decision-makers are intimately connected. Indeed, the sheer number is itself a signal of plurality. A causal matrix combining the two variables could illuminate the many variations between both poles: from more plural and more numerous to more homogeneous and smaller bodies. The latter would be more likely to reach consensus, hence clarity and certainty. The former would fare better in respect of the other deliberative promises, but only up to the point where the benefits of numerical and character-based plurality are more likely to break down.

Theories of deliberative democracy put a lot of hope on the diversity of deliberators.[58] If we assume that a constitutional court, in the light of its complex institutional assignment, cannot be too numerous,[59] there will be an inexorable limit on how plural and representative it can be. Elected parliaments, in that respect, would certainly score higher, however flawed the

---

[54] Vermeule, 2006, at 10.

[55] "In a range of settings, deliberation among the likeminded can make decisions worse, not better, than voting without deliberation" (Vermeule, 2006, at 20).

[56] Vermeule, 2006, at 21.

[57] ". . . differing views must be incorporated into the Court's decisionmaking process through structural representation—that there is no close substitute for having people of different views actually in the room where decisions are made" (Vermeule, 2006, at 26). For an argument that radicalizes the idea of "lay justices," based on the idea of representation rather than on expertise, like Vermeule's, see Ghosh (2010). He proposes a "Citizens' Court" in the form of a constitutional jury, which would enhance the overall legitimacy of the political system.

[58] See, for example, Fishkin (2009) and his idea of public consultation.

[59] In other words, if we assume that it cannot go beyond the approximate pattern of "the few," as I briefly mentioned at the beginning of the chapter.

electoral system happens to be. Diversity of decision-makers, limited though it may inescapably be in a constitutional court, can still augment the potential of the deliberation that takes place in such a setting.[60] The two following devices—mode of appointment and tenure—are also instrumental for that purpose.[61]

iv. Mode of appointment

In order to implement the value of diversity, or any other value regarding who should sit in a constitutional court, a procedure of appointment must be settled. Apart from an instrument for implementing the former variable (the character of judges), appointment may be a legitimating tool in itself: the nature of the political process that leads to appointment may open broader or narrower avenues for participation of diverse actors.[62] This is a primary normative question of institutional design: how should we choose those who will perform a specific function?

The existing techniques of appointment for constitutional courts tend to follow that initial dichotomy between the American and the European models: in the former, the president nominates and a Senate hearing confirms the nomination; in the latter, a more complex involvement of the houses of parliament takes place.[63] More importantly, the former tends to be a highly partisan process,[64] whereas the latter adopts mechanisms for a consensual bi-partisan decision.[65] Extant systems vary between the two ideal types.

Partisanship is at odds with deliberation. The sincere effort to argue and to persuade, to listen and to reflect upon the soundness of your own position in contrast to the alternative ones, is inimical to a default commitment to a pre-defined group in virtue of the mere membership to that group. Elections,

---

[60] Empirical researches indicate the number of deliberators that tends to optimize diversity with effective inter-personal engagement: "Finding the ideal mix of diversity and size requires the maximization of some combination of informational perspectives and participation in the group process. On this basis, many studies have concluded that *groups of four to six members* can best incorporate the perspectives of all members" (Hessick and Jordan, 2009, at 684, emphasis added).

[61] Although this section is entitled "character of decision-makers," it did not talk about "character traits" as conventionally uttered in virtue ethics. For a defence of virtues, rather than number and diversity, as a possible criterion for the selection and appointment of decision-makers, see Solum, 2004b and 2004c.

[62] "While courts are legislating, all of us have a legitimate interest in who sits on them" (Ferejohn, 2002, at 43).

[63] Some systems also involve the judiciary itself in the process of nomination, or other political actors. See, for example, the cases of the Chilean and Colombian constitutional courts. Different political actors are responsible for appointing for a specific number of slots in these courts.

[64] In the US, interest groups fight for staffing the courts with judges that embrace jurisprudential opinions that match their ideological positions: "Not surprisingly, it is easy to characterize judges and courts in partisan terms within such a system" (Ferejohn, 2002, at 64–65).

[65] The European model is less politicized in the partisan sense. For a comparative table about the recruitment and composition of European constitutional courts, see Stone-Sweet, 2000, at 49.

therefore, at least of the type that modern democracies consolidated—structured around political parties and the permission of re-election—cannot be replicated by the court. Elections may make judges vulnerable to behavioral incentives that are not easy to perceive or to control, and, besides, make them accountable to public opinion in a pernicious way. Elections would more likely be, in fact, a disincentive for deliberation. Such an instrument, however, does not need to be discarded out of hand. Impartial adjudication may not survive some kinds of elections, but there is little comparative experimentation to allow for quick generalizations. If plurality is one of the values to be pursued, a more carefully tailored combination of electoral techniques and delegation chains could profitably be tested.[66]

The defects of the current American mode of appointment have been widely voiced.[67] The suggested correctives are usually drawn from the empirical knowledge generated by European courts. Their accumulated experience turned into the current conventional wisdom of institutional behavior: supermajority appointment methods attract non-partisan members.[68] As far as their power of lawmaking is concerned, European courts are as political as any other. Their judges, however, tend to be "jurisprudential moderates by design"[69] rather than "ideological apologists."[70] The basic behavioral assumption of such a reform proposal is: the more centrist the court, the more inclined to deliberate; the more partisan and polarized, the opposite ensues, which would explain the non-deliberative reputation of the US Supreme Court. This empirical rule may be more or less generalizable in different contexts.

Instead of supermajorities, a well-known alternative way for protecting nominations against toxic partisanship and politicking are the "judicial appointment commissions."[71] Because such body is relatively insulated, or at least not controlled by the parties in power, the process is less likely to be politicized and more capable to promote more diversity.

The challenge for the designer concerned with deliberation is to craft a procedure that increases the chances of an optimal composition of the court, however it is defined by the inquiry underscored in the previous section. She

---

[66] To be sure, part of the members of the Chilean Constitutional Court, for example, is elected by the houses of parliament and the supreme court.

[67] The mode of appointment of the American Supreme Court has been widely criticized by a number of authors. Suggestions of change are prolific. For recent examples, see Ferejohn (2002), Ferejohn and Pasquino (2004), Dworkin (2006), and Eisgruber (2009).

[68] Ferejohn, 2002, at 66.   [69] Ferejohn, 2002b, at 67.

[70] Ferejohn, 2002, at 58. See also Ferejohn and Pasquino, 2004, at 1701.

[71] The UK Constitutional Reform Act 2005 created a judicial appointment commission in order to enhance judicial independence. Although the members of the UK Supreme Court are not selected by such commission, this arrangement stimulates reflection about less partisan forms of appointment to top courts.

will need to decide who should have the power to appoint and how discretionally this power should be exercised. If she has reasons not to trust that the appointer will make a judicious use of that power, such prerogative could be more strictly regulated. If diversity of whatever sort is to shape the court, the appointment procedure needs to be planned having these considerations in mind. Apart from being instrumental for promoting the deliberative promises that lurk behind the composition of the court, it can also realize a legitimating function of the court itself.

v. Tenure

One of the central instruments to forge judicial independence and impartiality is the guarantee that the judge will not be removed from office and will not have any concern of pleasing or upsetting a constituency. Such stability has been constructed through a single non-renewable tenure, as in European courts, or through life tenure, as in the US Supreme Court.[72] Several other variations in between, modulating the duration of the tenure or establishing an age for compulsory retirement,[73] do also exist.

Tenure and the appointment procedure are the joint mechanisms to tackle the risk of partisanship and other deliberative failures.[74] Arguably, there should be no premium for a judge who does comply with party lines, or a sanction for the one who does not. The amount of time judges stay in office and how the composition of the court is gradually and permanently renewed shape a certain group dynamics. Such dynamics, in turn, affects the quality of deliberation in positive or negative ways.

There is not much controversy about the importance of some measure of stability for the sake of collegiality. The optimal tenure model, under such behavioral assumption, should neither be too short, which would likely impede collegiality to flourish, nor too long, which would have a plausible tendency, in turn, to develop deliberative failures and to entrench intransigent positions. "Debts of deference" accumulated over time, for example, could induce "subtle, unarticulated vote trading."[75] A spirit of camaraderie could grow among groups of judges and, in turn, influence decisions in irrational ways.[76] Judicial socialization exerts a pressure towards homogenization, which would gradually diminish the epistemic weight that diversity of perspectives and opinions may play. And so on.

---

[72] For a reform proposal that changes the US system of life tenure, see Levinson (2006, chapter 4).

[73] Like the Brazilian system, in which the Constitution (art. 40) requires compulsory retirement at 70.

[74] For a defence of life tenure in UK House of Lords, see Parkinson (2007).

[75] Richman and Reynolds, quoted by Edwards, 2003, at footnote 22.

[76] Edwards, through a stronger notion of collegiality, has responded to those who "worry that, when members of a court have strong collegial relationships, judges may be reluctant to challenge colleagues

Thus, two vital questions emerge with respect to tenure. First, a designer needs to decide on tenure duration: whether it should extend for life, be fixed, or be regulated by an intermediate formula. Second, she decides how the seats will be renovated: whether there should be differentiated yet linear timings for each judge to retire, a system where larger blocs of judges get replaced at once, or some intermediary formula.

The critical shortcoming of extremely extensive tenure models, whether for life or not, is to allow for renovation at too slow a pace. It runs the risk of fossilizing positions and making the court unresponsive to fresh arguments and problems. The accountability dimension of the appointment system, moreover, gets diluted since judges entirely detach themselves from the political forces that originally appointed them. Mistakes get harder to be reversed. The court's deliberative energy and disposition is more likely to get exhausted. Its jurisprudence is plagued by long-lasting deadlock.

Life tenure, it is believed, would prevent judges from having further career plans after leaving the office, which would bias their decisions. The incentive to frame a decision with an eye on a post-office job can be alleviated through quarantine arrangements, but is inevitably a cost to be factored into the system if a shorter tenure is to be adopted. When such a system is coupled with an extremely partisan mode of appointment, like the US practice, the deliberative potential of the court is even more severely harmed: judges have the discretion to time their retirement according to the party in power and the court becomes incurably associated with partisan cleavages.[77]

4. PRE-DECISIONAL DEVICES: PROMOTING PUBLIC CONTESTATION, PREPARING FOR COLLEGIAL ENGAGEMENT

Devices	Dilemmas
vi. Docket-forming	Between discretionary and mandatory
vii. Agenda-setting	Between discretionary and mandatory
viii. Character of interlocutors	Between broader and narrower filters
ix. Mode of interaction	Form, procedure, and style

vi. Docket-forming

The pre-decisional phase starts when cases are brought to the court. There must be a decision about which and how many cases will be accepted. I refer to

---

and may join opinions to preserve personal relationships. They argue that 'less collegiality may thus increase independence—a virtue of good judging'" (Edwards, 2003, at 1646).

[77] Ferejohn and Pasquino, 2004, at 1704.

these qualitative and quantitative filters as docket-forming. Deliberation is a time-consuming enterprise, and an institution cannot be truly deliberative if that condition is not duly considered.[78] Priorities upon temporal resources, therefore, must be set.[79]

The design inquiry, here, addresses not only the optimal number of cases[80] and the relevant and opportune issues that should be addressed, but also who should take both decisions. A discretionary docket gives the court some leeway to manage both filters and more autonomy to ponder how long each case will demand on the basis of its own estimation.[81] It grants the court, additionally, the power to make its own political judgment on what constitutional issues should, either on the grounds of principle or expediency, be prioritized. The political temperature of the docket could hence be modulated.

A mandatory docket, on the other hand, despite having the risk of depriving the court of such convenient discretion, and of possibly overloading it with too many cases, may be beneficial in societies where it is reasonable to suspect that courts would perform such task in a biased and selective way, denying some unprivileged interests the opportunity to spark public contestation and to constrain the court to take a public stand on the most pressing controversies. Finally, mixed systems may combine both obligatory and discretionary jurisdictions with regard to different judicial actions.[82]

vii. Agenda-setting

Agenda-setting, as I define here, is related to the timing of decision (and of previous procedural acts) once a case was already accepted into the docket. The ordinary use of the term usually comprehends docket-forming. Conflating

---

[78] As Justice Powell has declared, the increase of the caseload may "reach the point when the competency of and craftsmanship of the Court will be perceptibly affected" (Bickel, 1973, at 14).

[79] Bickel even proposes a formula to reach the ideal docket, and factors, apart from time, the amount of pressure into the calculus: "Actual time—hours and days—is not the sole consideration. The proper equation is: burden = time + pressure. A docket of the size of the present one...does not merely exact time; it exerts pressure which drains energy and deflects attention" (1973, at 31).

[80] The workload has an obvious bearing on how meticulous the deliberation on each case can be. For evident reasons, the deliberative conditions of a court that decides twenty or thirty cases per year, like the South African Constitutional Court (see Roux, 2003, at 94), and one that decides almost a hundred thousand cases per year, like the Brazilian Supreme Court (see Veríssimo, 2008), are drastically different.

[81] The US Supreme Court, for example, uses the writ of certiorari to discretionally define its docket. The South African Constitutional Court can use both denials of direct access and denials of permission to appeal as means to manage its docket (see Klug, 2011).

[82] The Canadian Supreme Court, for example, have discretion to grant "leave of appeal" in some cases, but other must be "heard as of right." The Colombian Constitutional Court and the Brazilian Supreme Court are also hybrid with respect to discretion in docket-forming (Veríssimo, 2008).

both, however, may blur two distinct acts at stake. They are not redundant. To decide that a case will be processed is not the same as deciding when this will be done. In most constitutional courts, this distinction may seem gratuitous. It is assumed that if a case enters the docket, the court will necessarily decide within a definite timeframe, without much flexibility.

However, formally or informally, some courts have some additional leeway.[83] Again, agenda may benefit deliberation in multiple ways. The court may dose the rhythm and intensity through which a decision will be taken and public contestation will proceed. Issues that were not sufficiently debated in the public sphere, for example, may deserve to be postponed until they ripen. Instead of simply denying access to the case, the court can incorporate it into the docket but, at the same time, set a slow pace. It has a second chance, on the basis of principle or expediency, to set priorities. The power of prioritizing issues that are urgent in the public sphere might increase the quality and relevance of the public contestation managed by the court. On the other hand, the risk of discretionary agenda-setting is basically the same as discretionary docket-forming: the court may use it in unfair ways. In judicial cultures where a discriminatory predisposition exists, this may be harmful for the deliberative prospects of the court.

Discretionary docket-forming and agenda-setting make the principles of judicial passivity and of natural justice relative. For the sake of impartiality, courts are usually not allowed to choose the cases, let alone the timing. Since the core function of constitutional courts goes beyond solving individual conflicts (if this is a function at all), a strict acquiescence to those principles would significantly impoverish the other purposes such a court is supposed to pursue. With respect to the deliberative function, that blank adherence would deprive the pre-decisional phase of the flexibility and focus to which public contestation aspire, waste time with cases of lower political or legal import, and reduce the likelihood of collegial engagement and deliberative written decisions.

viii. Character of interlocutors

The choice between diversity and homogeneity does not only matter for defining who the decision-makers are. The degree of diversity of potential

---

[83] The Brazilian case provides again an interesting example. There are a number of tolerated informal practices that make it extremely difficult to predict whether a case will be decided in one, five, or more years by the Supreme Court. The Chief Justice, a position that is alternated every two years, has the power of defining the agenda. Individual judges, in turn, can interrupt public deliberation (which largely consists of public reading of individual opinions) and ask more time for himself, which could take between months or years. See Silva (2013). The US Supreme Court does not have such leeway. It has adopted an informal rule according to which it must dispose all argued cases before the recess: "This rule is designed to ensure that the court stays abreast of its workload, and it may encourage justices to reach a compromise sooner rather than later" (Hessick and Jordan, 2009, at 703).

interlocutors is also pivotal in determining the overall deliberative performance and, especially, of public contestation. Wendell Holmes once stated that "justice and high judicial performance require the company of the bench and the bar acting in concert."[84] The same advice applies for deliberative performance: openness to a various range of interlocutors may not only contribute to further increase the range of perspectives that will be addressed by the court, enhancing its epistemic capacity, but also has an important effect in terms of the psychological and educative effects of deliberation. The very same intrinsic and instrumental reasons for diversity of decision-makers, mentioned earlier, can be replicated vis-à-vis interlocutors as well.

The crucial point of this choice, therefore, is to set a list of actors that can be initiators of or contributors to a constitutional complaint.[85] In other words, it circumscribes who the court will be able to hear by way of its formal mechanisms. Although the court can always be attentive to what informal interlocutors argue in the public sphere, or even empathetically imagine points of view that were not voiced, empowering various actors to do so and increasing its formal porosity may facilitate such purpose.

Design, therefore, should devise a procedure that is versatile enough for channeling arguments from a heterogeneous set of interlocutors. Interlocutors may be of various sorts: the parties themselves, the advocates that speak on behalf of the parties and other sorts of interested actors and evidence-producers (like experts and *amici curiae*).

In this sense, individualistic rules of standing, which encapsulate reductionist definitions of "direct interest," seem to be at odds with a deliberative court.[86] As Thompson has suggested, the threshold of standing should not be too high, but rather "civic minded" and oriented to the development of the general moral principles.[87] When access to constitutional justice is reserved only for those who can afford a high "price of admission"[88]—be it political or strictly financial—the court is dispossessed of a large portion of its potential deliberative significance.[89]

---

[84] Quoted by Coleman, 1983, at 35.

[85] Instruments like "amicus curiae" and sessions of "public consultation" are well-known ways to make the court more permeable to the voices of diverse social groups.

[86] An interesting creation in that respect is the institution of Public Interest Litigation by the Indian Supreme Court, which substantially increased accessibility to the court. Mehta briefly explains: "the Court relaxes the normal legal requirements of 'standing' and 'pleading,' which require that litigation be pressed by a directly affected party or parties, and instead allows anyone to approach it seeking correction of an alleged evil or injustice. Such cases also typically involve the abandonment of adversarial fact-finding in favor of Court-appointed investigative and monitoring commissions" (2007, at 71).

[87] For Thompson, a more inclusive rule of standing would enhance judicial responsibility (2004, at 88).

[88] Thompson, 2004, at 88.

[89] Access to constitutional justice, in tune with Thompson's thoughts, can be conceptualized in the light of the ideal of participatory democracy. "Democratizing" the rules of standing, and making the value of

ix. Mode of interaction among decision-makers and interlocutors

During the pre-decisional phase, the mode of interaction between decision-makers and interlocutors may assume different forms, procedures, and styles. It structures public contestation and should supply the conditions for respectful curiosity to unfold. With respect to the form, the argument conduits of both interlocutors and decision-makers may combine face-to-face encounters in hearing sessions and written petitions. With respect to the procedure, the number of written petitions and the duration and amount of hearings may also be regulated in flexible ways in order to facilitate a broader assemblage of reasons.

On a more general level, a constitutional court needs to take some stand between the adversarial and inquisitorial styles of interaction. This is an old controversy of civil litigation. On the one hand, adversarial systems would guarantee that bilateral disputes, provided there is "equality of arms,"[90] are dealt with fairly. The judge has no duty to search for the truth, but simply to mediate between what is being said. It remains, therefore, inert. The inquisitorial principle allows the judge to more actively intervene on what is being argued by the parties. Such a principle would supposedly put impartiality under risk.

When it comes to constitutional scrutiny, it seems clear that a rigid attachment to an adversarial principle, which would force the court not only to stay silent while interlocutors speak, but also to contemplate, in order to take a decision, only what the interlocutors have said, would drastically diminish the likelihood of productive deliberation. If the court is not free to explicitly challenge the arguments of the interlocutors and to invite further response, and neither to imagine arguments that were not aired, and if the process is molded in a rigidly ritualistic and adversarial rather than in an open-ended and interactive way, its role as a deliberator drastically declines.[91]

When we talk about constitutional scrutiny, as defined in Chapter 3, we are not dealing with the elementary coordinates of adjudication. The court needs to be institutionally prepared to face polycentric issues. A polycentric problem, as Fuller defined it, can be pictured as a "spider web":[92] "A pull on one strand will distribute tensions after a complicated pattern throughout

diversity truly shape who the decision-makers and interlocutors are, may lead to courts that could hardly be called as "elitists." The example of the "acción de tutela," at the Constitutional Court of Colombia, an easy and little costly instrument to be used by any citizen, should not be detached from participatory democracy lenses (see Uprimny, 2003, at 61).

[90] Jolowicz, 2003, at 283.

[91] The South African Constitutional Court jurisprudence, for example, has already faced the question whether it can raise, regardless of the parties' arguments, a different constitutional issue in a case. Under certain conditions, it accepted to do so (Klug, 2011).

[92] Fuller, 1978, at 395.

the web as a whole." Such problems, therefore, would not fit well with a decisional method that mainly consists of distributing rights and duties in a bilateral dispute, for which adversarial tools may be serviceable.[93] Constitutional cases, more often than not, have discernible polycentric features and, indeed, could not be adequately handled by the typical principles of ordinary adjudication. Adversarial interaction, for sure, is one of them.[94]

5. DECISIONAL DEVICES: PROMOTING COLLEGIAL ENGAGEMENT

Devices	Dilemmas
x. Sessions	Between public and secret
xi. Mode of interaction	Between formal and informal, face-to-face and written
xii. Decisiveness	Between unanimity and majority

x. Sessions: between publicity and secrecy

It is an old question of deliberative theory whether external spectators should be able to watch deliberators while they interact. It is a problem that has always been faced by democracy itself. Spectators constrain the deliberators, especially when the latter feel, in some way, accountable to the former.[95] It should not be assumed, without further qualification, that deliberation must be public.[96]

The choice between publicity and secrecy, and the acceptable compromises between them, is thus a consequential one. As a general rule, a democratic culture has plenty of reasons to be suspicious of the legitimacy of secret governmental practices. Transparency is more than a powerful slogan, but a desirable mechanism of control. Nevertheless, counter-intuitive as the idea may sound, and depending on how it is implemented, transparency may also be harmful to

---

[93] Polycentric dimension is a "matter of degree": "There are polycentric elements in almost all problems submitted to adjudication" (Fuller, 1978, at 397).

[94] For Fuller "polycentric problems can often be solved, at least after a measure, by parliamentary methods which include an element of contract in the form of the political 'deal'" (1978, at 400). Although he had not deeply elaborated on what he meant by that, a constitutional court should rely on deliberation to reach such "political deal."

[95] Elster reminds that in the Athenian model of direct democracy, for example, a "democracy of orators" tends to prevail. There, orators do not intend to convince each other but only the audience who, in turn, does not speak. With the passage from a democracy of the public square to a democracy of parliament, a potentially more deliberative forum emerges. The fact that these members are accountable to constituents, though, still weakens deliberation (see Elster, 1998, at 2).

[96] For a philosophical approach to the dilemma between secrecy and publicity in deliberation, see Chambers (2004).

the quality of deliberation. Shapiro puts that eloquently: "Publicity has advantages for politics, though not unmitigated ones.... Whatever the advantages, they are not those of deliberation."[97]

Public sessions, therefore, may be an invitation to judicial demagoguery and foreclose genuine dialogue.[98] Judges may develop a public persona and a particular identity before the external audience.[99] They would have a plausible incentive to protect themselves against the "public ridicule."[100] Changing his mind, after all, may look like weakness of character or of intellect to the curious spectator. More generally, publicity runs counter to collegiality itself.[101] In order to avoid public shame or embarrassment, a judge might resist changing his mind.

A good deliberator is indifferent to personal recognition, incurious about how he will be publicly perceived.[102] Publicity does not particularly favor that individual trait. In secret sessions, in fact, deliberative flaws would simply become invisible and protected against public scrutiny. However, in public sessions, authentic deliberation might not even happen in the first place.[103] A measure of secrecy, as far as documented experience has shown, furnishes the proper institutional asepsis for deliberation to thrive. The institutional designer, therefore, must deal with the tension between publicity and

---

[97] Shapiro, 2002, at 198.

[98] Silva (2013, at 581). Justice Powell Jr. contends: "The integrity of judicial decision-making would be impaired seriously if we had to reach our judgments in the *atmosphere of an ongoing town meeting*... The confidentiality of this process assures that we will review carefully the soundness of our judgments" (2004, at 89, emphasis added).

[99] Ferejohn and Pasquino: "This 'anonymity' may well facilitate internal deliberative practices by making members amenable to compromise and mutual persuasion and not giving them a *reason to have pride* in their jurisprudential consistency as individual judges" (2004, at 1693, emphasis added). Ferejohn's reasons for internal deliberation presuppose a secret session, which would "shield members from *pressures of bribery or intimidation* from external groups" (Ferejohn, 2008, at 209, emphasis added).

[100] Justice Rehnquist follows that line: "This candor undoubtedly advances the purpose of the Conference in resolving the cases before it. No one feels at all inhibited by the possibility that any of his remarks will be quoted outside of the Conference Room, or that any of his half formed or ill conceived ideas, which all of us have at times, will be *later held up to public ridicule*" (2004, at 94–95, emphasis added).

[101] Like Sachs contended: "It would not be appropriate for me to publicize the internal debates we had amongst the eleven judges who heard the matter. Confidentiality and collegiality are integral to the proper functioning of any court" (2009, at 242).

[102] For Edwards, even the presence of a single social scientist in the conference room would harm the proper atmosphere of deliberation. He does not approve, for example, the authorization that Latour had received to observe the secret sessions of the French State Council: "I believe that the mere presence of a 'neutral,' even silent, observing anthropologist or sociologist in our deliberations would change the character and course of the deliberations among judges" (Edwards, 2003, at 1688).

[103] Judicial deliberation in public is, comparatively, a rare feature of constitutional courts. The Brazilian Supreme Court, nonetheless, has established this *sui generis* tradition for several decades. Letting the judges deliberate in public has been considered, by a certain Brazilian common sense, an exemplar model of transparency. An observer, however, can easily diagnose the artificiality of a public encounter that was

secrecy.[104] Some compromise between both might be profitably struck. Secrecy combined with future disclosure is, for Freund, the best way to do that.[105]

xi. Mode of interaction: between face-to-face and written, formal and informal

The dilemma between publicity and secrecy is not the only one to perturb the institutional designer when it comes to nudging collegial engagement. The interaction among decision-makers can be further regulated. Ingrained practices may both foster or suppress deliberation. The core deliberative promise of the decisional phase is the epistemic one, and an optimal mode for enhancing it may take different forms.

Reasons may be exchanged, again, through a face-to-face interaction and through written drafts.[106] In the latter case, part of the decisional phase would be merged with the post-decisional task of decision-drafting. Furthermore, decisional interaction may happen formally, through more disciplined conventions, and informally.[107] Which combination of these variables is more beneficial to deliberation is the hard question to be faced by each constitutional court.

---

transformed into a lengthy and non-interactive reading session of individual opinions, which damages not only the quality of deliberation, but also the rationality of the final decision itself. See Silva (2013).

[104] For an approach about the parliamentary context, see Bessette (1994).

[105] Paul Freund states: "What is wanted is an accommodation of two truths: that perfect candor in the conferences preceding judgments requires secrecy and that, in Lord Acton's phrase, whatever is secret degenerates... The problem of reconciliation has been met satisfactorily in other contexts: diplomatic correspondence is made public after an interval; Madison's notes of the debates in the Constitutional Convention were published a generation after the event" (Introduction to Bickel, 1957, at xvi). The practice of recording secret sessions for future disclosure, as practiced by the US Federal Reserve, is an example of middle ground. If a similar technique proves to mitigate the harms of publicity without undermining the conditions for deliberation in a constitutional court, that solution could be a wise answer to the dilemma. It would promote a differential sort of transparency, even if delayed. About the US Federal Reserve practices, see Ehrmann and Fratzscher (2005).

[106] The US Supreme Court, for example, adopts a blend of mechanisms: it starts by face-to-face "closed-door case conference," when majority opinion is defined, and is followed by months of opinion drafts circulation "deliberation-by-text" (Gastil, 2008, at 144). Internal communication, therefore, proceeds through written memos to the conference; circulation of draft opinions; comments upon the drafts. The conference, as several testimonies have revealed, have increasingly become a quick exchange to check whether there is consensus or not, not to actually argue (Cooper and Ball, 1997, at 224). For an extremely rich inventory of "non-published opinions," which were transformed during this circulation of drafts, see Schwartz (1985, 1988, and 1996).

[107] Le Sueur emphasizes the importance of the informal encounters to generate mutual trust (2008, at 33). Robertson once criticized the lack of engagement in the House of Lords formal deliberations: "English judges do not engage with each other intellectually—their positions largely slip past the alternative view with no comment" (2000, at 20). In private communication with Le Sueur and Cornes, a Lord of Appeal contested Robertson's statement. Apparently, Robertson would have missed the informal interactions: "Apart from formal meetings, there is a constant dynamic process of discussion about cases before they are heard, during the hearing of the cases, afterwards, at meetings, with reference to drafts circulated etc. We never seem to stop talking about our cases!" (2000, at 15).

As the interaction becomes more rigid and codified (like the ritual in which the order of individual votes follow a criterion of seniority[108]), deliberation naturally loses spontaneity. And although deliberation cannot be seen as mere "spontaneous conversation,"[109] hard rules of interaction may turn it artificial. The virtues of collegiality, epistemic ambition, epistemic modesty, and empathy do not emerge or evolve by formal design. The complete absence of rules, nonetheless, may also weaken those virtues and prompt deliberative failures.[110]

An infinite amount of formulas could possibly be imagined. Such formulas, of course, can build upon the historical practices of collegiate adjudication. One typical tradition ascribes a rapporteur a set of related functions: he would manage how the case evolves procedurally, conduct the internal deliberations and, further, be the chief drafter of the decision of the court (in case disagreement does not require someone else to write the majority opinion).[111] He is supposed, therefore, to exercise a leadership on the whole process.[112] The way such leadership is actually exercised and the other judges respond to it will be crucial for the prospects of deliberation. Other traditions of collegiate adjudication let the chief judge take the general lead of the process.[113] Others, yet, are more atomized and give either the rapporteur or the chief judge a marginal bureaucratic role.[114] Whatever the best strategy in each circumstance, the designer cannot underestimate how deliberation might be stimulated and improved by the internal rules of such kind.

xii. Decisiveness: between unanimity, simple majority, and qualified majority

Deliberation presupposes the need to take a collective decision, and there must be a standard of decisiveness to define when an authoritative settlement

---

[108] For Leflar, the order has implications "on a judge's opportunity to influence the decision" and, therefore, should be varied and not guided by seniority. He draws an interesting distinction between stating preliminary views and voting: "A statement of views and reasons may of course indicate how the judge expects to vote, but no judge should commit a final vote before hearing the analyses of everyone of the sitting judges. Those first to speak should leave themselves free to change their minds. It should be possible for all views to have effects upon each judge's vote" (1983, at 726).

[109] As Edwards contends: "Collegiality does not consist of spontaneous conversations by the water cooler. It consists primarily of ordered deliberation in which all views are aired and considered to every judge's satisfaction" (2003, at 1665).

[110] Some sort of constraint of participation on each judge, for example, can avoid that his views are not exposed to the group: "One of the biggest obstacles to achieving the benefits of diversity is ineffectiveness in extracting and integrating competing perspectives from group members" (Hessick and Jordan, 2009, at 683).

[111] The criterion to choose the rapporteur is sometimes thought of in deliberative terms. For example, the particular legal expertise of each judge may be taken into account in order to increase the epistemic potential of the decision and the efficiency in information gathering.

[112] See, for example, the process of the European Court of Justice.

[113] Like the US Supreme Court, for example.

[114] Again, I resort to the example of the Brazilian Supreme Court as archetype of atomistic court. See Silva (2013).

was reached and the process has come to an end. In other words, there must be a method for converting the "many" into "one." Such standard can range between unanimity rule, simple majority rule, or qualified majority rule. The choice of a standard of decisiveness should not be mixed up with the choice between *per curiam* or *seriatim* decisions, which I address later. Despite being counter-intuitive, a court could arguably decide on the basis of majority rule and publicly manifest itself through *per curiam* opinion, or even adopt unanimity rule but let individual judges write their own concurrent reasoning.[115]

The dynamics of deliberation may be substantially altered if different standards are adopted. When unanimity rule is in play, there tends to be a heavier pressure to deliberate.[116] Without extensive persuasion, principled compromise, or bargaining, the institution gets gridlocked. The downside is that the power of a single individual to impede decision may be excessively obstructive and force unacceptable compromises for the sake of consensus. Such a system, if not accompanied by a shared ethics of collegiality, may actually encourage bargaining instead of deliberation.[117] Even if internal fairness among judges, in the "one man one vote" fashion, is not seen as an intrinsic political value, unanimity rule may nonetheless be unwise if it ends up impeding deliberation.

Simple majority rule, on the other hand, is a traditional method of aggregation that has both a moral appeal—equal value of each individual—and a physicalist dimension—the greater force of the majority to prevail.[118] It is not at all obvious, however, that it should be adopted as a standard of decisiveness within a constitutional court. The extension of persuasion required by such rule is less ambitious and may encourage another type of internal strategic behavior: if not to reach consensus, bargaining may still be used to form coalitions. Some form of qualified majority may strike a reasonable balance between both extremes.

There is no single most deliberative method of aggregation. A deliberative court is not at odds with either alternative. The way each criterion will actually operate will heavily depend on how the judges understand their role within a collegiate body.[119]

---

[115] This distinction would only make sense, for sure, if the court deliberates in secret sessions.

[116] See, for example, Lasser's study about the French State Council (2004).

[117] The Italian Constitutional Court, for example, adopts unanimity rule: "The members meet and decide on cases face to face; deciding a single issue can take days of argument and persuasion. The members try hard to find a way to write a common opinion and, from the little that can be seen from outside, have devised various techniques of compromise and accommodation. Without the possibility of multiple opinions, the Justices are forced to try to persuade their brethren and reconcile themselves to a common decision" (Ferejohn and Pasquino, 2004, at 1693).

[118] See Waldron (1999).

[119] The "voting protocol" is a further complexity of decisiveness that will not be dealt with here. Kornhauser and Sager (1993) recommend that, in multi-issues cases, where the prospects of the "discursive

6. POST-DECISIONAL DEVICES: DRAFTING A DELIBERATIVE WRITTEN DECISION

Devices	Dilemmas
xiii. Public display of internal division	Between *per curiam* and *seriatim*
xiv. Decision-drafting	More or less interactive processes
xv. Communicating	Various instruments

xiii. Public display of internal division

The post-decisional phase has some bearing upon all four promises of deliberation. The decision is already taken, but how it will be publicly delivered raises further concerns. From the epistemic point of view, the written decision has both backward and forward-looking dimensions. It filters what precedents and what fresh arguments or information will be publicly recognized as relevant for the decision, establishes how it will stand as a new precedent for future cases, and how it adds to the diachronically constructed body of law. From the communitarian perspective, if the decision was not unanimous, it remains to be decided, as a second-order question, whether there are reasons for unity that outweigh the value of disclosing disagreement.[120] The psychological and educative functions, lastly, are intimately related to how the court communicates the decision: it should inculcate the feeling of respect on the interested parties and, additionally, enlighten them on the discussion of principle.

The primary choice to be made, therefore, is how the collegial nature of the court will be exhibited. It is one thing to establish a criterion for reaching a collective decision. It is another to define how occasional divisions, in case of non-unanimous standards of decisiveness, will be publicly displayed. Both factors may be merged in practice, but this is not necessary. Again, some courts may decide through majority voting, but communicate in unison.[121] Due to the lack of internal consensus, it may still choose to show unanimity

---

dilemma" are high, a meta-deliberation about voting protocol (the "meta-vote") should be undertaken. The question about which voting protocol (issue-by-issue or outcome-by-outcome) would turn the court more deliberative should not be taken for granted.

[120] This discussion may become almost futile, of course, if the internal sessions of deliberation are not secret. One might still ponder, however, that even if the disagreement is exposed thanks to the publicity of deliberation, it does not necessarily follow that it should be registered in the written decision itself.

[121] The Privy Council, for example, clearly distinguishes between decisiveness and public display. The decision of the majority is announced as decision of the whole. Occasional dissents remain publicly unrecognized (Zobell, 1958, at 186).

to the public. A judge might be in a minority, but prefer not to publish a dissenting opinion. Other courts may reach consensus, but let individual judges free to elaborate and publish their own converging votes in the spirit of *seriatim* traditions.

A deliberative written decision, as claimed by Chapters 4 and 5, does not require, in principle, a specific format. A single opinion is not the only possible translation of high deliberative performance. Neither is a plural opinion. Nevertheless, this should not mean that, from the point of view of the institutional designer preoccupied with instilling deliberation, incentives for judges "to indulge in their individuality"[122] are commendable.[123] Letting judges choose what to do without any collegial burden may curtail the likelihood of internal deliberation in the long run.[124]

For collegiality to exist, the centripetal vector needs to be stronger than the centrifugal one, even if the latter is still present.[125] Collegiality, in other words, does not require forcible integration, but also avoids unbound disintegration.[126] A blanket prohibition on dissents and concurrences, rather than enhancing collegiality, may damage the conditions to nourish it.[127] Besides, such prohibition deprives the public of one standard of criticism and control of the court's opinion.[128]

Single opinions, many believe, contribute to some formal qualities of the rule of law, like clarity and certainty. The obligation to reach a unitary text

---

[122] Ginsburg, 1990b, at 142.

[123] The House of Lords, for example, traditionally had an inertial leaning towards individualism and *seriatim*. For Arden, the recent creation of the UK Supreme Court is a rare historical opportunity to put that tradition under scrutiny (2010, at 9).

[124] This fear made the Italian Constitutional Court reject even the modest proposal of anonymous dissents: "In the end, even this modest but interesting proposal was rejected not only because it discouraged internal deliberation, but also because it encouraged too pluralistic a view of the Constitution" (Ferejohn and Pasquino, 2004, at 1696).

[125] Silva (2013).

[126] To return to an earlier distinction between deliberative or non-deliberative *seriatim* or *per curiam* opinions, a *seriatim* does not need to embody such "unbound disintegration" to the extent that the opinions converse among themselves.

[127] One might think that collegiality's tendency to accommodate would create ambiguity. However, it may also let judges freer to dissent: "collegiality may increase coherence because collegial groups, consisting of members who are comfortable expressing disagreement, may be more willing to dissent" (Hessick and Jordan, 2009, at 691).

[128] Douglas conceive of the right to dissent as an antidote against political subservience: "One cannot imagine the courts of Hitler engaged in a public debate over the principles of Der Fuehrer, with a minority of one or four denouncing the principles themselves" (1948, at 104). Nadelmann echoes the same idea: "Public control of the courts is weakened if dissents are hidden" (1959, at 430). Justice Hughes highlights the importance of dissents for the independence of judges: "When unanimity can be obtained without sacrifice of conviction, it strongly commends the decision to public confidence. But unanimity which is merely formal, which is recorded at the expense of strong conflicting views, is not desirable in a court of last resort, whatever may be the effect upon public opinion at the time. This is so because what

may, however, unexpectedly contribute to opacity and ambiguity rather than clarity. It may turn to "faux unanimity."[129]

Single opinions would still carry two other types of danger. The first would be epistemic: since they reflect the highest common denominator, they would lack attention to details and individual insights, and therefore hinder the development of the law. A relevant amount of deliberative energy would be wasted for future cases. Second, they could, at some stage, become oppressive (even if judicial independence is not conceived as an unlimited right to dissent). This is, for example, the gist of the case for the maintenance of the *seriatim* tradition of the UK Supreme Court.[130]

As it happens, costs exist on both sides, and trade-offs cannot but imply some loss. Specific circumstances and cultures may alleviate or intensify them. Forcing agreement at any rate or being too permissive to any sort of disagreement are usually unwise choices.[131] Letting judges publish anonymous dissents is a creative invention that may help cure judicial rhetoric and demagoguery.[132] Its effects, though, are yet to be investigated. The question of whether this trade-off should be set in advance by a general rule, or be decided in a case-by-case basis, relying on the internal culture, is a dilemma that does not admit to a single universal answer.

In the real world of constitutional adjudication, there is an array of traditions of collegiate decision-drafting. The French tradition provides the

---

must ultimately sustain the court in public confidence is the character and independence of the judges" (Douglas, 1948, at 106).

[129] This is a defect that Liptak (2010) identified in the US Supreme Court. He reverberates a recent stream of criticisms against the kind of unanimous decisions produced by the Roberts Court: "vague enough that both sides plausibly could and did claim victory." Owens and Wedekin (2010) also claim that an analysis of the legal clarity of US Supreme Court reveals that dissenting opinions tend to be clearer than majority opinions. See also West, 2006. The same complaint about the lack of clarity of *per curiam* opinions is usually made against the ECJ opinions (Le Sueur, 2008, at 31).

[130] As Le Sueur contended: "Would we really be better off if, for instance, we did not have the benefit of all the insights which Lord Hoffmann has produced over the years?... A single judgment, with all its inevitable compromises, would have given a spurious certainty to law which is genuinely uncertain" (2008, at 31). Ferejohn defends concurrences in a somewhat similar way. Concurrences would have the effect of "signalling the presence of conflicting viewpoints on the Court and (. . .) this has the capacity of enhancing the communicative capacity of Court opinions" (2000, at 98).

[131] The Italian Constitutional Court and the US Supreme Court seem to be the respective examples of the two extremes. The German and Spanish constitutional courts, on the other hand, by permitting dissents with restrictions (which are mainly cultural), have reached a middle ground that accommodates the centripetal and centrifugal vectors. For an overview of how the debate about the disclosure of dissents has inspired public discussions since the very creation of the post-war European constitutional courts, see Nadelmann, 1964.

[132] Ginsburg notes that the civil law tradition fuses anonymity with unanimity: "In the civil law pattern, anonymity (faceless or nameless judgments) and unanimity... go together" (1990b, at 138). Such fusion, however, is not inevitable, and individual judges may dissent but remain anonymous. This would be a way of de-personifying a *seriatim* decision.

stereotypically abridged version of a *per curiam* decision. The German tradition, in turn, is deemed as the stereotypically reasoned version of a *per curiam* decision. The British *seriatim* and US plurality styles complete this commonsensical comparative overview.[133] What these formal patterns gain or lose in terms of deliberative performance depend on further empirical investigation. What can probably be contended, at this level of generality, is that the French formulaic style certainly falls short of the post-decisional standards of deliberative performance.[134]

xiv. Process of decision-drafting

A written decision that congregates the position of more than one individual judge involves co-authorship. A unanimous opinion of the court, a majority opinion, or a joint dissent requires, therefore, some agreement on how to draft it collectively. An optimal team process needs to be set. This is not unproblematic. Sometimes the drafting process may be an extension of the face-to-face deliberation.[135] This variable seems to, and to some extent does, overlap with the written mode of interaction portrayed earlier.

Courts usually assign the task of drafting a joint decision to an individual judge. Where there is a rapporteur, such a task will be charged upon him, unless he ends up dissenting. For reasons of practicality and clearness, there seems to be a consensus, in the comparative landscape, that writing joint opinions is a one judge's job.[136] It would minimize the risk of ambiguity, despite not eliminating it.[137]

However the likelihood of a greater measure of ambiguity than in individual opinions, joint opinions have, in return, a greater chance of producing a clear *ratio decidendi* of the case. Unless there is a visible overlapping consensus pervading the various separate opinions of a *seriatim* decision, joint opinions

---

[133] For an enlightening distinction between "dissenting" and "defeated" opinions, which is central to understand the Brazilian type of *seriatim*, see Silva (2013, at 583).

[134] Lasser (2004) refuses to take a normative stand on the comparison he draws between the US Supreme Court, the European Court of Justice, and the French State Council, but he provides enough information for one to proceed through that critical step forward.

[135] Like the US Supreme Court process. Schwartz, for example, provides a rich compilation of the unpublished opinions of the Warren, Burger, and Rehnquist courts (Schwartz, 1986, 1988, and 1996). About the unpublished opinions of Brandeis, see also Bickel (1957).

[136] Justice Brennan expresses the difficulty of writing the opinion of the majority: "you have to artistically craft an opinion that is tolerable to one segment of the majority, while, at the same time, bearable to another segment... Writing an opinion that mollifies all individuals composing the majority will take all your skill, and intellect and artistry!" (Cooper and Ball, 1997, at 225). For Ginsburg, the possibility of dissent is an incentive for good court opinion writing: "The prospect of a dissent or separate concurring pointing out an opinion's inaccuracies and inadequacies strengthens the test; it heightens the opinion writer's incentive to 'get it right'" (1990b, at 139).

[137] See Owens and Wedekin (2010).

that decide on behalf of the court are more likely to make the court an effective precedent-setter, rather than a mere problem-solver.[138]

xv. Communicating

The written decision is the main instrument through which the court communicates with the public. The job of any rigorous interpreter of the decision, therefore, will be chiefly "paper-dependent."[139] There might be, however, supplementary communicative instruments. A court that praises its deliberative role should not ignore the variety of strategies it can adopt to communicate with the general public. Courts sometimes produce short statements of the *ratio decidendi* and implement other types of news-giving techniques. They may also consider oral mechanisms to trumpet its decisions or even dissents.[140] These, rather than the complex and usually long argumentative exposition of the decision may be crucial to how external deliberation will ensue.[141] Apart from communicating particular decisions, a constitutional court may create public momentum when, at a pre-decisional phase, it announces the agenda of forthcoming cases or, at the post-decisional one, it reports the cases that were decided over a certain period.

Different kinds of interlocutors will have different degrees of interest in the decision and diverse capacity to engage with it. There is a proper way to speak to the "continuous publics," like the legal community, and to the "intermittent publics,"[142] like the interlocutors somehow connected to a particular cause. The latter should be differently addressed if it is to be fully included and stimulated to participate as an interlocutor.

7. CONCLUSION

The optimal design of an institution ascribed with the function of everyday constitutional deliberation is, ultimately, an open question. This chapter did not offer, as it became clear, a 'one-size-fits-all recipe' for a deliberative

---

[138] One could still argue, for sure, that this would depend on what exactly consists the precedent: if it is just the *holding* of the decision, instead of its *ratio decidendi*, a *seriatim* decision with entirely disparate opinions, indeed, could constitute a precedent.

[139] That is how Greenhouse defines the nature of the US Supreme Court journalism: "When I arrived in Washington DC to take up my new assignment at the Supreme Court, I was met by silence" (1995, at 1540).

[140] Like, for example, Justice Stevens orally dissenting on *Citizens United* case (see Liptak, 2010).

[141] Le Sueur, for example, describes how recent debates about the UK Supreme Court have gone beyond the maxim that higher courts "spoke only through the words of their judgments" and reflect upon effective communication with the public: how to summarize judgements, to publish press releases, to organize information at the court's website, among other measures (2008, at 29).

[142] As Berkson qualifies the court's various audiences (1978, at 96–101). The author makes several other suggestions on communication strategies, like a committee on style, the avoidance of legalisms, and an office media.

constitutional court. Theories of institutional design conventionally start off with a self-protective caveat like this. No reputed theory of this sort, to be sure, has ever promised that much. It is an easy caricature to reject. Rather than a hollow commonplace, however, that warning reveals an immanent feature of constructing institutions of government.

Real-world constitutional courts provide a limited menu of institutional blends. Several choices became naturalized. They survive almost unquestioned and by unthinking default. One should not, however, take these contingent choices for granted and lose sight of alternatives that might be experimented. Even if one pragmatically grants that their basic backbones are historically consolidated, there are, below the radar screen of mainstream classifications, several additional paths for institutional improvement. Turning these courts more deliberative would require less than "root-and-branch overhaul."[143] Significant reforms can be done without having to change their grand features.[144] This chapter illuminated some of these paths.

Deliberation is surely not the only purpose to be factored into the design of a constitutional court. Each of the devices has other functions and justifications beyond facilitating deliberation. Their deliberative aspect, therefore, needs to be weighed with other sorts of concerns. The analysis did not do justice to the whole panoply of considerations involved in that balancing, but mainly shed light on the deliberative potential of each variable.

Constitutional courts, in sum, should be designed with, among other things, deliberative potential in mind.[145] Deliberation, though, is a multitask exercise and the case for it comprises a cluster of promises. Each promise, in turn, can be institutionally articulated in conflicting ways. Unfortunately, they are not optimally compossible. Balancing costs and benefits is unavoidable. That is all that design can foster.

There are two complementary focal points in theories of institutional design. One prioritizes the fairness of the inputs while the other analyzes the likelihood of desirable outputs. Fair procedures sometimes are unlikely to produce fair outcomes, and vice versa.[146] The chapter, to some extent, addressed both the self-standing angle and, through some empirical speculation, the consequentialist angle of the institutional devices. Some of the devices enumerated above do not only facilitate but are necessary conditions for deliberation in the multiple facets defined here. Some others are valuable per se.

---

[143] Burns (2009).   [144] This has also been pointed by Silva (2009).

[145] For a thorough analysis of the variables that turn the Brazilian Supreme Court particularly anti-deliberative, or that shape a unique style of "deciding without deliberating," see Silva (2013).

[146] See Ferejohn, 2000, at 89.

Deliberation and collegiality are collective ethical achievements that may wax and wane. It is a group phenomenon, as fluid and complex as the most intricate social relations. Devices may create more desirable conditions for it to flourish, but not much more than that.[147] As the previous chapter has claimed, deliberators also need to develop and cultivate deliberative virtues. Virtues cannot be mandated by design.[148] If the decisional culture is entirely averse to deliberation, it will simply not eventuate. Deliberation is a tortuous route between the emergence of a controversy and a collective decision. Procedural incentives are not enough to warrant the emergence of an impeccable deliberative process. They are, however, an indispensable resource for pursuing this and any other political aspiration.

---

[147] "It would be impossible to design consciously a system that would cultivate collegiality for a court or for any other group. Rather, collegiality is a goal whose characteristics are defined by those who pursue it in their interactions. It takes different forms in every court because it is a function of the individual themselves and the history of the particular institution" (Tacha, 1995, at 592).

[148] Like Shapiro asserted: "By its terms, deliberation requires solicitous good will, creative ingenuity, and a desire to get the right answer. These cannot be mandated. Even juries sometimes choose to bargain rather than to deliberate when they want to go home, and, when they do, there is little anyone can do about it" (2002, at 211).

7

The Legal Backdrop of Constitutional Scrutiny

I. INTRODUCTION

A constitutional court, many have contended, sits at the intersection between law and politics. The inexorability of this tension, demonstrated by positive political science but not easily stomached by normative legal theory, raises hard questions about the viability of the whole enterprise of a constitutional court itself. The reduction of constitutional adjudication to purely autonomous legal reasoning or to bare politics has proved to be inaccurate. Avoiding both positions puts the theorist in a rather uncomfortable situation. She is unable to provide, at this level of abstraction, solutions or normative guidance to dilemmas that depend on context and pragmatic accommodation as much as on a reasonable interpretation of constitutional norms.

Constitutional courts articulate their positions and arguments through the medium of constitutional law, but cannot but practice a modicum of pragmatism that is inescapable in the domain of constitutional adjudication. Legal materials and political pressures are the food for distinct decisional exercises. However, they come together in every case and are difficult to set apart. The legal backdrop defines the sort of public reason that this forum requires, whereas the political circumstances define the major components of the political thicket in which the court is entangled. How the court answers to the former will shape its legal identity. How it handles the latter will fashion its political outlook. Legal identity and political outlook, however, are sides of the same coin.

This chapter and the next do not offer an in-depth treatment of the hedges of constitutional deliberation. That would extrapolate their purposes. An argument about deliberative performance would remain fragmentary, however, if it had not pointed to what lies behind the core meaning. It is not a minor detail. It actually encompasses the most intricate theoretical discussions about constitutional theory today. Both chapters, admittedly, go "all over the place." The brief brush of each section leaves theoretical complications aside. But its aim is justifiably delimited, or so I hope. To combine constitutional adjudication with the ideal of deliberation is a large project. The book takes up the challenge of outlining such a project, and considers that there is a value in presenting a comprehensive picture in spite of losing in depth. If there is something new in such picture, it is certainly not in each piece individually considered, but rather in trying to put them together in a coherent way, recognizing tensions and deriving some normative guidance for courts that face them. The hedges are not exclusive of deliberative courts. Any court in charge of constitutional scrutiny comes across them. Deliberative courts may face them in a particular way.

One may argue that the role of the constitution is exactly to insulate some fundamental substantive content from open and unbridled discussion. It would be of the essence of modern constitutions to protect non-negotiable norms. The point of constitutional deliberation, though, is not to negotiate the extent to which the constitution will be compromised. Deliberation is here defended as a proficient and more desirable way to construct rather than to discover what the constitution entails. Constitutional meaning is not a given that can be set in stone, but is subject to serious deliberative contestation. A deliberative court does not hide this inexorable feature of constitutional reasoning.

What follows is structured in two further sections. The next section presents the five components of the legal backdrop. It claims that, ideally, a deliberative court openly recognizes the moral quality of the constitutional language, forges a coherent jurisprudential thread through its precedents, plays a coordinating function with respect to lower courts, perceives itself as a participant of a continuing inter-branch conversation, and appreciates the constitutionalist ideal as a cosmopolitan venture, hence giving due regard to foreign solutions to similar constitutional dilemmas. The third section characterizes the exoteric nature of deliberation on the basis of the legal backdrop, as opposed to the esoteric character of the considerations about political circumstances, to be examined in the next chapter.

2. DELIBERATING ABOUT THE CONSTITUTION

A model of deliberative performance needs to shed light and regulate the reasons that are acceptable in each deliberative forum. Law is not averse to deliberation, but it institutes a formal grip on argumentation. Political reasoning under the rule of law is framed by legal boundaries. In the case of constitutional courts, the argumentative canon that makes their decisions legitimate comprises several sources or addressees, as I enumerate below.

There is a minimalist theory of constitutional reasoning underlying these constraints. It is not a full-fledged theory of interpretation. For the purpose of deliberative performance, different interpretative strategies of these constraints might, themselves, be open for discussion among judges. I delineate how the reasoning of a deliberative constitutional court looks like without delving, as much as possible, into the delicate controversies about methods of interpretation. Before embracing one particular method, a deliberative court needs to commit itself to a certain approach towards the legal sources. My argument is placed at this previous stage and lays down how a deliberative court should assimilate these sources.

The quality of reasons invoked, on top of how deliberators interact, matters for the assessment of deliberative performance. However, this assessment does not need to adopt a substantive standard of correctness, neither a full interpretive recipe. A deliberative court should seek to steer a conception of law that is most hospitable to deliberation. The line between legal and non-legal reasons, or the perimeter of law's formality, may be drawn in different places, as argued in Chapter 2. The list below partially draws that tentative line and indicates the genres of constitutional argument that may enhance a court's deliberative potential. The list is not beyond disagreement (and some of its components more debatable than others). The more a court rejects this list, I claim, the lesser will be its deliberative potential with respect to the amplitude of disposable reasons. However intense the argumentative interaction among deliberators might be, constitutional deliberation will not accomplish its full potential if the reasons available do not do justice to the legal and political complexity of the controversy.

i. The moral quality of the constitutional language

Modern constitutionalism has embedded the language of constitutional essentials in abstract moral concepts.[1] Rights and structural norms are mostly announced through succinct and vague principles. As a consequence, the political condition of individuals and, to some extent, the operational machinery of government, receive from constitutional texts little substantive filling. The responsibility for loading supplementary content to the norm is bestowed upon constituted authorities. There are more or less deliberative ways of doing so. Insofar as constitutional scrutiny is exercised within such a diluted normative backdrop, a genuinely deliberative approach requires candor to the contested character of these abstract concepts.[2] Candid reasoning,

---

[1] Constitutional texts surely include, apart from compact and abstract constitutional essentials, several provisions that are clear-cut too (Tushnet considers the institutional implications of the elementary distinction between abstract and precise constitutional provisions—Tushnet, 2006, at 360). This is a fair generalization of contemporary constitutional democracies. On average, their style of constitutional drafting is strikingly similar. Ordinary non-constitutional laws may also comprise abstract language, but the implications for politics and adjudication are different, as explained in Chapter 3.

[2] Dworkin called it "transparency and sincerity": "The sole ground of their legitimacy—the sole ground—is the discipline of the argument: Their institutional commitment to do nothing that they

on this account, depends on disclosing the theory of justice that lies at the root of that sort of political claim. Such reflexive disclosure allows the consistency of that theory to be probed.

This is a restatement of an approach that was most forcefully and repeatedly emphasized by Dworkin.[3] To deny that constitutional judges delve into moral considerations, for him, is a "costly mendacity."[4] Besides, I would add, it harms the deliberative potential of constitutional courts.[5]

A deliberative court, therefore, adheres to the Dworkinian ideal of the moral reading of the constitution without necessarily fleshing it out with the precise Dworkinian liberalism. It upholds, first of all, an interpretive attitude towards the constitutional text. The point of arrival will be a product of deliberation. Deliberative judges should display, in other words, activated theoretical awareness. A legal culture that, consciously or not, shadows these core substantive dilemmas behind a "curtain of legalisms"[6] renounces the possibility of open deliberation at the arena of constitutional interpretation. Judges (or legislators) that want to profit from deliberation cannot conceal or ignore the moral judgments that constitutional texts request. To lay responsibility elsewhere for the choices they inevitably make in applying the constitution would be, at best, self-deceptive.[7] At worst, it would make for bad constitutional jurisprudence and leave judges unaccountable.

The limit, or the very possibility, of a deliberative constitutional scrutiny is determined by how constitutional language is treated. A court that, for

are not prepared to justify through arguments that satisfy, at once, two basic conditions. The first is sincerity...The second is transparency" (2002, at 54).

[3] The confidence in the power of argument to constrain legal interpretation is his indelible mark: "The vice of bad decisions is bad argument and bad conviction; all we can do about those bad decisions is to point out how and where the arguments were bad or the convictions unacceptable" (1994, at 146).

[4] "Constitutional politics has been confused and corrupted by a pretense that judges...could use politically neutral strategies of constitutional interpretation. Judges who join in that pretense try to hide the inevitable influence of their own convictions even from themselves, and the result is a costly mendacity. The actual grounds of decision are hidden both from legitimate public inspection and from valuable public debate" (Dworkin, 1996, at 37).

[5] Sachs also recognizes that challenge: "In the end we had to make value judgments and we soon became aware of the need to spell out as fully and accurately as we could the basis for these judgments" (Sachs, 2009, at 208).

[6] Justice Handy's expression in his opinion at the "Case of the Speluncean Explorers," celebrated allegory written by Lon Fuller.

[7] For Berkowitz, the fear and abdication of judgment in the US Supreme Court betrays its role as a court: "The movements to ground judgments in an 'original intent,' in 'bright line rules,' and in invocations of *stare decisis*—indeed, the now bipartisan opposition to judicial judgment of any sort—are born of a denial of the very essence of being a judge." And he quotes Justice Souter to show the inevitability of moral choice: "We want order and security, and we want liberty. And we want not only liberty but equality as well. These paired desires of ours can clash, and when they do a court is forced to choose between them, between one constitutional good and another one. The court has to decide which of our approved desires has the better claim, right here, right now, and a court has to do more than read fairly when it makes this kind of choice" (Berkowitz, 2010, at 64).

whatever reason, does not manage to escape the fetish of textualism, understood as the non-volitional search for hidden meanings under the written words, is deservingly vulnerable to the objections that Waldron and others have made.[8] Deliberation, indeed, cannot be safely squared with a tight formalistic straitjacket. Textualism, though, is a convenient and widely used strategy to assure judicial legitimation. Clean statements about the application of rules would inculcate in the public the impression that it is the collective will translated into general law that is neutrally being applied. Otherwise, the public would supposedly perceive adjudication as something dominated by impressionistic, hence rationally uncontrollable, judicial beliefs. Nevertheless, constitutional courts will only manage to be deliberative institutions as long as they can drop this heavy baggage inherited from traditions of thought that tried to sever legal reasoning from morals and sanitize the application of the law.

Where, when, and how that open take on constitutional interpretation is feasible is a question of political history, not of normative theory.[9] Legal traditions, indeed, can be averse to such reflexivity at which deliberation aims. A mature political culture with regards to constitutional reasoning should not be surprised with the compass of interpretive power that any institution in charge of applying the constitution has. Open acknowledgement of such power is the background condition, to be sure, for keeping it in check.

ii. Historical depth: precedents

The stance against textualism does not suppose that the constitutional text has no interpretive grip whatsoever. Neither does it assume that deliberative judges should be pure moralists, who simply take their personal "raw morality" into account, and nothing else.[10] It accepts that the text is a vital point of departure in the pursuit of constitutional meaning, a documentary level playing field for a constrained type of moral engagement. The normative character of constitutional law, especially with respect to the typically open-textured provisions mentioned above, cannot be exhausted by the constitutional text alone. It only supplies a shared language for political claims.

---

[8] See Waldron (2009a, 2009b, 2006), Zurn (2007), Glendon (1993).

[9] The landscape of contemporary constitutional courts has examples of various sorts. The US Supreme Court has a mixed and eclectic tradition. The German, Canadian, and South African courts have adopted, in the last decades, argumentative practices that more openly engage with moral considerations (see Goldsworthy, 2006). The French Constitutional Council, in turn, conserves its telegraphic style (see Lasser, 2004).

[10] MacCormick (1989) draws the distinction between "raw moral argument" and a "legalistic" argument that may be imbued with moral considerations.

Despite this light normative grip of the constitutional text, courts are not devoid of further textual footing for deciding. Their catalogue of precedents creates a burden of narrative coherence that is derivative from the general principle of "deciding like cases alike."[11] This stock of past decisions determines a large portion of what the constitution actually means and carries out a crucial constraint. Deliberative courts, such as any other rational enterprise, are committed to coherence and accountable to their own former decisions. The ethical context in which precedents operate, therefore, is shaped by the ideal of fairness.

In practice, this constraint has been translated into diverse techniques of precedent-following, which vary according to three main factors: first, the criterion of identity that enables one to single out a precedent; second, the method to construct the holding or *ratio decidendi* for future cases; third, the normative weight that is granted to these precedents themselves. Different technical choices as to these variables form distinct precedent systems. Each adopts its particular pattern of likeness and binding force. Each will occupy some spot of a spectrum between a system of strict deference to horizontal *stare decisis* and one of loose persuasive authority.[12]

Whatever particular technical variables a constitutional court endorses, its deliberative potential can be enhanced by a mindful construction of jurisprudential density. Density consists in developing an incremental rationality that is both prospective and retrospective. It avoids gross institutional amnesia, a restart of the constitutional history at every new case. It does not ignore, on the other hand, that interpretation is subject to development and mutation, and does not ascribe blank deference to former positions. The historical thread remains clear even when a precedent is ultimately rejected. A critical attachment to precedents, on this account, generates historical depth to a court's decision-making, without tying it to a stationary position. As a memorial practice, precedent-following selects, for example, what to remember and what to forget. In "forgetting," however, a deliberative court does not conceal the existence of a precedent, but accounts for its unsustainability.

Deliberative courts feel the pressure for coherence and face it openly.[13] They are candid as to why they follow or overrule a precedent and to what extent precedents remain as an independent reason to decide. In addition to an argumentative constraint, precedents give the court a fertile repertoire

---

[11] On "narrative coherence," see MacCormick, 2005, chapter 11.

[12] For a comprehensive conceptual elaboration on the forces of precedents and a comparison between the practices of precedent-based reasoning in central Western legal systems, see MacCormick and Summers (1997).

[13] Dworkin's notions of "integrity," "gravitational force of precedents," and "chain novel" (1986), MacCormick's conception of "narrative coherence" (2005), Raz's claims on coherence (1979), and the idea of "common law constitutionalism" (Strauss (1996), Waluchow (2007), among others), are primary

of arguments that can be revisited. By inquiring into its "usable past," the court maximizes its deliberative capacity and economizes its scarce deliberative energy. It is able to build its institutional memory and to recognize the value of prior deliberations. It becomes more acutely responsive, a virtue defined in Chapter 5. A deliberative court, though, does not confer absolute weight on a precedent. By taking a critical approach to its past, the court can mitigate its conservative pull and avoid being hostage to path dependence.

A court that takes its precedents seriously manages to deliberate with its past and future selves. It is, in other words, self-reflective in a deeply historical way. Because deliberation is a long-term process, the accumulation of precedents and the experimentation they offer on each topic should likely amplify the epistemic quality of the court's further decisions.[14] A deliberative written decision, as noted in Chapter 4, retains an epistemic value to the extent that it is received as a precedent by future cases.

The flipside of this attribute is that a sufficiently deliberated reserve of precedents is a justified disincentive to new deliberative exercises. The longevity of a particular controversy has a bearing on the need for new deliberations. In a case of first impression, the deliberative load is fresher and more onerous. If a court, however, has a sequence of consonant precedents and considers that there is nothing new to say, similar cases do not need to involve time-consuming deliberation. The challenge for a court that accepts that good precedents exempt it from extra deliberative rounds is to remain alert to the nuances that new cases may bring to old controversies. Courts

---

references to build up a normative theory of constitutional precedents that is generally applicable both to common law and to civil law systems. This dichotomy, at the level of constitutional scrutiny, is increasingly less accurate to describe or compare courts from either system (despite some remaining stylistic specificities between both traditions). The conventional wisdom according to which in civil law countries the constitutional court does not have a duty to follow precedents, as opposed to common law, where the opposite would obtain, is doubly mistaken: from the point of view of normative theory, it overlooks the importance of precedent to the very idea of the rule of law; from the historical point of view, it ignores both the fact that common law courts are not and have rarely been so uncritically obedient to precedents, and that civil law judges, in turn, do follow precedents, regardless of their being recognized as formal sources of law. Justice Douglas gives a clue on that: "Stare decisis has small place in constitutional law. The Constitution was written for all times and all ages. It would lose its great character and become feeble, if it were allowed to become encrusted with narrow, legalistic notions that dominated the thinking of one generation" (Douglas, 1948, at 106). A cursory reading of the constitutional jurisprudence of courts as different as the US, the Canadian, the Brazilian, or the Argentine supreme courts, or the Spanish, German, South African, and Italian constitutional courts shows that the important differences that may exist between them are hardly captured by the dichotomy. See MacCormick and Summers (1997). A pragmatic normative approach to precedents competes with the coherentist one. Whereas the latter is concerned with fairness, the former prioritizes predictability and certainty. See Posner (1999).

[14] This claim underlines a "knowledge-based" account of integrity. As Walker has put it, "only to the extent that a legal system self-consciously evolves as a system, rather than as a mere aggregation of rule and cases without any robust requirement of internal coherence across time and subject-matter, will it then be in a position to exploit effectively its historical and systemic reservoir of experience and practical reason" (Walker, 2010, at 56).

may reach bedrock positions over time and not be too keen on reopening them. A deliberative court needs to avoid the risk of blinding itself and keep active its historical sensitivity.

iii. Intra-judiciary coordination

The two previous sections conveyed an old controversy about the allegedly dual nature of law. Dworkin articulated it through the ideal of "integrity": a merging between "fit" and "justice," a commitment to a moral engagement with the legal materials on the basis of the deep principles that justify the whole system. The three additional constraints that I include in what follows are not often regarded as such. Not explicitly, at least. Likewise, these three constraints can also be read in the light of the ideal of deliberation. I start by intra-judiciary coordination.

The relationship that a deliberative constitutional court may have with the judicial system is not only based on top-down hierarchical authority (encapsulated, for example, by a mechanism of vertical *stare decisis*). It is also argumentative in a special way. There is more to intra-branch interaction than hierarchical deference or *intra-corporis* judicial politics.[15] Arguments flow through its channels and are vital to the sustenance of the system's coherence.

It is a fact that, comparatively, there is a large variation with regards to where constitutional courts are placed in relation to the rest of the judiciary.[16] This is the result of each contingent national history of designing judicial independence and insulating constitutional scrutiny. Each judicial system will thus have a particular internal dynamics.[17] In some, perhaps, the constraint of intra-branch communication may well not be a significant concern. Still, many courts in charge of operating constitutional scrutiny have the responsibility of taking lower courts past and future decisions into account when choosing and justifying its course of action.

This constraint, thus, is manifested in two ways. First, as a matter of input, the constitutional cases that reach the court may have already sparked argumentative exchanges and decisions in lower levels of the judiciary long before the

---

[15] Friedman highlighted this political aspect (2005, at 295).

[16] The most common classification is between the American model, with a Supreme Court placed at the top of the judicial appeal system, and the "Kelsenian" constitutional courts, with the constitutional court placed outside the judiciary and empowered to do abstract control (Cappelletti, 1984). Between the ideal types of diffuse and concentrated forms of review, several mixed systems have also emerged, like that of Brazil, Colombia, or South Africa.

[17] The difference, for example, between a system in which only the top court has the power to declare the unconstitutionality of a statute, like the Kelsenian type, and a system where lower judges also have this power to recognize the unconstitutionality of a statute in a concrete case, is crucial to determine the relevance and intensity of the constraint here explained.

final appeal.[18] Second, as a matter of output, the constitutional court's decision will impact how the lower courts will interpret and apply the constitution from then onwards (regardless of the existence of binding vertical *stare decisis*).[19]

A deliberative court is constrained in both directions: it needs to listen to what the legal system has previously produced and to communicate its decisions in a way that preserves a coherent historical thread. This is more than coordinating authority within the judiciary, more than commanding or enforcing particular decisions from the top. It involves communicating a constitutional interpretation in an intelligible, persuasive, and manageable way. In some systems, the constitutional court will mandate, whereas in others it will suggest a certain legal solution for the rest of the judiciary.[20] In both circumstances, however, a deliberative court is constrained to be responsive to the large set of lower judicial arguments that may have experimented with various kinds of solutions. As with its own precedents, a constitutional court enhances its deliberative performance if it engages with the decisions delivered by the other instances of the judiciary.

iv. Deliberation of powers

The separation of powers is an apparatus associated with dissipation of authority, the institutional hallmark of liberal constitutionalism. It sets in motion an engine known as checks and balances, through which institutions would control each other without the predominance of any. It would serve the value of liberty by diluting the menace of tyranny.[21] Its inner logic does not fit well with the establishment of a fixed internal sovereign.[22] As a

---

[18] The South African Constitutional Court, for example, is reluctant to grant direct access and to sit "both as a court of first and last instance." Justice Ngcobo justifies the preference for appeal jurisdiction because the decisions would be "greatly enriched by being able to draw on the considered opinion of other courts." See *The AParty et al. v Minister for Home Affairs et al.* [2009] ZACC 4 [56].

[19] Liptak reverberates the recent critiques against the decline in the "quality of the court's judicial craftsmanship" of the US Supreme Court under Chief J. Roberts. Part of this decline is attributable to the Supreme Court's failure "to provide clear guidance to lower courts, sometimes seemingly driven by a desire for unanimity that can lead to fuzzy, unwieldy rulings" (Liptak, 2010).

[20] The distinction between "mandating" and "suggesting" is not far-fetched, despite being uncommon. The Brazilian system of constitutional review, for example, is one of the most complex in that respect. It not only instantiates a mixed variant of the American v. Kelsenian dichotomy, because of the co-existence of diffuse and concentrated control, but also gives discretion to the Supreme Court to determine whether its decision on a final appeal will have binding effect on the judiciary or not. This binding effect, to add another complicated layer, is not operated by the Supreme Court decision as a whole, but by a "binding summa"—a short rule-like normative statement that defines the *ratio decidendi* of the case.

[21] The question about whether separation of powers amounts to a division of functions or rather to a mechanism that holds diverse forces under check was one of the classic debates between Federalists and Anti-Federalists. See Manin (1994).

[22] This feature pre-dates modern state, and can be found in the tradition of the "mixed constitution," which, rather than separating powers and functions, sought to strike an equilibrium between social strata (see Von Fritz, 1954).

requisite of the modern rule of law, however, the decisional circuit needs to stop somewhere and a final collective decision must be settled. Legality, as this theory assumes, would not survive the anarchical tendencies of unending disputes of power.[23]

A certain democratic persuasion requires that the people be personified within this structure.[24] It indicates elected parliaments as the natural candidate for that political and symbolic role of supremacy, and parliamentary legislation as the primary source of legal authority. Still, legislative acts must abide by the constitution. To that effect, for theorists of another stripe, an agency that checks the constitutionality of the everyday parliamentary decisions would be needed. This function had been typically ascribed to constitutional courts. Accordingly, when it comes to constitutional meaning, courts would have the final say. Thus, a key political challenge of the regimes organized under these cornerstones is to find a formula for articulating the roles of parliaments and courts and their exact terms of co-existence and engagement.

This is an abridged version of the theoretical story that undergirds a significant part of contemporary debates on judicial review, as described in Chapter 3. Theories of dialogue tried to break that gridlocked search for supremacy and devised a middle ground.[25] Despite some disparities, dialogic theses minimally share the stance that the "last word" is an overstated concern of political legitimacy, and that parliaments continuously have the opportunity, over time, to respond to judicial decisions in more or less perceptible ways.[26] And vice versa. These theories skip the question of who should have the last word and reflect upon the standards that should guide inter-branch interaction. The exaggerated anxiety for locating the last word would have buried this latter question and, above all, obfuscated more fecund inquiries about the contributions of each branch to that ceaseless process.[27]

---

[23] This concern was expressed, among others, by Schauer and Alexander (1997).

[24] This runs against the classic comprehension of the principle of "popular sovereignty" advanced by Sièyes. The principle refers to a pre-institutional and non-formalized manifestation of "the people" as "pouvoir constituant," to which all "pouvoir constitué" are subordinated. See Waldron (2002).

[25] Silva (2009).

[26] Not only in "weak" models of judicial review, where the legislative response is formally institutionalized, like in Canada (see Hogg and Bushell, 1997 and 2007), but also in "strong" models, where legislative responses may sneak in less formal ways, like in the US system (see Fisher, 1988, or Fisher and Devins, 2004, or Friedman, 2003). Whether strong or weak, therefore, legislative responses to judicial review are ever-present possibilities, both in the wholesale and in the retail. Political circumstances, rather than the constitutional text, better explain when this happens or not.

[27] Eskridge and Ferejohn, for example, draw an interesting contrast between "deliberation-ending" judicial review (which imposes judicial supremacy), that they reject, and, on the other hand, "deliberation-inducing" (which invites the legislature to respond), "deliberation-respecting" (which concedes to the quality of legislature's arguments), and "deliberation-protecting" (which safeguards the conditions of public debate) judicial review (2008, at 1285–1295). Ginsburg also observes the tone that

Among its important insights, these theories noticed that what the constitution happens to mean rarely depends exclusively on who has the last word. Meanings emerge from a more intricate process of "action-response-rejoinder"[28] that some conceptions of judicial supremacy simply fail to catch. More importantly, they reveal an under-explored face of the separation of powers: alongside the dispute of forces between branches, there is, or there can be, an inter-branch exchange of reasons. Put differently, there is both a political and a deliberative tension that co-exist and mold collective decision-making in the circuit of separation of powers. They embody two parallel constraints.

This counter-intuitive double face captures both the defensive and the constructive facets of the separation of powers. It recognizes that there is political life after "last words" and defends dialogue as an attractive way to, at least partially, discipline such unending interaction.[29] The principle of the separation of powers expresses, in other words, a fact to be perceived—the provisionality of collective decisions or the continuity of politics—and an ideal to be pursued—a deliberative mode of interaction.[30]

Separation of powers, thus, may be sensitive to reasons.[31] This feature can be grasped as a constraint of law that has a bearing upon courts. Deliberative performance, in the overlapping space that parliaments and constitutional courts occupy, is a useful metric through which such interaction can be regulated and criticized. Each participant of this interaction carries deliberative responsibilities. A deliberative court engages with the reasons provided by the other branches. It assesses their respective deliberative performances and, on that basis, decides whether it should challenge them with better reasons. As observed in Chapter 3, the partial functional redundancy between

---

invites dialogue or not: "Roe v Wade, in contrast, invited no dialogue with legislators. Instead, it seemed entirely to remove the ball from the legislators' court" (1992, at 1204).

[28] As Mehta envisions in the Indian Supreme Court's interaction with the legislator: "episodes in an iterative game of action-response-rejoinder that can be played out any number of times" (2007, at 75).

[29] For Thompson, judicial supremacy would trigger a "one-sided monologue," a general deferential respect to the "forum of principle." Judicial responsibility, in turn, would require a "two-sided dialogue," one in which the court could be an "agora of principle": "Instead of the 'forum of principle,' we should think of the judicial process as the 'agora of principle.'" The court cannot speak alone, and it would be relevant to enhance "the other side of the conversation." The only legitimate way to deal with the fact of reasonable disagreement, for him, is "to accept the problem as permanent—to let many minds deliberate" (2004, at 85).

[30] This attempt to strike a point of equilibrium between last word and dialogue in the long run is surely not devoid of difficulties. A consistent dialogue theory is not exempt of facing the questions of when it is justifiable for a branch to strike down the acts of the other, where the "last word," even if provisional, should be placed and, in overall, what the division of labour should be. I suggested a context-based answer to this question (Mendes 2008b, 2009a, 2009b).

[31] Thompson's position is also in tune with the idea of deliberation of powers. For him, the culture of judicial monopoly about constitutional meaning "restricts the opportunity of citizens to join in that deliberation." A responsible judicial role would have to abdicate of such monopoly and encourage others "to take part in making judgments about fundamental values for society" (2004, at 91).

parliaments and courts can be beneficial if understood and practiced through deliberative lenses.

The court's attentiveness to inter-institutional deliberation implies the rejection of unmitigated judicial supremacy, of a view that does not regard legislative acts as genuine constitutional interpretations. A deliberative court does not understand itself as the only and ultimate say about the constitution.[32] In a context of continuous interaction, it addresses the parliament as an agent to be persuaded, but that can equally persuade in return. It stimulates a deliberative exchange rather than a zero-sum game between winners and losers. Branches are authorized for challenging each other, as long as they listen and present new reasons. Courts, on this account, are not only a counter-power, but become a counter-argument.

More concretely, to join the deliberative track of the separation of powers is to construct a doctrine of deference based on deliberative performance.[33] The timeframe of each single case decided by the court may not always be squared with the span of collective or inter-institutional persuasion. Persuasion demands argument, but it also requires real-world experimentation that only the passage of time permits. It may require more than a single deliberative round. Collective decisions, emerging either from constitutional courts or from parliaments, are the community's works-in-progress.[34] Therefore, the exact stage and the quality of the conversation are relevant variables to determine when to defer and step out or when to keep pressing for new reasons and rounds of inter-branch discussion.[35]

Practical difficulties surely arise in the attempt to implement the ideal of inter-branch conversation. Parliaments and courts do not speak alike. They convert multiple voices into one through different formal mechanisms. For a court to enter into a "dialogue" and to identify the arguments behind statutes could end up flirting with mystifying entities like original intent or

---

[32] Waldron attacks that judicial posture: "For the courts to refuse ever to defer to such a contribution is for them to insist that serious constitutional choices are to be made by them—all by themselves" (Waldron, 2002, at 28).

[33] A doctrine that would inform, in the words of Eskridge and Ferejohn (2008), a "deliberation-respecting" judicial review. Judicial standards of deference are "self-imposed." Policies of justiciability, precedent etc. have this endogenous nature. See Ferejohn, 2002, at 49. Waldron states the same idea: "every case in which the courts decide to overturn a legislative decision is also a case in which the courts decide that they themselves are not required to defer to the legislature" (Waldron, 2009d, at 141).

[34] A judicial decision would be "only one segment of a continuing public dialogue" (Greenhouse, 1995, at 1544), or an "episode in the ongoing dialogue" (Greenhouse, 2005, at 7). For Sachs, a "dialogic relation" between judiciary and government is inherent, for example, to the South African constitution: "the underlying assumption is that there will be civilized conversation rather than rude discourse between the three branches" (Sachs, 2009, at 147). The literature on dialogue is numerous and arguably comprises empirical and normative strands. For a comprehensive review, see Bateup (2006).

[35] The notions of "stage" and "quality" of the conversation would demand qualifications that go beyond the purpose of the chapter. The basic intuition is that constitutional scrutiny is exercised in different

legislator's will. But this does not have to be the case. Some existing doctrines of deference similarly practiced in various jurisdictions have been shaped by concerns that are not so dissimilar to those indicated above. A deliberative court perceives itself within the separation of powers in a particular way. It is neither a modest nor a self-sufficient way, but curious and open to the arguments that may run against or for its positions. A sense of fallibility and provisionality, virtues highlighted in Chapter 5, can only be squared with this conception of the separation of powers.

Waldron sympathizes with a similar approach once he suspends his wholesale rejection of the "very existence" of judicial review as a choice of institutional design,[36] and gets down to the "way it is exercised." He avoids conflating judicial review with judicial supremacy and considers the latter a particular posture in the exercise of the former. The notion of posture is an illuminating one and captures what is at stake here.[37] He deplores a court that "refuses to look beyond judicial materials," one that that uses its "aura of legality" to silence other voices of the formal and informal public sphere.[38] Deliberation of powers attends to this exact concern. It praises a constitutional court that is attuned to outer deliberations and that demarcates its space accordingly.

---

legislative contexts, each of which may raise completely different legitimacy burdens and reasons for deference. Context, here, is shaped by several variables: the age of the statute (it is different to overrule a statute enacted generations ago from striking down a statute enacted by the current majority with fresh arguments); the deliberative quality of a statute (overarching codifying statutes have a weightier pedigree than expedient and short-lived ones—super-statutes, as Ferejohn and Eskridge call them, "penetrate public normative and institutional culture in a deep way" (2001, at 1215); the relation to parliaments omission or commission: filling the vacuum of legislative inertia is not the same as revoking a statute. Blunt objections against judicial review turn a blind eye to these nuances. The so-called "second-look cases," where the court assesses a sort of "legislative response," prompted in Canada a large debate about whether the "second-look" quality should be sufficient reason to defer. Justice McLachlin, from the Canadian Supreme Court, refused that sort of bland and non-deliberative deference: "The healthy and important promotion of a dialogue between the legislature and the courts should not be debased to a rule of 'if at first you don't succeed, try, try again'" (*Sauvé v. Canada*, 2002 SCC 68). See also Hogg (2007). Waldron, in turn, criticized the US Supreme Court for getting stuck with its own precedent in a second-look case. In *City of Boerne v. Flores* (521 U.S. 507 [1997]), the court did not engage with the new legislative reasons and sent congress a defiant message, which typically characterized, for him, the "posture" of judicial supremacy (Waldron, 2002, at 25).

[36] Like in his broadly debated objections to judicial review (1999, 2001, 2006a).

[37] Waldron echoes the old Thayer's doctrine of the clear mistake to define what the posture of supremacy entails: "supremacy has to do with the posture that the courts adopt—and the deference that is accorded to that posture—when the demands of the constitution are unclear" (2002, at 21). And he adds: "Judicial supremacy may be represented as the posture of a court that refuses to look beyond judicial materials. It is the posture of a court that refuses to take any guidance from the legislature or from the executive or from plebiscitary resolutions of the people as to how the choice that faces the court should be resolved" (2002, at 25).

[38] Waldron, 2002, at 34.

v. Cosmopolitan reverberations

The US Supreme Court has recently waved towards a new standpoint with regards to foreign case-law.[39] The episode erupted an intense scholarly awareness to the possible implications of that fact.[40] Comparatively, cross-national mutual citation is not a novel practice. Other constitutional courts around the world have been reading and quoting themselves, with more or less frequency, since their very creation.[41] This practice is not yet backed, however, by an appropriate theory. It is still not clear what is at stake when national constitutional courts do refer to each other. We still do not have an overall picture of what are the political principles that may explain, justify, and demand this growing judicial custom.

Waldron detected that gap and proposed a normative framework to regulate such phenomenon. He did so by articulating two main arguments. First, he claimed that courts should identify in foreign case-law the modern *ius gentium*, a set of converging decisions that can be incorporated as a "source of insight." As opposed to natural law, derivable from a purely rational exercise, the *ius gentium* is a product of repeated multinational experiences that crystallize a series of common solutions to similar problems. It is no "guarantor of truth," but builds upon the "accumulated wisdom of the world on rights and justice."[42] Neither is it simply a descriptive consensus, but rather a reflective equilibrium between the provisional settlements of positive law and a sense of justice.[43] It is, on this account, an interpretive construct.

Second, Waldron argues that a court should strive for a global expansion of integrity in the realm of rights' jurisprudence. Foreign decisions should not, for sure, be understood as binding precedents but, as he claims, as decisions

---

[39] The articles invariably started by listing a special set of cases, like *Printz v. United States*, 521 U.S. 898 (1997); *Lawrence v Texas*, 539 U.S. 558 (2003); *Roper v. Simmons*, 543 U.S. 551 (2005), among others. See, for example, Choudhry (2006).

[40] This is a hot topic in US contemporary constitutional literature, and has already echoed in other countries. It is worthy to start by Waldron (2005), Slaughter (2003), Jackson (2005 and 2010), Choudhry (2006), or McCrudden (2008). An interesting defense of an open approach of the American Supreme Court towards foreign case-law is given by Glendon (1992).

[41] Sachs stressed this aspect of his judicial experience: "we live in a period when I have felt myself proud not only to be a judge in South Africa, with its exceptional Constitution, but to belong to a world-wide community of judges who believe that basic rights and freedoms matter" (Sachs, 2009, at 33). He points to the universality of this process, despite differences: "for all the differences between the work of our new Court and that of, say, the mature United States Supreme Court, my sense is that we simply write large what are universal processes of evolving judicial reasoning, wherever and whatever the court" (2009, at 52). In many other passages of his memories, he restates the duty of a constitutional judge to be aware of foreign precedents, even if to set them aside. For him, the same dilemmas have been moving across constitutional traditions. Those cases would contribute to an "emerging world jurisprudence" (at 212), to which the South African court, in his opinion, struggled to contribute even when domestic legal materials were more useful (at 243).

[42] Waldron, 2005, at 138–139.   [43] Waldron, 2005, at 136.

that deserve "some weight," regardless of their correctness. Political communities that share some basic moral commitments should embrace, for him, this cross-national ideal of integrity.[44] The purpose of such a practice, in his opinion, is not to "expand our sense of agency," but "our sense of community." In such a bottom-up approach, a conception of "law as reason" outbalances the conception of "law as will."[45]

This phenomenon raises an intriguing question to my inquiry. A deliberative constitutional court is not necessarily cosmopolitan. Neither is a parochial court necessarily non-deliberative (as far, at least, as the core meaning and the four previous elements of the hedges are concerned). A court that fails to take its own precedents into account, for example, may be objectionable on the grounds of incoherence and casuistry. Deliberative performance is more clearly impaired in that case. This fault, nevertheless, is not at stake here. Neglecting foreign case-law, instead, leads to a self-exclusion of a transnational endeavor.

I shall contend that a constitutional court may enhance its deliberative capacity by engaging with comparative jurisprudence. This connection is soft and calls for a more extensive elaboration. Why and how to compare are the elemental questions that must be addressed at the outset of any comparative enterprise. However, the answers to both questions do not provide sufficient guidance to a different concern: why and how should courts use foreign law as a valid source of legal argument? These two levels—comparison per se and comparison as an aid for judicial decision—are not always distinguished. When a court lets a foreign decision be part of its *ratio decidendi*, it ascribes that decision some sort of legal authority.[46] Comparison, at this second level, becomes more than an enlightening intellectual habit; it supplies a further source of law.

The ethics of comparative law comprises three principles: (i) self-understanding, (ii) self-improvement, and (iii) mutual cooperation. The first is an identitarian one: by comparing we gain unexpected insights about our own character.[47] We may realize that apparent differences are actual

---

[44] Waldron qualifies what he means by global community: "I am not talking about an all-purpose global community. I am talking about something like a club of us all, dedicated specifically to advancing the idea of human rights" (2007, at 32). Discontinuities with foreign decisions should be seen as a "sort of potential embarrassment," specially if grounded on a cursory appeal to our cultural particularities rather than on good reasons (2007, at 37).

[45] Waldron, 2007, at 53.

[46] This act will need to follow some "metaprinciple of legal authority" (see Walker, 2008). According to Walker, among the different kinds of authority that inhabit the global legal landscape, the dialogue between courts is the product of "sympathetic consideration." This can be read through a modest cognitive prism—courts pragmatically see that "like problems may require like considerations," or through a more ambitious one—constitutional democracies share a similar moral grounding and foreign decisions may deserve some weight (2008, at 383–384).

[47] Braudel offers a better image: "Live in London for a year, and you will not get to know much about the English. But through comparison, and in the light of your surprise, you will suddenly come to understand

commonalities and vice versa. As Michelman phrased it, by the "comparative encounter" we may "clarify our picture of ourselves."[48] The second is an immediate derivation of the first: by comparing, apart from a deeper comprehension, we are also enabled to formulate a critical stance about ourselves. It allows for reflexivity and may induce moral improvement. These two values are a commonplace. The third one, though, captures a less obvious and more ambitious aim. Mutual cooperation appreciates that we are part of a single, despite thin, community. Morally meaningful comparisons, on this account, assume a sense of partnership and reciprocity. The first and the second are inward-looking: we observe the outside for the sake of ourselves. The third one is outward-looking: we contemplate the outside because we are concerned with what we share with the *alter*. We compare ourselves to others for the sake of both.

By applying these three general principles to the more specific realm of constitutional jurisprudence, we may refine them a further layer: as a matter of self-understanding, to compare rights' decisions enables us to perceive our own particular dialect within the language of rights;[49] furthermore, we can also refine our dialect and incorporate previously unobserved nuances; finally, as a matter of reciprocity, we may jointly build a coherent narrative and breed a sense of common enterprise.[50]

The language of rights has a universalistic take and its morals are not jurisdiction-bound. Of course, at the moment this language is institutionalized through bills of rights, it becomes part of a municipal legal system and tied to a more precise linguistic formula that will be interpreted and proceed into its own doctrinal developments. Still, comparisons unfold the contingency and the very limitations of these local dialects.

It makes sense to try to harmonize our national rights' practices as long as our sense of transnational community can reasonably hold. Harmonization does not call for sheer homogeneity. It implies the pursuit of consistency, conceived not as plain uniformity, but as an open give and take of reasons. Or, to put it differently, it can be envisioned as a constraint to "decide like cases alike" with a more context-sensitive criterion of "likeness." Consistency is a sophisticated enough property of practical reason to allow for distinguishing between relevant dissimilarities, which is part and parcel of precedent-based or analogical reasoning. Countries that share political ideals should be

---

some of the more profound and individual characteristics of France, which you did not previously understand because you knew them too well" (see Glendon, 1992, at 520).

[48] Michelman, 2003, at 1758.   [49] Glendon (1970).

[50] One might argue that this jurisprudential phenomenon is not restricted to the domain of rights. However sound this assertion could be, it is historically undeniable that rights' jurisprudence do more easily travel across jurisdictions than structural provisions, which are much more subject to the local correlation of forces.

able to engage in this kind of cross-fertilization without overlooking local peculiarities.

The value of comparative law does not immediately justify, however, that national courts incorporate comparative material. It does not follow, from the possibility that a particular rights' jurisprudence "travels" by academic or political argument, that it should formally travel through a judicial decision. This shortcut is not obvious. One could argue that there are more legitimate ways to internalize foreign solutions. We still need, thus, complementary normative reasons that articulate a "metaprinciple of authority."[51]

It does not suffice to highlight the importance of learning with the experience and insight of others in constitutional reasoning. Self-understanding and self-improvement do not lead us that far. Mutual cooperation seems to do a better job, but still does not address the legitimacy anxiety. We need to supplement that case with extra arguments. This extra work could be made by a mixture of three claims: that democratic legitimacy, apart from majority voting of a *demos* situated in time and space, entails respect for the core collective decisions based on public reasons; that the cosmopolitan ideal, which demands an equal moral status for every individual, impacts the content of public reasons;[52] that the rule of law in general, and constitutionalism more specifically, should be permeable to a kind of authority based on persuasion besides sheer bindingness.[53]

The ideal of cosmopolitan conversation adds flesh to this argument and provides a sense of direction. It is a derivation of the ethics of comparative law generally conceived applied to the interaction between constitutional courts. There are alternative institutional routes for the pursuit of the same ideal, but a "global community of courts"[54] has been an active one, if not the most. This is the route that concerns this book.[55]

What emerges from this process is not a top-down set of constitutional solutions. It is, instead, a rational reconstruction of disperse legal decisions, a multilingual "chain novel"[56] connected by a shared moral project. Constitutional scholars and judges can help to sew this global patchwork. It is selective, but not necessarily arbitrary: it picks and chooses foreign decisions according to a certain theory of justice that informs the act of recognizing the members of a broader community. It does not have the normative

---

[51] Walker (2008).

[52] As contended by Perju, to engage with foreign case-law strengthens rather than weakens self-government (Perju, 2005 and 2010).

[53] Waldron (2005) supports a similar argument.   [54] Slaughter (2003).

[55] For a somewhat analogous approach that considers the legislative route for this international conversation, see Barak-Erez (2006).

[56] Dworkin, 1986, chapter 7.

authority of the sword, but accounts for a relevant constraint once judges accept the attractiveness of cosmopolitan cooperation.

To participate in the development of this patchwork is an option that courts may or may not wish to make. Some courts may prefer to concentrate on a regional dialogue, or on a dialogue with courts embedded in closer cultural and linguistic traditions. Some may opt to stay outside of this collective construction altogether.[57] But there is a deliberative cost in self-isolation.

The particularity of a local tradition is not a compelling excuse against collaborating with this cross-national deliberation. Contextual uniqueness may, indeed, justify diverse solutions that cannot be exported. The facile recourse to "context," however, does not release courts from engaging with the reasons that are ventilated in this cosmopolitan conversation about a similar set of moral dilemmas.[58] Constitutional courts should engage with foreign case-law in the light of sound normative principles. That is the soul of the comparative message inspired by moral cosmopolitanism.[59]

Risks, for sure, do also exist. Comparative constitutional law is not a neutral activity. On the one hand, it can play valuable roles and serve moral and political progress. On the other, it can be of service to authoritarian and hegemonic purposes. The danger of converting this exercise into an instrument of geopolitical oppression is not negligible.

The terms of the interaction, according to that ideal, cannot be set a priori by the centers of political and intellectual power, without the sense of mutuality required by the ethics of comparative law. We do not have to turn a blind eye, of course, to how the geopolitics of comparative jurisprudence has traditionally worked: from north to south, rich to poor, powerful to powerless. The subversion of this longstanding logic, in favor of a sounder ethics of comparison, is the challenge ahead. Among the many comparative sins, geopolitical subservience, or the unqualified deference towards the influential

---

[57] The disengagement of the US Supreme Court in that matter is a paradigmatic example. Sotomayor's hesitation to elaborate on the role of foreign precedents in the Senate confirmation hearings is a recent evidence of that. Dworkin has lamented that event: "We share traditions, problems, and challenges with many other nations with similar cultures, and the fact that almost all of them have concluded that certain individual rights are of fundamental importance provides a reason, though of course not necessarily a decisive one, for us to suppose that it is of fundamental importance for us too. We should always carefully re-examine our own moral convictions when we find that no one else shares them... We pay an increasingly heavy price for our stubborn fidelity to a foolish myth" (Dworkin, 2009).

[58] As Carozza put it: "The failure to acknowledge and engage the universal human values that underlie human rights does more than deprive us of the most important language of cross-cultural dialogue about the requirements of justice in the world. Ultimately, it diminishes our ability to understand ourselves and our own moral resources... The price of that insularity is a self-satisfaction that can blind us to our own humanity" (Carozza, 2003, at 1088).

[59] As to the moral cosmopolitans in constitutional jurisprudence, Waldron's notion of "ius gentium," Carozza's suggestion of a "ius commune of human rights," and Slaughter's idea of a "global community of courts" denote very similar proposals.

and the neglect towards less prestigious constitutional regimes, is a crucial obstacle to the ideal. The constitutional history of developing countries is pervaded by that reverential attitude towards canonical courts.[60] It sees the foreign as a moral and intellectual authority, as a conversation-stopper, not as a partner. These countries basically function as passive "sites of reception," that import constitutional solutions from the "sites of production."[61]

Foreign case-law is not an authoritative legal source, as skeptics seem to fear. A deliberative court that is inclined to take foreign decisions into account does not assume that acclaimed foreign decisions are substantively good. Neither does it simply try to maximize information as if being well informed about the world, or knowing more rather than less, were always instrumental for better decisions. Foreign jurisprudence can well be thought of as an experimental laboratory in moral reasoning, but there is more to it. The value highlighted here is not epistemic, but political: the display of an associative disposition to integrate a broader deliberative chain.

Partnership implies that communities recognize themselves as members of a single enterprise and take the responsibility to do the best they can for constructing a shared narrative. The performative act of recognition—a judgment about the communities you acknowledge as partners—is a constitutive one. A court with a cosmopolitan curiosity and that assimilates that ideal is likely to enrich its deliberative potential. Walker perceived a tension between the exploration of this global "richness of resources" and the ideal of integrity.[62] The challenge brought by this additional source of "reasons to decide" is not qualitatively different from the others listed above: a deliberative court, again, has the burden of making judgments that are attentive to this multi-directional pull of arguments. Deliberative judgments do not manage to fit the legal system by mechanically embracing any of these arguments, but through its commitment of responsiveness towards them.

3. RESPONDING TO LAW: EXOTERIC DELIBERATION THROUGH PUBLIC REASONS

Constraints of law form the exoteric argumentative thicket of constitutional adjudication. They are addressed to, and supposed to be understandable by, the general citizenry. They shape the public reasons that justify a constitutional court's decision. There lies its exoteric character, as opposed to an esoteric one, defined in the next chapter.

---

[60] The rhetorical obsession of so many courts with the German constitutional court or US Supreme Court is a key example.

[61] See Medina (2004).

[62] "There is a fine line between external enrichment of a legal order and disregard of its integrity" (Walker, 2010, at 58).

I have sketched an approach to a set of argumentative sources. This approach, rather than refractory to, intends to profit as much as possible from the ideal of deliberation. The court may drop one or more elements of this list at the cost of missing some fruitful deliberative opportunities. A constitutional court will hardly succeed in stimulating public contestation, in promoting collegial engagement and in drafting a deliberative written decision, as defined by the core meaning of deliberative performance, if not by an approach to legal reasoning that unknots legalistic strictures.

The court can do that as long as it is sensitive to the moral texture of constitutional language (rather than searching for escape routes from the responsibility of judging); to the value of jurisprudential density (rather than ignoring or indiscriminately following precedents); to the deliberative facet of intra-branch communication and separation of powers (rather than relying on its purely formal authority); and to the cosmopolitan character of the constitutionalist enterprise (rather than remaining averse to learning and cooperating with foreign courts).[63]

A deliberative constitutional court should be accountable to the legal backdrop outlined above. There is more in it than just amplifying the range of arguments or multiplying information for the sake of a better decision. It is also a matter of being solicitous about the construction of an argumentatively accessible legal system. I shed light on how these sources of constitutional reasoning may enhance or spoil the quality of constitutional deliberation. There is not one single approach to the legal backdrop. Some approaches, however, make constitutional reasoning more deliberative than others. In legal cultures that are refractory towards these minimal recommendations, courts will be less than exemplar deliberative forums. However, this conclusion should not be too quickly universalized, as if every constitutional court were gridlocked within the legalistic business.[64]

---

[63] The legal backdrop has a close connection to the core meaning of deliberative performance, defined in Chapter 4. If you amplify the temporal scope of the collective enterprise under analysis and go beyond the actual group of judges that is presently deliberating and taking decisions in a collegiate court, other layers can be included in the measurement of the quality of deliberation. Kornhauser and Sager provide a fitting summary: "We may consider a single, multi-judge court at a particular time, such as the Supreme Court of the United States in 1992, as the enterprise. Or we might consider the Supreme Court of the United States from its inception through today as the enterprise. This second entity has changing personnel, and analysis of this entity requires articulating not only the obligation of a sitting judge to other judges sitting at the same time but also to judges who sat before and who will sit in the future. A third enterprise might be the entire federal court system at a given time. A fourth might be the 'law' or the 'common law' as a whole. This all-encompassing enterprise apparently has a somewhat different character than the single court to which we shall attend" (1993, at 5). The core meaning of deliberative performance refers to the first enterprise (judges interacting among themselves), whereas the legal backdrop relates to the three further enterprises.

[64] A generalization that Waldron (2009a and 2009b) seems to promote from his diagnosis of the US Supreme Court habits of reasoning.

8

The Political Circumstances of Constitutional Scrutiny

"The specter of a government of judges does not reflect political reality."[1]

I. INTRODUCTION

Constitutional courts do not decide in a political vacuum. Inasmuch as legislation is not confined to elected parliaments, neither is politics.[2] This oft-repeated truism, if not so much heard by legal scholars, has important implications. As a condition of intelligent and effective decision-making, if not of institutional survival itself, courts need to be perceptive and reactive to the surrounding political climate.[3] The third chapter identified two political aspects of constitutional scrutiny: the polity-framing character of its decisions and the corresponding political voltage of the conflicts it is faced with.[4] While the former quality raises a question of political theory, concerned with moral legitimacy,

---

[1] Vanberg, 2005, at 177.

[2] Courts are not immune from the pressures, as Ferejohn puts it, "associated with the exercise of legislative power": "Whenever general and prospective rules are made, there can be disagreement... The contest among these competing ideas is intrinsically political in the sense that the choice of one rule or interpretation over another must be justifiable in some sense to those whom the rule affects... The people have a rightful stake in lawmaking, wherever it occurs" (2002, at 51–53).

[3] This is a common premise in studies of the politics of adjudication, an empirical truth with which normative theories still need to come to terms. Ferejohn echoes this shared point of departure: "I am assuming that courts will tend to exercise their authority within political constraints. That is, they will not adopt courses of action that lead to regular and repeated reversals or other sharp reactions by the political branches" (2002, at 59).

[4] There are several ways by which constitutional adjudication is associated with politics or regarded as "political." First, by legislating and shaping the boundaries of the political; second, when it has discretion thanks to the thin and malleable character of legal parameters; third, by following and reacting to partisan politics; fourth, because judges would be ideological and policy-oriented, even if not partisan allies; fifth, because judges form coalitions within the court and behave in a strategic rather than collegial way; finally, because the court responds to external political circumstances, calculates its impact and anticipates the reactions. I want to address the "political character" in the latter sense. Chapter 3 accepted the two first senses. A deliberative court, for reasons developed in the course of the book, resists the other three.

the latter points to a problem of political sociology and presents challenges of concrete political capacity and factual legitimation.

Constitutional scrutiny galvanizes multiple social forces. Insulated as though courts may be from electoral pressure, they are not safe from the rule of actions and reactions in politics. Theoretical approaches to the role of courts would better not be indifferent to that fact. Constitutional courts need to factor into the modulation of their decisions the occasional dormant threats of non-compliance (or of partial compliance). They tend to work, at least part of the time, under extreme political duress. Pressure comes in different shapes and sizes, from expected and unexpected sources.

Explanatory stories for the expanding space occupied by constitutional courts in contemporary democratic regimes cannot, thus, be exhausted by the constitutional text, judicial ideologies, or by methods of interpretation. They rely a great deal on the circumstances that enabled each court to seize new attributions or that frustrated their institutional ambitions and forced them to step back.[5]

Political actors do not usually perceive a constitutional court as an inoffensive agent.[6] Courts may be a strategic ally to be co-opted or, sometimes, an obstacle to be ousted. Resistance against unwelcome judicial decisions come in various shapes, some of which lie outside institutional procedures and arenas. Constitutional courts may face, in some circumstances, heavy challenges towards the effectiveness of their decisions. A successful management of these challenges goes beyond legal interpretation. It depends upon political dexterity.

A constitutional court usually has a number of instruments to play this specific hidden politics of constitutional scrutiny. It does not necessarily amount to partisan politics. Neither should it be seen as the confirmation of the soundness of theories that deem constitutional adjudication as politics by other means. It is rather a program of self-protection and self-affirmation.

The court, to some extent, must rely on its own instincts to anticipate backlashes and to measure its ability to keep them under control. Put straightforwardly, it must be a tactician. The constraints of politics comprise a set of more or less unavoidable non-legal decisions the court needs to make. These are choices that lie beyond the four corners of law. It is the space for pragmatic and consequentialist considerations. Institutional design has a bearing on how some of these political constraints might emerge,[7] but

---

[5] There are several explanatory hypotheses for the process of judicialization of politics that took place in the last few decades. See, for example, Shapiro and Stone-Sweet (2002).

[6] This is an empirical statement that obtains, to varying degrees, in most contemporary democracies. See Vanberg (2005).

[7] Restricting procedural discretion by design (like matters of agenda-setting, for example) may be useful to protect the court from unwieldy political pressure on how to exercise that discretion. It may be unwise,

cannot entirely domesticate them. These constraints transcend formal discipline and can only be captured by a different sort of lens. Their intensity and exact configuration will surely vary from court to court and from case to case.[8]

The chapter is structured around three additional sections. The second enumerates the five main political choices a constitutional court is faced with. The third characterizes what the political facet of constitutional scrutiny entails for the court's internal deliberation. The fourth puts forward the notions of prudence and courage as supplementary virtues that shape the ethics of deliberation and assist the court to handle those political constraints.

2. DEVISING POLITICAL STRATEGIES

The notion of a court with a political strategy must be elaborated with utmost care. The terrain is polemical and has already staged inflamed theoretical debates. The stakes are high and any vague wording may easily lead to misinterpretation. This would harm an already gridlocked topic in normative theory, which is at pains to accept, let alone to provide guidance, to a fact that has been ignored or become almost a taboo in some circles of judicial scholarship.

What follows, then, is a menu of the chief strategic choices that constitutional courts need to make. These choices pertain to the timing of judgment (which include agenda-setting and duration), the style of judgment (which cuts across questions of width, depth, and tone), the diverse symbolic messages behind either single or plural decisions, the level of intrusion on the other branches and of deviation from public opinion. These are the main extra-legal variables that make up this residual black box of constitutional adjudication.

The surrounding politics adds esoteric ingredients into the court's deliberation. These ingredients concern the tests of circumstances that are part of second-order deliberation, explained in the first chapter. The sections below draw on empirical hypotheses that are largely accepted by judicial studies.[9] They echo a certain common sense about correlations in political behavior. It is up to the specific court to check, in each circumstance, the best path for maintenance of its political purposes.

---

however, to deprive courts of at least some of the political cards that grant them political maneuver to play, with greater proficiency, the political game. Sometimes, in any event, informal procedural practices may circumvent formal limitations.

[8] Differences with respect to the court's design, to the legal tradition under which it operates and to the political context have obvious implications on how the constraints will materialize.

[9] See Shapiro and Stone-Sweet (2002).

A constitutional court that is unknowledgeable or too innocent about such constraints may become vulnerable to external assaults. It may risk unnecessary confrontation and gradually shrink. If, on the other hand, it plans to make the most of its deliberative potential, it cannot but participate in that game. This does not need to compromise judicial independence and impartiality. It rather preserves them, as much as it is realistic to expect. The choices a court makes with respect to these variables will reflect its political profile.[10]

i. Timing: agenda and duration

Justice Frankfurter had once declared, in a denial of certiorari, that "wise adjudication has its own time for ripening."[11] Justice Brandeis, in turn, coined another famous maxim of judicial review: "The most important thing we do is not doing."[12] More than advancing a philosophy of self-restraint, they discerned a pivotal non-legal variable of constitutional adjudication that has been largely unexamined by constitutional theory. Both aphorisms inspired and, to some extent, summarize much of Bickel's well-known prudential claims in constitutional law. For Bickel, the writ of certiorari was one of the main opportunities for the exercise of "passive virtues."

The sense of judicial timing that they incite is manifested, I submit, in two moments. The court asks itself when deliberation should start—by incorporating a case to its agenda and scheduling the subsequent procedural acts—and when it should stop—by taking a decision. It is true that these variables may be settled by design or convention beforehand: compulsory jurisdiction and a deadline to decide may restrict or even abolish such discretion.[13] However, to the many constitutional courts that have both a discretionary

---

[10] The Supreme Court of the Lochner era, as opposed to the one of New Deal era, for example, has shifted in political posture rather than merely in hermeneutics. I am concerned with what Ferejohn and Pasquino call "institutional considerations": "Because their desire for expansive authority conflicts with the interests of political officials capable of diminishing judicial authority, its pursuit must (in any political system) be tempered by *institutional considerations*. Like the first (ideological) conflict, the institutional conflict is political in the sense that it is rooted in desires to maintain or increase authority and is not necessarily connected to norms of legality themselves" (2003, at 258, emphasis added).

[11] *Maryland v. Baltimore Radio Show*, 338 U.S. 912 (1950). The longer passage: "A case may raise an important question but the record may be cloudy. It may be desirable to have different aspects of an issue further illumined by the lower courts. Wise adjudication has its own time for ripening."

[12] Bickel, 1962, at 71.

[13] The French Constitutional Council, for example, cannot discretionally play with the temporal variable. Because it reviews a bill before the statute is promulgated, it has to act quickly in the midst of a politically heated situation. In such scenario, there is temporal coincidence between the bill to be checked and the sitting legislature that elaborated it (see Ferejohn and Pasquino, 2002, at 32). It cannot benefit from temporal dissonance, as it happens with the US Supreme Court and most Latin American and European courts.

power of agenda and some procedural leeway to postpone or accelerate judgment, they remain as fundamental devices to calibrate the temperature of the docket.[14] A default criterion of temporal fairness—first come, first served—may not always be adequate to order the cases and attend to their respective urgency or political susceptibility.[15]

A good deliberative institution is that which responds in adequate time, not too early, not too late. It has a sense of priority among the cases of its docket. Sometimes it is better to respond promptly than seeking the best answer indefinitely. It is, therefore, sensitive to the case duration in two ways: (i) it recognizes when deliberation is not working anymore and gets entrenched in a deadlock that does not allow further persuasion or otherwise beneficial reason-giving; (ii) it accepts that, even when there is hypothetically more room for preference transformation, or for argument refinement, the urgency or the costs of delay may outweigh the potential benefits of further deliberation. Deliberation is, among other things, at the service of better decisions (in the diverse dimensions outlined earlier). Sometimes, though, urgency does not allow for a full exploration of deliberation's potentials. The inquiry about whether deliberation is viable, productive, and timely, and the search for its optimal amount are primary responsibilities.

Time and energy are scarce political resources to be judiciously allocated. In the light of scarcity, priorities need to be set. A sense of opportunity may help a constitutional court to decide when to step in or out. Sometimes, less deliberation is better than more. A deliberative court is opportunistic in grasping the proper momentum for its decisions. It is, in other words, temporally strategic in order to handle its political dynamites.[16] The timing of the case is one of the determinants of the various repercussions triggered

---

[14] The US Supreme Court writ of certiorari is an example. Reasons for granting certiorari may be more technical and sometimes prudential (see Ginsburg, 1995, at 2123). For a broad picture of these considerations, see J. Stevens, opinion at *Singleton v. Commissioner*, 439 U.S. 940 (1978). Constitutional courts sometimes devise instruments to keep the debate in the public agenda for a long time, letting other actors speak while they remain silent and then pacing the publication of the decision itself in gradual portions. The Brazilian Supreme Court, for example, has developed a complex mixture of alternatives to lengthen the duration of a case: it may take a "preliminary" decision and postpone the "definitive" decision for years, it may suspend the judgment session, under request of one individual judge, after several judges have publicly manifested their opinions, and come back to the case months or years later. In the meantime, public debate alternates moments of noise and quietness.

[15] Greenhouse connects this sense of timing to the stage of inter-branch conversation: "Sometimes a case arrives rather early, sometimes even too early, in that dialogue and sometimes, as with affirmative action, it arrives when it appears there might be nothing left to say." She points to timing as a relevant variable for deliberation: "the Justices concluded that the time had come when they could no longer remain silent—even if it was not clear at the time what they would eventually say" (2005, at 7–8).

[16] Joseph Weiler noted this feature of the German Constitutional Court: "It is not more relevant than the *Conseil Constitutionel*, the Italian Constitutional Court or the UK Supreme Court. But it has an uncanny ability to time and communicate its decisions. It barks without biting" (Oral intervention at a Fellows' Forum with Dieter Grimm, NYU Law School, November 2009).

by a judicial decision. Some occasions may be better than others for biting. Provided there is discretion in that regard, a deliberative court should manage it through wise political calculation. Deciding to decide is a first delicate choice of second-order deliberation.

ii. Width, depth, and tone

Once a constitutional court has solved the occasional dilemmas of agenda and duration, it still has to ponder over how to communicate a decision. Part of it involves delineating its width, depth, and tone. These are choices that, again, are imbued with political resonance.[17] Width and depth are terms forged by Sunstein to advance his minimalist theory of judicial review. The former dimension operates on a horizontal scale and directs the variety of future cases that the case at hand will reach as a precedent. The latter, in turn, stands on a vertical scale and refers to the level of abstraction of the decision's groundings. It may hinge from grand principles to minute case-specific reasons.[18]

Judicial minimalism is the practice of saying not more than necessary to justify a result, and of leaving most other arguable things undecided.[19] To use Sunstein's jargon, it praises narrow rather than wide, shallow rather than deep decisions. It would facilitate the production of "incompletely theorized agreements,"[20] which enable judges who disagree on principles to agree on outcomes. Apart from a technique to reduce disagreement, it would also stimulate, for Sunstein, public deliberation through the "constructive use of silence."[21]

There is more to constitutional adjudication than the declaration of either constitutionality or unconstitutionality. The numerous subtle ways of practicing such power can hardly be disciplined by law. Sunstein articulates the categories of width and depth by which he advocates a specific judicial posture. Without committing myself with minimalism, I borrow these formal categories in order to shed light on another variable upon which the court must work. A deliberative court does not need to be as confident as Sunstein about the putative effects of silence. Rather than fully embracing minimalism,

---

[17] After "deciding to decide," the court has to balance the terms of decision. Greenhouse sheds light on this further choice of what she calls "analytical path": "the Court had come to the conclusion that it was time to confront Bowers and to dismantle it... The only question were how broadly the Court would rule and what analytical path it would take" (2005, at 9).

[18] I have explored Sunstein's theory elsewhere (Mendes, 2009b, at 204–209). [19] Sunstein, 2001, at 3.

[20] Sunstein (1994).

[21] Studying what judges say is, therefore, as important as noticing what they do not say. Sunstein highlights the potential purposes of silence: "Judges often use silence for pragmatic, strategic and democratic reasons" (2001, at 5).

it may consider that some circumstances call for maximalism. It does not presume, as Sunstein, the default superiority of one over the other. The question of whether it will decide minimally or maximally, or the dilemma between being a problem-solver for the present or a lawmaking body that sets broad regulative patterns for the future,[22] remains a topic for case-by-case deliberation. The vertical and horizontal scopes of the lawmaking effects of the court's decision will depend on such choice.

Alongside width and depth, the decisional tone is not a negligible strategic factor to the external deliberative intentions of constitutional courts. Judges may converge on the degree of width and depth, they may even share the legal concepts and principles that affect the controversy. It is still politically sensible, however, to choose the right words to express or qualify what they want to convey. Deciding to speak out loudly or to talk mildly involves acute political judgment.[23] The potential vocal resonation of their decisions, and the more or less explicit messages sent through *obiter dicta*, is another variable to be administered.

This refers, in other words, to the rhetorical side of constitutional scrutiny. The reputation of rhetoric has surely not been stable or linear throughout the history of political philosophy. Rhetoric, for some strands, would be at odds with deliberation.[24] It would serve for deceiving, misleading, and manipulating the audience. It would appeal to passion at the expense of rational engagement.

As Chambers has argued, a certain type of rhetoric is, indeed, a threat to deliberation and to democracy itself. This type is aimed exclusively at getting the allegiance of the listener, whatever means and motivations are instrumental to this specific aim. She contrasts this plebiscitary type with the deliberative one, which puts emotions at the service of frank argumentation.[25]

Rhetoric, as the way an argument is communicated in parallel with its content, is obviously inherent to any communicative interactions, and deliberation cannot be sterilized against it.[26] Even the dry and expert sounding

---

[22] Gutmann echoes this classic distinction between legislation as a broad, general, all encompassing norm, and adjudication as a narrow, case-bound norm (2006, at x). Such distinction is also important for common law constitutionalism (see Vermeule, 2006b).

[23] This is the virtue that Toobin highlights on Justice Stevens' craftsmanship to write a careful majority opinion in *Rasul v. Bush* (542 U.S. 466 [2004]), "which was written in an especially understated tone, in notable contrast to the bombastic rhetoric that accompanied the war on terror" (2010, at 45).

[24] Rhetoric is a controversial topic in contemporary and classic deliberative theory. Its occasional tension with deliberation is well mapped by Chambers (2009), Dryzek (2010), and Fontana et al. (eds) (2004).

[25] Plebiscitary rhetoric would be "strategically focused on getting the numbers," whereas deliberative rhetoric would focus on "engaging, persuading, and informing citizens" (Chambers, 2009, at 341).

[26] Iris Young grasps as follows: "Understanding the role of rhetoric in political communication is important precisely because the meaning of a discourse, its pragmatic operation in a situation of communicative interaction, depends as much on its rhetorical as its assertoric aspects" (2000, at 65).

that legal discourse takes in some areas of law, or some traditions or legal reasoning, cannot be seen as anti-rhetorical but as a particular and not necessarily illegitimate rhetorical mode. Constitutional language, at any rate, generally tends to be much less hospitable to such mode. Young warned that dispassionate discourse mimics neutrality and excludes voices that are not prepared to speak in the same accent.[27] Her claim has a special leverage in the realm of constitutional scrutiny.

A deliberative written decision, as stated in Chapters 4 and 5, has a dignitarian commitment of responding to the reasonable claims that were addressed to the court. The tone of this response, though, brings an inevitable political ingredient. This is an area of large discretion, little controllable by design.[28] The court basically needs to choose among the various ways to phrase the response it deems correct. The role of deliberation, therefore, does not end when a decision is made. The choice of the wisest way to speak to the external public is a burdensome remainder.

If a court is to play a conscious deliberative role in public debate, it must have a strategy of public communication. One portion of this strategy relates to width, depth, and tone: the court modulates the purview of the precedent it produces, graduates the abstraction of its reasons and fine-tunes its rhetoric. There are circumstances that invite more or less vocal formulations. Courts with a penchant for messianic narratives are not always welcome, not always helpful to fulfill its constitutional mandate. In some contexts, heroic styles may be counterproductive and self-harming.[29]

iii. Degree of cohesion

The *per curiam* or *seriatim* formats are not definitive and indubitable indicators of collegial engagement. This formal criterion, as claimed by Chapters 4 and 5, fails to grasp the deliberative quality of the written decision, let alone of the preceding phases. There is still more at stake though. Provided the discretionary choice of the specific written format is not precluded by institutional rules, a constitutional court may have the opportunity to delve into various considerations before selecting what degree of cohesion will be

---

[27] "What such privileging takes to be neutral, universal, and dispassionate expression actually carries the rhetorical nuances of particular situated social positions and relations" (Young, 2000, at 63).

[28] One might say, though, that some judicial traditions have so entrenched writing styles, as the French telegraphic one, that discretion simply evaporates. Such restriction, however, is set by a cultural canon, not by design.

[29] On how the Colombian Constitutional Court, for example, despite intense activism against presidential emergency powers, did not develop consistent doctrine and strategically used ambiguity, see Uprimny, 2003, at 65; on how the South African Constitutional Court developed context-sensitive doctrinal standards, in order to leave discretion for future cases and reduce the risk of incoherence, see Roux, 2009, at 133.

formally documented and displayed to the public.[30] Unanimous decisions, on the one hand, and majority opinions with concurrences and dissents, on the other, carry multiple symbolisms and may be explored according to the peculiar circumstances.

For one, the manifestation of organic institutionality through a single opinion favors legal certainty as a formal property of the rule of law. But beyond this reason of principle, this format tends to obtain greater political force. It denotes self-assurance in interpreting the law and may command broader deference towards the court. The mere sum of individualities usually falls short of that standard. Courts may prefer to keep disagreement internal for strategic reasons.[31] The image of neutrality offered by a single opinion is sometimes perceived as a value in itself.[32] Besides, it can also be a tougher weapon to be used as a strategy of survival in the face of likely external resistance.[33]

Fragmentation and atomicity, in turn, disclose the resilience of internal disagreement. They may stimulate more debate and candidly expose the uncertainty that still shapes the case.[34] This format conveys respect not only

---

[30] This section, like the previous one, concerns the written decision. To the extent that the variations of width and depth may also be used as a way to reduce disagreement and to reach a workable majority or unity (that is, to shape the sort of cohesion), both sections are interrelated.

[31] This tactic had been widely used, for example, by the US Supreme Court, notably during Marshall and Warren courts (Ferejohn, 2008, at 209). In the last 30 years, that court went the opposite way, but, as widely agreed among commentators, it has gone too far: "Is it good for the U.S. Supreme Court to show that the policies established in Roe v. Wade and ensuing cases remain open to severe constitutional doubts, and even more, remain vulnerable as the composition of the Court shifts?" (Ferejohn and Pasquino, 2004, at 1698). Other examples involve the German court, which only started to accept dissenting opinions in 1969, in a very controlled way, and the Italian court, which has debated the topic but still prohibits it. The German and Italian experiences confirm the idea that new courts "cannot afford, or do not think they can afford, to present a public image of discord" (at 1698).

[32] A good example of a pursuit of consensus for the sake of the value of neutrality is the case in which the majority of the Italian Court faced a very resilient minority and felt forced to concede: "So to avoid the internal split of the Court, the majority accepted a much weaker fallback position in order to conceal the internal divisions in the Court and to allow it to present itself as a neutral arbiter among the political contestants... Then again, there are reasons to believe that Zagrebelsky really thinks that neutrality is a value in itself, not merely a strategy of survival in the transitional periods, and that neutrality necessarily involves compromise and not mere accession to majoritarian decisions" (Ferejohn and Pasquino, 2004, at 1693, footnote 98).

[33] The series of single opinions of the Warren Court in de-segregation cases give a uniquely fitting example of the political dimension of unanimous decisions. The Supreme Court before Warren feared to overturn *Plessy v. Ferguson* by close majority. Warren's alleged accomplishment was to restore collegiality and craft a unanimous decision in a fractured court: "Earl Warren came to the court in October 1953, facing a divided and noncollegial group of justices. In the course of the next seven months, under Warren's astute leadership, the Court went from a four to four split to a unanimous decision in Brown" (Cooper and Ball, 1997, at 202). Zobell endorses the same claim: "the impact of the decision was in large measure due to the unanimity with which it was announced" (1958, at 206).

[34] Continental lawyers, for MacCormick, tend to prefer keeping the "faith in the relative certainty of the law" instead of revealing its relative uncertainty. He underscored the advantage of a *seriatim* opinion: "It follows from the practice of permitting each judge to state publicly his own opinion, that the judges in effect enter into public argument among themselves" (MacCormick, 1978, at 10).

for the dissenting and concurrent judges, but also for the dissenting interlocutors. The court sends a clearer sign that the majority of judges may be wrong. Artificial consensus, thus, is not always advantageous for the court.[35] Through the public exposure of disagreement, the court echoes other voices that might feel ignored by a single opinion.[36] The written demonstration of the deliberative effort, even if resulting in a plurality decision, may outweigh the value of a single opinion. The risk, though, is that fine line when, as Greenhouse contends, it starts being perceived as an "institution locked in mortal combat where sheer numbers rather than force of argument" control the outcome.[37]

This is, in rough terms, the political trade-off. In some circumstances, it might be better to concede to a single voice (at the cost of silencing dissents and restricting itself to a common denominator below what would be achievable by the majority). In others, the pronouncement of multiple voices may deepen external deliberation. Assuming that first-order deliberative energy was drained without agreement, there are second-order reasons of a political kind for pushing for compromise and crafting a *per curiam* opinion or for letting a *seriatim* decision take hold. A deliberative court may use this variable consciously. Between unity and diverse levels of plurality, it chooses which degree of cohesion is politically commendable.[38]

The tension between a public image of concord or discord is, as MacCormick called it, a "technical legal-cum-political question."[39] Unity, on the one hand, favors the stable rule-generating task of the rule of law. On the other, especially in the realm of constitutional scrutiny, it invigorates the court and better shields it against political pressure.[40] Plurality may also be seen through these two prisms. From a principled point of view, it gives a stronger official

---

[35] Shapiro hints to the occasional downside of consensus: "deliberation need not lead to agreement, and when it does this may not be advantageous" (2002, at 199).

[36] Consensual courts, like the Italian, are deprived of such political card and cannot balance both sides.

[37] For many analysts, this is the current state of the US Supreme Court. For Greenhouse, the growing frequency of "close cases" can give this harmful impression (1995, at 1551).

[38] For example, there currently is a high degree of anxiety among American constitutional scholars about an occasional Supreme Court decision that strikes down the healthcare reform by a close majority. Barry Friedman declared: "For the good of the republic, it's better if it's not 5-to-4" (Liptak, 2011). Party alignment in the US Supreme Court has become more predictable than ever after the decisions of *Bush v. Gore* (2000) and *Citizens United* (2010). A new divided decision, it is contended, would further damage the legitimacy of the court.

[39] MacCormick, 1978, at 10.

[40] As stated by Learned Hand: "disunity cancels the impact of *monolithic solidarity* on which the authority of a bench of judges so largely depends" (1964, at 71, emphasis added). Jerome Frank also highlights that: "Dissents and concurrences need to be saved for major matters if the Court is not to appear indecisive and quarrelsome, for the appearance of indecision and quarrelsomeness are *drains on the energy* of the institution, leaving it in weakened condition at those moments when the call upon it for public leadership is greatest" (quoted by Ginsburg, 1992b, at 201, emphasis added).

acknowledgement of the plausibility of the defeated positions and stimulates new rounds of public deliberation. But it incurs the cost of leaving law unsettled. From a pragmatic perspective, dissents may encourage the interlocutors who were defeated to persist, through new cases, in their effort of persuasion.[41] But, in some circumstances, they may also feel encouraged to react in less institutional ways.[42]

iv. Cooperation of powers

Not only may a constitutional court be able to avoid, delay, or take up certain issues by means of its agenda-setting power; to alleviate or intensify the rhetorical repercussions of its decisions by means of its freedom to draft them; to show itself as an organic or divided body by communicating, respectively, through single or plural decisions. It may, in more substantive terms, ultimately back off from too intrusive decisions or, contrariwise, interfere and collide with the positions of external actors. The three previous sections described formal variables that can be politically dosed. The measure of such dose can be calculated according to how a court anticipates the reactions of the two main vectors of outer political forces: the other branches of government and public opinion. I start with the former.

"Cooperation of powers" is an expression of Barry Friedman that attempts to assimilate the political complexity of how branches interact. "Cooperation" does not naively suggest the absence of conflict, but actually discerns inevitable interdependent aspects of the separation of powers. The tendency to conceive this arrangement as a purely adversarial fight, as a competition for supremacy and last word, has obfuscated the way public policies actually emerge. The court lacks power to enforce its decisions and needs the joint action of the other branches in order for those decisions to be effective. Inter-branch cooperation combines decisions and non-decisions, acts and omissions, systoles and diastoles. It functions on the basis of prudential accommodations apart from legal interpretation, of politics apart from principle. Like a door with many locks, in Friedman's words, each branch cannot have all the keys.[43]

---

[41] Dissenting opinions, in this sense, may play a wise political role of allowing the court's decision to comply with extant majorities, but sending a message about the direction the court may pursue in the near future. The court's decision may be read, in other words, as a compromise for the time being, but convoking public mobilization for finally effectuating a deeper change in a later case.

[42] See Ferejohn and Pasquino, 2004, at 1699.

[43] Friedman, 1992, at 772: "Separation of powers—and other structural limitations—may just as well be thought of as a 'cooperation of powers.' Each branch or governmental unit has a special role to play, but goals cannot be advanced unless the branches work together at some extent. Picture a door secured with several locks, the key to each in another's hands. If the door is to be unlocked, the keyholders must reach agreement to do so."

"Deliberation of powers," as depicted in the previous chapter, conveys the ideal of impregnating such ongoing interaction by reasons. Yet, it does not show the whole picture. It is complemented by an intricate disputation that, despite conflict, must come up with joint products. This is not done without mutual negotiation and compromise. The inner logic of the "checks and balances" apparatus can hardly be captured by an abstract blueprint, set in advance. The lines between each branch are constantly redrawn. Instead of relying on normative barriers enshrined on a legal document, its limitation mechanism is concrete and existential: the branches contend with each other in order to demarcate their proper space. Clashes and adjustments between institutions, not simple obedience to written rules, better describe such process. That is a mainstream conception classically formulated by Madison and reverberated ever since.

A constitutional court, therefore, needs to know, and usually knows, that it cannot go wherever the constitutional text imaginably leads it. The boundaries of constitutional scrutiny fluctuate with the winds of politics. Without the collaboration of the other branches, the court becomes impotent. The recourse to the constitutional text will be futile when other political forces are robust enough not to comply.

v. Public opinion

A somewhat similar stance applies to public opinion. Public opinion is actually not just a political constraint, but relates to adjudication in other ways too. Theories of constitutional adjudication have already offered guidelines about how to process public opinion as a matter of principle rather than of politics. Some understand that the court has a duty to interpret the constitution according to the evolving state of public opinion.[44] On the opposite side, others have argued that it should be ignored so that rights and the constitutional structure are not put under risk. The very idea of a court as a bastion of rights is based on its capacity to be insulated against such forces.[45] If the court were always and inevitably hostage or subservient to public opinion, there would not be much point in constitutional scrutiny.

Alongside that controversial principled dimension, again, politics creeps in inadvertently. Public opinion may be, at least sometimes, a heavy burden on the constitutional court's autonomy to decide. Empirical evidences in

---

[44] See, for example, *Trop v. Dulles*, 356 U.S. 86 (1958) a landmark decision in determining the evolving sense of "cruel and unusual punishment" in US Constitution. *Roper v. Simmons*, 543 U.S. 551 (2005) is a more recent case. Theories of "living constitution" sometimes accept that public opinion is itself a legitimate determinant of how constitutional interpretations evolve.

[45] Marshall, 2008, at 13–14.

comparative politics largely support this claim.[46] Having a radar of public opinion, therefore, helps the court in defining which directions it can go. Without compensating unpopular decisions with popular ones may be, again, an impediment for the court's enforcement ability.[47]

The empirical connections between public opinion and constitutional decisions can be visualized in a bi-directional way.[48] First, one can study how the latter impact the former. From this perspective, public opinion may actually remain indifferent to, shift in favor of or turn against the court's decision.[49] Public opinion as a political constraint, however, relates to the inverse causal direction. It does not concern the actual effect of a decision already taken on public opinion thereafter, but how the trends of pre-decisional public opinion affect and shape the judicial decision. Gauging how much a decision should stray from current public opinion, estimating the impact it will promote, and the court's capacity to cope with that impact is the political calculus at stake.[50]

Thus, public opinion—both in its pre-decisional crude state and in the way the court predicts it will react to a decision—is not something the court can ignore. It cannot afford the political price of overlooking public opinion.[51] They risk losing political stature. This is not just an empirical given furnished by political science, a raw political force that may debilitate the court's credibility. It is also a datum to be argumentatively processed and responded to. A deliberative court does not defer to public opinion without engaging with it. It may launch, through individual decisions, "constitutional trial balloons"[52] and pin down whether future decisions may dig a bit deeper in the

---

[46] Friedman (2010), Vanberg (2005), Roux (2009).

[47] Historically, for example, the US Supreme Court has rarely been "tone-deaf to the public mood." As a matter of fact, the court has never strayed too far from it. More often than not, it stays in tune (even if against parliament). This practice has allegedly been rigorously followed by the Roberts' Court. That is why the content and bad timing of *Citizens United v. FEC* (130 S.Ct. 876 [2010]) was, for many, all the more surprising. See Friedman and Lithwick (2010).

[48] The literature on the relationship between the US Supreme Court and public opinion is vast. See Marshall (1989 and 2008), Persily (2008), and Friedman (2010).

[49] These are, for Persily, the "null hypothesis," when public opinion simply does not care; the "legitimation hypothesis," when public opinion adjusts and aligns with the court's decision; and the "backlash hypothesis," when the judicial decision spawns a counter reaction (2008, at 9–12), as the temporary antigay backlash in the face of *Lawrence v. Texas* (539 U.S. 558 [2003]).

[50] This political calculus is certainly not elementary and straightforward. The basic variables to be considered when one categorizes public opinion are the kind of case in question (which could vary between salient and non-salient cases), the kind of support (which will vary between diffuse endorsement to the institution and specific support to the case) and the time span (short term and long term). Institutions construct diffuse political capital in the long term and manage it in more or less popular specific decisions. Its range of action is not given *en bloc*. It varies from topic to topic, according to the particularities the conflict. See Friedman (2010) and Marshall (1989).

[51] See Roux (2009) and Vanberg (2005). [52] Friedman and Lithwick (2010).

same line of action. Observing these signals is what enables the court to make the most of its argumentative and political power. A deliberative court should be politically sensitive precisely because it is aware that deliberation, in non-ideal circumstances, is a risky endeavor.

3. MANAGING THE CONSTRAINTS OF POLITICS: ESOTERIC POLITICAL INSTINCT

Politics hides at the backdoor of constitutional adjudication. It is no excuse for the absence of collegial engagement, but a reminder that some considerations compete with the practice of pure exoteric deliberation. It demands a judgment of circumstances. I indicated above five instances in which an extra-legal dilemma emerges. A deliberative court has to be aware of its limitations for the sake of its effectiveness. "Giant strides," as Ginsburg recognized, would risk "a backlash too forceful to contain."[53] It measures its power, perceives when it had gone too far, when its grand decisions were counter-productive, when risk-taking is worthwhile or pointless. It senses when there is space to be occupied or a political opportunity to advance. It detects and manages the undeclared rules of politics. In the words of Ferejohn, constitutional courts "need to take care"[54] in the face of the political weight of its function.

Constitutional decisions promote controversial impact, may face resistance, and cannot but rely on the allegiance of political partners to be enforced. A court that is insensitive towards that fact is less capable of carrying on its constitutional assignment. It must avoid, therefore, impolitic moves that erode its reservoir of energy and respectability. The attempt to be anti-political may undermine its very political viability.

Courts, therefore, do not only pursue right decisions from the standpoint of law. Political survival is also a primary pragmatic concern. The court has to guess the consequences of its decisions in a zone of deep uncertainty. The faculty of political foresight has to integrate its decisional arsenal. This can be better translated as the "esoteric morality" behind constitutional decision-making.[55] Esoteric morality comprises considerations that often

---

[53] Ginsburg, 1992, at 1208.

[54] "There is a need, therefore, for courts to take care when they relocate specific legislative issues to legal settings, and taking such care requires the formulation of normative standards to guide the allocation of legislative authority" (Ferejohn, 2002, at 64–65).

[55] Singer and Lazari-Radek made a recent case for esoteric morality as a partial commitment of consequentialism in the domain of personal ethics. The basic proposition of esoteric morality is: "it may be right to do and privately recommend, under certain circumstances, what it *would not be right to advocate openly*" (2010, at 37, emphasis added).

cannot be publicly unveiled. Courts may play with several political cards, but political success largely depends on keeping these choices secret, under pain of being de-legitimized or defeated. At least some of them, thus, should remain inscrutable. What exactly should remain esoteric will, to some extent, depend on how the court is perceived by a political culture and how trusted it is to play certain kinds of roles.

This does not mean, however, that observers cannot engage in critical debate about political choices that, on their face, courts are taking. The mode of debate, in this case, is not shaped by or accessible through public reasons. It is not possible to entertain a frank dialogue with the court about its strategic choices if these choices are not openly articulated. Because consequences are at stake, only history will tell what acts were politically wise. These choices can be judged retroactively, with hindsight.[56]

It may happen that the design of the court obstructs its ability to delve into this kind of esoteric consideration collectively (that is, engaging all members of the collegiate). If the court does not have any closed-doors encounter, for example, this sort of political hunch will be, if at all, individual. The risk, in such a case, is that the sum of different individual strategies may result in an arbitrary or unwise institutional strategy. The final political outlook of a court can be partially controlled by design, but some leeway for instinctive choices is both inescapable and desirable.

Sometimes deliberation produces harm, and this harm may be of such a kind that cancels out any intrinsic value that deliberation may have. Intrinsic reasons cannot be sustained all the way down. That was a pivotal claim of Chapter 1. When it comes to institutions, which detach decision-makers from interlocutors, this concern remains significant. Intuiting this threshold between tolerable and intolerable harm is for decision-makers to do.[57] It takes place at the level of second-order deliberation.

Thompson rejects the "esotericism" of political choices. He claims that political calculations should be open and that such publicity is the only way to promote judicial responsibility.[58] For him, "citizens deserve to know when

---

[56] For an example of this sort of speculative analysis of the political wisdom underlying the decisions of the South African Constitutional Court, see Roux, 2009. See also Couso, 2003 (about the Chilean Constitutional Court), Uprimny, 2003 (about the Colombian Constitutional Court), and Mehta, 2007 (about the Indian Supreme Court).

[57] About the "tolerance interval" of political branches that courts should respect, see Roux, 2009, at 113. Vanberg also circumscribes the realistic role of courts, which cannot overstep the "tolerance threshold of governing majorities," unless it musters enough public support for the confrontation (2005, at 14).

[58] In respect of Justice Neely's assertion that he doesn't necessarily write in his decisions all the considerations that were necessary to decide, Thompson contends: "Perhaps he calculated that voicing these political calculus would defeat his political purposes. But his political reasoning—at least as supplement to the constitutional and other arguments—may be a necessary part of justification" (Thompson, 2004, at 80).

judges decide partly on the basis of such claims." He does not deny that political calculation is sometimes an inevitable part of adjudication,[59] but calls for "a more refined test of what should count as a principle in legal reasoning—one that rejects reasons that assert mere preferences or prejudices, but admits reasons that express relevant political factors."[60]

The defense of a legal rationality that incorporates political judgment is a controversial one, the acceptability of which will vary across canons of legal reasoning. However plausible, it cannot go far enough. The reasons that ground some political choices cannot be publicized because their secrecy is the very source of their potential success. A court cannot declare: "We will not go as far as we take the constitution to require because we do not have enough political capital to enforce it." Confessing its political weakness is an unwise way of constructing and managing its public reputation.

Political instinct is not a purely irrational act or, in Bickel's words, a "craftsman's inarticulable feel."[61] Empirical evidences about the level of public support the court enjoys and the historical record of the court's political interactions can help the court to gauge the viable political choices.[62] At any rate, consequentialist predictions will be done in contexts of large uncertainty. Political deliberation, even of the specific type performed by a constitutional court, cannot work itself pure. Its impurities have implications for a normative theory of constitutional adjudication.[63]

4. BETWEEN PRUDENCE AND COURAGE: A DELIBERATIVE COURT AS A TIGHTROPE WALKER

Hercules does not compromise. A "mortal judge" does. Hercules, unlike the mortal judge, does not face practical problems. He is rather "free to concentrate on the issues of principle" without bothering about real-world disturbances. Dworkin accepts, though, that an actual judge, particularly in a constitutional court, may have to "adjust what he believes to be right" in order to face the "press of time and docket," and to "gain the votes of other justices" so

---

[59] "If the judicial norm of rationality is interpreted as it usually is to exclude political calculations of this kind, then the judicial process itself contributes to judicial irresponsibility...The judge should either make the reasons public, or reconsider the decision itself." (2004, 80–81).

[60] Thompson, 2004, at 80.   [61] Bickel, 1957, at 30.

[62] Solum calls it practical wisdom: "The practically wise judge has an intuitive sense of how real-life lawyers and parties will react to judicial decisions" (2003, at 193). "Whether one calls it prudence, practical wisdom, practical reason, pragmatism, or situation-sense, in the end it comes down to an exercise of judgment" (Sherry, 2003, at 797).

[63] "Hence, there is no outcome that is purely deliberative, as opposed to political in the full sense of that term" (Walzer, 2004, at 107).

that their joint decision is "sufficiently acceptable to the community."[64] These mundane pressures do not concern Hercules. After all, he is just a heuristic construct to make clear that "the compromises actual justices think necessary" are "compromises with the law."[65]

For all impressive accomplishments of Dworkin's normative theory of adjudication, apart from advising judges to "adjust" their decisions to what is "acceptable to the community," it leaves them adrift when "practical problems" of that sort emerge. In the realm of constitutional adjudication, though, such practical problems are not merely anomalous incidents of turbulent days,[66] but rather an inherent part of its quotidian operation.

The first chapter presented a contextual case for deliberation by asking what its realistic aspirations could be and elucidated some tests of circumstances that call for second-order deliberation in the light of consequentialist prerequisites. The current chapter tries to give effect to that milestone in the domain of constitutional scrutiny. It explains when and how a constitutional court has to come to grips with politics, alongside law, and why this is an issue for a model of deliberative performance.

Constitutional courts cannot only be concerned with the principled quality of their decisions and of the reasons that back them. Neither should they indulge in a purely political contest. Either perspective, alone, does not do justice to the experience of sitting at the constitutional bench and frustrates the normative expectations that are or should be bestowed on courts.

Deliberative performance largely depends on the court's ability to harmonize first-order and second-order, or to reconcile exoteric and esoteric deliberation. Normative theory needs to find out how to keep both balls in the air without undermining law or hiding politics. Can a court do both, without letting the latter erode the former? Do the political animal and the principled deliberator fit in the same picture? Can a court learn how to sustain a constructive relation between them?

Constitutional adjudication is impure in a strong sense. In such a decisional setting, the fine line between law and politics becomes extraordinarily erratic. Politics may well colonize law. Legal constraints may well lose their grips and submerge into sheer politicking. These are pressing risks for the project of constitutionalism, which remains viable to the extent that those in

---

[64] Dworkin, 1986, at 380. Dworkin, in this concise passage, touched upon at least four of the political elements listed above: timing, cohesion, cooperation of powers, and public opinion.

[65] Dworkin, 1986, at 380.

[66] It might be fairly said that this is an even more pressing problem of constitutional adjudication in "new democracies," as a large literature indicates (see Roux, 2003, 2005, and 2009, and Couso, 2003). This does not mean that, in more consolidated regimes, courts do not face obstacles of similar nature. See Vanberg (2005) and Friedman (2010).

charge of constitutional scrutiny recognize the dual nature of the constraints they face and commit themselves to handling them appropriately.

Bickel had once contended that courts, as any other political institution, face the inexorable and simultaneous conflict between principle and expediency. This would be part of the DNA of politics, from which a court could hardly be insulated. Courts are not only confronted by differences of principled opinions in society, but also by a "trial of political strength."[67] There would be no way out of this "Lincolnian tension," as he labeled it.[68] This fate would not imply, for him, a compromise of principle. Rather, through the exercise of passive virtues, the court should evade deciding whenever possible. That is how Bickel believed to have solved that tension. For him, the court cannot decide but on the basis of principle, which is rigid and uncompromising.[69] When prudence recommends, then, the court should simply opt not to decide, to remain silent as to the substance of the matter.[70] The court should not and would not be able to bring about social change apace, through the simple enunciation of principle. A "blitzkrieg" court, like the Warren Court of his time, would simply not endure. By evading decision, the court escapes the burden of giving the official status of principle to solutions that society is not yet prepared to accept.[71]

Sunstein, with a similar minimalist drive, proposes something more audacious. As outlined above, he argues that in order to encourage external deliberation, the court, instead of not deciding, should decide as little as possible. Passive virtues, for him, lie in the aptitude of the decision not to overstep the minimal needs of the case. Grand declarations of principle and a broad precedential scope would hamper further debates in other arena. Unlike Bickel, Sunstein notices that a court can be prudent not only when it bypasses decision, but when it decides modestly.

The advices offered by both authors are insightfully inspired by political circumspection, but are still unsatisfactory. The solution to the "Lincolnian tension," rendered by Bickel, is too rigid: not deciding is the only alternative for the court to circumvent the risk of settling a principled solution when circumstances supposedly do not recommend. Sunstein's proposal, in

---

[67] Bickel, 1962, at 130.

[68] "No attempt to lift the Court out of the Lincolnian tension can be successful" (Bickel, 1962, at 131).

[69] Bickel, 1962, at 69: "judicial review as a principle-defining process that stands aside from the marketplace of expediency."

[70] The refusal to grant certiorari and several other doctrines of deference and justiciability were his suggestions (1962, at 42).

[71] Bickel compares, for example, the problems of school de-segregation and capital punishment. For him, society was not prepared to embrace the unconstitutionality of the latter, but was already going in the direction of the former before the Supreme Court decisions: "Even as of 1954, national consensus on the racial problem was immanent; it is not on the abolition of capital punishment" (1962, at 241).

turn, remains too hesitant as to the role of courts. The presumptive superiority of minimalism, and the causal assumption that external deliberation would be impoverished if the court's decision happens to be far-reaching, is under-demonstrated and hard to generalize.

Still, both authors seem to accept that a strategic attention is unavoidable in decision-making. Their unease with this expedient facet, however, is pronounced. In order to minimize the harms that unanticipated decisional effects may cause, and having in mind the court's fragile popular pedigree, they favor a self-effacing institution. For Bickel, silence would not amount to "uncharted discretion," to mere "hunch" or "predilection," but simply to "prudence."[72]

Realpolitik, again, sneaks behind constitutional scrutiny. Prescriptions for judicial behavior need to take that fact into account. Courts do not play a significant constitutional role without nurturing public support and managing their political resources skillfully. Their space for action, as positive political science has been constantly showing, waxes and wanes. The relation between politics and law, in such domain, becomes symbiotic.

Although the myth of judicial neutrality has long been debunked, the one of judicial independence perseveres (both by those who celebrate it and by those who attack its democratic deficit). It is already common to acknowledge, thus, that personal convictions influence judicial decision. Not so many take notice, though, that judicial behavior is also determined, to some extent, by external political constraints. It is generally assumed that, since the court has autonomy from election, the judge is constrained, for the more optimistic, only by law, and, for others, not even by that.

Positive political science breaks down this latter common sense. It shares three empirical claims that qualify what judicial independence can credibly mean: (i) courts are often politically vigilant and test their capacity to implement decisions and to withstand occasional backlashes; (ii) the separation of powers is a dynamic phenomenon, and a fixed division of labor is not able to capture this constant redistribution of boundaries; (iii) the very social legitimacy of each participant of the game oscillates, and this oscillation is responsible for the greater or lesser space that each branch will occupy in the overall arrangement. Political reactivity, prudential accommodations, and fluctuations of legitimacy are, respectively, phenomena envisaged by the Federalists[73] and confirmed by empirical research. The radiography of the

---

[72] Bickel contends, for example, that not deciding would not "concede unchanneled, undirected, uncharted discretion. It is not to concede decision proceeding from impulse, hunch, sentiment, predilection, inarticulable and unreasoned. The antithesis of principle in an institution that represents decency and reason is not whim or even expediency, but prudence" (1962, at 132–133).

[73] See *Federalist Papers* n. 47–51, where Madison described his theory of inter-branch interaction.

separation of powers looks different over time. Institutions do not successfully participate in this game without political skills.

Therefore, even if interpretive methods do not constrain judges to the extent that some have wished, politics does.[74] Some well-known historical examples may illustrate this hypothesis. The (post-war) German and (post-apartheid) South African constitutions and respective constitutional courts were born with a common characteristic: in an environment of deep distrust against electoral political bodies, they signaled a rupture with an authoritarian past and pointed to a program of extensive social transformation. Both constitutional courts are deemed to have actually played, since their foundation and with significant force, a major role in the promotion of rights. But that path has not been smooth and free of political struggle.[75] This role cannot be explained by hermeneutics.

The development of the Indian Supreme Court also gives prominence to the connection between the interpretive discourse publicly announced and the political atmosphere. Since the country's independence, and still embedded in the British culture of parliamentary sovereignty, the court occupied a timid space. In the 1970s, however, this scenario was inverted as Indira Ghandi's authoritarian government undermined the reputation of the representative bodies. It created a propitious political vacuum for the court to reconstruct its image.[76] The extremely interventionist decision that overruled a constitutional amendment on the basis of the "basic structure" doctrine dates back to this period. The three aforementioned courts, in the heydays of activism, managed to have their decisions complied with and did not face any fatal objection against their legitimacy. Their force sprang from the political surroundings.

The Australian case gives us the opposite example. The extremely apprehensive and legalist posture of the court is, many believe, the only way it manages to maintain a minimum of respectability and independence.[77] In the only moment in which the court rehearsed a modicum of "creativity"—the construction of an implicit bill of rights—multiple attacks from all sides led it to abandon the plan and resume its limited place. Finally, the history of the American Supreme Court provides prolific examples to illustrate the political factors that have driven these judicial systoles and diastoles. These pendulous oscillations are sometimes explained as a tradition of "interpretive eclecticism."[78]

Political science gives straightforward political advice to a constitutional court: if it is going to confront the other branches, it would better have wide

---

[74] Friedman called them as "concentric circles of influence and constraint" (2005, at 263).
[75] Goldsworthy (ed), 2006, at 320 and 339.   [76] See Mehta (2007).
[77] Goldsworthy (ed), 2006, at 145.   [78] See Tushnet (2006).

public support; if it is to confront public opinion, it would better have strong allies among the other branches.[79] It needs, in sum, enough political ammunition to make itself respected. If that is not the case, it should back off, to an acceptable measure, from its ideal conclusions of principle. This would not only explain the successful political role played by the South African Constitutional Court,[80] but also, for example, the alleged conservatism of the Chilean Constitutional Court,[81] and the activism of the Colombian Constitutional Court.[82]

The political science literature naturally does not hesitate to explain these events through the elucidation of political causalities. They have not simply described it as products of different traditions and methods of constitutional interpretation.[83] The palpable unsuitability of purely legal categories to spell

---

[79] Vanberg, 2005, at 170; Roux, 2009, at 110.

[80] Roux (2009) considers that the mix of principle and pragmatism explains the record of such court. He contrasts two groups of cases to show how the political circumstances either allowed the court to follow principle or forced it to compromise. With respect to the former type of case, he describes how the court managed to declare the unconstitutionality of the death penalty, against strong opposition of public opinion, thanks to the alliance with government (*State v. Makwanyane*, 1995); and managed to enforce the distribution of retroviral drugs to pregnant women, despite strong government's opposition, thanks to strong mobilization of public opinion (*Treatment Action Campaign*, 2002). In the other set of cases, Roux finds plausible evidence to infer that, rather than a simple mistake, the court actually compromised on principle in order to maintain its institutional security.

[81] For Couso, what would explain why the Chilean courts gradually granted a more liberal interpretation to the Amnesty Law was not the emergence of a new jurisprudential or political ethos within the court, but a new correlation of forces. The conservative leaning of judges is insufficient explanation for their retreat from their constitutional powers. The main evidence, for Couso, is that they have been as timid in property rights as they are in civil and political rights. Thus, it would be neither a literalist legal culture nor a conservative ethos that would explain the courts' extreme deference to political branches. Such behavior would actually be a survival strategy after traumatic events against judicial independence in Chilean history. As Couso summarizes: the "deliberate passivity" of the Chilean courts is a "reasonable response by a judicial system that gives priority to its survival" (2003, at 88). Gargarella offers an opposite explanation for the failure of the Argentine Supreme Court to protect basic human rights in a variety of cases in which the key determinant was the judicial elitist culture rather than the danger of backlash. These decisions, for him, were "not the product of the political dependence of the judges but instead owed to their unfounded conservatism or lack of commitment to democracy" (2003, at 194).

[82] The new Colombian Constitution, of 1991, created a Constitutional Court that has been one of the most interventionist courts in the world. Uprimny explains that, besides some favourable institutional elements, the court was able to take advantage of a political context of distrust of representative politics and, allying itself with specific social sectors, managed to fill in a vacuum of power despite the strong opposition that is has sparked. In his words, the "court has been on the knife's edge," resisting counter-offensives of reform that were not far from succeeding: "The court's progressivism is made possible, in turn, by the relative weakness until now of the forces that oppose it and the failure of the attempts at constitutional counter-reform" (2003, at 62–63). From this list of examples related to "new democracies," one should not infer that the political environment of courts in consolidated democracies is unconstrained. For sure, judicial review will be more or less able to accomplish intrusive constitutional mandates depending on each country's stage of political development. Successful judicial review would require, for Couso, a consolidated democracy (2003, at 88). However, serious problems of implementation also exist in the latter countries. See the cases of non-compliance in the German Constitutional Court and American Supreme Court given by Vanberg, 2005, at 3–6.

[83] Like, for example, the book in comparative constitutional interpretation edited by Goldsworthy (2006).

out the greater or lesser judicial activism of the episodes above is symptomatic of the limits of that approach. The unstated, yet more plausible, explanatory account is that each court, apart from grappling with their legal sources, has measured the degree of intervention according to the social expectation about its role.

The recourse to binary taxonomies relating to methods of legal interpretation falls short of telling the whole story.[84] Facts of politics are not usually incorporated as parts of the explanation offered by legal scholars. There are more variables in play, though, than traditional legal theory acknowledges. If such variables are inescapable, theoretical prescriptions that ignore them tend to be innocuous. This is not to say that, in all those cases, interpretive methods were invoked as mere rationalizations of political choices. Those examples actually indicate how the attempt to isolate the causal determinant of judicial behavior in either politics or law ultimately fails. It disregards their intricate and inseparable link.

Empirical evidences and normative arguments still fail to communicate, at the expense of both.[85] Hercules is the figure that best epitomizes such detachment from working institutions. The constraints faced by a judge are givens of the constitutional system. He does not have a choice, but to take them into account.[86] Conventional wisdom does not accept that political skills are part of a court's decisional repertoire. But compliance with judicial decisions cannot be taken for granted. How can constitutional scrutiny come out of politics alive?

This chapter takes issue with this theoretical challenge. It inquires whether it is possible to instill a measure of pragmatism without losing the dimension of principled reasoning.[87] It departs from the premise that a tenable ideal of constitutional judging cannot be portrayed as a formulaic and apolitical exercise, and needs to be sincere about the inevitability of political obstacles. Normative claims need to have a sensible grasp of what may realistically

---

[84] Courts that are supposedly more attached to the text are characterized as positivists, formalists, or textualists, whereas courts that feel freer to expand their role are understood as applying structural, systemic, teleological, or purposive. See Goldworthy, 2006, at 334.

[85] Friedman, among others, has been echoing this methodological manifesto about the importance of approximating the findings of empirical research with normative elaboration (2005 and 2006).

[86] "That Hercules is a judge and not just any other political actor is a fact of enormous significance; still, Hercules must do his judging in a political world" (Friedman, 2005, at 260).

[87] That is Roux's argument: "some combination of principle and pragmatism seems likely to provide the best way for a constitutional court in a new democracy to establish its legal legitimacy while safeguarding its institutional security. 'Principle,' because deciding cases according to law is what legitimates courts in the legal sense; and 'pragmatism,' because constitutional courts in new democracies, given the inherent weakness of their position, must perforce temper their commitment to principle with strategic calculations about how their decisions are likely to be received" (2009, at 108).

shape judicial behavior and, therefore, of what can actually be delivered. On the basis of these facts, can any appealing normative story be told?[88]

Friedman does not shy away from this normative question, but his suggestions are still incipient. For him, the court basically needs to strike an optimal balance between the two poles within which it moves: deferential majoritarianism and leadership, alignment and dissonance, dynamism and finality, visionary and reactionary moments.[89] The virtuous management of these cycles would be, for him, the major task of consequential normative investigations.

His shorthand advice, read under Bickel's terms, adds active virtues to passive virtues, complements prudence with courage. His court is a prudent yet courageous political animal, aware of its limits but open to take risks. He does not specify the proper ratio of each, or whether it is preferable to err on the side of over-cautiousness or fearlessness. Neither does Bickel elaborate on the acceptable trade-off between principle and expediency.

Prudence and courage should steer the political calculation in adjudication.[90] The primary feature of a normative theory that incorporates the tension between law and politics is its inability to come up with stable abstract recommendations. Political circumstances are shaped by a multitude of singular and incommensurable factors. The normative guideline, if it can be called so, is an open one: the court should decide, again, according to its political instinct.

The court does not need to abdicate the dictates of law. Exoteric legal arguments are not just a veneer for esoteric hunch. Rather, political considerations help to modulate the intensity of the court's decisions and to

---

[88] "Judicial review can be understood as attractive precisely because it is embedded in politics, but is not quite of it. Politics and law are not separate, they are symbiotic. It would be remarkable to believe judicial review could operate entirely independent of politics or would be tolerated as such" (Friedman, 2005, at 333).

[89] "The judiciary can be at times visionary, and at times reactionary, but never too much of either...The judiciary is both visionary and reactionary simply because it is always somewhat out of sync with the waves of more political branches—always inching ahead of lagging behind" (1993, at 678). Friedman repeats it in various places: "Finality would curtail the evolution of our constitution; dynamism encourages it...Of course, there is a *balance to be struck* between dynamism and finality" (1993, at 652, emphasis added); "The Constitution does grant Hercules a certain degree of independence, but it also embeds him in politics. This is no accident: The Constitution represents a deliberate *balance* between, on the one hand, separation and independence of the branches and, on the other, accountability and the idea of checks and balances." (2005, at 260); "The trick is *striking a balance* between too little and too much judicial responsiveness" (2003, at 2599, emphasis added).

[90] Sherry, in a similar spirit, proposes a balance between humility and courage in adjudication: "In the end, humility and courage are like other constitutional dualities: there is no mechanical device that can mediate between them. But judges who are inclined both to doubt themselves and to risk being wrong are more likely to reach a happy medium then judges who are too strongly inclined towards arrogance or timidity" (2003, at 810). This is the short normative advice that Vanberg offers: "To be successful in shaping policy, judges must adjust their decisions to the political environment in which they work. They cannot simply act as jurists. They must be prudent jurists" (2005, 177).

adjust the law's interpretive possibilities. They help the court to reach a pragmatic equilibrium.[91] Politics will not engulf law if judges are able to perceive when it has enough support to face opposition and when it should alleviate its degree of intrusion. A deliberative court has a plan of the constitution in the long run, is aware of the possibly ephemeral nature of its decision, and may advance piecemeal changes or wholesale reforms according to this balance.[92] It equilibrates itself between the exigencies of law and the constraints of politics.

Constitutional courts can certainly refuse to accept the reality of political constraints. After all, insulation from electoral competition and all other ideals of good adjudication allegedly proscribe such influence. It would let chance instead of conscious strategy handle the matter. The risk is downright political failure.

5. CONCLUSION

A deliberative constitutional court not only provokes its formal and informal interlocutors in order to collect reasonable arguments in the pre-decisional phase, have judges who seriously deliberate among themselves in the decisional phase, and drafts a deliberative written decision in the post-decisional phase; it does so within a specified legal and political context. The core meaning is a formal depiction of the process. The hedges, in turn, flesh out what it comprises, give content to what can be said and done in public contestation, collegial engagement and deliberative written decision.

---

[91] To use an analogy to Rawls's notion of "reflective equilibrium," as a method for justification in ethics, pragmatic equilibrium would be a way of acting in politics.

[92] Justice Yacoob, from the Constitutional Court of South Africa, commenting on the famous case of Grootboom (2000), related to the right to housing, has once orally stated: "Unless we develop this area of law carefully, it will explode." This is a clear formulation of an incremental jurisprudential strategy to develop the content of a right with the passage of time.

9

Concluding Remarks

NO HEROIC COURT, NO HEROIC JUDGES

Some theories of judicial review have entrusted to constitutional judges a daunting task. Accordingly, judges are supposed to listen to diverse voices and back their decisions with good public reasons to which a political community can be expected to adhere. This book argued that their responsibility runs deeper. What matters for a decent constitutional court is not just what voices are heard, what decisions are taken, or what grounds justify them, but the particular way this is done. The distinction is subtle but serious. Deliberation, in its variegated manifestations, is a decent way of recognizing and coping with the chronic openness of constitutional disputes and with the heavy political burden of constitutional scrutiny. The question of *how* is as important as *what* a court decides. Constitutional theory has been mostly concerned with the latter and remained oblivious as to the former.

A deliberative constitutional court should not be seen as an institutional counterpart of Hercules. It is not composed of clones of that mythological figure. This is not to say that the blended standards of deliberative performance portrayed here are not comparably demanding and idealistic. The moral style they convey, however, does not hinge exclusively on the aspiration of finding the right answer for constitutional dilemmas. The commitment for pursuing the promises of deliberation, with an acute awareness of its limitations, is a more complex and less solitary endeavor.

A constitutional court, to be sure, might not care about being deliberative. One could even argue, perhaps, that there is nothing in the nature of constitutional adjudication, historically or theoretically, that requires or presupposes that institutional ethos. However plausible that descriptive contention might be, a court that is concerned and, somehow, succeeds in being deliberative profits from a powerful legitimating credential and makes a distinct contribution for a political regime. A non-deliberative court may still be, for other reasons, functional and justifiable, but it misses a special political opportunity. It implies a loss, and the book tried to explicate what that loss entails.

A quick recapitulation of the argument is in order. The book could be summarized in four main steps: it first highlights the role of political deliberation in general, then specifies it to collegiate adjudication, further qualifies it in constitutional courts, and finally describes how it is ideally exhibited in such forum. Chapter 1 provides a definition of political deliberation, which is followed by an overview of the intrinsic moral values it carries and the instrumental expectations it inspires. Furthermore, it pays attention to the circumstances in which deliberation is desirable and elaborates on the very different sites it may be practiced. The chapter, in sum, rather than a general and unconditional case for political deliberation, embraces a situated one. Deliberation is a highly attractive practice, but only under some conditions of time and space. And it depends on its participants' ethos as well.

Chapter 2 starts off with a conceptual discussion about the connection between legal reasoning and deliberation. It shows that, with the exception of the outdated phonograph view of law application, other schools of legal thought share the deliberative character of legal reasoning itself. The chapter proceeds to a discussion about the institutional face of that connection: collegiate adjudication involves group decision-making, and this primary feature, if not requires, at least benefits from a deliberative mode of interaction.

The following chapter studies the particular nature of constitutional scrutiny and its location within the poles of law-making and law-application. It accepts the legislative (or "co-legislative") nature of such enterprise. But it argues that, despite the functional redundancy, it cannot be seen as merely equivalent to parliamentary institutions. The chapter then describes in what ways a constitutional court has been noted and defended as a deliberative forum, but diagnoses the insufficiency of the arguments so far presented. It maintains that we still lack a comprehensive view of what a deliberative court looks like and an evaluative standard that enables the observer to assess different degrees of deliberative performance.

Chapter 4 furnishes the core meaning of deliberative performance. It portrays a deliberative court in practice, breaking down its processual phases and indicating what particular responsibilities each phase demands. Public contestation, collegial engagement, and a deliberative written decision are the respective goals of the pre-decisional, decisional, and post-decisional phases. The chapter draws a particular institutional style, regardless of a precise argumentative canon or legal profile.

Chapter 5 further fleshes out the core meaning by elaborating on the virtues they are deemed to exercise in each of the phases. It outlines, in other words, the ethics of deliberation, or the personal character without which that political ideal gets impoverished or untenable.

The next chapter maps the institutional devices that facilitate deliberation. Under the assumption that procedures may be important tools to constitute and encourage deliberation, whoever the deliberators happen to be, I pointed to the inevitable trade-offs the design of a deliberative court has to settle. As a multiple-purpose practice, a balance needs to be struck when the aims of deliberation conflict. Devices do not entirely determine the political behavior that will supervene, but are not just epiphenomenal either. As a measure of output, deliberative performance cannot be assured, but only nudged, by institutional design.

The two last chapters of the book address the hedges of deliberative performance, the substantial boundaries in which judicial deliberation takes place. Chapter 7 takes issue with the legal backdrop of constitutional scrutiny and contends that optimal deliberation requires certain minimal commitments on how to approach and interpret constitutional law. The acknowledgement of the moral quality of constitutional language, the diachronic thread of precedents, the demand of intra-judiciary coordination, the deliberative facet of the separation of powers, and the cosmopolitan dimension of the constitutionalist ideal, may enhance the court's argumentative moorings, hence its deliberative performance.

Chapter 8 finally deals with the strategic choices a constitutional court needs to make in order to manage and retain its respectability and the compliance to its decisions. In such circumstances, difficult dilemmas about how the court will calibrate its principled decisions in the light of political pressures emerge. A deliberative court, therefore, has a "will for self-preservation and the knowledge that they are not a 'bevy of Platonic guardians.'"[1] The chapter holds that prudence and courage are the virtues that should animate a constitutional court to make the best of its deliberative capacities. A good deliberator is not politically insensitive and knows that sometimes circumstances recommend less rather than more deliberation.

A deliberative constitutional court is anything but an ultimate guardian. It is a respectful body for the opposite reason: it is aware and sincere about its fallibility, but still audacious enough to press the hard constitutional questions and, when advisable, to tackle the political system's silent inertia and argumentative idleness.

WHAT IS NEW?

What is new in relation to the good old arguments? Chapter 3 presented a broad survey of the literature that somehow envisions a specific deliberative virtue in the function of judicial review of legislation. I claimed that this mainstream is incomplete in a number of ways. It relies on a too hastily

---

[1] Ginsburg, 1992, at 1208.

accepted assumption about the unique deliberative capacity of constitutional courts thanks to their institutional location.

I engaged in a more extensive theoretical investigation in order to fill the gaps that I diagnosed in that literature. Supplementary questions were raised and, through the analysis of the different deliberative aspects that stand out in each moment of the decisional process, a more complete portrait of a deliberative court was drawn. The answers to those questions, if tentative, rehearse some ways to enhance the moral and political status of constitutional adjudication.

I am a partner, not an adversary, of the theoretical enterprise that relates deliberation with constitutional courts. But I am less automatically so. My basic quibble, from where I structure my argument, is that those authors did not go far enough. We remain deprived of standards that do not only put constitutional courts in their best light, but that are also crystal clear about the various ways they may fail and to what extent. Moreover, this theory should be able to identify potential causes of failure and the avenues for improvement. The normative dispute is not necessarily lost if a court falls short of delivering what advocates expect it to, as long as they are still able to point to an attractive and feasible ideal not yet realized.

The book is not just adding one more image to the ever-growing imagery about what constitutional courts do or promise to realize. It sheds light, through a numerous set of variables, on a fecund way to classify judicial review of legislation. It cuts across the classificatory categories of institutional design (abstract and concrete, weak and strong, etc.), political posture (activist and self-restrained) or interpretive method (formalist, historicist, interpretive, purposive, etc.) and does not have any immediate causal relation with them.

The continuum that ranges between deliberative and non-deliberative courts can capture other insightful aspects on how to compare, criticize, and refine constitutional adjudication. As Chambers reminds, "more or less are important deliberative categories" and we must have a "critical yardstick by which to evaluate how we are doing" and to highlight "degrees of deliberativeness."[2] This book puts together, if not a yardstick with a sharp grip, a theoretical path to pursue it.

WHAT NEXT?

A broad research agenda naturally springs from this book. Comparing the deliberative performance of actual constitutional courts will demand a thorough reflection on the empirical testability of the evaluative model here

---

[2] Chambers, 2009, at 344.

outlined. Numerous technical questions of empirical methodology still need to be untangled in order to measure and contrast the extent to which the ideals of public contestation, collegial engagement, and deliberative written decision are accomplished in each court, or how differently they may be instantiated.

The book, as the introduction explained, proposes an argument of middle-level normative theory. As such, it expects to be broadly applicable across a range of actual constitutional courts, each working within different legal traditions and political circumstances but yet sharing minimal common denominators that prompt similar theoretical questions. For the very same reason, though, it does not fashion a full-fledged theoretical equipment for inspecting each specific court. Jurisdiction-bound considerations certainly have to complete that enterprise.

On top of the empirical development, theoretical consequences may also ensue. I concentrated on conceptualizing and defending a constitutional court as a deliberative court. I did not directly address the age-old comparative legitimacy debate: whether courts or parliaments, according to the democratic principle, should have the last word on constitutional meaning. Assessing the book's implications for that debate is a possible step to be taken on the theoretical terrain.

The democratic objection to judicial review per se, or to judicial activism in particular, is one of the most stubborn commonplaces of constitutional theory. Reduced to its core, it basically criticizes the very judicial power (or the amount thereof) to overrule the acts of elected parliaments. It has, undoubtedly, a different resonance and weight in each jurisdiction. Sooner or later, however, it inevitably accompanies constitutional courts wherever they go.

The answers to the democratic objection, in turn, come from various mutually complementary fronts. One type of answer stems from the field of legal interpretation. The court would be, for that strand, simply enforcing the constitution. As long as it follows a certain interpretive methodology, there would be little to fear. The court, rather than a second-guesser, who substitutes its will for the one of the parliament, would be just following the will of the constitutional founders. A second type of answer explores the concept of democracy itself, and attempts to show that election and majority rule are not the single and undefeatable litmus-tests of what democracy means. Democracy would comprise a diverse set of competing decision-making principles that can interrelate in multiple ways. The monolithic picture of parliamentary supremacy, therefore, would not exhaust the equally valid democratic alternatives of institutionalization. Constitutional scrutiny, discretionary though it might be, would be an acceptable component of that project. And such a defense has been done both on the basis of instrumental and intrinsic reasons.[3]

Two other answers put the debate on a more empirically informed setting. They try to show that the empirical premise that apparently embeds the abstract debate is overstated and unrealistic. Real world courts are not unbounded or unconstrained. Real world parliaments, at the same time, are shaped by inherently fallible electoral systems and legislative processes. Flaws would unavoidably be built-in. Metaphors that insinuate that judicial supremacy leads to a "government of judges," or that legislative supremacy instantiates a more genuine sort of political equality would be, if not a gross mistake, a deceitful rhetorical abuse. Critics of courts would, on the one hand, overestimate the power of courts to promote, on their own, such momentous damage to a putative democratic will, and, on the other, underscore unique perspectives and positive net effects that a court may insert in collective decision-making over time.

The ideal of a deliberative constitutional court endorsed in this book contributes to that answer too. It stems, though, from another front. It provides a gradualist output-measure of legitimacy, and prescribes that the legitimacy of constitutional courts varies according to their deliberative performance, an everlasting project. A court will be more or less legitimate for what it does, not for the power that it has formally received. People might disagree, for sure, about the correctness of what the court does (as they disagree about the correctness of any other political decision). This cannot prove that a political community, as Waldron could suggest, should automatically resort to majority rule as the single and paramount decisional method.[4] A court that shares the ethical and institutional backbones outlined in this book has an irreplaceable contribution to make. This normative statement could be applicable to three imaginable theoretical scenarios.

A "modest third-best answer" could react to the democratic objection by pointing to circumstances in which there is no decent structure of electoral representation to fuel the practical and symbolic democratic value of an elected parliament. As Waldron himself concedes, judicial review (even through non-deliberative courts) might be justifiable in "non-core cases."[5] In less than ideal circumstances for electoral politics to thrive, and provided that courts would not repeat the same corrupting features, a constitutional court, be it deliberative or not, would be a desirable device. It would be difficult to

---

[3] Kumm (2007).   [4] See Waldron, 2001 or 2006a.

[5] "Non-core cases," as opposed to "core cases," are non-ideal circumstances in which judicial review would be defensible and parliamentary supremacy undesirable. It comprises a set of empirical features connected to political culture and institutional practices (Waldron, 2006a).

deny that, if judicial review per se is justified in the first place, the court can further enhance itself if it becomes deliberative in the politically sensitive way defined here.

An "underestimated second-best answer" could assert that, if we accept that judicial review is a historical given, a deliberative court is less vulnerable to the democratic objection than a non-deliberative one. It is a defensive argument that tries to accommodate judicial review within majoritarian and populist theories of democracy. If constitutional courts are just "out there," and we are not in a moment of constitutional foundation when large-scale institutional reforms may be promoted, the "least anti-democratic" behavior of courts, according to these conceptions of democracy, would be a deliberative one. Given the contingencies of institutional history, in other words, the best constitutional court a democratic regime could have would be the one sketched in this book.

One could still put forward an "ambitious first-best answer" that investigates how a court, rather than a lamentable remedy to a pathological situation (third-best), or a merely regretful historical accident that a political community is forced to tolerate (second-best), can be a constitutive part of democracy, provided this regime is conceived under the more controversial deliberative frame. Such theoretical stance would not necessarily denote a "bias for the courtroom"[6] or exclude other attractive deliberative forums. It appreciates, though, the singular character of the court's deliberation.[7]

The purest case for a deliberative constitutional court would be the one that not only denies elected parliaments a presumptive democratic pedigree, but also manages to demonstrate that, whatever deliberative performance a parliament may have, a deliberative court adds a non-fungible institutional capacity forged by its numerous distinctive procedural features. Under this theoretical prism, a constitutional court is not accorded an easy democratic title, but may chase and seize it through good quality deliberation. In both ideal and non-ideal environments, thus, a deliberative constitutional court would have a dignified space to occupy. Deliberative democrats would better not ignore how constitutional courts might enhance their political project. That is a question worth asking.

My analysis suspended and bypassed the traditional frame in which the democratic legitimacy of constitutional courts has been approached. It tried to avoid the risk of getting stuck in the binary straitjacket that pictures an

---

[6] This is a quality that Walzer identifies in the American debate on deliberative democracy (2004, at 91). Courts are the place, he regrets, "where the nuts and bolts of membership and equality [have been] most often addressed" in recent times (2004, at xiii).

[7] Silva offers a similar formula of legitimacy: "'The more the internal organizational rules and customary practices of a given court function as incentives for rational deliberation, the more legitimate the judicial review exercised by this court" (2013, at 559).

all-or-nothing opposition between elected parliaments and unelected—hence allegedly elitist—courts. This gridlocked debate passes over a significant number of institutional variables and ends up missing different degrees of legitimacy that standards of performance might capture. Irrespective of whether we accept the presumptively superior legitimacy of elected parliaments, there is a lot of theoretical work to be done in order to put courts in their best light and reform them accordingly.

The book, therefore, is by no means an unqualified or overconfident apology for constitutional courts. The stereotypical socio-political character of a court's composition, wherever you go in time and space, has more often been on the side of conservation than on the side of transformation. This historical baggage has generated, in a prevailing democratic era, a large repertory of anti-judicial slogans.

Against this backdrop, a reader may infer from this book a case for an "intra-curial senatorial deliberation," based on elite ethos and virtue.[8] That skeptic hesitation might be sociologically grounded. Still, when one needs to think about alternative paths for designing and improving constitutional courts within democracy, that hasty judgment can be cognitively paralyzing. The dignity of a deliberative court is not connected with the bells and whistles of the courtroom's mystifying liturgies, but with something more pedestrian and meaningful. However plausible the skepticism might be as a matter of political history, and however silent it usually remains with regards to the distinctly elitist character of parliaments, the book does not preclude alternative ways of designing the place and function of a constitutional court. It does, instead, invite further institutional experimentation.

[8] I thank the Oxford University Press reviewer for reminding me of this.

Bibliography

Ackerman, Bruce (1984). "The Storrs Lectures: Discovering the Constitution." *Yale Law Journal* 93: 1013–1072.

—— (1995) *We The People: Foundations*. Cambridge: Harvard University Press.

Alarie, Benjamin, Green, Andrew, Iacobucci, Edward (2011). "Is Bigger Always Better? On Optimal Panel Size, with Evidence from the Supreme Court of Canada." U Toronto, *Legal Studies Research Paper 08-15*.

Alexy, Robert (1989). "On Necessary Relations Between Law and Morality." *Ratio Juris* 2, 2: 167–183.

—— (2002). *The Argument From Injustice: A Reply to Legal Positivism*. Oxford: Oxford University Press.

—— (2005). "Balancing, Constitutional Review, and Representation." *International Journal of Constitutional Law* 3, 4: 572–581.

—— (2007). "Thirteen Replies." In *Law, Rights and Discourse*, ed. George Pavlakos. Oxford: Hart.

—— (2010). *A Theory of Constitutional Rights*. Oxford: Oxford University Press.

Alford, Roger (2006). "In Search of a Theory of Constitutional Comparativism." *UCLA Law Review* 52: 639–714.

Araujo, Robert (1991–1994). "Moral Issues and the Virtuous Judge: Reflections on the Nomination and Confirmation of Supreme Court Justices." *Catholic Lawyer* 35: 178–213.

Arden, Lady Justice (2010). "A Matter of Style? The Form of Judgments in Common Law Jurisdictions." Available at: <http://www.judiciary.gov.uk>.

Atria, Fernando (2002). *On Law and Legal Reasoning*. Oxford: Hart.

—— (2009). *La Forma Del Derecho*. Book manuscript with the author.

Barak, Aharon (2006). *The Judge in a Democracy*. Princeton: Princeton University Press.

Barak-Erez, Daphne (2006). "An International Community of Legislatures?" In *The Least Examined Branch: The Role of Legislatures in the Constitutional State*, T. Kahana and R. Bauman (eds.), Cambridge: Cambridge University Press.

Bateup, Christine (2006). "The Dialogic Promise: Assessing the Normative Potential of Theories of Constitutional Dialogue." *Brooklyn Law Review* 71.

Bauman, Richard and Kahana, Tsvi (eds.) (2006). *The Least Examined Branch: The Role of Legislatures in the Constitutional State*. Cambridge: Cambridge University Press.

Bennett, Robert W. (1990–1991). "A Dissent on Dissent." *Judicature* 74: 255–260.

Berkowitz, Roger (2010). "Why We Must Judge. It's Not All Relative: Without Judgment, a Society Loses its Sense of Justice." *Democracy Journal* 18: 56–69.

Berkson, Larry Charles (1978). *The Supreme Court and Its Publics*. Lanham: Lexington Books.

Bessette, Joseph (1994). *The Mild Voice of Reason*. Chicago: University of Chicago Press.

Bhagwati, P. N. (1992). "The Role of the Judiciary in the Democratic Process: Balancing Activism and Judicial Restraint." *Commonwealth Law Bulletin* 18.

Bickel, Alexander (1957). *The Unpublished Opinions of Mr. Justice Brandeis*. Chicago: University of Chicago Press.

—— (1961). "Foreword: The Passive Virtues." *Harvard Law Review* 75: 40–79.

—— (1962). *The Least Dangerous Branch: the Supreme Court at the Bar of Politics*. Indianapolis: Bobbs-Merrill.

—— (1973). *The Caseload of the Supreme Court (and What, if Anything, to Do about It)*. Domestic Affairs Studies 21, Washington: American Enterprise Institute for Public Policy Research.

Bohman, James (1998). "The Coming of Age of Deliberative Democracy." *The Journal of Political Philosophy* 6, 4: 400–425.

Brady, Michael and Pritchard, Duncan (2003). "Moral and Epistemic Virtues." *Metaphilosophy* 34, 1: 1–11.

Brennan Jr., William (1985). "In Defense of Dissents." *Hastings Law Journal* 37: 427–438.

Brown, Donald E. (2004). "Human Universals, Human Nature & Human Culture." *Daedalus* 133, 4: 47–54.

Burns, John (2009). "Beneath a British Scandal, Deeper Furies." *New York Times* 23/05/2009.

Cappelletti, Mauro (1984). *O Controle Judicial de Constitucionalidade das Leis no Direito Comparado*. Porto Alegre: Fabris.

Cardozo, Benjamin (1934). *Law and Literature*. New York: Harcourt Inc.

Carozza, Paolo (2003). "'My Friend is a Stranger': The Death Penalty and the Global Ius Commune of Human Rights." *Texas Law Review* 81: 1031–1090.

Chambers, Simone (2003). "Deliberative Democratic Theory." *Annual Review of Political Science* 6: 307–326.

—— (2004). "Behind Closed Doors: Publicity, Secrecy and the Quality of Deliberation." *The Journal of Political Philosophy* 12, 4: 389–410.

—— (2009). "Rhetoric and the Public Sphere: Has Deliberative Democracy Abandoned Mass Democracy?" *Political Theory* 37: 323–350.

Choudhry, Sujit (1999). "Globalization in Search of Justification: Toward a Theory of Comparative Constitutional Interpretation." *Indiana Law Journal* 74: 819–892.

—— (2006). "Migration as a New Metaphor in Comparative Constitutional Law." In *The Migration of Constitutional Ideas*, ed. Sujit Choudhry. Cambridge: Cambridge University Press.

—— (2008). "Ackerman's Higher Lawmaking in Comparative Constitutional Perspective: Constitutional Moments as Constitutional Failures?" *International Journal of Constitutional Law* 6, 2: 193–230.

Christiano, Thomas (1997). "The Significance of Public Deliberation." In *Deliberative Democracy: Essays on Reason and Politics*, ed. James Bohman and William Rehg, 243–277. Cambridge: MIT Press.

Coffin, Frank Morey (1980). *The Ways of a Judge: Reflections from the Federal Appellate Bench*. Boston: Houghton Mifflin.

Cohen, Joshua (1997a). "Deliberation and Democratic Legitimacy." In *Deliberative Democracy: Essays on Reason and Politics*, ed. James Bohman and William Rehg, 67–91. Cambridge: MIT Press.

—— (1997b). "Procedure and Substance in Deliberative Democracy." In *Deliberative Democracy: Essays on Reason and Politics*, ed. James Bohman and William Rehg, 407–437. Cambridge: MIT Press.

Cohen, Morris R. (1914). "The Process of Judicial Legislation." *American Law Review* 48: 161–198.

—— (1915). "Legal Theories and Social Science." *International Journal of Ethics* 25, 4: 469–493.

Coleman Jr., William T. (1938). "The Supreme Court of the United States: Managing its Caseload to Achieve its Constitutional Purposes." *Fordham Law Review* 52: 1–35.

Collier, Helen V. (1992). "Collegiality Among Judges: No More High Noons." *Judges Journal* 31: 4–10.

Condorcet, Marquis de (1976). "Essay on the Application of Mathematics to the Theory of Decision-Making." In *Condorcet: Selected Writings*. Indianapolis: Bobbs-Merrill.

Cooper, Phillip and Ball, Howard (1997). *The United States Supreme Court: From the Inside Out*. New Jersey: Prentice Hall.

Couso, Javier (2003). "The Politics of Judicial Review in Chile in the Era of Democratic Transition, 1990–2002." *Democratization* 10, 4: 70–91.

Davidson, Donald (1991). *Inquiries Into Truth and Interpretation*. Oxford: Oxford University Press.

Delli Carpini, M.X., Lomax Cook, F., Jacobs L.R. (2004). "Public Deliberation, Discursive Participation, and Citizen Engagement: A Review of the Empirical Literature." *Annual Review of Political Science* 7: 315–334.

Douglas, William (1948). "The Dissent: A Safeguard of Democracy." *Journal of American Judicial Society* 32: 104–107.

Dryzek, John S. (1994). *Discursive Democracy: Politics, Policy, and Political Science*. Cambridge: Cambridge University Press.

—— (2000a). *Deliberative Democracy and Beyond: Liberals, Critics, Contestations.* Oxford: Oxford University Press.

—— (2000b). "Discursive Democracy vs. Liberal Constitutionalism." In *Democratic Innovation: Deliberation, representation and association*, ed. Michael Saward London: Routledge.

—— (2010). "Rhetoric in Democracy: A Systemic Appreciation." *Political Theory* 38: 319–339.

Duff, R.A. (2003). "The Limits of Virtue Jurisprudence." *Metaphilosophy* 34, 1.

Duverger, Maurice (1964). *Political Parties*. London: Methuen.

Dworkin, Ronald (1978). *Taking Rights Seriously*. Cambridge: Harvard University Press.

—— (1985). *A Matter of Principle*. Cambridge: Harvard University Press.

—— (1986). *Law's Empire*. Cambridge: Harvard University Press.

—— (1990). "Equality, Democracy and Constitution: We the People in Court." *Alberta Law Review* 28, 2: 324–346.

—— (1994). *Life's Dominion: An Argument About Abortion, Euthanasia, and Individual Freedom*. New York: Vintage.

—— (1995). "Constitutionalism and Democracy." *European Journal of Philosophy* 3: 1–11.

—— (1996). *Freedom's Law: a Moral Reading of the American Constitution*. Cambridge: Harvard University Press.

—— (1998). "The Partnership Conception of Democracy," *California Law Review* 86, 3: 453–458.

—— (2004). "The Secular Papacy." In *Judges in Contemporary Democracy*, ed. Robert Badinter and Stephen Breyer, 67–79. New York: New York University Press.

—— (2002). "Introduction." In *A Badly Flawed Election*, ed. Ronald Dworkin. New York: The New Press.

—— (2006). *Is Democracy Possible Here?* Princeton: Princeton University Press.

—— (2009). "Justice Sotomayor: The Unjust Hearings." *New York Review of Books*, September 24.

—— (2010). "The Temptation of Elena Kagan." *New York Review of Books*, August 19.

—— (1991). *Justice for Hedgehogs*. Cambridge: Harvard University Press, 2011.

Edwards, Harry T. (1991). "The Judicial Function and the Elusive Goal of Principled Decision-Making." *Wisconsin Law Review* 5: 837–865.

—— (1998). "Collegiality and Decision-Making on the D.C. Circuit." *Virginia Law Review* 84: 1335–1370.

—— (2002). "Race and the Judiciary." *Yale Law and Policy Review* 20: 325.

—— (2003). "The Effects of Collegiality on Judicial Decision Making." *University of Pennsylvania Law Review* 151, 5: 1639–1689.

Ehrmann, Michael and Fratzscher, Marcel (2005). "Transparency, Disclosure and the Federal Reserve." *ECB Working Paper 457*, at ssrn.

Eisgruber, Christopher L. (2009). *The Next Justice: Repairing the Supreme Court Appointments Process*. Princeton: Princeton University Press.

Elster, Jon (1997). "The Market and the Forum: Three Varieties of Political Theory." In *Deliberative Democracy: Essays on Reason and Politics*, ed. James Bohman and William Rehg. Cambridge: MIT Press.

Elster, Jon, ed. (1998). *Deliberative Democracy*. Cambridge: Cambridge University Press.

Ely, John Hart (1977). "Toward a Representation-Reinforcing Mode of Judicial Review." *Maryland Law Review 37*: 451–487.

——— (1980). *Democracy and Distrust: a Theory of Judicial Review*. Cambridge: Harvard University Press.

Epp, Charles (1998). *The Rights Revolution: Lawyers, Activists, and Supreme Courts in Comparative Perspective*. Chicago: University of Chicago Press.

Eskridge, William and Ferejohn, John (2008). "Constitutional Horticulture : Deliberation-Respecting Judicial Review." *Texas Law Review 97*: 1273–1302.

Estlund, David M. (1993). "Making Truth Safe for Democracy." In *The Idea of Democracy*, ed. David Copp, Jean Hampton, and John Roemer. Cambridge: Cambridge University Press: 71–100.

——— (2000). "Jeremy Waldron on Law and Disagreement." *Philosophical Studies* 99: 111–128.

——— (2004). "Deliberation Down and Dirty: Must Political Expression Be Civil?" The Poynter Center for the Study of Ethics and American Institutions, Indiana University.

——— (2008). *Democratic Authority*. Princeton: Princeton University Press.

Estlund, David M., Waldron, Jeremy, Grofman, Bernard, Feld, Scott (1989). "Democratic Theory and the Public Interest: Condorcet and Rousseau Revisited." *American Political Science Review 83*, 4: 1317–1340.

Fallon, Richard H. (2005). "Legitimacy and the Constitution." *Harvard Law Review* 118: 1787–1853.

Farber, Daniel and Sherry, Suzanna (2009). *Judgment Calls: Principle and Politics in Constitutional Law*. Oxford: Oxford University Press.

Ferejohn, John (2000). "Instituting Deliberative Democracy." In *Nomos XLII: Designing Democratic Institutions*, ed. Ian Shapiro and Stephen Macedo. New York: New York University Press.

——— (2002a). "Judicializing Politics, Politicizing Law." *Law and Contemporary Problems 65*, 3: 41–68.

——— (2002b). "Constitutional Review in the Global Context." *New York University Journal of Legislation and Public Policy 6*: 49–59.

——— (2007). "Accountability in a Global Context." *IILJ Working Paper 2007/5*, NYU Law School.

—— (2008). "The Citizen's Assembly Model." In *Designing Deliberative Democracy: The British Columbia Citizens' Assembly*, ed. Mark Warren and Hilary Pearse, 192–213. Cambridge: Cambridge University Press.

Ferejohn, John and Pasquino, Pasquale (2002). "Constitutional Courts as Deliberative Institutions: Towards an Institutional Theory of Constitutional Justice." In *Constitutional Justice, East and West*, ed. Wojciech Sadurski, 21–36. The Hague: Kluwer Law International.

—— (2003). "Rule of Democracy and Rule of Law." In *Democracy and the Rule of Law*, ed. J.M. Maravall and A. Przeworski, 242–260. Cambridge: Cambridge University Press.

—— (2004). "Constitutional Adjudication: Lessons From Europe." *Texas Law Review* 82: 1671–1704.

—— (2010). "Constitutional Adjudication: Italian Style," proceedings of a conference at University of Chicago, October 2009, ed. Tom Ginsburg.

Ferejohn, John and Eskridge, William (2001). "Super-Statutes." *Duke Law Journal* 50: 1215–1276.

Fischer, Louis (1988). *Constitutional Dialogues: Interpretation as Political Process*. Princeton: Princeton University Press.

Fischer, Louis and Devins, Neal (2004). *The Democratic Constitution*. New York: Oxford University Press.

Fishkin, James (2009). *When the People Speak: Deliberative Democracy and Public Consultation*. Oxford: Oxford University Press.

Fontana, Benedetto, Nederman, Cary J., Remer, Gary (eds.) (2004). *Talking Democracy: Historical Perspectives on Rhetoric and Democracy*. University Park: The Pennsylvania State University Press.

Freeman, Samuel (2000). "Deliberative Democracy: a Sympathetic Comment." *Philosophy and Public Affairs* 29, 4: 371–418.

Friedman, Barry (1992). "When Rights Encounter Reality." *S. Cal. Law Review* 65: 735–797.

—— (1993). "Dialogue and Judicial Review." *Michigan Law Review* 91: 577–682.

—— (1994). "Leadership and Majoritarianism: A Response." *Constitutional Commentary* 11.

—— (2003). "Mediated Popular Constitutionalism," *Michigan Law Review* 101: 2596–2636.

—— (2005). "The Politics of Judicial Review." *Texas Law Review* 84, 2: 257–337.

—— (2006). "Taking Law Seriously." *Perspectives on Politics* 4: 261–276.

—— (2010). *The Will of the People: How Public Opinion Has Influenced the Supreme Court and Shaped the Meaning of the Constitution*. New York: Farrar, Straus and Giroux.

Friedman, Barry and Lithwick, Dahlia (2010). "Speeding Locomotive: Did the Roberts Court misjudge the public mood on campaign finance reform?" *Slate* 25/10/2010.

Fuller, Lon (1958). "Positivism and Fidelity to Law: A Reply to Professor Hart." *Harvard Law Review* 71, 4: 630–672.

——— (1960). "Adjudication and the Rule of Law." *American Society of International Law and Process* 54:1–8.

——— (1968). *The Morality of Law*. New Haven: Yale University Press.

——— (1978). "Forms and Limits of Adjudication." *Harvard Law Review* 92: 353–409.

Fung, Archon (2005). "Deliberation Before the Revolution: Toward an Ethics of Deliberative Democracy in an Unjust World." *Political Theory* 33, 3: 397–419.

Gallie, W.B. (1964). "Essentially Contested Concepts." In *Philosophy and the Historical Understanding*, London: Chatto & Windus.

Gardbaum, Stephen (2001). "The New Commonwealth Model of Constitutionalism." *American Journal of Comparative Law* 49, 4: 707–760.

——— (2010). "Reassessing the New Commonwealth Model of Constitutionalism." *International Journal of Constitutional Law* 8, 2: 167–206.

Gargarella, Roberto (1996). *La Justicia Frente al Gobierno—Sobre ele carácter contramayoritario del poder judicial*. Barcelona: Ariel.

——— (2003). "In Search of a Democratic Justice—What Courts Should Not Do: Argentina, 1983–2002." *Democratization* 10, 4: 181–197.

Gastil, John (2008). *Political communication and deliberation*. Thousand Oakes: Sage Publications.

Ghosh, Eric (2010). "Deliberative Democracy and the Countermajoritarian Difficulty: Considering Constitutional Juries." *Oxford Journal of Legal Studies* 30, 2: 327–359.

Ginsburg, Ruth Bader (1990a). "On Muteness, Confidence and Collegiality: a Response to Professor Nagel." *Colorado Law Review* 61.

——— (1990b). "Remarks on Writing Separately." *Washington Law Review* 65: 133–150.

——— (1992a). "Speaking in a judicial voice." *NYU Law Review* 67, 6: 1185–1209.

——— (1992b). "Styles of Collegial Judging." *Federal Bar News & Journal* 39, 3: 199.

——— (1995). "Communicating and Commenting on the Court's Work." *Georgetown Law Journal* 83: 2119–2128.

Glendon, Marry Ann (1992). "Rights in the Twentieth-Century Constitutions." *The University of Chicago Review* 59, 1: 519–538.

——— (1993). *Rights Talk: The Impoverishment of Political Discourse*. New York: Free Press.

Goldsworthy, Jeffrey (ed) (2006). *Interpreting Constitutions: A Comparative Study*. Oxford: Oxford University Press.

Goodin, Robert (2003). *Reflective Democracy*. Oxford: Oxford University Press.

——— (2006). "Democratic Deliberation Within." In *Debating Deliberative Democracy*, ed. Peter Laslett and James Fishkin. Oxford: Blackwell Publishing.

Greenhouse, Linda (1995). "Telling the Court's Story: Justice and Journalism at the Supreme Court." *Yale Law Journal* 105: 1537–1561.

—— (2005). "What got into the court? What happens next?" *Maine Law Review* 57.

Grimm, Dieter (2000). "Constitutional Adjudication and Democracy," in Mads Andenas (ed.), *Judicial Review in International Perspective, Liber Amicorum in Honour of Lord Slynn of Hadley*. Dordrecht: Kluwer.

—— (2003). "To Be A Constitutional Court Judge." Distinguished Fellow Lecture Series—A Conversation with Professor Dieter Grimm, NYU School of Law, Hauser Program, March 3. Transcriptions available at NYU website.

—— (2009). "Constitutions, Constitutional Court and Constitutional Interpretation at the Interface of Law and Politics." In Bogdan Iancu (ed.), *The Law/Politics Distinction in Contemporary Public Law Adjudication*. The Hague: Eleven Publishing.

Gutmann, Amy (2006). "Foreword: Legislatures in the Constitutional State." In *The Least Examined Branch: The Role of Legislatures in the Constitutional State*, ed. T. Kahana and R. Bauman, Cambridge: Cambridge University Press.

Gutmann, Amy and Thompson, Dennis (1996). *Democracy and disagreement*. Cambridge: Harvard University Press.

—— (2002). "Deliberative Democracy Beyond Process." *The Journal of Political Philosophy* 10, 2: 153–174.

Habermas, Jürgen (1996). *Between Facts and Norms: Contributions to a Discourse Theory of Law and Democracy*. Trans. William Rehg. Cambridge: MIT Press.

—— (1997). "Popular Sovereignty as Procedure." In *Deliberative Democracy: Essays on Reason and Politics*, ed. James Bohman and William Rehg, 35–65. Cambridge: MIT Press.

—— (2005). "Concluding Comments on Empirical Approaches to Deliberative Politics." *Acta Politica* 40: 384–392.

Hamilton, Madison, and Jay (2003). *The Federalist*. ed. Terence Ball. Cambridge: Cambridge University Press.

Hand, Learned (1964). *The Bill of Rights*. New York: Atheneum Books.

Hart, Herbert (1958). "Positivism and the Separation of Law and Morals." *Harvard Law Review* 71, 4: 593–629.

—— (1961). *The Concept of Law*. Oxford: Clarendon Press.

Hessick, F. Andrew and Jordan, Samuel P. (2009) "Setting the Size of the Supreme Court." *Arizona State Law Journal* 41: 645–708.

Hirschl, Ran (2008). "The 'Design Sciences' and Constitutional 'Success.'" *Texas Law Review* 97: 1339–1374.

Hoecke, Mark Van (2001). "Judicial Review and Deliberative Democracy: A Circular Model of Law Creation and Legitimation." *Ratio Juris* 14, 4: 415–423.

Hogg, Peter and Bushell, Allison (1997). "The Charter Dialogue Between Courts and Legislatures (Or Perhaps the Charter of Rights Isn't Such a Bad Thing After All)." *Osgoode Hall Law Journal* 35: 75–124.

Hogg, Peter, Bushell, Allison, Wright, Wade K. (2007). "Charter Dialogue Revisited—Or Much Ado About Metaphors." *Osgoode Hall Law Journal* 45, 1: 1–66.

Hursthouse, Rosalynd (2002). *On Virtue Ethics*. Oxford: Oxford University Press.

Iffil, Sherrilyn (2000). "Racial Diversity on the Bench: Beyond Role Models and Public Confidence." *Washington and Lee Law Review* 57: 405–496.

Jackson, Vicki (2005). "Constitutional Comparisons, Convergence, Resistance, Engagement." *Harvard Law Review* 119: 108–128.

——— (2010). *Constitutional Engagement in a Transnational Era*. Oxford: Oxford University Press.

Jolowicz, J.A. (2003) "Adversarial and Inquisitorial Models of Civil Procedure." *International and Comparative Law Quarterly* 52: 281–295.

Kelman, Maurice (1985). "The Forked Path of Dissent." *Supreme Court Review*: 227–255.

Kelsen, Hans (1931). "Wer sol der Hueter der Verfassung sein?" *Die Justiz* 6: 576–628.

——— (1942). "Judicial Review of Legislation: A Comparative Study of the Austrian and the American Constitution." *The Journal of Politics* 4, 2: 183–200.

Kennedy, Duncan (1998). *A Critique of Adjudication*. Cambridge: Harvard University Press.

Klug, Heinz (2011). "Finding Its Place." *Constitutional Court Review* 3: 33–44.

Kornhauser, Lewis and Sager, Lawrence (1986). "Unpacking the Court." *The Yale Law Journal* 96, 1: 82–117.

——— (1993). "The One and the Many: Adjudication in Collegial Courts." *California Law Review* 81, 1: 1–59.

Kumm, Mattias (2007). "Institutionalizing Socratic Contestation." *European Journal of Legal Studies*, 1, 2: 1–32.

Lasser, Mitchell (2004). *Judicial Deliberations*. Oxford: Oxford University Press.

Leflar, Robert (1983). "The multi-judge decisional process." *Modern Law Review* 42.

Legrand, Pierre (1996). "How to Compare Now," *Legal Studies* 16.

Le Sueur, Andrew (2008). "A report on six seminars about the UK Supreme Court." *Queen Mary School of Law Legal Studies Research Paper* 1/2008, at ssrn.

Le Sueur, Andrew and Cornes, Richard (2000). "What Do Top Courts Do?" UCL Constitution Unit Papers. Available at: <http://www.ucl.ac.uk/spp/publications>.

Levinson, Sanford (2006). *Our Undemocratic Constitution*. Oxford: Oxford University Press.

Liptak, Adam (2010a). "In a Polarized Court, Getting the Last Word." *New York Times*, 08/03/2010.

——— (2010b). "Justices Are Long on Words but Short on Guidance." *New York Times*, 17/11/2010.

——— (2011). "Doing the Judicial Math on Health Care." *New York Times*, 05/02/2011.

Llewellyn, Karl (1960). *The Common Law Tradition: Deciding Appeals*. Boston: Little Brown & Company.

Lutz, Donald (2006). *Principles of Constitutional Design*. Cambridge: Cambridge University Press.

MacCormick, Neil (1978). *Legal Theory and Legal Reasoning*. Oxford: Oxford University Press (reprinted 2003).

—— (1989). "The Ethics of Legalism." *Ratio Juris* 2, 2: 184–193.

—— (1995). "The Relative Heteronomy of Law." *European Journal of Philosophy* 3, 1: 69–85.

—— (2005). *Rhetoric and the Rule of Law*. Oxford: Oxford University Press.

MacCormick, Neil and Summers, Robert (1997). *Interpreting Precedents: A Comparative Study*. Farnham: Ashgate Publishing.

Manin, Bernard (1987). "On Legitimacy and Political Deliberation." *Political Theory* 15: 338–368.

—— (1994). "Checks, Balances and Boundaries: the Separation of Powers in the Constitutional Debate of 1787." In *The invention of modern republic*, ed. Biancamaria Fontana. Cambridge: Cambridge University Press.

—— (1997). *The Principles of Representative Government*. Cambridge: Cambridge University Press.

—— (2005). "Democratic Deliberation: Why Should We Promote Debate Rather Than Discussion." Paper delivered at the Program in Ethics and Public Affairs Seminar, Princeton University.

Manin, Bernard and Lev-On, Azi (2009). "Happy Accidents: Deliberation and Online Exposure to Opposing Views." In *Online Deliberation: Design, Research and Practice*, ed. Todd Davies and Seeta Peña Gangadharan. Stanford: CSLI Publications.

Mansbridge, Jane, Bohman, James, Chambers, Simone, Estlund, David, Føllesdal, Andreas, Fung, Archon, Lafont, Cristina, Manin, Bernard, Martí, José Luis (2010). "The Place of Self-Interest and the Role of Power in Deliberative Democracy." *The Journal of Political Philosophy* 18, 1: 64–100.

Marshall, Thomas R. (1989). *Public Opinion and the Supreme Court*. Boston: Unwin Hyman.

—— (2008). *Public Opinion and the Rehnquist Court*. New York: State University of New York Press.

Martí, Jose Luis (2006). "The Epistemic Conception of Deliberative Democracy Defended." In *Deliberative Democracy and Its Discontents*, ed. Samantha Besson and Jose Luis Martí. Farnham: Ashgate.

Mavcic, Arne (2010). *A Tabular Presentation of Constitutional/Judicial Review around the World*. Available at: <http://www.concourts.net> (December 2010).

McRudden, Christopher (2008). "Human Dignity and Judicial Interpretation of Human Rights." *Oxford Legal Studies Research Papers* 24, at ssrn.

Medina, Diego Lopez (2004). *Teoria Impura del Derecho*. Bogotá: Legis.

Mehta, Pratap Bhanu (2007). "The Rise of Judicial Sovereignty." *Democracy* 18, 2.

Mendes, Conrado Hübner (2008a). *Controle de Constitucionalidade e Democracia*. São Paulo: Elsevier.

—— (2008b). *Direitos Fundamentais, Separação de Poderes e Deliberação*. Doctoral dissertation approved by the Department of Political Science at the University of São Paulo.

—— (2009a). "Is it All About the Last Word?" *Legisprudence* 3, 1: 69–110.

——— (2009b). "Not the Last Word, But Dialogue." *Legisprudence, 3*, 2: 191–246.
Michelman, Frank (1986). "Traces of Self-Government." *Harvard Law Review* 100: 4–77.
——— (1999). *Brennan and Democracy*. Princeton: Princeton University Press.
——— (2003). "Reflection—Comparative Avenues in Constitutional Law." *Texas Law Review 82*, 7: 1737–1761.
——— (2008). "On the Uses of Interpretive Charity: Some Notes on Application, Avoidance, Equality and Objective Unconstitutionality from the 2007 Term of the Constitutional Court of South Africa." *Constitutional Court Review 1*: 1–61.
Mill, John Stuart (1998). Considerations on Representative Government. In *John Stuart Mill On Liberty and Other Essays*, Oxford: Oxford World Classics.
Miller, Laurel (ed) (2010). *Framing the State in Times of Transition: Case Studies in Constitution Making*. Washington: United States Institute of Peace Press.
Minow, Martha and Rosenblum, Nancy (eds.) (2003). *Breaking the Cycles of Hatred: Memory, Law, and Repair*. Princeton: Princeton University Press.
Mouffe, Chantal (2000a). *The Democratic Paradox*. London: Verso.
——— (2000b). "Deliberative Democracy or Agonistic Pluralism." Institute for Advanced Studies, Vienna.
Mukhopadhaya, Kaushik (2003). "Jury Size and the Free Rider Problem." *The Journal of Law, Economics, and Organization 19*, 1: 24–44.
Murphy, Walter (2008). "Designing a Constitution: Of Architects and Builders." *Texas Law Review 97*: 1303–1337.
Mutz, Diana (2008). "Is Deliberative Democracy a Falsifiable Theory?" *Annual Review of Political Science 11*: 521–538.
Nadelmann, Kurt (1959). "The Judicial Dissent: Publication v. Secrecy." *American Journal of Comparative Law 8*, 4: 415–432.
——— (1964). "Non-disclosure of dissents in constitutional courts: Italy and West Germany." *American Journal of Comparative Law 13*, 2: 268–275.
Nelson, William E. (2000). *Marbury v. Madison: The Origins and Legacy of Judicial Review*. Lawrence: University Press of Kansas.
Neumann, Franz (1986). *The Rule of Law: Political Theory and the Legal System in Modern Society*. Oxford: Berg Publishers.
Nino, Carlos S. (1996). *The Constitution of Deliberative Democracy*. New Haven: Yale University Press.
Oakley, Justin (1996). "Varieties of Virtue Ethics." *Ratio 9*, 2: 128–152.
O'Connor, Francis (1998). "The Art of Collegiality: creating consensus and coping with dissent." *Massachusetts Law Review 83*: 93–96.
Onwuachi-Willig, Angela (2006). "Representative Government, Representative Court? The Supreme Court as a Representative Body." *Minnesota Law Review 90*: 1252–1274.
Orth, John (2006). *How Many Judges Does It Take to Make a Supreme Court?* Lawrence: University Press of Kansas.

Owens, Ryan J. and Wedeking, Justin (2010). "Justices and Legal Clarity: Analyzing the Complexity of Supreme Court Opinions." At ssrn.

Paterson, Alan (1982). *The Law Lords*. London: Macmillan Press.

Parkinson, John (2007). "The House of Lords: A Deliberative Democratic Defence." *The Political Quarterly* 78, 3: 374–381.

Pasquino, Pasquale (1998). "Constitutional Adjudication and Democracy. Comparative Perspectives: USA, France, Italy." *Ratio Juris* 11, 1: 38–50.

—— (1999). "Lenient Legislation: the Italian Constitutional Court." Unpublished, provided by the author.

Pateman, Carole (1970). *Participation and Democratic Theory*. Cambridge: Cambridge University Press.

Perju, Vlad (2005). "Comparative Constitutionalism and the Making of A New World Order." *Constellations* 12, 4: 464–486.

—— (2010). "Cosmopolitanism and Constitutional Self-Government." *Boston College Law School Legal Studies Research Paper 201*, at ssrn.

Persily, Nathaniel (2008). "Introduction." In *Public Opinion and Constitutional Controversy*, ed. N. Persily, J. Citrin and P. J. Egan. Oxford: Oxford University Press.

Pettit, Philippe (1997). *Republicanism: A Theory of Freedom and Government*. Oxford: Oxford University Press.

—— (2004a). "Democracy and Common Valuations." *Associations* 8: 71–75.

—— (2004b). "Depoliticizing Democracy." *Ratio Juris* 17, 1: 52–65.

—— (2005). "Two-dimensional Democracy, National and International." *IILJ Working Paper 2005/8*, at ssrn.

—— (2006). "Deliberative Democracy, the Discursive Dilemma, and Republican Theory." In *Debating Deliberative Democracy*, Peter Laslett and James Fishkin (eds). New Jersey: Blackwell Publishing.

Pickerill, J. Mitchell (2004). *Constitutional Deliberation in Congress: the Impact of Judicial Review in a Separated System*. Durham: Duke University Press.

Posner, Richard (1999). *The Problematics of Moral and Legal Theory*. Cambridge: Harvard University Press.

Pound, Roscoe (1953). "Cacoethes Dissentiendi: The Heated Judicial Dissent." *ABA Journal*, September: 794–795.

Powell Jr., Lewis (2004). "What Really Goes on at the Supreme Court." In *Judges on Judging: Views From the Bench*, ed. David O'Brien. Washington: CQ Press.

Przeworski, Adam (1998). "Deliberation and Ideological Domination." In *Deliberative Democracy*, ed. Jon Elster. Cambridge: Cambridge University Press.

Przeworski, Adam, Alvarez, Michael, Limongi, Fernando, Cheibub, J.A. (1996). "Classifying Political Regimes." *Studies in Comparative International Development* 31, 2: 3–36.

Putnam, Robert (1993). *Making Democracy Work: Civic Traditions in Italy*. Princeton: Princeton University Press.

Quick, Brenda Jones (1991). "Whatever happened with respectful dissent?" *ABA Journal*, June: 62.

Rawls, John (1971). *A Theory of Justice.* Cambridge: Harvard University Press.

—— (1997a). "The Idea of Public Reason." In *Deliberative Democracy: Essays on Reason and Politics*, ed. James Bohman and William Rehg. Cambridge: MIT Press.

—— (1997b). "The Idea of Public Reason Revisited." *The University of Chicago Law Review* 64, 3: 765–807.

—— (2005). *Political Liberalism.* New York: Columbia University Press.

Raz, Joseph (1979). *The Authority of Law.* Oxford. Oxford University Press.

—— (1986). *The Morality of Freedom.* Oxford: Oxford University Press.

Rehnquist, William (2004). "The Supreme Court's Conference." In *Judges on Judging: Views From the Bench*, ed. David O'Brien. Washington: CQ Press.

Remer, Gary (1999). "Political Oratory and Conversation: Cicero versus Deliberative Democracy." *Political Theory*, 27, 1: 39–64.

Robertson, David (2000). "The House of Lords as a Political and Constitutional Court: Lessons from the Pinochet Case." In *The Pinochet Case: A Legal and Constitutional Analysis*, ed. Diana Roodhouse. Oxford: Hart Publishing.

—— (2010). *The Judge as a Political Theorist: Contemporary Constitutional Review.* Princeton: Princeton University Press.

Rostbøll, Christian (2005). "Preferences and Paternalism: on freedom and deliberative democracy." *Political Theory* 33, 3: 370–396.

—— (2008). *Deliberative Freedom: Deliberative Democracy as Critical Theory.* Albany: State University of New York Press.

Rousseau, Jean-Jacques (1994). *Discourse on Political Economy and the Social Contract.* Transl. Christopher Betts. New York: Oxford University Press.

Roux, Theunis (2003). "Legitimating Transformation: Political Resource Allocation in the South African Constitutional Court." *Democratization* 10, 4: 92–111.

—— (2005). "The constitutional framework and the deepening democracy in South Africa." *Policy Issue & Actors* 18, 6: 1–17.

—— (2009). "Principle and pragmatism on the Constitutional Court of South Africa." *International Journal of Constitutional Law* 7, 1: 106–138.

Ryfe, D.M. (2005). "Does deliberative democracy work?" *Annual Review of Political Science* 8: 49–71.

Sachs, Albie (2009). *The Strange Alchemy of Life and Law.* Oxford: Oxford University Press.

Sandel, Michael (2010). *Justice: What's the Right Thing to Do?* New York: Farrar, Straus and Giroux.

Sanders, Lynn (1997). "Against Deliberation." *Political Theory* 25, 3: 1–17.

Sartori, Giovani (1970). "Concept misformation in comparative politics." *The American Political Science Review* 64, 4: 1033–1053.

Schauer, Frederick (1992). "Deliberating about Deliberation." *Michigan Law Review* 90: 1187–1202.

Schauer, Frederick and Alexander, Larry (1997). "On Extrajudicial Constitutional Interpretation." *Harvard Law Review* 110, 7: 1359–1387.

Schmitt, Carl (2000). *The Crisis of Parliamentary Democracy*. Transl. Ellen Kennedy. Cambridge: MIT Press.

—— (2007). *The Concept of the Political*. Chicago: University of Chicago Press.

—— (2008). *Constitutional Theory*. Transl. Jeffrey Seitzer. Durham: Duke University Press.

Schmitter, Philippe C. (2005). "Two cheers for deliberation." *European Political Science* 4: 430–435.

Schroeder, Christopher H. (2002). "Deliberative Democracy's Attempt to Turn Politics into Law." *Law and Contemporary Problems* 65, 3: 95–132.

Schwartz, Bernard (1985). *The Unpublished Opinions of the Warren Court*. Oxford: Oxford University Press.

—— (1988). *The Unpublished Opinions of the Burger Court*. Oxford: Oxford University Press.

—— (1996). *The Unpublished Opinions of the Rehnquist Court*. Oxford: Oxford University Press.

Shapiro, Ian (2002). "Optimal Deliberation?" *The Journal of Political Philosophy* 10, 2: 196–211.

Shapiro, Martin and Stone-Sweet, Alec (2002). *On Law, Politics and Judicialization*. Oxford: Oxford University Press.

Sherry, Suzanna (1986). "The Gender of Judges." *Law and Inequality* 4: 159–169.

—— (1998). "Textualism and Judgment." *The George Washington Law Review* 66: 1148–1152.

—— (1998b). "Judicial Independence: Playing Politics with the Constitution." *Georgia State University Law Review* 14: 795–815.

—— (2003). "Judges of Character." *Wake Forest Law Review* 38: 793–812.

—— (2004). "Hard Cases Make Good Judges." *Northwestern University Law Review* 99, 1: 3–32.

—— (2005). "Politics and Judgment." *Missouri Law Review* 70: 973–987.

Sherry, Suzanna and Farber, Daniel (2009). *Judgment Calls: Principle and Politics in Constitutional Law*. Oxford: Oxford University Press.

Silva, Virgílio Afonso da (2006). "Duverger's Laws: Between social and institutional determinism." *European Journal of Political Research* 45: 31–41.

—— (2009). "O STF e o controle de constitucionalidade: diálogo, deliberação e razão pública." *Revista de Direito Administrativo* 250.

—— (2013). "Deciding Without Deliberating." *International Journal of Constitutional Law* 11, 3: 557–584.

Silva, Virgílio Afonso and Mendes, Conrado Hübner. "Habermas e a jurisdição constitucional." In *Direito e democracia: um guia de leitura de Habermas*, ed. M. Nobre and R. Terra. São Paulo: Malheiros, 2008.

Singer, Peter and Lazari-Radek, Katarzyna de (2010). "Secrecy in Consequentialism: a Defence of Esoteric Morality." *Ratio* 23, 1: 34–58.

Slaughter, Anne-Marie (2003). "A Global Community of Courts." *Harvard International Law Journal* 44, 1: 191–219.

Solum, Lawrence B. (2003). "Virtue Jurisprudence: A Virtue-Centred Theory of Judging." *Metaphilosophy* 34, 1: 178–213.

—— (2004a). "The Aretic Turn in Constitutional Theory." *University of San Diego School of Law, Public Law and Legal Theory Research Paper Series Research*, 04-03.

—— (2004b). "Judicial Selection: Ideology versus Character." *University of San Diego School of Law, Public Law and Legal Theory Research Paper Series*, 04-07.

—— (2004c). "A Tournament of Virtue." *University of San Diego School of Law, Legal Studies Research Paper Series*, 05-16.

Sottomayor, Sonia (2009). "A Latina Judge's Voice." *New York Times*, 14/05/2009.

Stack, Kevin (1996). "The Practice of Dissent in the Supreme Court." *Yale Law Journal* 105: 2235–2259.

Stokes, Susan (1998). "Pathologies of Deliberation." In *Deliberative Democracy*, ed. Jon Elster. Cambridge: Cambridge University Press.

Stone, Alec (1992). *The Birth of Judicial Politics in France*. Oxford: Oxford University Press.

Stone-Sweet, Alec (2000). *Governing With Judges*. Oxford: Oxford University Press.

Strauss, David A. (1996). "Common Law Constitutional Interpretation." *University of Chicago Law Review* 63, 3: 877–935.

Sunstein, Cass (1994). "Incompletely Theorized Agreements." *Harvard Law Review* 108: 1733–1772.

—— (1996). "The Supreme Court, 1995 Term—Foreword: Leaving Things Undecided." *Harvard Law Review* 110: 4–101.

—— (1998). *The Partial Constitution*. Cambridge: Harvard University Press.

—— (2000). "Constitutional Agreements Without Constitutional Theories." *Ratio Juris* 13, 1: 117–130.

—— (2001). *One Case at a Time: Judicial Minimalism on the Supreme Court*. Cambridge: Harvard University Press.

—— (2002). "On a Danger of Deliberative Democracy." *Daedalus* 131, 4: 120–124.

—— (2005). "Testing minimalism: a reply." *Michigan Law Review* 104: 123–130.

Tacha, Deanell Reece (1995). "The 'C' Word: on Collegiality." *Ohio State Law Journal* 56: 585–592.

Talbot, Margaret (2010). "A Risky Proposal: Is it Too Soon to Petition the Supreme Court on gay marriage?." *New Yorker*, January 18.

Taylor, Matthew M. (2009). "Curbing the Courts: Latin American Lessons on Curtailing Judicial Independence." Paper presented at the 2009 Meetings of the American Political Science Association, Toronto, Canada, September 1-4.

Thayer, James B. (1893). "The Origin and Scope of the American Doctrine of Constitutional Law." *Harvard Law Review* 7, 3: 129–156.

Thibaut, John and Walker, Laurens (1978). "A Theory of Procedure." *California Law Review* 66, 3: 541–566.

Thompson, Dennis F. (2004). *Restoring Responsibility: Ethics in Government, Business, and Healthcare.* Cambridge: Cambridge University Press.

—— (2008). "Deliberative Democratic Theory and Empirical Political Science." *Annual Review of Political Science* 11: 497–520.

Toobin, Jeffrey (2010). "After Stevens." *New Yorker*, March 22.

Troper, Michel (1999). "La máquina y la norma. Dos modelos de Constitución." *Doxa* 22: 330–347.

Tsebellis, George (2002). *Veto Players: How Political Institutions Work.* Princeton: Princeton University Press.

Tushnet, Mark (2006). "Interpretation in Legislatures and Courts: Incentives and Institutional Design." In *The Least Examined Branch: The Role of Legislatures in the Constitutional State*, ed. T. Kahana and R. Bauman. Cambridge: Cambridge University Press.

Twining, William (1973). *Karl Llewellyn and the Realist Movement.* London: Weidenfield and Nicolson.

Uprimny, Rodrigo (2003). "The Constitutional Court and Control of Presidential Extraordinary Powers in Colombia." *Democratization* 10, 4: 46–69.

Urbinati, Nadia (2008). *Representative Democracy: Principles and Genealogy.* Chicago: University of Chicago Press.

—— (2004). "Reading J.S. Mill's The Subjection of Women as a Text of Deliberative Rhetoric." In *Talking Democracy*, ed. Benedetto Fontana et al. University Park: Pennsylvania State University Press.

—— (2010). "Unpolitical Democracy." *Political Theory* 38, 1: 65–92.

Vanberg, Georg (2005). *The Politics of Constitutional Review in Germany.* Cambridge: Cambridge University Press.

Veríssimo, Marcos Paulo (2008). "A Constituição de 1988 Vinte Anos Depois: Suprema Corte e Ativismo Judicial à Brasileira." *Revista Direito GV* 4, 2: 407–440.

Vermeule, Adrian (2006a). "Should We Have Lay Justices?" *Harvard Public Law Working Paper 134*, at ssrn.

—— (2006b). "Constitutional Amendments and the Constitutional Common Law." In *The Least Examined Branch: The Role of Legislatures in the Constitutional State* ed., T. Kahana and R. Bauman. Cambridge: Cambridge University Press.

—— (2007). *Mechanisms of Democracy: Institutional Design Writ Small.* New York: Oxford University Press.

Vermeule, Adrian and Garrett, Elizabeth (2001). "Institutional Design of a Thayerian Congress." *Duke Law Journal* 50: 1277–1333.

Volcansek, Mary L. (2000). *Constitutional Politics in Italy.* New York: St. Martin's Press.

—— (2001). "Constitutional Courts as Veto-players: Divorce and Decrees in Italy." *European Journal of Political Research 39.*

Von Fritz, K. (1954) *The Theory of the Mixed Constitution in Antiquity: A Critical Analysis of Polybius' Political Ideas.* New York: Columbia University Press.

Waldron, Jeremy (1999). *The Dignity of Legislation.* Cambridge: Cambridge University Press.

—— (2001). *Law and Disagreement.* Oxford: Oxford University Press.

—— (2002). "Judicial Power and Popular Sovereignty." In *Marbury versus Madison: Documents and Commentary,* ed. Mark A. Graber and Michael Perhac. Washington: CQ Press.

—— (2005a). "Foreign Law and the Modern Ius Gentium." *Harvard Law Review* 119: 129–147.

—— (2005b). "Legitimacy and Electoral Legitimacy." Unpublished manuscript, file with the author.

—— (2006a). "The Core of the Case Against Judicial Review." *Yale Law Journal* 115: 1346–1406.

—— (2006b). "How Judges Should Judge." *New York Review of Books,* August 10.

—— (2007). "'Partly Laws Common to All Mankind': Foreign Law in American Courts." *Storrs Lectures 2007,* Yale Law School, September 10-12, available at Yale Law School website.

—— (2009a). "Judges as Moral Reasoners." *International Journal of Constitutional Law* 7, 1: 2–24.

—— (2009b). "Refining the question about judges' moral capacity." *International Journal of Constitutional Law* 7, 1: 69–82.

—— (2009c). "Legislatures Judging in Their Own Cause." *Legisprudence 3,* 1: 125–145.

—— (2010). "Dignity and Defamation: the Visibility of Hate." *Harvard Law Review* 123: 1596–1657.

Walker, Neil (2003). "After the Constitutional Moment." *The Federal Trust for education & research,* online paper 32.

—— (2008). "Beyond Boundary Disputes and Basic Grids: Mapping the Global Disorder of Normative Orders." *International Journal of Constitutional Law* 6, 3: 373–396.

—— (2009). "Beyond the Holistic Constitution?" *University of Edinburgh School of Law Working Paper 2009/16,* at ssrn.

—— (2010). "Final Appellate Jurisdiction in the Scottish Legal System." Scottish Government, Legal Division. Available at: <http://www.scotland.gov.uk/publications>.

Waluchow, Wil (2005). "Constitutions as Living Trees: An Idiot Responds." *Canadian Journal of Law and Jurisprudence 18:* 1–58.

—— (2007). *A Common Law theory of Judicial Review: The Living Tree.* Cambridge: Cambridge University Press.

Walzer, Michael (2004). *Politics and Passion: Toward a More Egalitarian Liberalism.* New Haven: Yale University Press.

—— (2008). "Preface." In *Global Politics After 9/11: The Democratiya Interviews*, ed. Alan Johnson. London: Foreign Policy Centre.

—— (1990). "Review Essay: The virtue of incompletion." *Theory and Society* 19: 225–229.

—— (1989). "Two Kinds of Universalism." *The Tanner Lecture on Human Values.*

West, Sonja (2006). "Concurring in Part & Concurring in the Confusion." *Michigan Law Review* 104: 1951–1960.

Williams, K.Y. and O'Reilly, C.A. (1998). "Demography and Diversity in Organizations: A Review of 40 Years of Research." In *Research in Organizational Behavior* 20, ed. L.L. Cummings and B.M. Staw. Greenwich, CT: JAI Press.

Wills, Garry (2010). "Behind Obama's Cool." *New York Times*, 07/04/2010.

Wolfe, Alan (2006). "Why Conservatives Can't Govern." *Washington Monthly*, July/August.

Wollheim, R. (1962). "A Paradox in the Theory of Democracy." In *Philosophy, Politics and Society*, ed. P. Laslett et al. Oxford: Blackwell.

Woolman, Stu and Bishop, Michael (eds.) (2008). *Constitutional Conversations.* Pretoria: PULP.

Young, Iris Marion (1996). "Communication and the Other: Beyond Deliberative Democracy." In *Democracy and Difference*, ed. S. Benhabib. Princeton: Princeton University Press.

—— (2000). *Inclusion and Democracy.* Oxford: Oxford University Press.

—— (2001). "Activist Challenges to Deliberative Democracy." *Political Theory* 29, 5: 670–690.

Zobell, Karl M. (1958) "Division of Opinion in the Supreme Court: a History of Judicial Disintegration." *Cornell Law Quarterly* 44: 186–214.

Zurn, Christopher (2007). *Deliberative Democracy and the Institutions of Judicial Review.* Cambridge: Cambridge University Press.

REPORTS

"The Report of the Advisory Panel on Judicial Diversity 2010." UK Ministry of Justice, 24/02/2010. Available at: <http://www.equality-ne.co.uk/downloads/759_advisory-panel-judicial-diversity-2010.pdf>.

Index

adjudication 54, 58, 61, 73–82, 212
   collegiate adjudication 53, 61–70, 71, 221
   constitutional adjudication 72, 113, 176, 211–12, 223
   monocratic adjudication 61–70, 72
   ordinary adjudication 74–8, 113, 164
   politics of adjudication 11, 196–8
aggregation 12, 19, 65–6, 168
Alexy, Robert 5, 56–7, 87, 89, 90, 92

bargaining 19, 27, 65, 130, 168
Bickel, Alexander 83, 90, 131, 133, 160, 172, 199, 211, 213–14, 218

Choudhry, Sujit 80–1, 189
civil law v. common law 111, 149, 171, 181–2, 195
collegial engagement 105–8, 111, 114–15, 117–18, 128, 134–5, 141, 164, 203, 209, 219
compromise 12, 27–8, 65, 67, 84, 94–5, 130–1, 140, 168, 199, 207, 211, 216
consensus 12, 14, 16, 22, 26–7, 28–32, 39–40, 44, 48, 97–8, 109, 114–15, 128–31, 151, 155, 168–70, 189, 205
constitutional courts 1, 72, 101
   as deliberative institutions 38, 43, 45, 47, 54, 82, 87, 93, 114, 141
   imagery 1, 86, 223
constitutional scrutiny 73–82, 99, 163, 176, 183, 196, 207, 214, 220
   adjudication v. legislation 54–5, 58, 74, 76–7, 81, 99, 202
   co-legislation and co-legislators 77
   functional redundancy v. institutional equivalence 77, 186, 221
   positive legislation 76
constitutionalism 2, 78, 84, 89, 96, 144, 178, 184, 212

deliberation
   adjudication and 54–61
   circumstances of deliberation 35, 36, 104, 176, 196
      persuasion and 12, 16–7, 21, 26, 30, 45, 51, 67, 98, 114, 124, 134, 139–40, 168, 187, 200

constitutional deliberation 173, 178, 195, 120, 141, 177
deliberation of powers 184, 188, 207
deliberative institutions 38, 43, 45, 47, 54, 82, 87, 93, 114, 141, 221, 224
deliberative performance 51, 73, 98, 101, 102–3, 106, 119–20, 145, 147, 176–8, 187, 190, 212, 222–3, 225
   core meaning 103, 105, 115, 117, 176, 195
   facilitators 103–4, 145
   hedges 103–4, 177, 190
deliberative phases 46, 105
   decisional 105, 111, 114, 128
   post-decisional 105, 114, 136, 169
   pre-decisional 105, 114, 116, 127, 159
deliberative potential 104, 120, 142, 147, 174, 178–9, 181, 194, 199
deliberative tasks 105, 119, 122
   collegial engagement 105–8, 111, 114–15, 117–18, 128, 134–5, 141, 164, 203, 209, 219
   deliberative written decision 105, 107, 109–10, 114, 117, 136, 138, 169, 203
   public contestation 105, 114–15, 122, 127–8, 159, 161
deliberative virtues 92, 98, 126–7, 140, 175, 222
   clarity 127, 137–9, 155, 171
   cognitive ambition 126, 134–5, 141
   cognitive modesty 126, 134–5, 141
   collegiality 126, 128–9, 131–3, 154, 165, 170
   empathy 14, 45, 126, 128, 135–6
   respectful curiosity 126–8
   responsiveness 18, 36, 45, 127, 136–8, 194
   sense of fallibility and provisionality 127, 136, 138, 188
deliberativeness 61, 96, 111
esoteric deliberation 177, 198, 209–10, 212, 218
ethics of deliberation 14, 16, 122–4, 141
exoteric deliberation 194, 209, 212, 218
first-order and second-order deliberation 28, 39, 40, 42, 51, 69, 169, 198, 201, 205, 210, 212
internal and external deliberation 90, 95–7, 103, 105, 113, 116, 173, 205, 214

deliberation (Cont.)
  intramural and extramural
    deliberation 46–7, 107–8
  intrinsic and instrumental reasons for
    deliberation 13, 22, 44, 49–50, 114–15, 162
  inversion of logical priority between
    instrumental and intrinsic reasons
    (instrumental threshold) 50, 69
  legal deliberation 60
  political deliberation 12, 14, 19, 22, 36, 42
  promises of deliberation 36, 70, 114, 124, 141
    communitarian promise 23, 26, 31, 34, 70,
      114, 119, 128, 152–3, 169
    educative promise 22, 32, 34, 68, 88, 114,
      169
    epistemic promise 66, 70, 114, 119, 135,
      152, 154
    psychological promise 22–3, 31–2, 48, 67,
      114–15
  sites of deliberation 35, 42, 107, 122
democracy 6, 44, 80, 83–4, 87–90, 164, 202,
  224, 226
  constitutional democracy 5–6, 99, 104
  deliberative democracy 14, 43, 84–5, 89, 155
  democratic legitimacy of judicial
    review 82–3, 192, 226
dialogue 70, 72, 90, 92, 96, 165, 185–7,
  193, 210
disagreement or dissensus 19–20, 22–3, 26–7,
  64, 67, 98, 109, 115, 128, 130, 138, 140, 169,
  201, 204
Dworkin, Ronald 3, 5, 21, 24–5, 29, 33, 56–7,
  62, 75, 85, 87–9, 91–2, 140, 178–9, 181, 183, 193,
  211–12

Elster, Jon 19, 26, 29, 40, 49, 164
Ely, John Hart 85

Ferejohn, John 3, 16–7, 38, 93–8, 109, 117, 130,
  143, 144–6, 148, 156–7, 159, 165, 168, 170–1, 174,
  185, 187–8, 196, 199, 204, 206, 209
Fuller, Lon 10, 73, 138, 146, 163–4

Grimm, Dieter 24, 83–4, 91, 101, 117, 131, 133
Gutmann, Amy 14, 17, 22, 25, 36, 40, 84, 202

Habermas, Jürgen 17–19, 26, 33, 42, 48, 77, 85,
  90, 92, 140
Hart, Herbert 30, 40, 57–8,

institutional design
  constitutive devices 147, 149
  decisional devices 164
  post-decisional devices 169
  pre-decisional devices 159

judicial opinion
  concurrent opinion 65, 139, 168, 205
  dissenting opinion 65–6, 111–12, 130, 131–3,
    139, 171–2, 204–6
  joint opinion 61, 64–5, 111, 172, 207, 212
  majority opinion 66, 111, 132, 166–7, 172
judicial review of legislation
  democratic legitimacy of judicial review 11,
    82–3, 90, 93, 192, 226
  legal backdrop of judicial review 176
  political circumstances of judicial
    review 196

Kumm, Mattias 85, 87, 89–90, 92, 116, 225

legal reasoning 53, 56, 58, 60, 65, 138, 176, 180,
  195, 203, 211, 221
legitimacy 11, 20, 22, 25, 32, 43–4, 47, 51, 69,
  82–4, 87–9, 93, 98, 101–2, 116, 138, 164, 192, 196,
  214–15, 224–6

MacCormick, Neil 60, 112, 180–2, 204–5
majority 67, 131, 168, 204
  majority opinion 66, 111, 132, 166–7, 172
  majority rule 30, 168, 224–25
  majority voting 28, 169, 192
  qualified majority 167–8
  simple majority 167–8
Manin, Bernard 14, 20, 30, 32–3, 38, 42, 69, 184
Michelman, Frank 83, 91–2, 134, 140, 191
middle-level theory 5, 7–9, 76, 102, 113, 117,
  148–9, 224

Pasquino, Pasquale 3, 93–8, 109, 117, 130, 143–5,
  159, 165, 168, 170, 199, 204, 206
per curiam decision 64, 96–7, 111–13, 128, 136,
  168–9, 172, 203, 205
Pettit, Philippe 8, 13, 20–21, 90, 116,
pragmatic equilibrium (between esoteric and
  exoteric deliberation) 219
precedent 133, 169, 173, 181–2, 201, 203
public contestation 105, 114–15, 122, 127–8,
  159, 161

Rawls, John 3, 5, 16, 20, 29, 30, 48, 87–8, 90,
  92–4, 219
rights 1, 3, 84, 88, 101, 120, 178, 189, 191–3, 207, 215
  language of rights (or rights-talk) 178, 191
Roux, Theunis 160, 203, 208, 210, 212, 216–17

separation of powers 2, 44, 77, 93, 184,
  186–8, 195, 206, 214–15, 222,
  and dialogue 90, 185, 187
  deliberation of powers 184, 188, 207

seriatim decision 63–5, 68, 96–7, 111–13, 129, 136, 168–72, 203, 205
Silva, Virgílio Afonso da 24, 76, 93, 129, 142, 144, 161, 165–7, 170, 172, 174, 185, 226
Solum, Lawrence 125–6, 134, 139, 156, 211
Sunstein, Cass 26, 29, 33–4, 36, 85–6, 96, 201–2, 213

Thompson, Dennis 14, 17, 22–3, 25, 36, 40, 84, 136–8, 162, 186, 210–11

Waldron, Jeremy 4, 6, 9, 24, 30–2, 40, 57, 84–5, 118, 151, 168, 180, 185–90, 192–3, 195, 225

Ingram Content Group UK Ltd.
Milton Keynes UK
UKHW020615200323
418662UK00015B/373

9 780198 759454